D1592761

The Rise of American Naval Power

1776 - 1918

By

Harold & Margaret Sprout

☆ ☆

☆ ☆

PRINCETON UNIVERSITY PRESS

PRINCETON

London-Oxford University Press

Fifth Printing 1966

PRINTED IN THE UNITED STATES OF AMERICA

Authors' Introduction to the 1966 Edition

Nearly thirty years have elapsed since we finished writing *The Rise of American Naval Power.* The book was published in the spring of 1939. A year and a half later Princeton University Press published the sequel, *Toward a New Order of Sea Power. The Rise* closed with the victory of 1918. The sequel carried the story of American naval policy and development through the Washington Conference on Limitation of Armaments (1921-1922). We were well started on a third volume when the attack on Pearl Harbor diverted our efforts (permanently, as things turned out) into other channels.

The torpedoes and bombs that sank the United States battleships inside Pearl Harbor and the subsequent course of naval operations in World War II stimulated long overdue questions regarding some of the most hallowed concepts of American naval policy. The process of reevaluation was further stimulated by the development of nuclear explosives, long-range ballistic missiles, the fantastic growth of airborne transport, nuclear ship propulsion, and other technological advances, as well as by radical and still continuing changes in the structure and patterns of international politics.

The period covered by *The Rise of American Naval Power* (1776-1918) ended a generation before any of these later events occurred. In a narrow sense that earlier period belongs to the dead past, and may seem to have slight if any relevance to the issues that confront our policy makers today. In a broader sense the past is always relevant. The present is a product of the past. A different past would have produced a different present. The present is scarcely comprehensible except in terms of images of the past. Moreover, many of the ideas that guided those responsible for American naval policy and development in the past still live in the Navy's traditions and doctrines, and in people's thinking about the Navy's mission in American statecraft.

The Rise of American Naval Power was conceived as a political history of American naval policy and development. No such work existed in the 1930's. There were naval histories, largely devoted to narratives of naval battles and campaigns. There were a few technical works on naval architecture and technology. The United States Naval Institute had published serially in its *Proceedings* a pioneering history of American naval administration. The diplomatic missions of American naval officers had received some attention. A few officers had published noteworthy memoirs. Above all, there were the voluminous writings of Captain Alfred T. Mahan, notable for their flashes of insight intermingled with rambling narratives of naval operations, discursive technical discussions of strategy and tactics, and propaganda for expanded foreign commerce, overseas expansion, a more active foreign policy, and a bigger and better navy. However, no one (least of all Mahan) had examined and synthesized in broad historical perspective the ideas and forces that had produced the ships, the shore establishments, the public attitudes, and the traditions and doctrines of the American Navy. That was the task we set for ourselves in *The Rise of American Naval Power.*

In the Foreword, dated February 15, 1939, we summarized the lines of inquiry and analysis more specifically as follows:

"(1) the problem of naval defense as envisaged by different persons, groups, classes, and sections, at each stage in the territorial, economic, and political expansion of the United States;

"(2) the continuing historic debate over the nature and scope of the Navy's functions in peace as well as in war;

"(3) the arguments of successive generations as to the size and kind of navy required to perform these functions;

"(4) the evolution of ideas as to the principles of naval strategy and warfare;

"(5) the strategic and political implications of advances in naval architecture and technology;

"(6) the like implications of changing ideas as to the organization, disposition, and management of the forces afloat;

"(7) the like implications of the problems of Navy Department and navyyard administration;

"(8) the processes of formulating and enacting naval legislation within the American political system;

"(9) the respective roles of organized groups and unorganized public opinion; and—

"(10) the international repercussions and consequences of the rise of American naval power."

Subsequent research by other scholars, while correcting some errors and considerably extending available knowledge of some of the above issues, has confirmed in the main the book's major conclusions. *The Rise* is still the most comprehensive overview of the first 130 years of American naval policy and development. There is relatively little that we could do to make it a better book. But we are concerned with certain perspectives and emphases in *The Rise* that we ourselves have come to query and modify with the passage of time.

It seems clear in retrospect that we were initially swayed too much by some of Mahan's interpretations and theories. In *The Rise* we accepted rather too readily his denigration of cruiser warfare, his doctrine of fleet concentration, and his thesis (only slightly qualified) that American imitation of British naval doctrine and policy would yield for the United States military capabilities and political leverages on a scale comparable to those wielded by Great Britain in the heyday of the Pax Britannica.

We began to question these points shortly after *The Rise* was published. Some of our doubts are reflected in the opening chapters of *Toward a New Order of Sea Power*, published in 1940. In a very real sense, those chapters are an addendum to *The Rise*. The ideas expressed therein underwent further modification in our later books and articles. Because of their relevance to what we had said in *The Rise*, we have brought together and reproduced here some of our matured thinking about Mahan's theories and interpretations, and their bearing on American naval policy.[1]

It is difficult to exaggerate the indirect influence of British naval history on American naval policy and development in the 1890's and 1900's. Mahan's theories of naval power and his prescriptions for naval policy were derived in large part from his reading of British experience. Through the impact of his writings and through the activities of his influential political friends (especially Theodore Roosevelt and Henry Cabot

[1] In addition to chs. 1 & 2 of *Toward a New Order of Sea Power*, Princeton University Press, 1940, the relevant later writings include: "Atlantic Ocean, Command of," in *Encyclopedia Britannica*; ch. 10 of *Foundations of International Politics*, Van Nostrand, 1962; and "Geopolitical Hypotheses in Technological Perspective," in *World Politics*, Jan. 1963, v. 15, pp. 187, 193 ff.

Lodge) Mahan's interpretations of British policy and practice found their way into the naval legislation and doctrine of the United States. For this reason it is relevant to examine with special care both his reading of British naval history and its relevance (or lack of relevance) to the situation of the United States at the turn of the twentieth century.

By the end of the Napoleonic Wars (in the words of Mahan's contemporary, the British geographer Halford J. Mackinder) Britain "could deny all the ocean to the fleets of her enemies, could transport her armies to whatsoever coast she would and remove them again, could carry supplies home from foreign sources, could exert pressure in negotiation on whatsoever offending state had a sea-front."[2] Though Mahan never put it so concisely, his reading of the Pax Britannica is virtually the same as Mackinder's.

Mahan attributed Britain's world position largely, though not exclusively, to certain strategic and tactical principles which, after generations of trial and error, had come to govern British naval deployment and operations in war. Britain's immunity from invasion, he contended, had not been achieved by dispersing the Royal Navy along the coasts of the British Isles, or by distributing its ships among the oversea colonies. The British Admiralty in time of war had not guarded the Empire's sea communications by scattering its ships around the oceans by one's and two's. The guiding principles had been concentration of force and aggressive fleet strategy to destroy or drive enemy forces from the seas.

Mahan supported the principle of concentration of force with the following argument: Individual ships and small squadrons might supplement land forces in repelling invasion; but these could neither prevent nor break up blockade of the ports. Solitary roving cruisers might raid the enemy's coast and commerce, and conceivably do much damage. But hit-and-run raiding could never by itself yield decisive results. It could not even seriously harass the enemy unless one's cruisers could restock and refit at ports conveniently close to the heavily traveled routes of enemy commerce. In short, Mahan argued, hit-and-run raiding, a sort of naval counterpart to guerilla

[2] H. J. Mackinder, *Democratic Ideals and Reality*, Henry Holt & Co., 1919, 1942, p. 58.

operations on land, while sometimes useful as a supplement, was not an effective substitute for command of the sea achieved by superior concentrations of capital ships capable of sinking enemy forces or driving them to cover; capable of blockading enemy ports and thereby paralyzing the enemy's internal economy; and capable also of supporting one's own seaborne troop and cargo movements.

It is essential to remember that British seapower derived from a number of conditions besides a superior navy and a particular strategic doctrine. Britain achieved naval dominance in an era of primitive overland communications. There were few all-weather roads, no motor road vehicles, and only the beginnings of a railway grid. Large-scale movement of people and bulky freight overland, even for relatively short distances, was slow and costly. The advantage of water-borne transport was nearly everywhere decisive. Under these conditions blockade of a country's ports could be a paralyzing experience. Furthermore, it was generally quicker and cheaper in those days to travel around Europe than to cross it. Though the island of Britain lies on the periphery of Europe, the superior mobility of movement by sea rendered the British position strategically central vis-à-vis every continental country, so long as the British Navy controlled the sea.

Britain controlled the sea by controlling the ocean portals of Europe. Broadly speaking, European countries could gain access to the oceans only through narrow seas—the English Channel, the North Sea, the Strait of Gibraltar, and (after 1869) the Suez Canal and Red Sea. By occupying one or both shores of those narrow seas, and by maintaining superior naval forces, the British government wielded at all times a potential control of the use of those ocean portals.

The pattern was duplicated on a lesser scale in the Indian Ocean and in other distant seas. At the summit of her world power, Britain held strategically located shore positions close to all the passages into and out of the Atlantic, Indian, and Pacific oceans—with one exception: the potential (but still unbuilt) seaway across the American isthmus. With negligible exceptions, each of these naval outposts was located upon an island, or at the foot of a peninsula or promontory, or upon a coast backed by a formidable desert, jungle, or mountain range.

Before the advent of submarines and aircraft, and before the development of transcontinental railways, these British outposts were as secure from attack as the British homeland itself. As long as the British Navy retained control of the water's surface, both the insular homeland and the oversea bases remained secure with minimal outlay for garrisons or other land defense.

The geographical structure of international politics added significantly to the edifice of British seapower. Until late in the nineteenth century, Britain's only rivals were located upon the European mainland. As long as these conditions continued, control of the narrow seas gave Britain not only a potentially strangling leverage on Europe but also a virtually global command of the sea. In the metaphor coined by Mackinder, British naval power, though deployed mainly in European waters, in effect "enveloped" the "world promontory" of Eurasia "which stands forward to the Cape of Good Hope from between the [island of] Britain and Japan."[3] Or, in Admiral Lord Fisher's even more colorful metaphor: Britain held the "five keys" which "lock up the world"—Dover, Gibraltar, Alexandria, the Cape of Good Hope, and Singapore.[4]

Mahan understood all this well enough. He repeatedly emphasized the superior capabilities of seaborne transport as compared with haulage overland. He dwelt on the advantages Britain derived from the configuration of the European coastline and narrow seas. He clearly had some sense of the significance of the geographical pattern of nineteenth-century world politics. On one occasion he observed that Britain defended its scattered dominions and colonies "not indeed by local superiorities in their several waters, an object at once unattainable and needless, but by concentrated superiority of naval force in Europe. . . ." On another occasion, he said: "So long as the British fleet can maintain and assert superiority in the North Sea and around the British Isles, the entire imperial system stands secure."

Mahan was considerably less percipient when he came to apply British doctrine and practice to American conditions. The strategic geography of the United States differed from

[3] *ibid.*, pp. 52, 56.

[4] Quoted in A. J. Marder, *The Anatomy of British Sea Power,* Alfred A. Knopf, 1940, p. 473.

Britain's in nearly every essential respect. Because of the absence of powerful, potentially hostile neighbors in North America, the United States was, from the perspective of military geography, as insular as Britain. Everything Mahan said about the advantages of insularity applied as much to the United States as to the British Isles. But right there the parallel ended!

Because the Atlantic Ocean is immensely wider than the English Channel and North Sea, and because no American state approached the greater powers of Europe in military potential, the homeland of the United States could be made more secure at lower cost than was ever possible in the case of Britain. Distance, as Mahan once put it, was a "factor equivalent to a certain number of ships." For this reason the minimum naval requirements for defense of the continental United States were proportionally smaller—and Mahan said so.

From the standpoint of world politics, and for purposes of waging large-scale offensive war against the Great Powers overseas, however, the American position was infinitely weaker than Britain's. For geographical reasons, obvious though too often ignored by Mahan and his empire-minded friends, no exercise of naval power within the Western Hemisphere could possibly produce political results comparable to those that flowed from Britain's historic command of Europe's narrow seas. There were no narrow seaways in the Americas comparable in international importance to the English Channel and the Strait of Gibraltar.

Naval theorists often drew an analogy between the Caribbean and the Mediterranean seas. Mahan and others confidently prophesied that the opening of an isthmian canal would transform the Caribbean into a trunk route of world commerce, rivalling Suez and the Mediterranean as a short-cut to the Far East. But they failed to appreciate, or at least neglected to state, that the Panama Canal would never be a thoroughfare politically and strategically vital to any Great Power except the United States.

American statesmen and their naval advisers might, and did, conclude (under the tutelage of Mahan) that military control of the oceanic approaches to the United States required building capital ships and organizing these into one, or at most two, battle fleets. But it is difficult to see, Mahan and his disciples to the contrary notwithstanding, how any fleet, however powerful, or any strategic doctrine, however sound, could have given the United States government a leverage on other Great Powers even remotely approaching that exercised from London down to the end of the nineteenth century.

Mahan's persistent denigration of cruiser warfare was unquestionably influential in shifting American naval doctrine to a capital fleet strategy. Mahan was historically correct when he reiterated that hit-and-run raiding had crippled neither Britain in the War of 1812 nor the North in the American Civil War. At the same time, it could be argued that hit-and-run raiding was the only offensive strategy available to the United States in more distant seas—at least under technological conditions prevailing well into the twentieth century. The geographical isolation of the United States from Eurasia, lack of advantageously located naval ports close to the trunklines of seaborne commerce to and from Europe, and the limited steaming radius of early twentieth-century naval ships, severely restricted the offensive operations that the United States could have conducted against any European enemy. Mahan recognized these limitations, yet ambivalently advocated a capital fleet strategy not merely as a necessity for continental defense but also as a presumably effective military and political instrument vis-à-vis the Great Powers overseas.

At the same time, alternative opportunities already on the horizon went largely or completely unnoticed in Mahan's vision of the future. In the 1890's and 1900's, evidence of accelerating technological change was discernible in all directions. But Mahan's intellectual universe was deeply rooted in the seventeenth and eighteenth centuries. It was largely from that perspective that he interpreted events and estimated future possibilities. Nearly all his generalizations reflected judgments as to what would have been possible or impossible on the day of Trafalgar.

Mahan paid scarcely any attention to the future political-naval implications of the spreading railway networks that were in his time already reducing dependence on seaborne movement. He beheld the early development of highway motor vehicles, submarines, and aircraft; yet there is hardly any evidence that, to the day of his death in 1914, he anticipated in the slightest the revolutionary effects that these and other mechanical inventions would produce in the years just ahead. Essentially a conservative thinker, Mahan seems to have taken it for granted that the future would not be very different from the immediate past.

Without Mahan the history of American naval policy and development would unquestionably have been different. Had Mahan's thinking been less firmly rooted in an already obsolescent past, had he been a little more imaginative and prescient, the future impact of his ideas might also have been considerably different. That his teachings—especially on fleet organization and cruiser warfare—rendered the Naval Service more doctrinally conservative and resistant to new thinking than they might otherwise have been after World War I, and even as recently as World War II and after, is at least an arguable thesis. In any case, these are some of the issues implicit in *The Rise of American Naval Power,* issues that seem especially relevant in the longer historical perspective from our vastly changed world of the 1960's.

Contents

	Introduction	v
I.	Chart and Compass	1
II.	Sea Power and American Independence (1776-1783)	7
III.	Independence Without Sea Power (1783-1789)	16
IV.	Federalist Policy: Naval Expansion and Cruiser Warfare (1789-1801)	25
V.	Jeffersonian Policy: Retrenchment and Passive Coast Defense (1801-1812)	50
VI.	Strategic Lessons of the War of 1812 (1812-1815)	73
VII.	The Neglected Lessons of 1812 (1815-1837)	86
VIII.	From Sails to Steam: The First Phase (1837-1845)	110
IX.	Naval Policy, Manifest Destiny, and Slave Politics (1845-1861)	127
X.	The Civil War: Strategic Lessons and Technical Progress (1861-1865)	151
XI.	Last Years of the Old Navy (1865-1881)	165
XII.	Beginnings of the New Navy (1881-1889)	183
XIII.	Alfred Thayer Mahan: Sea Power and the New Manifest Destiny (1889-1897)	202
XIV.	Mahan Vindicated: The War with Spain (1897-1901)	223
XV.	Mahan Triumphant: The Policy of Theodore Roosevelt (1901-1909)	250
XVI.	Rooseveltian Policy Without Roosevelt (1909-1913)	286

Contents

XVII. Politics and Policy on the Eve of the Great War (1913-1914) 304

XVIII. Europe at War: Neutrality and Preparedness (1914-1917) 317

XIX. America at War: Strategic Lessons and Political Consequences (1917-1918) 347

XX. The Log Reviewed 378

Notes on Methods and Materials 387

Index 393

CHAPTER ONE

☆ ☆

Chart and Compass

THURSDAY, December 26, 1918, was a gray winter day in New York City. Fog and "swirling snow and rain" filled the air, almost shutting out the magnificent spectacle for which cheering crowds lined the waterfront of lower Manhattan. Ten American battleships which had served in the war overseas were returning home. These great war machines, looming one after another through the mist, were a far cry from the picturesque, long-vanished sailing ships in which John Paul Jones and other Revolutionary captains had challenged the overwhelming sea power of Great Britain. The ten dreadnoughts which steamed slowly up the Bay on that December morning nearly one hundred and fifty years later symbolized the American Navy's inexorable march to equality with the historic mistress of the seas. And it was fitting that the rise of American naval power, begun in hostility to Great Britain, should thus approach its climax in the return of the American battle squadrons from intimate association in a common cause with the world's first naval Power.

In many ways the World War marked the final stage in the formative period of American naval development. That is not to say that naval progress had come to an end. The post-war generation would witness many changes and improvements, but the basic principles and broad pattern of policy were now established. In general, the organization of Great Britain's Grand Fleet, in which one squadron of the American battleships had served for a year with unostentatious distinction, was much the same as that of the United States Fleet twenty years later. The main components of a fighting fleet today—battleships, cruisers, destroyers, submarines, aircraft, and aircraft carriers—were all present in the Grand Fleet at the close of the World War. The strategic and tactical principles which governed that Fleet's operations were substantially those in vogue today. The complex processes of administration—building, servicing, and repairing ships; training and handling personnel; providing ammunition, fuel, and the thousand other supplies necessary to maintain a great fighting fleet; building and operating drydocks, machine shops, and other industrial plants on which the forces afloat ultimately depend—these were well established, and destined to change comparatively little in the ensuing years.

A visitor to the Navy Department in 1919, and again in 1939, would have discovered remarkable continuity in the activities of that establishment. An observer in the galleries, committee rooms, and lobbies of Congress during the weeks preceding passage of the great naval bill of 1916, and again during the proceedings on the Vinson naval bill of 1938, would have noted marked similarity in the procedures and tactics of legislation. The tremendous "preparedness" drive which preceded the 1916 Act anticipated in almost every particular the "rearmament" campaign a generation later. The merging of naval policy with foreign policy was at last effected as a result of the war. And today's ominous struggle for armed security upon the sea is but the resumption of a process perceptible before the war, accelerated during and as a result of that struggle, and partially if temporarily arrested by the Washington Conference of 1921–1922. In short, if a navy-minded Rip Van Winkle had fallen asleep following the return of the American battleships from Europe in the winter of 1918–1919, and awakened twenty years later, he would have beheld changes, it is true, but no revolutionary alteration of the principles of naval technology, strategy, and organization; of the processes of naval administration and policy determination; of the general atmosphere of public opinion; of the relation of naval development to internal politics; or of the impact of American naval power and policy on international politics in Europe, Eastern Asia, and the Western Hemisphere.

If, however, our Rip Van Winkle had awakened in 1918, after a twenty-years' sleep beginning in December 1898, he would have been amazed at the startling developments that had taken place. The *Oregon,* best American ship in the war with Spain, was little more than a gunboat compared with the battleships which steamed into New York Harbor on the day after Christmas in 1918. In 1898 the further development of naval architecture which culminated in the dreadnought, the all-big-gun battleship, lay still in the uncharted future. Destroyers were just coming into use. The submarine was still an experimental toy, the immense potentialities of which no one could then foresee. And few men had even dreamed of the development of aircraft into powerful instruments of maritime defense and into indispensable components of a fighting fleet.

In fact, the very conception of a permanent American fighting fleet was in 1898 still in its infancy. As a result of the Spanish War and the teachings of Captain Alfred Thayer Mahan, then at the zenith of his fame, the doctrine of command of the sea was officially accepted, it is true. And there was some appreciation of the corollary principle of concentration of power. But there was little agreement, even in theory, as to the proper composition of a fighting fleet. And scarcely anyone then envisaged the "fleet" as a permanent institution, in peace as well as in war; a collective entity with ships and men forged into an instrument of power through long association and constant training.

The visitor from 1898 would have been astonished in 1918 also by the greatly enhanced importance of the Navy in the international relations of the American people. Foreign affairs and international crises had frequently stimulated naval development during the nineteenth century. But naval policy had rarely influenced foreign relations in any great measure. The oversea expansion accompanying the war with Spain, however, had transformed the United States from a continental Power to a world empire, although few men in 1898 grasped the naval implications of this fact. Even fewer foresaw the larger participation of the United States in world politics which took place under Secretary of State John Hay (1898–1905) and President Theodore Roosevelt (1901–1909). Oversea possessions and world politics projected the threat of American naval power into the geographic spheres of other Great Powers, especially Japan. The unprecedented development of the fleet under Roosevelt produced further international repercussions. The adoption in 1916 of a new standard of power summed up in the slogan, "a navy second to none," foreshadowed the possibility of a naval race with Great Britain. The defeat of Germany heightened the danger of an Anglo-American struggle for supremacy upon the sea. The war in Europe destroyed the balance of power in the Far East, stimulated Japanese imperialism, and left the United States, at least temporarily, as the chief guardian of Western interests in Eastern Asia. And this result, together with the rapid rise of American naval power, foreshadowed a grave crisis and the possibility of an early war in the Pacific. In short, the American Navy had evolved in twenty years from an important instrument of national policy into an object of such worldwide concern that it was no exaggeration to regard naval policy in 1918 as a branch, and at least momentarily the paramount branch, of the foreign policy of the United States.

Although no political developments comparable to these had occurred during the twenty years preceding 1898, the United States had, in that period, made revolutionary progress in naval strategy and technology. If our Rip Van Winkle's slumbers had spanned the years from 1878 to 1898, he would have wakened in a world strange almost beyond recognition. The wooden navy had vanished, and its place had been taken by one of steel. He would have missed the tall masts, the maze of rigging, and the wide sails which still distinguished cruisers of the Old Navy in the decade following the Civil War. Instead of muzzle-loading guns, mostly smooth-bores, he would have discovered new breech-loading rifles, firing shells weighing hundreds of pounds, so destructive that one well placed hit could have sunk the best cruiser that flew the American flag in 1878.

Revolutionary developments had also taken place in the strategic sphere. As late as 1888 the American people had not progressed beyond their eighteenth century conceptions of commerce raiding cruiser warfare and passive coast and harbor defense. The advent of Captain Mahan in 1890 finally brought about the long overdue subordination of those ancestral conceptions to the modern and fundamental doctrine of command of the sea. Official acceptance of Mahan's philosophy of sea power had in turn effected radical changes in the naval building policy of the United States.

Important developments in both the technical and political spheres had taken place during the preceding middle decades of the century. Captain John Paul Jones could have stepped upon the deck of any American man-of-war in the early 1830's and felt as much at home there as upon the quarter-deck of his own *Bonhomme Richard* (1779). The ship-of-the-line, that massive wooden sailing fortress, mounting sixty to one hundred or more smooth-bore, muzzle-loading pieces, served by hundreds of manual workers, was still the essential basis of naval power. But when Martin Van Buren entered the White House in 1837, steam was coming into use in the American Navy. And in the next fifty years sails were gradually to disappear. This half century (1837–1887)—the naval counterpart of the mechanical revolution in industry—witnessed other sweeping technological advances. The solid projectile finally gave way to explosive shells. The once great wooden warship, degraded to a shambles by the increasing destructiveness of gunfire, and lacking the structural strength to support heavy marine engines, gradually retreated, despite official reluctance, before the inexorable advance of ironclad warships, which in turn were to evolve into the great battleship of the twentieth century.

In this middle period of the nineteenth century, the American people also passed political milestones important in the rise of American naval power upon the sea. Westward expansion to the Pacific (1846–1848) raised the problem of two-ocean defense. This strategic puzzle made the interoceanic canal a necessity. And its eventual construction, while partially resolving one strategic impasse, was to create the further problem of defending the canal itself.

Finally the first half-century of our national existence, that still more remote period from the Revolution to the inauguration of Andrew Jackson, had laid the foundation of American naval power. The distinctively American methods of formulating naval policy dated from those early years. It was then that the Navy became entangled in domestic politics, victimized by patronage and the pork-barrel. It was then that oceanic, continental, sectional, economic, and partisan influences gave rise to strategic theories and political attitudes which were strikingly to affect the growth of naval power for a century and more to come. It was then that statesmen and publicists formulated the arguments which were to feed the fires of propaganda incessantly raging around the Navy to the present day. And to those early years of our national life we now turn for the halting but supremely important first steps in the rise of American naval power.

CHAPTER TWO

☆ ☆

Sea Power and American Independence (1776–1783)

THE naval epic of the United States may be said to have begun with the War of the American Revolution. One could, it is true, trace the conceptual foundation of early American naval policy back into a still more remote age. It is also true that the United States Navy was not permanently established until more than a decade after the close of the Revolutionary struggle. But there are at least three reasons for beginning at the Revolution in a study of the rise of American naval power. First, because sea power played so vital a part in the winning of American independence. Second, because the events of that struggle started a discussion of national defense, and of the Navy's rôle therein, which has continued to this day. And third, because Captain Alfred Thayer Mahan's reinterpretation, more than one hundred years later, of the naval operations of the Revolution, figured so conspicuously in the rise of the strategic principle which is today the basic doctrine of American naval policy.

FOUNDATIONS OF REVOLUTIONARY NAVAL POLICY

The strategic situation and maritime interests of Great Britain and the Colonies conditioned the naval policy of Revolutionary America. The outstanding fact was the overwhelming superiority of the British Navy. No one entertained the slightest hope of improvising a naval force that could cope with the larger vessels and squadrons of that Navy. It was doubtful if the Colonies could themselves assemble upon the ocean enough force even to compel a concentration of British detachments in American waters.[1]

A second conditioning factor was the economic importance and political power of maritime interests in the Colonies. Maritime enterprises—foreign trade, intercolonial commerce, whaling, and the fisheries—engaged a large portion of the capital and inhabitants, especially of the New England Colonies. War with the world's greatest naval Power immediately exposed these properties and enterprises to destruction, a matter of the greatest concern to the maritime interests which swayed the politics of the Northern Colonies, and wielded a large influence in the Continental Congress.[2]

A third factor was the opportunity which the war afforded to plunder the commerce of the British Empire. The merchant shipping and military transports of Great Britain were viewed as a legitimate source of military supplies and other merchandise, desperately needed in the Colonies. And prospective profits from plundering this shipping appealed irresistibly to colonial shipowners and maritime adventurers in general.[3]

A fourth conditioning factor was the strategic situation of the Colonies. The ocean was the chief highway of intercolonial communication. All the principal cities were seaports. Population was concentrated within a narrow zone stretching a thousand miles along the Atlantic seaboard. The configuration of that seaboard rendered the Colonies highly vulnerable. Hostile occupation of Chesapeake Bay, Delaware Bay, or the Hudson River, and their tributary waters, would disrupt overland communication which, though primitive, was vitally important in

[1] C. O. Paullin, *The Navy of the American Revolution* (1906), pp. 156–8, 163. This is the standard work on the navy and naval policy of Revolutionary America.

[2] C. W. Upham, *The Life of Timothy Pickering* (1873), Vol. II, pp. 143–4.

[3] Paullin, *Navy of the Revolution,* pp. 147–50.

a war with a superior maritime Power. The line of the Hudson was especially important. This great marine highway, together with Lake Champlain and the Richelieu River, provided a virtually continuous waterway from the Atlantic to the St. Lawrence. Hostile possession of this thoroughfare would isolate New England, and quite possibly result in irretrievable disaster to the Revolutionary cause.[4]

Naval Strategy and Operations

The naval efforts of the Continental Congress developed along three lines. During the siege of Boston, in the first year of the war, Congress authorized fitting out a temporary force to prey on the military transports carrying supplies to the British army in that city.[5] Following the unsuccessful assault on Quebec, the same year, Congress sought to place a naval force upon Lake Champlain to resist the expected counter-offensive on the part of the British forces in Canada.[6] And simultaneously, it embarked upon the much larger undertaking of providing a sea-going navy.[7]

The initiative for this larger undertaking came, logically enough, from Rhode Island, the maritime interests of whose citizens were suffering from the depredations of British men-of-war and privateers. As was to be expected, the representatives

[4] *ibid.*, pp. 34, 153–4.

[5] *ibid.*, pp. 61–9.

[6] The makeshift force assembled upon the lakes played a rôle of the greatest strategic importance. Though ultimately overpowered, it held back the British advance from the north until 1777, preventing a junction of these forces with those in New York, which, if it had taken place, might well have ended the war in the autumn of 1776. This delay, together with the poor generalship of the British command, saved the Revolutionary cause, and gave time for the American agents in Europe to prepare the way for treaties of commerce and alliance with France, which were concluded after the surrender of Burgoyne's army in northern New York in October, 1777. See Captain A. T. Mahan, "Major Operations of the Royal Navy, 1762–1783" in *The Royal Navy* (edited by W. L. Clowes, 1898), Vol. III, pp. 353–70; and Paullin, *Navy of the Revolution*, pp. 71–9.

[7] E. P. Oberholtzer, *Robert Morris, Patriot and Financier* (1903), pp. 91–6; and Paullin, *Navy of the Revolution*, Chap. III.

of the other New England Colonies strongly supported this proposal to provide a sea-going navy. And as was likewise to be expected, it was the South, less concerned with maritime enterprise, that offered the principal opposition. But this opposition, while delaying action for weeks, could not prevent the adoption and execution of measures resulting in the creation of the Continental Navy.[8]

The operations of this Navy reflected opportunistic adjustments to prevailing conditions, rather than adherence to fundamental principles of strategy. Unable to drive off, or even to engage with any hope of success, the larger vessels of the British Navy, the operations of the Continental cruisers were at all times severely limited. These cruisers attempted to afford some protection to American merchant shipping by making war on hostile privateers and smaller men-of-war, and by convoying merchant vessels out to sea past the enemy's hovering warships. They cooperated to some extent with the Continental land forces around certain port towns. They attacked the enemy's military communications and oversea commerce. And they even raided the coasts of the British Isles and of outlying parts of the British Empire.[9]

Several States raised their own naval forces.[10] While these State navies included a few deep-sea cruising vessels, they consisted chiefly of makeshift gunboats, barges, and other improvised floating defenses for local protection.[11] These forces played a minor rôle, and might perhaps be ignored altogether, but for the fact that they foreshadowed a kind of passive coast defense, which was to have great vogue under President Jefferson (1801–1809), and recurrently thereafter was to disturb American naval policy.

Privateering supplemented, and in the end virtually sup-

[8] Paullin, *Navy of the Revolution,* pp. 81–5; and *Letters of Members of the Continental Congress* (edited by E. C. Burnett, 1921), Vol. I, pp. 230, 236.

[9] Paullin, *Navy of the Revolution,* Chap. VI.

[10] *ibid.,* Chaps. XI–XVII.

[11] *ibid.,* p. 152.

planted, the deep-sea operations of the Continental and State navies. Privateers, as their name suggests, were privately owned war vessels, sailing under licenses issued by a belligerent government. Hundreds of such vessels were fitted out in America, to raid and plunder the merchant shipping of the British Empire. The profits of this business went to the owners and crews, making service in the privateers far more popular than in the Continental Navy. Indeed, the resulting difficulty in procuring seamen was an important factor in the steadily declining activity of the Continental cruisers in the later stages of the war. It is estimated that the privateers took some six hundred prizes, worth altogether about eighteen million dollars, as compared with less than two hundred prizes, worth six million dollars, accredited to the Continental Navy.[12]

The exploits of Continental naval captains in general, and of John Paul Jones in particular; the fabulous profits of lucky privateersmen; and the chorus of protests and lamentations raised in the British Empire—all tended to create an impression that American cruisers and privateers played a vital rôle in the Revolutionary struggle. Such, however, was not the case. They did, it is true, bring in much needed cargoes of military supplies and other merchandise which incidentally were usually sold at exorbitant prices.[13] But American naval efforts signally failed to protect American shipping from equally heavy losses at the hands of British cruisers and privateers. They failed to cripple either the oversea commerce or the military communications of the British Empire. They also failed to draw off the British forces operating in American waters. And they utterly failed to frighten the British government into suing for peace.

Command of the sea, on the other hand, gave Great Britain a tremendous advantage. The British forces enjoyed a mobility denied to those of the revolutionaries chiefly dependent upon

[12] E. S. Maclay, *A History of American Privateers* (1899), pp. viii–ix; and Paullin, *Navy of the Revolution*, pp. 144–52.

[13] Paullin, *Navy of the Revolution*, pp. 150–1.

primitive overland communications.[14] Command of the sea enabled the British to capture New York and other important seaports, which thereafter became military and naval bases and havens of refuge for the British armies. Without sufficient naval power to drive off the British squadrons, it was always difficult and usually impossible for the Continental armies to win decisive victories. The ultimate failure of Great Britain to suppress the revolt in America must be attributed in no small degree to the failure of the British Command to exploit its apparently overwhelming advantage upon the ocean.[15]

Several factors contributed to this result. Weather conditions, which meant everything to a navy under sail, were peculiarly unfavorable. The British Admiralty's traditional reliance upon New England for first-class spars, and its failure to develop other sources of supply, quickly reduced the Royal Navy to dire straits when American forests were no longer available.[16] In addition, there developed a critical shortage of other essential supplies. And these conditions, in conjunction with inadequate docking and service facilities, lack of confidence in commanding officers, constant interference from London, and other handicaps, seriously reduced the effective power of the British Navy on the coast of America.[17]

The entry of France into the war, in 1778, aggravated the difficulties of Great Britain, while immensely improving the strategic position of the Colonies. France had a strong navy which played a decisive part in the struggle. For a brief period in 1781, a combination of circumstances gave naval supremacy in American waters to the French fleet of Admiral Comte de Grasse, and this rendered possible the capture of General Cornwallis's army at Yorktown.[18]

[14] W. M. James, *The British Navy in Adversity* (1926), p. 423.

[15] Captain A. T. Mahan, *The Influence of Sea Power upon History* (1890), pp. 342–3.

[16] R. G. Albion, *Forests and Sea Power, The Timber Problem of the Royal Navy* (1926), Chap. VII.

[17] James, *British Navy in Adversity*, Chap. XV, and *passim*.

[18] *ibid.*, pp. 297–300.

Naval Lessons of the Revolution

While it remained for Captain Alfred Thayer Mahan, writing more than a century later, to revive and to popularize the naval lessons of the Revolutionary struggle,[19] certain contemporary observers grasped the fundamental principles involved. Within a month after the victory at Yorktown, General Washington was writing to Lafayette that "no land force can act decisively, unless it is accompanied by a maritime superiority. . . . For proof of this, we have only to recur to the . . . ease and facility with which the British shifted their ground, as advantages were to be obtained at either extremity of the continent, and to their late heavy loss the moment they failed in their naval superiority."[20]

A few weeks later, in another letter to Lafayette, Washington appealed for additional help from France, on the ground that "a naval superiority would compel the enemy to draw their whole force to a point. . . ." And as a result, their armies would have to relinquish areas "which they effect to have conquered," or else, deprived of naval support, suffer being "cut off in detail."[21]

In May 1781, James Madison, who would one day reluctantly lead the American people into the costly and fruitless War of 1812, noted that naval superiority had enabled the enemy to shift the theater of war from one point to another along the coast, wearing down the American forces compelled to march overland.[22]

In 1782, Robert Morris, the Revolutionary financier who also wielded a large influence over Continental naval policy,

[19] *The Influence of Sea Power upon History*, Chaps. X–XIV.

[20] *The Writings of George Washington* (edited by Jared Sparks, 1834–1837), Vol. VIII, pp. 203, 205.

[21] *ibid.*, p. 224.

[22] *The Writings of James Madison* (edited by Gaillard Hunt, 1900–1910), Vol. I, p. 145.

advocated a naval force strong enough to compel the British to reinforce their squadrons, or else to accept inferiority in American waters. The former, he held, would give an advantage to our French allies in other parts of the world; the latter would spell disaster for the British armies in America.[23]

Especially remarkable, in view of later developments, was Thomas Jefferson's penetrating analysis of the naval situation of the United States in future wars with European powers. "To aim at such a navy as the greater nations of Europe possess," he wrote in 1781, "would be a foolish and wicked waste of the energies of our countrymen." Our situation rendered such a course unnecessary. "Providence has placed . . . [the] richest and most defenseless possessions" of these powers "at our door; has obliged their most precious commerce to pass, as it were, in review before us. To protect this, or to assail [us], a small part only of their naval force will ever be risked across the Atlantic. The dangers to which the elements expose them here are too well known, and the greater dangers to which they would be exposed at home were any general calamity to involve their whole fleet. They can attack us by detachment only; and it will suffice to make ourselves equal to what they may detach. Even a smaller force than they may detach will be rendered equal or superior by the quickness with which any check may be repaired with us, while losses with them will be irreparable till too late. A small naval force then is sufficient for us, and a small one is necessary."[24]

From statements such as these, it would appear that some of the leaders of Revolutionary America had learned at least two of the naval lessons of the war with Great Britain. They had perceived that conclusive naval superiority to a considerable distance from shore was necessary to prevent disruption of coastwise commerce, blockade of the country's seaports, and invasion of its seaboard. And they had grasped the equally

[23] Paullin, *Navy of the Revolution*, pp. 242–3.

[24] "Notes on Virginia" in *The Writings of Thomas Jefferson* (edited by H. A. Washington, 1853–1854), Vol. VIII, pp. 413–14.

fundamental principle that naval power was relative, both to the place of its exercise and to the general international situation—in short, that America's continental insularity and the chronically unstable balance of power in the Old World prevented any European Power from ever sending all, or anywhere nearly all, of its naval power against the United States.

It may be doubted whether the men whose statements we have just cited realized fully the broader implications of their words. It is indisputable that some of them in later years failed to act on the lessons which they appeared to have derived from the Revolutionary struggle. It is impossible, moreover, to discover how extensively the naval aspects of that conflict affected contemporary opinion regarding national security. One suspects that the lessons went largely unlearned. At any rate, the Continental Congress had neither the financial resources nor the inclination to maintain a navy in time of peace. Even Morris felt compelled, in 1783, after the close of the war, to withdraw his earlier recommendation. Congress gradually liquidated the improvised Revolutionary Navy. By the end of 1785, all of the ships had been sold or given away, leaving the United States, under the Articles of Confederation, with neither a navy nor a naval program.[25]

[25] Paullin, *Navy of the Revolution,* pp. 244–51.

CHAPTER THREE

☆ ☆

Independence Without Sea Power (1783–1789)

LACK of a navy unquestionably contributed to the sorry diplomatic record of the United States under the Articles of Confederation. Inability to back up demands with anything stronger than words was certainly an important, if incommensurable, factor in the failure of American statesmen to hold Great Britain to the terms of the Peace Treaty of 1783, to force Spain to open the lower reaches of the Mississippi River, and to secure access on more favorable terms to the home and colonial markets of the Great Powers.[1] Without a navy, Congress could neither punish nor overawe the North African Barbary Powers, whose piratical cruisers were plundering American merchant shipping in the Mediterranean.[2] In the event of another war among the European Powers, regarded as imminent during these troubled years, it seemed highly doubtful if the Continental Congress would be able, without any tangible symbol of national power upon the sea, either to forestall belligerent aggression against neutral American shipping, or even to prevent the United States from being drawn into the conflict. "A nation, despicable by its weakness,"

[1] See, for example, Jefferson to Washington, Dec. 4, 1788, *The Writings of Thomas Jefferson* (P. L. Ford's ed., 1892–1899), Vol. V, pp. 56, 58. And see, in general S. F. Bemis, *Diplomatic History of the United States* (1936), Chap. V.

[2] See, in general, R. W. Irwin, *The Diplomatic Relations of the United States with the Barbary Powers* (1931).

it was contended, "forfeits even the privilege of being neutral."[3]

No statesman of post-Revolutionary America grasped these implications of naval impotence more clearly than did Thomas Jefferson who served as Minister to France from 1785 to 1789. In theory, Jefferson favored abandoning the sea and directing the energies of his countrymen to agriculture. But, he frankly admitted, "We are not free to decide this question on principles of theory only." "Our people" were determined to "share in the occupation of the ocean," he declared, with a solicitude for the shipping interests in marked contrast to his later attitude as leader of the great agrarian movement. It was the duty of national statesmen, he continued, "to conform themselves to the decided choice of their constituents"—in this instance, "to preserve an equality of right . . . in the transportation of commodities, in the right of fishing, & in the other uses of the sea."

To realize these ends, Jefferson believed, a navy was indispensable. Without one we could not command respect for our own citizen's maritime interests, and the resulting aggression might easily lead to war. Without a navy we could neither protect our shipping nor defend our coast in case of war with the great maritime Powers. Even a small navy would give us a commanding strategic position. "Our vicinity to the West India possessions [of these Powers] & to [their Atlantic] fisheries" was, as he had previously pointed out in his "Notes on Virginia," "a bridle which a small naval force on our part could hold in the mouths of the most powerful of these countries."[4]

The piracy of the Barbary Powers seemed to Jefferson a convenient and suitable occasion for beginning a navy. We could not "begin it in a better cause nor against a weaker foe."[5] A

[3] Alexander Hamilton to the People of New York, Nov. 24, 1787, *The Federalist* (E. M. Earle's ed., 1937), No. 11, p. 65.

[4] Jefferson to Jay, Aug. 23, 1785, *The Writings of Jefferson* (Ford's ed.), Vol. IV, pp. 87, 89–90.

[5] Jefferson to Gates, Dec. 13, 1784, *ibid.*, pp. 23–4; and see also, Jefferson to Monroe, Nov. 11, 1784, *ibid.*, pp. 4, 11.

display of force upon the sea would enhance the prestige of the United States; it would "procure us respect in Europe"; and it would "arm the federal head [the Continental Congress] with the safest of all the instruments of coercion over its delinquent members [the States], . . ."[6]

Formidable constitutional obstacles, however, stood in the way of establishing a navy. The policy-determining organ under the Articles of Confederation was the Continental Congress. This body had power to "allow" expenditures for the "common defense," but no power to levy taxes or to compel the States to contribute funds to the "common treasury." The Articles authorized Congress to appoint a committee consisting of one delegate from each State to manage the "general affairs" of the Confederation between sessions of Congress, and this "Committee of the States" was expressly empowered "to build and equip a navy." But it could take no step toward this end until nine or more of the thirteen States "in Congress assembled" should "ascertain the sums and expenses necessary for the defense . . . of the United States," and "agree upon the number of vessels of war to be built or purchased. . . ."[7]

These constitutional limitations, in conjunction with the sectional cleavage which had impeded the naval efforts of the Revolutionary Continental Congress, blocked the only serious effort made under the Articles of Confederation to reestablish a navy. This effort followed a report on the depredations of the Barbary pirates, submitted in the winter of 1785–1786, by John Jay, foreign secretary of Congress. In this report Jay raised squarely the question: "Whether it would be more wise in the United States to withdraw their Attention from the Sea, and Permit Foreigners to fetch and Carry for them; or to persevere in concerting and pursuing such Measures as may conduce to

[6] Jefferson to Adams, July 11, 1786, *The Writings of Thomas Jefferson* (H. A. Washington's ed., 1853–1854), Vol. I, pp. 591–2; and see also Jefferson to Monroe, Aug. 11, 1786, *Writings of Jefferson* (Ford's ed.), Vol. IV, pp. 262, 264–5.

[7] Text in E. M. Earle's edition of *The Federalist*, pp. 580, 582, 583.

render them a maritime Power?"[8] Delegates from the eastern and middle States were generally for the "latter system," while those from other quarters were inclined to favor the former, and to "throw cold water" on schemes for increasing the maritime power of the United States.[9] Torn by divided counsels, and unable either to enforce its decisions or to replenish its dwindling financial resources, the moribund Congress could make little headway. After months of delay a committee brought in a report endorsing a navy in principle and recommending further study of the question. But even this innocuous measure was allowed to die of inaction.[10]

Naval Policy in the Constitutional Struggle

While the fragmentary records of the Constitutional Convention of 1787 contain very few references to naval affairs, and no extended discussions of the subject whatever, the work of that assembly was nevertheless a landmark in the evolution of American naval policy. The new Constitution invested Congress with power "to lay and collect taxes . . . to pay the debts and provide for the common defense and general welfare of the United States." And it specifically authorized Congress "to provide and maintain a navy." This latter provision supplanted the clause in the Articles of Confederation which had empowered the Continental Congress "to build and equip a navy." This weaker phraseology which was carried over into early drafts considered by the Constitutional Convention, was strengthened by unanimous consent and without debate.[11] "The palpable necessity of the power to provide and maintain a

[8] *Journals of the Continental Congress* (Library of Congress ed., 1904–1937), Vol. XXIX, pp. 842–4; and see William Jay, *The Life of John Jay* (1833), Vol. I, pp. 202–3.

[9] Jay to John Adams, Nov. 1, 1785, *Diplomatic Correspondence of the United States, 1783–1789* (Rives' three-volume ed., 1855), Vol. II, p. 430.

[10] *Journals of the Continental Congress,* Vol. XXX, pp. 152–3.

[11] *Debates on the Adoption of the Federal Constitution* (Jonathon Elliot's 2nd ed., 1861), Vol. V (Madison's Journal), pp. 130, 379, 445, 561.

navy," noted James Madison, an influential member of the Convention, "has protected that part of the Constitution against a spirit of censure, which has spared few other parts."[12]

Broadly speaking, Madison's statement held true, not only for the Constitutional Convention, but also for the post-Convention struggle for ratification within the several States. Still, national defense in general and naval policy in particular were by no means ignored in the State ratification campaigns. In several States the need of a Federal navy was cited as one of the reasons for ratifying the Constitution. Without a navy, it was argued, the country was and must remain at the mercy of every strong maritime Power. It was an "old observation," declared Edmund Randolph, in the Virginia Convention, "that he who commands the sea will command the land . . ."[13] While the "European powers were so far removed from us that it would be very dangerons [for them] to send a considerable force against us"; and while their West Indies trade passing near our coast "naturally lay at our mercy," it was still a fact, contended John Rutledge, in the South Carolina Convention, that "we must hold our country by courtesy, unless we have a navy. . . ."[14] The Southern States, argued Charles Cotesworth Pinckney, in the same assembly, were peculiarly vulnerable to attack. Because of the "nature of our climate and the fewness of our inhabitants, we are undoubtedly weak," he admitted, urging "close union with the Eastern States," and "increase [in] that species of strength [a navy] which will render them of most service to us both in peace and war. . . ."[15] The object of naval policy uppermost in the minds of these spokesmen of the Southern tidewater aristocracy apparently involved little more than security for the lands which were the source of both their wealth and their political power.

In the eyes of James Madison, whose views of national policy

[12] James Madison to the People of New York, Jan. 22, 1788, *The Federalist* (Earle's ed.), No. 41, p. 266.

[13] Elliot's *Debates*, Vol. III, p. 78.

[14] *ibid.*, Vol. IV, p. 299.

[15] *ibid.*, p. 284.

extended somewhat beyond the boundaries of his Virginia plantation, a navy was not merely an agency for territorial defense, but also an instrument with which to compel respect for other national interests and policies. Looking forward to an early outbreak of war between France and Great Britain, Madison spoke at some length, in the Virginia Convention, on the imperative need of a navy with which to safeguard the neutral interests of the United States. We were "remote from Europe, and ought not to engage in her politics and wars." Neutrality would enable our merchantmen to "carry on the commerce of the contending nations." Here was a source of wealth, he argued, "which we ought not to deny to our citizens." But such a commerce would invite belligerent reprisals. Unless we could compel respect, we would be "insulted and attacked." With sufficient power upon the sea, however, our ships could enjoy the "great advantages of carrying on the commerce of the nations at war; for none of them would [then] be willing to add us to the number of their enemies."[16]

A still broader conception of national interest in a navy was developed by Alexander Hamilton during the constitutional struggle in New York State. A regular navy was, first of all, as Madison had said, an indispensable instrument of national policy in dealing with foreign nations. ". . . Continuance of the Union under an efficient government," Hamilton contended, "would put it in our power, at a period not very distant, to create a navy which, if it could not vie with those of the great maritime powers," could at least hold the balance of power within this hemisphere. In view of European colonial interests in the West Indies, "our position" was, "in this respect, a most commanding one." With even "a few ships-of-the-line whose intervention would often be sufficient to decide the fate of a campaign" in this region, American statesmen could "bargain with great advantage for commercial privileges. A price would be set not only upon our friendship, but upon our neutrality."

[16] *ibid.*, Vol. III, pp. 249–50, 309.

And we might "hope, erelong, to become the arbiter of Europe in America, and to be able to incline the balance of European competitions in this part of the world as our interests may dictate." And in Hamilton's view these interests, which included access to foreign markets, the ocean carrying trade, the Atlantic fisheries, and free navigation of the Mississippi, were objects of concern not only to particular localities and sections, but also to the national economy as a whole.

Hamilton also believed that institution of a navy would have an internally unifying and stimulating effect on this national economy. Each section would benefit not only from the display and exercise of naval power, but also from the process of naval development. Each possessed "some peculiar advantage for this essential establishment." The Southern States, for example, produced especially fine ship timber and naval stores; the Middle States yielded "a greater plenty of iron, and of better quality"; while seamen would be drawn chiefly from the North. And the force thus created by the joint efforts of the whole country would provide the people of America with a tangible symbol of their national unity and power.[17]

Hamilton's theory of a general, country-wide interest in a navy stood in marked contrast to the sectionalism of numerous spokesmen chiefly of the agrarian West and South. When James Duane of New York City "spoke [in the New York Convention] of the necessity, that might in future exist, of maintaining large armies and navies," and "hoped yet to see the United States able, as well by sea as by land, to resent any injuries that might be offered them,"[18] he drew a vigorous dissent from Melancthon Smith of Poughkeepsie, leader of the anti-Federalist forces. Voicing a sentiment current in the interior, Smith "thought it would be wild and ridiculous to attempt a project of that kind for a considerable length of time, even if the treasury were full of money."[19]

[17] *The Federalist* (Earle's ed.), No. 11, pp. 64-5.
[18] Elliot's *Debates*, Vol. II, p. 379.
[19] *ibid.*, p. 381.

In the Virginia Convention, Patrick Henry, a self-appointed champion of Western interests,[20] left no doubt regarding his opposition to a Federal navy. A navy was an instrument of imperial ambition.[21] It would place a heavy financial burden upon the people.[22] And it would be an unnecessary burden, for such was the "condition of European affairs, that it would be unsafe for them [the European Powers] to send fleets or armies" against us.[23]

Even more forthright was the uncompromising stand of William Grayson, a Virginia lawyer and politician who was deeply interested in the "development of the western country. . . ."[24] Adverting to Madison's argument that a navy was necessary to compel respect for the interests of neutral shipping, he declared that even if this were so, "the profits that might arise from such a transient commerce could not compensate for the expenses of rendering ourselves formidable at sea, or the danger that would probably result from the attempt." The European Powers with West Indian possessions would take alarm, he believed, "at any extraordinary maritime exertions" on our part, and would provoke a war in order to "crush us in our infancy." An attempt to maintain a navy, moreover, would tend to withdraw men from the land, to the detriment of agriculture which was the only source of real prosperity for a country as sparsely populated as the United States.[25] A Federal navy, moreover, would benefit the North at the expense of the South. Northern shipbuilders would monopolize the construction of the vessels. Northern politicians would control their movements. The South would have to share the "expenses without having equal emoluments." Indeed, there was grave danger that the South would be left undefended in case of war. For these reasons, Grayson thought that it would be "very im-

[20] W. E. Dodd, "Patrick Henry," *Dict. Am. Biog.*, Vol. VIII, pp. 554–9.
[21] Elliot's *Debates*, Vol. III, p. 53.
[22] *ibid.*, p. 157.
[23] *ibid.*, p. 153.
[24] F. E. Ross, "William Grayson," *Dict. Am. Biog.*, Vol. VII, p. 525.
[25] Elliot's *Debates*, Vol. III, pp. 288–9.

politic to give this power [to provide and maintain a navy] to Congress without any limitation."[26]

Viewed as a whole, the period of the Confederation appears not only as an interregnum in the development of American naval power, but also as an important stage in the evolution of American naval policy. The scattered references to naval affairs in this period, when assembled, reveal two antithetical patterns of thought which have persisted down to the present day. To the argument that a navy was needed to defend the coast and commerce of the United States against hostile attack in war, it was replied that distance and the unstable balance of power in the Old World would prevent any European Power from carrying war to the coast of America, and that oversea commerce was not worth the cost of defense. To the argument that a navy was an essential adjunct of diplomacy to compel respect for national interests and policies, it was replied that a navy so conceived would become an instrument of imperialism and a provocation to war. To the claim that a navy would stimulate and unify the national economy, it was answered that the profits would accrue only to certain sections, and that the more fundamental economic effect would be to increase taxes and to impoverish the people as a whole.

These discussions reflected a fundamental difference of opinion in post-Revolutionary America, both as to the national interest in power upon the sea, and as to a navy's potentialities in the country's political economy. The cleavage thus revealed coincided substantially with a sectional, economic, and social grouping which was soon to find political expression in the Hamiltonian-Federalist and the Jeffersonian-Republican Parties. And this alignment foreshadowed the future politics of American naval development in general, and in particular the partisan struggle that was soon to rage around the Federalist drive to establish a regular sea-going navy.[27]

[26] *ibid.*, pp. 428–30. For words of similar import, see the argument of Rawlins Lowndes in the South Carolina Convention. *ibid.*, Vol. IV, p. 309.

[27] The basis and ramifications of the Federalist-Jeffersonian alignment are most fully developed in the writings of Dr. Charles Beard. See in particular, his *The Idea of National Interest* (1934), Chap. II.

CHAPTER FOUR

☆ ☆

Federalist Policy: Naval Expansion and Cruiser Warfare (1789–1801)

THE next stage in the evolution of American naval policy spanned the first twelve years under the Constitution—from 1789 to 1801. During these years, the Federalist Party was the dominant influence in the new system. This party, which derived its chief support from the commercial and shipping interests of the North Atlantic seaboard and from the tidewater planting aristocracy of the South,[1] embraced precisely those groups whose spokesmen had cited the need of a Federal navy as one of the reasons for ratifying the Constitution. The prospect, therefore, was that the Federalists would soon turn to the congenial task of creating such an establishment.

This project was discussed intermittently during President Washington's first term (1789–1793), but Congress took no action until 1794, when a new wave of Barbary piracy enabled the Federalists to force the issue. With that problem on the way to solution, attention shifted to the larger question of protecting American shipping from belligerent aggression in the War of the French Revolution. And naval policy presently became entangled in the bitter partisan struggle which marked the rise and triumph of the Jeffersonian-Republican Party. All these developments, especially the last, influenced the course of naval development, not only during the Federalist period,

[1] See A. N. Holcombe, *Political Parties of Today* (1924), p. 83.

but also during the succeeding years of Jeffersonian supremacy, and on into the indefinite future.

EARLY STRAWS IN THE WIND

Naval policy received comparatively little attention during Washington's first term. Even strong advocates of a navy felt constrained to wait until the government's fiscal position should have improved. Not until 1794 did Congress take any positive steps toward creating a navy. And possibly for this reason, naval historians have generally ignored a number of incidents and utterances during those early years of Federalist supremacy.

One of these was a brief allusion to naval policy in the congressional tariff debate of 1789. Speaking before the House of Representatives, James Madison advocated legislation favoring the merchant marine which would, he held, "form a school for seamen," and "lay the foundation of a navy."[2]

Then there was a provision of the congressional Act of 1789, creating the War Department, which stipulated that the Secretary of War, under the President, should have jurisdiction over the naval forces, as well as the land forces, of the United States. Although no record was taken of the debate on this measure, its phraseology clearly suggests an intention to establish a navy as soon as possible.[3]

A step in this direction was made in the autumn of 1790, when General Henry Knox, the Secretary of War, made inquiries regarding the expense of building and equipping a sea-going navy.[4] In 1791, Thomas Jefferson, who had recently returned from France to become Secretary of State, recommended fitting out a naval force strong enough to chastise

[2] *Annals of 1st Congress*, pp. 196–7.

[3] *ibid.*, pp. 49, 57, 434, 615, 631; and *Stat. at Large*, Vol. I, p. 50.

[4] C. O. Paullin, "Early Naval Administration under the Constitution," *Proceedings of United States Naval Institute*, Vol. XXXII (1906), pp. 1001–2. This is one of a large group of excellent papers by Dr. Paullin on naval administration which have greatly facilitated our study of the related subject of naval policy.

the Barbary Powers who were holding a considerable number of American seamen for ransom.[5] This proposal, together with a report by the Secretary of War on the cost of a navy,[6] created a stir in congressional circles. The House discussed the matter in secret session.[7] A Senate committee brought in a report advising a naval force "as soon as the state of the public finances will admit."[8] And the question apparently aroused a good deal of feeling among the members.

On this point, there is the testimony of Senator William Maclay of Pennsylvania, whose journal contains the following entry, dated February 1, 1791: "This day I had much to say against the report of a committee which went to declare war against the Algerines. It is not suspicion that the designs of the court [i.e., the Administration] are to have a fleet and army. . . . Eleven unfortunate men, now in slavery in Algiers, is the pretext for fitting out a fleet to go to war with them. . . . It is urged that we should expend half a million dollars rather than redeem [i.e., ransom] these unhappy men. . . . This thing of a fleet has been working among our members all the session. I have heard it break out often."[9]

More perhaps than any other member of that Congress, Maclay was the national spokesman of the rural interior,[10] whose hostility to a navy had flared up in the Continental Congress, and in the debates on the Constitution. Maclay was voicing the sentiments of that potentially powerful though still unorganized interior region, when he confided to his diary that "war is often entered into to answer domestic, not foreign purposes";[11] when he denounced the navy proposal as part of a scheme to destroy "freedom in America";[12] and when he rejoiced at the collapse of the movement to fit out a naval force

[5] *State Papers and Public Documents of the United States,* Vol. X, pp. 46, 60.
[6] Paullin, "Early Naval Administration," p. 1002.
[7] *Annals, 1st Cong.*, p. 1886.
[8] *American State Papers, Foreign Relations,* Vol. I, p. 108.
[9] *Journal of William Maclay* (edited by E. S. Maclay, 1890), p. 383.
[10] Mary R. Beard, "William Maclay," *Dict. Am. Biog.*, Vol. XII, pp. 123–4.
[11] Jan. 21, 1791, *Maclay's Journal,* p. 375.
[12] Feb. 11, *ibid.*, p. 390.

for the Mediterranean.[13] Here, plainly, was a harbinger of the storm that would break when the Federalists should come forward with a specific legislative proposal to establish a navy. That moment arrived less than three years later, in 1794, following the outbreak of the European War of the French Revolution.

The Naval Act of 1794

The outbreak of the war gave rise to a new wave of piracy. Ostensibly as a war measure, British statesmen arranged a truce between Algiers and Portugal whose navy had previously kept the Algerian corsairs confined within the Mediterranean. This truce enabled the latter to venture out into the Atlantic. It was widely believed that this stroke, aimed ostensibly at the commerce of Britain's enemy, France, was designed also to destroy the merchant shipping of the United States, Britain's chief competitor for the ocean carrying trade.[14]

Four courses lay open. The United States Government might do nothing at all, leaving American shipping to take care of itself as best it could. President and Congress might follow the old European custom of paying blackmail to the Barbary Powers. They might hire some European Power to provide naval protection for American shipping. Or they might fit out a naval force of their own for that purpose.

The Federalists, with whom, on this issue, Jefferson was still in accord,[15] strongly favored the last-mentioned course. Early in January 1794, they carried through the House of Representatives a resolution that the government ought to provide

[13] Feb. 26, *ibid.*, pp. 406–7.

[14] Timothy Pitkin, *Political and Civil History of the United States* (1828), Vol. II, pp. 402–3; *The Writings of George Washington* (Jared Sparks' edition, 1834–1837), Vol. X, pp. 401–2; *State Papers and Public Documents*, Vol. X, pp. 278, 280; and R. W. Irwin, *Diplomatic Relations with the Barbary Powers* (1931), Chap. IV.

[15] *The Writings of Thomas Jefferson* (Memorial ed., 1903–1904), Vol. XV, pp. 397, 400.

a naval force to protect American commerce against the Algerian corsairs, and that a committee be designated to consider that question.[16] The committee appointed for this purpose was heavily loaded with pro-navy Federalists,[17] and included only one outspoken anti-navy man,[18] despite the close division of opinion in the House on the desirability of fitting out any naval force at all.[19]

This committee's report recommending a force of six frigates[20] provoked a heated debate.[21] The anti-Federalists, especially the representatives of inland districts, savagely attacked the proposal. Such a force, they argued, would prove utterly inadequate; yet it would cost more than our Mediterranean commerce was worth. It would be cheaper to buy a "peace," or, if that proved impracticable, to hire some European navy to convoy our shipping. The presence of an American naval force in European waters, moreover, would tend to involve us in war; the British would probably come to the aid of Algiers; British men-of-war would provoke a crisis by stopping and searching American naval vessels; and there was grave danger that the Powers allied against France would pick a quarrel in order to destroy our naval power in its infancy.

Finally, it was feared that this measure was but the entering wedge for a standing navy, which the back country opposed on still other grounds. Such an establishment, argued the inlanders, would dangerously enlarge the power of the Federal Executive; it would tend to increase the public debt; it would neces-

[16] *Annals, 3rd Cong.*, pp. 154–5, 250.

[17] The committee contained nine members—six Federalists and three Anti-Federalists. Four of the six Federalists not only represented predominantly commercial constituencies, but were themselves merchants and shipowners. These four were Thomas Fitzsimmons of Philadelphia, Benjamin Goodhue of Salem, Francis Malbone of Newport, and Jeremiah Wadsworth of Hartford. *ibid.*, p. 155.

[18] Nathaniel Macon of North Carolina. For Macon's lifelong opposition to the Navy, see J. G. deR. Hamilton, "Nathaniel Macon," *Dict. Am. Biog.*, Vol. XII, p. 158.

[19] *Annals, 3rd Cong.*, pp. 154, 459.

[20] Frigates were large, square-rigged men-of-war, second only to ships-of-the-line in fighting power.

[21] *Annals, 3rd Cong.*, pp. 250, 433–97.

sitate higher taxes; and it would foster the growth of a tax-collecting bureaucracy—altogether, a system nicely calculated to fasten a financial tyranny upon the necks of the common people, especially the small landowners of the interior.[22]

Advocates of a navy, in their turn, ranged over an equally wide field. They argued that our Mediterranean commerce was a great national interest; that the proposed force would prove quite adequate to protect it; and that the mere existence of such a force would overawe the corsairs, and incidentally effect great savings in marine insurance. They stressed the national humiliation of paying blackmail to the Dey of Algiers, or of hiring a foreign navy to protect our shipping. There was danger that such a reputation of weakness would encourage the Algerines to extend their depredations, even to the point of raiding our continental seaboard. Against such perils, the argument of cost had no validity. A navy was admittedly expensive and we did have a "very heavy debt; but still it was better to bear debts than depredations."[23]

A resolution endorsing the naval committee's proposal was carried by two votes.[24] And so determined was the opposition that the outcome continued in doubt to the end. To reassure those opposed to a standing navy, but not to a temporary force to chastise the Algerines, an ingenious amendment was added, stipulating that there should be "no further proceeding . . . under this act," in case the United States made "peace" with Algiers.[25] Thus amended, the bill finally passed the House by a vote of 50 to 39. In due course it passed the Senate also, received the President's signature, and became law on March 27, 1794.[26]

[22] See, in particular, James Madison (Va.), Abraham Clark (N. J.), William B. Giles (Va.), *ibid.*, pp. 433–4, 436–7, 438, 446–7, 486–91.

[23] See, in particular, Samuel Smith (Md.), Fisher Ames (Mass.), Zephaniah Swift (Conn.), Thomas Fitzsimmons (Pa.), William Vans Murray (Md.), and William Smith (S. C.), *ibid.*, pp. 434–6, 438–9, 439–41, 492–6.

[24] The division was 43 to 41. *ibid.*, p. 459.

[25] This amendment did not deceive William B. Giles of Virginia, an outspoken anti-navy man who foresaw that this was but the entering wedge for further legislation to create a standing navy. *ibid.*, p. 490.

[26] *ibid.*, pp. 65, 70, 71, 497, 1426.

The accompanying table shows that the two critical votes in the House reflected the sectional cleavage previously noted in the debate. Maritime New England, where commercial, shipping, and shipbuilding interests predominated, stood 25 to 1 for a navy. The Middle Atlantic States divided 14 to 8 for the bill; the South Atlantic States, 11 to 27 against it; and the frontier States of Vermont and Kentucky supplied three more

SUMMARY OF ROLL CALLS IN THE HOUSE OF REPRESENTATIVES[27]

ON (1) THE SPECIAL NAVAL COMMITTEE'S PROPOSAL FOR A NAVAL FORCE OF SIX FRIGATES (FEB. 21, 1794), AND (2) THE FINAL PASSAGE OF THE BILL EMBODYING THIS PROPOSAL IN AMENDED FORM (MARCH 10, 1794)

	Vote on (1)			*Vote on (2)*		
	yes	*no*	*n. vtg.*	*yes*	*no*	*n. vtg.*
Maritime New England						
New Hampshire	0	3	1	2	1	1
Massachusetts	11	2	1	14	0	0
Rhode Island	2	0	0	2	0	0
Connecticut	5	0	2	7	0	0
Totals	18	5	4	25	1	1
Middle Atlantic States						
New York	6	2	2	7	3	0
Pennsylvania	5	4	4	4	5	4
New Jersey	4	0	1	3	0	2
Totals	15	6	7	14	8	6
South Atlantic States						
Delaware	1	0	0	0	0	1
Maryland	5	1	2	5	1	2
Virginia	2	14	3	4	14	1
North Carolina	0	9	1	0	9	1
South Carolina	2	2	2	2	1	3
Georgia	0	2	0	0	2	0
Totals	10	28	8	11	27	8
Frontier States						
Vermont	0	1	1	0	2	0
Kentucky	0	1	1	0	1	1
Totals	0	2	2	0	3	1
Grand totals	43	41	21	50	39	16

[27] *ibid.*, pp. 459, 497.

negative votes. Many of the Southern affirmative votes came from representatives of tidewater constituencies, with whose pro-navy tendencies we are already familiar. And a large proportion of the negative votes, both North and South, came from representatives of the rural interior.

The partisan alignment was equally significant. Although the Federalists comprised a minority of the House at this time,[28] the Naval Act of 1794 was distinctly a Federalist measure. Anti-Federalists were generally opposed, but enough of them—chiefly representatives of seaboard constituencies[29]—joined with the Federalists to secure passage of the act.[30]

In the majority of cases, sectional interests and partisan loyalties seem to have coincided. When it is recalled that the Federalist Party derived its strength mainly from an alliance between the mercantile interests of the Northern and Middle Atlantic States and the planting interests of the South, the basis of that party's stand on naval policy is at once apparent. When it is noted further, that the backbone of the rising opposition party was the multitude of small farmers, especially those of the interior,[31] it is clear why naval policy was from the outset a partisan as well as a sectional issue.[32]

[28] See George Gibbs, *Memoirs of the Administrations of Washington and John Adams, Edited from the Papers of Oliver Wolcott* (1846), Vol. I, p. 116; and Richard Hildreth, *History of the United States* (rev. ed., 1885), Vol. IV, p. 450.

[29] Hildreth, *History*, p. 480.

[30] This conclusion is believed to be well founded, although the fluidity of partisan loyalties at that time, as well as insufficiency of available data regarding some of the members of that Congress, render positive conclusions difficult, if not impossible.

[31] See Holcombe, *Parties of Today*, p. 83.

[32] It should be noted in this connection that Thomas Jefferson, the leader of this rising agrarian party, was soon to renounce his earlier advocacy of a navy, either from change of conviction, or merely to conform to the prevailing sentiment of the back-country, especially within his own State of Virginia whose representatives in Congress voted 14 to 4 against the naval bill of 1794. See *Writings of Jefferson* (Mem. ed.), Vol. X, pp. 89–95, 97–9. And it was likewise significant that James Madison, who was to be Jefferson's chief political lieutenant, led the all but solid opposition of the Virginia delegation against this bill, thereby renouncing implicitly, if not expressly, the views which he had frequently voiced as to the desirability of a navy not only to defend our

Development of Federalist Naval Policy

It was apparent from the outset that the Federalist Administration had in view an object larger than a mere temporary force directed against Algiers—although the Act of 1794 had been expressly limited to that. Instead of purchasing vessels as the Act certainly contemplated, it was decided to build them, although such a course must seriously delay putting a force upon the sea. Instead of building the vessels of such materials as were readily available, it was decided to use live oak and red cedar, which would require months to cut before construction could begin. And it was the avowed aim of the Administration, that these vessels "should combine such qualities of strength, durability, swiftness of sailing, and force, as to render them equal, if not superior, [not merely to the Algerian corsairs, but] to any frigates belonging to any of the European Powers."[33]

This reference to European navies is the key to Federalist naval plans. During the winter of 1793–1794, while Congress was debating the proposal to fit out a naval force against Algiers, the belligerent spoliation of American commerce, as well as the routine discriminations which the European Powers still imposed upon that commerce, were producing lively discussion in American governmental circles.[34] One group, consisting mainly of the pro-French anti-Federalists, advocated commercial reprisals—a policy nicely calculated to injure not only Great Britain, the worst offender, but also the politically powerful maritime interests which constituted the backbone of

coast, but also to protect American shipping and to sustain the prestige of the United States abroad. For commentaries on Madison's inconsistency, see John Marshall, *Life of George Washington* (1807), Vol. V, pp. 523–30; and J. C. Hamilton, *History of the Republic* (1859), Vol. V, p. 488. For a defense of Madison, see W. C. Rives, *Life and Times of James Madison* (1868), Vol. III, p. 436.

[33] *American State Papers, Naval Affairs,* Vol. I, p. 6, and also pp. 8, 17, 19.

[34] See, in particular, Jefferson's "Report . . . on the Privileges and Restrictions on the Commerce of the United States in Foreign Countries," *A. S. P., Foreign Relations,* Vol. I, p. 300; and the debate on this report in *Annals, 3rd Cong.,* pp. 155*ff*.

the Northern wing of the Federalist Party.[35] These interests, while resisting a policy of retaliation that might easily prove fatal to their rapidly expanding commerce with the European belligerents, nevertheless utilized foreign discriminations and depredations as an argument for building a navy, not to fight their best customers, but to compel the latter to respect the claims and interests of American merchant-shipowners.

Such a course was likewise urged by the Administration's agents in Europe. In December 1793, for example, David Humphreys[36] had written from Madrid, pleading for a naval force, not merely to overawe the Barbary pirates, but also to safeguard American shipping from aggressions arising out of the European war. A navy, he believed, "would tend more towards enabling us to maintain our neutrality in the actual critical state of affairs in Europe, than all the declarations, reasonings, concessions, and sacrifices that can possibly be made."[37]

To much the same effect ran the argument of Gouverneur Morris, another Federalist diplomat, who wrote from Paris in May 1794 urging a more aggressive foreign policy. He believed "that we could now maintain twelve ships of the line, perhaps twenty, with a due proportion of frigates and smaller vessels." He was "tolerably certain" that, "with twenty sail of the line at sea, no nation on earth" would "dare to insult" the United States. And he was thoroughly convinced, that, if we failed to "render ourselves respectable," we should "continue to be insulted."[38]

It was no simple task, however, to build a navy of such proportions, or, indeed, to build any navy at all. Not only had timber to be cut and seasoned, but other necessary materials collected, the vessels designed, shipyards built or rented, skilled

[35] Madison was the sponsor and chief advocate of this plan which was laid before Congress at exactly the same time as the naval proposal discussed in the preceding section. *Annals, 3rd Cong.*, pp. 155, 255, 366.

[36] For Humphreys' background and identification with the mercantile interest, see S. T. Williams, "David Humphreys," *Dict. Am. Biog.*, Vol. IX, pp. 373–5.

[37] *State Papers and Public Documents*, Vol. X, pp. 326–8.

[38] *A. S. P., Foreign Relations*, Vol. I, pp. 408, 409.

workmen employed, the work of construction rigidly supervised, ordnance secured, stores and supplies purchased, competent officers found and commissioned, crews recruited and assembled—all these and many other details, before the ships would be ready for sea.[39]

In laying out the work of construction, the Administration followed a course which was not without political significance for the future. To "distribute the advantages," as well as to compare the work of different sections, it was decided to build one ship at each of six seaports—Portsmouth, N. H., Boston, New York, Philadelphia, Baltimore, and Norfolk.[40] At each of these points, the government rented a shipyard, and set up a business organization to carry on the work. Meanwhile, the Treasury Department was collecting and arranging for the necessary materials and equipment. Timber was secured from the States of North and South Carolina and Georgia. Timber-cutting crews and carpenters were recruited in Massachusetts, Rhode Island, Connecticut, and Delaware, and supplies for them purchased in New London, Conn., New York City, and Philadelphia. Contracts for cannon were signed with Maryland and Connecticut firms, and for cannon ball and iron ballast with producers in New Jersey and Pennsylvania. Then there was a contract for sails with a Boston concern, and miscellaneous smaller purchases at different places.[41]

While the limited facilities of any single seaport, as well as the location of particular materials and industries, would have necessitated considerable distribution of work and contracts in any event, there is every indication that the Administration deliberately spread its shipbuilding operations over as large an area, and among as many individuals and companies as possible. It is also evident that home industries were patronized as much as possible. And it would seem a fair inference, from

[39] Paullin, "Early Naval Administration," pp. 1001, 1005–8; H. I. Chappelle, *History of American Sailing Ships* (1935), pp. 78*ff*.; and *A. S. P., Naval Affairs*, Vol. I, pp. 6*ff*.

[40] *A. S. P., Naval Affairs*, Vol. I, p. 6.

[41] *ibid.*, pp. 6–10.

official utterances as well as from circumstantial evidence, that the Administration aimed to popularize the Navy in a sufficient number of States and communities, to insure legislation continuing it on a permanent basis.

Word that an American diplomatic agent had concluded a "peace" with Algiers threatened, early in 1796, to bring everything to a standstill. According to the statute, the President should have stopped all work at once. Instead, with the manifest object of securing legislative sanction to go ahead, he sent a message to Congress asking for instructions.[42] The Senate, still under Federalist control, promptly passed a bill directing the President to finish at least three and, at his discretion, all six frigates.[43] This measure provoked a stormy debate in the House, with one side charging duplicity and bad faith,[44] and the other reiterating the arguments for a navy and blandly maintaining that it had all along been understood that these frigates were to be the nucleus of a standing navy.[45] Once again the struggle ended in a compromise, the measure, as finally passed and signed, April 20, 1796, authorizing the President to go ahead with work on only three of the unfinished vessels.[46]

During the summer and autumn of 1796, the Administration's naval policy underwent further development at the hand of Alexander Hamilton, Secretary of the Treasury, and chief architect of the "Federalist System." We have already noted Hamilton's exposition of national interest in a navy, set forth in 1787 during the struggle for ratification of the Constitution.[47] Early reestablishment of a navy had been assumed in Hamilton's system of fiscal and commercial policy as embodied

[42] *ibid.*, p. 25.

[43] *ibid.*, p. 25; *Annals, 4th Cong.*, pp. 60, 61, 62.

[44] See, in particular, John Williams (N. Y.), James Madison (Va.), and John Nicholas (Va.), *Annals, 4th Cong.*, pp. 872*ff.*, 877*ff.*, 879.

[45] See, in particular, William Smith (S. C.), *ibid.*, p. 885. Other prominent spokesmen for the affirmative included Benjamin Bourne (R. I.), Samuel Smith (Md.), Josiah Parker (Va.), Theodore Sedgwick (Mass.), Fisher Ames (Mass.), and John Swanwick (Pa.), *ibid.*, pp. 869–91, *passim.*

[46] *ibid.*, p. 891; *Stat. at Large*, Vol. I, p. 453.

[47] See pp. 21–2, *supra.*

in his "Opinion as to the Constitutionality of the Bank of the United States" (February 1791),[48] and his "Report on Manufactures" (December 1791).[49] The unifying rôle of maritime power in the national economy was implicit in certain passages which Hamilton contributed to President Washington's "Farewell Address" (September 1796).[50] And Washington's eighth and last annual message to Congress (December 1796) included a final plea for a permanent standing navy in words which unquestionably reflected Hamilton's continuing influence on the Administration's policy.

An "active external commerce," declared the President, required a "naval force" to protect it. This proposition was "manifest with regard to wars in which a State is itself a party." It was just as true with respect to wars between other Powers, for "our own experience" showed that "the most sincere neutrality" offered in itself little protection "against the depredations of nations at war." Only "a naval force organized and ready to vindicate it from insult or aggression," could "secure respect to a neutral flag. . . ." Such a force might "even prevent the necessity of going to war" at all. For these reasons, the United States should "set about the gradual creation of a navy . . . so that a future war of Europe may not find our commerce in the same unprotected state in which it was found by the present."[51]

The President's message prepared the way for a plea for additional appropriations necessary to complete even three of the frigates.[52] The introduction of measures to provide funds for finishing, fitting out, and manning the vessels, immediately drew the fire of the anti-navy forces who were determined to

[48] *Papers on the Public Credit, Commerce, and Finance by Alexander Hamilton* (edited by Samuel McKee, Jr., 1934), pp. 100, 123.

[49] *ibid.*, pp. 177, 228.

[50] See V. H. Paltsits, *Washington's Farewell Address* (1935), pp. 144*ff.*, 184*ff.*

[51] *Messages and Papers of the Presidents* (Richardson's 1st ed.), Vol. I, p. 201. This passage drew a favorable response from the Federalist majority in the Senate, but was completely ignored in the formal reply of the Anti-Federalist House, *ibid.*, pp. 205, 207-9.

[52] *A. S. P., Naval Affairs,* Vol. I, pp. 25–8.

stop work on the ships if possible, and, at any cost, to prevent fitting out and manning them for actual service at sea. Another protracted debate culminated in an impasse which once again threatened to bring everything to a standstill.[53]

Naval Policy and the Quasi-War with France

At this juncture, an international crisis temporarily rescued the Navy from the quicksands of domestic politics. Back in 1794, the pro-English Federalist leaders had staved off a rupture with Great Britain over alleged violations of neutral rights. They had done this by entering into the so-called Jay Treaty which, in return for adjustment of several long-standing American claims against Great Britain, granted some of Britain's harsh contentions as to the rights of belligerents to interfere with neutral shipping. This treaty was regarded in France as a violation of the Franco-American Alliance of 1778, and as tantamount to an alliance between the United States and England. The French forces accordingly continued their depredations on American commerce. When James Monroe, our francophile minister in Paris, failed to press American claims, President Washington recalled him, and sent in his place Charles Cotesworth Pinckney, an aristocratic Southern Federalist. French statesmen, angered at the recall of Monroe, whom they liked, refused to receive Pinckney, whom they decidedly did not like. This rebuff, together with ever increasing aggressions against American shipping, brought on a diplomatic crisis in 1797. And when the French Government refused to deal honorably with a special mission sent to restore friendly relations, the Federalists resorted to reprisals which culminated in an undeclared naval war.[54]

The rapidly developing French crisis gave a great impetus to naval development during the first two years of President John

[53] *Annals, 4th Cong.*, pp. 1671, 1893, 2049–56, 2111–51, 2200–8, 2329, 2339–52, 2784*ff*., 2939, 2955.

[54] See, for example, S. F. Bemis, *Diplomatic History of the United States* (1936), pp. 99–125.

Adams's administration, which took office March 4, 1797. With a navy-minded Federalist in the presidency,[55] and Federalist majorities in both branches of Congress,[56] bill after bill was passed, rushing the partially built frigates to completion, establishing a separate Navy Department, authorizing the President to construct, purchase, or rent additional men-of-war, and even to accept gifts of such vessels from groups of public-spirited citizens.[57]

Creation of a separate Navy Department was an event of the greatest importance. Such an institution might do more than anything else to put the Navy upon a solid, permanent foundation. Inland anti-Federalist leaders who still cherished hopes of abolishing the Navy clearly foresaw this result, and stubbornly fought the Navy Department bill at every stage of its progress through Congress. And they almost defeated it in one critical division in the House of Representatives.[58]

Almost as important as the Act creating the Navy Department, was President Adams's choice of Benjamin Stoddert, of Georgetown, Maryland, as first Secretary of the Navy. Stoddert, a staunch Federalist and prosperous merchant, proved also to be an energetic executive and competent administrator. Serving from June 1798 to March 1801, he directed the Navy's mushroom growth during the hostilities with France, and labored tirelessly to build a solid foundation for a sound future development of the Navy.[59]

[55] John Adams, long a strong advocate of a navy, had played a leading part in organizing the Continental Navy in our Revolutionary War.

[56] See James Schouler, *History of the United States* (1880), Vol. I, pp. 351–2. Despite the split between Adams and Hamilton, the Federalist Party was fairly united on the naval issue.

[57] *Annals, 5th Cong.*, pp. 3689, 3717, 3722, 3724, 3743, 3751, 3791, 3804.

[58] The bill was ordered to a third reading by the close vote of 47 to 41. *ibid.*, p. 1553. For the progress of the bill through Congress, see *ibid.*, pp. 534, 535, 539, 540, 541, 1426, 1522, 1545–54.

[59] Paullin, "Early Naval Administration," pp. 1001, 1015*ff*; C. W. Garrison. "Benjamin Stoddert," in *Dict. Am. Biog.*, Vol. XVIII, pp. 62–4. One can gather some idea of the immense volume of work which Stoddert carried on by glancing through the pages of the Navy Department's voluminous collection of *Naval Documents Relating to the Quasi-War Between the United States and France*, seven volumes of which have thus far been published under the able editorship of Captain Dudley W. Knox.

When Stoddert took office, the United States and France were rapidly drifting toward war. On May 28, 1798, Congress had authorized hostilities against armed French vessels hovering off the coast of the United States.[60] One improvised man-of-war had already put to sea; the *Constellation,* first to be completed of the frigates authorized back in 1794, was about ready to sail, and others were building or fitting out at different points along the coast.[61] On July 9, less than a month after the organization of the Navy Department, Congress went a step further, authorizing American warships and privateers to capture any armed French vessel, whether public or private, anywhere upon the sea—a declaration of war in everything but name.[62]

Stoddert's first task was virtually to create a navy with a war already in progress. In this, he was remarkably successful. With congressional support and the help of individuals and groups in the principal seaports, he assembled a force of more than fifty vessels, ranging from large, heavily armed frigates, down to small revenue cutters carrying a dozen or so light cannon.[63] Some of these were simply merchant vessels converted into makeshift men-of-war. Others, while especially designed for war service, were hastily built of unseasoned timber and inferior materials. But still others were exceptionally fine ships, destined to become famous in American naval annals. Such was the 44-gun frigate *Constitution,* familiarly known to posterity as "Old Ironsides." And such also was the 44-gun frigate *President,* a sister ship of the *Constitution,* and said to have been, in its day, the finest warship of its class in existence.[64]

Without entering into the details of this undeclared war upon the ocean which lasted from the summer of 1798 to the fall of 1800, we may note briefly the general course of events,

[60] *Quasi-War with France,* Vol. I, pp. 87–8.

[61] *ibid.,* pp. 1–122, *passim.*

[62] *ibid.,* pp. 181–3.

[63] Chappelle, *American Sailing Ships,* p. 182.

[64] *ibid.,* p. 91. A detailed account of the design and construction of the men-of-war assembled between 1798 and 1800 must await the promised publication of volumes devoted to this subject in the Navy Department's series of documents on the *Quasi-War with France.* See Vol. I, p. vi.

and their effect on American naval policy and development. American naval vessels provided convoys for merchant shipping trading in the West Indies.[65] And these men-of-war, supplemented by a large and miscellaneous collection of privateers and armed merchantmen,[66] patrolled a large area in the Caribbean and Western Atlantic.[67] With the heavy fighting ships of France unable to keep the sea in the face of the superior sea power of Great Britain, with whom France was still at war, the American cruisers had to contend only with French privateers and a few cruisers still at large. And against these hostile raiders, the American men-of-war and privateers operated with considerable success, suffering a few reverses, but winning many victories, some of them spectacular ones against superior forces.[68]

In the meantime, the undeclared war upon the ocean had given a fresh impetus to the discussion of naval policy within the United States. This discussion culminated in a comprehensive report, submitted by Secretary Stoddert to Congress in December 1798, which marked the high-water mark of Federalist naval policy.[69] Stoddert's report opened with a statement of Federalist naval objectives which were, he declared, "protection of our Coast . . . safety of our important Commerce; and our future peace when the Maritime Nations of Europe war with each other. . . . To make the most powerful nations desire our friendship—the most unprincipled respect our neutrality," we must have at least "twelve Ships of Seventy-four Guns, as many Frigates, and twenty or thirty smaller Vessels. . . ."[70] Such a force would command the respect of the

[65] *ibid.*, index to each volume, title "convoys."

[66] See E. S. Maclay, *A History of American Privateers* (1899), Part II; and George Coggeshall, *History of the American Privateers* (1856).

[67] See *Quasi-War with France*, index to each volume, title "vessels."

[68] Captain A. T. Mahan, *The Influence of Sea Power upon the French Revolution and Empire, 1793–1812* (1892), Vol. II, pp. 258–9; and *Quasi-War with France*, all volumes, *passim.*

[69] This report is available both in *A. S. P., Naval Affairs,* Vol. I, pp. 65–6; and in *Quasi-War with France,* Vol. II, pp. 129–34.

[70] *Quasi-War with France,* Vol. II, p. 129.

strongest maritime Power, for an oversea enemy would require "more than double the Number of Ships of equal force, to convoy her armies, provisions, and Stores, and to keep the communications open between her armies, and her own Country."[71]

Turning to ways and means, Stoddert strongly urged building such a navy at once, if necessary borrowing the money to do it. He also advised building the ships within the United States, and, as far as possible, of domestic materials. Such a course would insure procuring the best ships obtainable. It would distribute the benefits "amongst our own Citizens. . . ." And it would build up the industries necessary "to render ourselves independent of Foreign Countries, for articles so essential to our defense. . . ."[72]

Finally, a navy of such magnitude would need an extensive shore organization. To build and maintain the ships would require well equipped shipyards, with large store-houses and dry-docks. Stoddert recommended a judicious distribution of such establishments along the seaboard. And he would locate them at easily defensible places, near to large commercial cities where materials and workmen would always be easily available.[73]

This is, in several respects, a remarkable document. It revealed a keen appreciation of the desirability of enlisting as many parts of the country as possible in the cause of naval development. It suggested, by implication, the political advantage that electioneering Congressmen might derive from a judicious distribution of expenditures. It showed a clear grasp of the naturally strong strategic position of the United States, and at least a partial knowledge of the function and utility of capital ships in a system of strategy calculated to make the most of our geographical isolation.

The point as to capital ships perhaps needs a further word of

[71] *ibid.*, p. 130.
[72] *ibid.*, pp. 130–1.
[73] *ibid.*, pp. 132–4.

explanation. There were several recognized classes of sea-going men-of-war in this period. At the bottom of the scale stood a miscellaneous group of small vessels rating less than twenty guns, and classified as brigs, schooners, cutters, etc., according to the number of masts and the shape and arrangement of their sails. Three-masted square-riggers, rating less than twenty-four guns, mounted on a single deck, were called sloops in the American Navy. Larger, similarly rigged ships, rating twenty-eight to forty-four guns, mounted on one or two decks, were known as frigates. Sloops and frigates were the light and heavy cruisers of the sailing ship era, and were the most powerful types possessed by the United States until after the War of 1812. Although, as previously noted, the early American frigates were the finest ships of their type in existence, they were no match for seventy-four gun ships, seventy-fours, line-of-battle-ships, or ships-of-the-line, as the eighteenth-century forerunners of the modern dreadnought battleship, were variously called. The ship-of-the-line was a massive sailing fortress, carrying sixty to one hundred or more guns on two or three decks. Formidable under any conditions, seventy-fours attained their greatest power and efficiency when operating in squadrons and fleets. Such vessels constituted the backbone of the British and other European navies. Without comparable ships, the United States Navy could never prevent the squadrons of a strong maritime enemy from penetrating into American waters, driving our frigates, sloops and lighter men-of-war to cover, blockading our seaports, and opening the way for hostile invasion of our seaboard.

While there are indications, just noted, that Stoddert at least partially understood the importance and function of heavy capital ships, members of Congress had only the vaguest ideas of the reason for introducing such vessels into the American Navy. Such, at any rate, would seem a fair inference from the debate which preceded passage of acts authorizing the President to take steps safeguarding future timber needs of the Navy, to commence work on two docks, and to lay down six 74-gun ships-of-the-line.[74] Though perceiving that the remarkable security of the lands and shipping of the British Empire was somehow related to the superior power of the British Navy, even the strongest congressional advocates of the capital-ship bill showed little or no knowledge of the basic principles of British naval strategy.[75]

While the congressional debate on introducing 74-gun line-of-battle-ships into the American Navy disclosed general ignorance of the function of such men-of-war, it did reveal growing appreciation of certain aspects of our strategic situation. In reply to the argument that we could not afford a great navy, and that a small navy was worse than no navy at all, it was maintained that our geographical isolation, viewed in relation to the general international situation, rendered a huge navy unnecessary, but a small and efficient navy indispensable.

"Placed at a vast distance from those Great Powers, and in the neighborhood of those possessions which contribute most to the support of their commerce and their navies [i.e., the West Indies], we can attack them in a weak, and yet a vital part, with our whole force, while but a small part of their force can at any time be brought against us." Even Great Britain, the greatest of all Powers upon the sea, could attack us with only "that part" of her navy "which she can spare from Europe, after securing her preponderance there."[76] For the same reason, a small, well organized naval force would suffice to command respect for American commercial interests in periods of war among the maritime Powers of Europe. At such times, it was contended, "we can throw our force into the scale against that nation which shall dare to insult our commerce; or it is probable that the idea that we may do so, without our doing it, will preserve us from insult."[77]

[74] *A. S. P., Naval Affairs,* Vol. I, pp. 68–70; and *Annals, 5th Cong.,* pp. 3804–6.

[75] See, in particular, Josiah Parker (Va.), Robert Goodloe Harper (S. C.), Harrison Gray Otis (Mass.), and Samuel Smith (Md.), *ibid.,* pp. 2832–51, 2874–83.

[76] Rep. Harper (S. C.), *ibid.,* p. 2841. And to much the same effect, Rep. Parker (Va.), *ibid.,* p. 2838, and Rep. Otis (Mass.), *ibid.,* p. 2874.

[77] Rep. Smith (Md.), *ibid.,* p. 2880.

These arguments, ironically enough, were practically identical with those which Thomas Jefferson had put forward eighteen years before in his "Notes on Virginia."[78] And the Chairman of the Naval Committee now quoted at length from this earlier work, to confound Jefferson's own political followers who were lined up solidly in opposition to any augmentation of the Navy.[79]

The congressional leader of this opposition was now Albert Gallatin. This brilliant young man, a native of Switzerland who had emigrated to America and settled in Western Pennsylvania, was the preeminent spokesman of the agrarian frontier, a financial genius second to none in his day, and a pillar of strength in the rising Jeffersonian Party. Gallatin scouted the idea of attack from overseas. Even assuming the possibility of such an attack, "the bravery of the mass of the people," without any navy, would amply suffice to turn back the invader.

Passing to the question of commercial defense, he denied that a navy was essential to a healthy commerce with foreign nations, and cited recent events in proof thereof. "During the course of the present war," both France and Great Britain had "plundered" American commerce "in a most shameful manner. . . . Yet, notwithstanding all these depredations . . . year after year our exports and imports have increased in value. . . ." Even the carrying trade had prospered. All this, in Gallatin's eyes, proved "that a commerce can be protected without a navy, whilst a nation preserves its neutrality."

As an instrument of power to give "this nation a certain weight in the general scale of European politics," Gallatin viewed a navy as a positive menace. "No man could doubt . . . that if, in 1793, we had had twelve ships-of-the-line, we should have been involved in the present war, on one side or the other, according to the fluctuation of public opinion." He was alarmed at the desire of American statesmen to play a rôle in the politics of the Old World. He "had conceived,

[78] See p. 14, *supra*.
[79] *Annals, 5th Cong.*, p. 2835.

when contemplating the situation of America, that our distance from the European world might have prevented our being involved in the mischievous politics of Europe, and that we might have lived in peace without armies and navies. . . ." On the contrary, it now appeared that "our navy is intended for the common service of mankind"; and that "the united banners of Mahomet and of America," as he sarcastically put it, "are to establish true religion in France."

Finally, Gallatin was opposed to building up a powerful sea-going navy, because the cost of such a navy, chiefly beneficial to the commercial and financial interests, must fall, first or last, mainly upon agriculture which would derive little or no benefit. Taxes sufficient to carry the cost—whether customs duties, excises, or taxes on land—would put a heavy burden upon the farmers. The Federalist policy of borrowing to meet a part of the cost was calculated to increase even further the ultimate burden upon agriculture. Under this policy, the country's taxpayers, of whom the farmers constituted the largest group, would have to pay not only the cost of the Navy, but also interest on the sum to the money-lenders, and these would prove to be, in many instances, the very merchants and financiers who were deriving the chief benefits from a powerful navy.[80]

One should view this politico-economic argument against the background of the fiscal situation which was rapidly developing in the United States. During the four years of the Adams administration (1797–1801), national expenditures increased from about $6,000,000 to nearly $11,000,000 per year. To procure additional revenue, the Federalists levied new and heavier taxes, including a tax on land which raised a storm of protest in the back country where people were still smarting under an unpopular liquor excise. Heavier taxation, however, failed to keep pace with the rising cost of government, and in 1800, the last year of the Federalist régime, the national debt jumped

[80] *ibid.*, pp. 2823–32, 2859–71.

from $78,400,000 to $82,900,000. A large part of this increase was directly attributable to the naval expenditure accompanying the undeclared war with France, a fact which further intensified the opposition of the Jeffersonians to both the naval and fiscal policies of the Federalists, and foreshadowed a savage assault on the Navy if and when the agrarian party should get control of the Federal government.[81]

One should also view the naval debate of 1799, as well as the earlier debates on establishing a Navy Department and augmenting the Navy for war with France, against the background of political and social crisis which had taken form simultaneously with the international crisis. Generally speaking, the common people—small farmers, urban workers and tradesmen who comprised so large a part of the rising Jeffersonian Party—had enthusiastically acclaimed the French Revolution, and had taken sides against the monarchical enemies of Revolutionary France. These groups, especially the small farmers of the back country, naturally felt little inclination to support a navy which they regarded as unnecessary to their own security; which they viewed as an instrument calculated to enhance the prestige, power, and profits of the hated, pro-English Federalists; which they believed would certainly in-

[81] See, in general, C. A. Beard, *Economic Origins of Jeffersonian Democracy* (1915), especially Chaps. IX–XIV; and D. R. Dewey, *Financial History of the United States* (6th ed., 1918), Chap. V. A significant harbinger of the approaching storm appeared early in 1800, in the form of a resolution passed in the House of Delegates of the Virginia Legislature. This resolution, introduced with the support of, and possibly drafted by, James Madison, soon to become Secretary of State in the Jefferson administration, accurately foreshadowed the position which that Administration was to assume on taking office the following year. Declaring "that a navy has ever in practice been known more as an instrument of power, a source of expense, and an occasion of collisions and war with other nations, than as an instrument of defense, of economy, or of protection to commerce," the Jeffersonian majority instructed the Virginia Senators in Congress "to prevent any augmentation of the Navy, and to promote any proposition for reducing it . . . within the narrowest limits compatible with the protection of the sea-coasts, ports, and harbours of the United States, and of consequence a proportionate reduction of the taxes." *The Virginia Report of 1799–1800, Touching the Alien and Sedition Laws; Together with the Virginia Resolutions . . . and Several Other Documents* (compiled by J. W. Randolph, 1850), pp. 238, 242, 243, 246.

crease the taxes of the common people; and which they strongly feared would get us into a full-fledged war with France.

TABULAR SUMMARY OF ROLL CALLS IN THE HOUSE OF REPRESENTATIVES[82]

ON (1) ORDERING THE NAVY-DEPARTMENT BILL TO A THIRD READING (APR. 25, 1798), AND ON
(2) FINAL PASSAGE OF THE BILL AUTHORIZING SIX "SEVENTY-FOURS" (FEB. 11, 1799)

	Vote on (1)			Vote on (2)		
	yes	*no*	*n. vtg.*	*yes*	*no*	*n. vtg.*
Maritime New England						
New Hampshire	3	0	1	4	0	0
Massachusetts	10	2	2	11	2	1
Rhode Island	2	0	0	2	0	0
Connecticut	6	0	1	6	0	1
Totals	21	2	4	23	2	2
Middle Atlantic States						
New York	4	5	1	6	4	0
New Jersey	4	0	1	3	0	2
Pennsylvania	2	5	6	4	8	1
Totals	10	10	8	13	12	3
South Atlantic States						
Delaware	1	0	0	1	0	0
Maryland	6	1	1	7	1	0
Virginia	4	11	4	4	14	1
North Carolina	1	8	1	2	7	1
South Carolina	3	3	0	3	2	1
Georgia	0	2	0	0	1	1
Totals	15	25	6	17	25	4
Frontier States						
Vermont	1	1	0	1	0	1
Kentucky	0	2	0	0	2	0
Tennessee	0	1	0	0	1	0
Totals	1	4	0	1	3	1
Grand totals	47	41	18	54	42	10

Passage of the oppressive Alien and Sedition Acts of 1798 intensified opposition to the Navy. These enactments, aimed ostensibly at treasonable agitators in general, and foreign-born radicals in particular, were actually used in an attempt to sup-

[82] *Annals, 5th Cong.*, pp. 1553, 2883.

press and to overawe the rising opposition to the Federalist régime.[83] Earlier suspicions now hardened into a widespread conviction that the Federalists really wanted an army and a navy, not so much to defend the United States against foreign enemies, as to gratify the personal ambitions of certain Federalist leaders, and even to perpetuate the Federalist Party in power. In these circumstances, it was perhaps inevitable that the Navy, even thus early in its existence, should have become a political football; that partisan clamor should have taken the place of rational discussion of national defense; and that arguments put forward in the heat of partisan debate should have hardened into dogmas that predetermined the naval policy of the Jeffersonian Republican Party which swept into power in the presidential and congressional elections of 1800.[84]

[83] Albert Gallatin, congressional leader of the Jeffersonian opposition, was one of the intended victims of these oppressive enactments.

[84] See, in this connection, *The Virginia Report,* pp. 242, 243.

CHAPTER FIVE

☆ ☆

Jeffersonian Policy: Retrenchment and Passive Coast Defense (1801–1812)

THE triumph of the Jeffersonian Republican Party, in the presidential and congressional elections of 1800, foreshadowed radical changes in naval policy. The Federalist defeat meant a shift of political power from the seaboard to the interior, and from commerce and finance to agriculture. It was altogether probable that the victorious agrarians would repudiate the Federalist policy of developing a strong sea-going navy. The most that could be expected of the Jeffersonians was preparation for defending the coast against actual invasion. And it was not beyond the realm of possibility that the new régime might abolish the sea-going Navy altogether.

NAVAL POLICY IN TRANSITION

The final year of the Adams administration and the first year of the Jefferson régime present an interesting study in contrasts; and in no sphere were the contrasts sharper or more fundamental than in naval policy and administration.

The program which President Adams and his Secretary of the Navy, Benjamin Stoddert, were pushing forward during their final months in office envisaged a comprehensive naval development along three lines—ships, personnel, and a supporting organization of yards and docks.

Congress had enacted legislation in 1799 appropriating $1,000,000 toward construction of six 74-gun ships-of-the-line, $200,000 for purchase of timber and timber lands for the future needs of the Navy, and $20,000 toward construction of two dry-docks.[1] The Adams administration had construed this legislation as permitting not merely the specified acts, but also the purchase and development of sites for shipyards in which to build the authorized vessels and docks, and in which to store timber and other materials.[2] Pursuant to this dubious statutory interpretation, Secretary Stoddert had selected sites and acquired land for navy yards at Portsmouth, N. H., Boston, New York, Philadelphia, Washington, and Norfolk. These works, hastily undertaken without proper statutory authority in the last weeks of a defeated administration, represented an attempt to lay the foundation for a permanent shore organization before the Navy should fall into the hands of the hostile Jeffersonians.[3]

With respect to personnel, Stoddert had striven to inaugurate equally far-sighted reforms. He had revised the code of regulations governing the Navy. He had begun construction of a naval hospital. He had recommended changing the existing law, which authorized no rank higher than that of captain, to allow appointment of admirals, vice-admirals, and rear-admirals.[4] Recognizing that a drastic reduction of personnel would have to follow restoration of peace with France, he had sought to compensate discharged officers, and to prepare for future emergencies by organizing such officers into what would have been virtually a reserve corps. Members of this reserve were to receive half-pay and be subject to recall at any time.[5]

Stoddert had taken an equally far-sighted view of the ship problem. He had commenced work on the six seventy-fours

[1] *Annals of the 5th Congress*, pp. 3804–6.

[2] *American State Papers, Naval Affairs*, Vol. I, pp. 74, 86–7.

[3] C. O. Paullin, "Early Naval Administration under the Constitution," *Proceedings of the United States Naval Institute*, Vol. XXXII (1906), pp. 1001, 1024–8.

[4] *ibid.*, pp. 1023–4.

[5] *A. S. P., Naval Affairs*, Vol. I, p. 75.

authorized in 1799.[6] To clear the way for a sound future development, he had recommended selling all the jerry-built and improvised men-of-war acquired during the hostilities with France, and retaining only thirteen vessels whose size and condition gave promise of continuing usefulness. At the same time, he had recommended new construction sufficient to bring up the Navy's strength to twelve ships-of-the-line and twenty-four heavy frigates, and additional purchases of timber and timber lands to provide for a still greater expansion in an emergency.[7]

Most of Stoddert's legislative recommendations had died in Congress. While the Federalists had a nominal majority in each chamber from 1799 to 1801, the reaction that set in following the undeclared war with France had prevented practically all constructive naval legislation. The Jeffersonian opposition had stalled off Stoddert's plan for appointing admirals,[8] and had mustered enough votes to defeat his scheme for creating a naval reserve.[9] Instead, Congress had directed the President to discharge, with four months' pay, all officers except 9 captains, 36 lieutenants, and 150 midshipmen, and to give these full pay only when engaged in active service. This same act had given the President discretion to sell all save the thirteen vessels which Stoddert had recommended keeping. It had further invested the President with authority to take seven of these out of active service.[10] And the naval appropriation acts of 1800 and 1801, while authorizing large expenditures for work already in hand, had been conspicuously silent on the subject of new construction.[11]

All this legislation, which left a great deal to presidential discretion, opened the way either for a conservative forward movement, or for a devastating assault on the Navy, depending

[6] *ibid.*, p. 74.
[7] *ibid.*, pp. 74–5.
[8] *Annals, 6th Cong.*, pp. 676-8.
[9] *ibid.*, pp. 1056–8.
[10] *ibid.*, pp. 1057–8, 1557.
[11] *ibid.*, pp. 1523, 1570.

on the attitude and policy of the Jefferson administration which entered office March 4, 1801.

Two men dictated the naval policy of the new régime—President Jefferson and his Secretary of the Treasury, Albert Gallatin.[12] Jefferson's attitude toward the Navy still remains something of an enigma. Back in the 'eighties, as we have previously noted, he had advocated a sea-going navy not only to overawe and chastise the pirates of the Mediterranean, but also to command respect for American shipping during periods of war among the maritime Powers of Europe.[13] He had supported the movement which had led, in 1794, to passage of the first naval bill.[14] But after leaving President Washington's Cabinet in that year, he had gravitated toward the anti-navy position. He had opposed the naval expansion that accompanied the hostilities with France.[15] And although the advocates of a strong navy could, and did, cite a famous passage from one of his earlier writings[16] in support of their demands,[17] it was scarcely to be expected that Jefferson, as President and as leader of the agrarian party, would show much solicitude for an institution so Federalist in its origin and tendencies, and so generally unpopular with all but a small fraction of his political supporters.

[12] Jefferson's Secretary of the Navy, Robert Smith of Maryland, belonged to a prominent family long associated with shipping and commerce. Family tradition and interest, as well as personal inclination, naturally aligned him with a small pro-navy faction within the Jeffersonian Party. But Smith, who was an easy-going gentleman with little capacity or apparent desire for leadership, exercised slight influence on policy. See M. W. Williams, "Robert Smith," in *Dict. Am. Biog.*, Vol. XVII, pp. 337–8; Henry Adams, *History of the United States* (1889), Vol. I, pp. 219–22; and C. O. Paullin, "Naval Administration under Secretaries of the Navy Smith, Hamilton, and Jones," *Proc. U. S. Naval Inst.*, Vol. XXXII (1906), pp. 1289, 1291, 1300.

[13] See p. 17, *supra*.

[14] See p. 28, *supra*.

[15] See Jefferson's letters to Lewis, Jan. 30, 1799; to Madison, Jan. 30; and to Monroe, Feb. 11. *The Writings of Thomas Jefferson* (Mem. ed., 1903–1904), Vol. X, pp. 89, 92, 98.

[16] "Notes on Virginia," published in 1781. The passage in question is quoted and paraphrased on p. 14, *supra*.

[17] *Annals, 5th Cong.*, p. 2835.

While there was perhaps some room for doubt as to the President's inner convictions, there was none whatever regarding the attitude of his Secretary of the Treasury. As congressional leader of the Jeffersonian opposition, Gallatin had repeatedly set forth the political economics of the agrarian movement, and it will be recalled that in the notable debate on the capital-ship bill of 1799, he had mercilessly attacked, on political as well as fiscal grounds, the Federalist policy of building up a strong seagoing navy.[18]

Gallatin entered the Jefferson administration with a determination to deflate the fiscal system of the preceding régime. His plan called for retirement of the entire national debt—now exceeding $83,000,000—within sixteen years. He proposed to do this, moreover, while simultaneously relieving the country of all internal taxes, and holding down customs duties to their existing low level. From a total anticipated revenue of less than $10,000,000 per year, he aimed to set aside more than $7,000,000 for the debt, leaving considerably less than $3,000,000 for all the running expenses of the Federal Government. Naval expenditures alone had reached nearly $3,500,000 in the last year of the Adams administration. While some reduction would have followed naturally from cessation of hostilities against France, the Federalists' plans for future naval development envisaged a continuing annual outlay well in excess of $2,000,000. Gallatin, however, proposed to allot less than that sum to the Army and Navy together. It would be politically unwise to deal too harshly with the Army, which the agrarian frontier regarded as a bulwark against the Indian menace, but no such consideration restrained him from proceeding against the Navy which, with the undeclared war with France at an end, and the European conflict drawing to a close,[19] was more

[18] See pp. 45–6, *supra*.

[19] The Peace of Amiens, finally concluded in March 1802, brought to a formal conclusion the War of the French Revolution.

than ever regarded by the Jeffersonians as an expensive and possibly dispensable luxury.[21]

Liquidation of the Navy was begun at once and vigorously prosecuted. Pursuant to the discretion conferred by the Act of March 1801, the Administration sold a large number of vessels and laid up seven of those retained. Work was discontinued on the seventy-fours under construction. And the President projected a ship-building policy limited to collecting materials for use in case of an emergency.[22] A simultaneous assault on personnel resulted in the wholesale discharge of purchasing agents and navy-yard employees, and a drastic reduction of commissioned officers and enlisted men.[23] Work on dry-docks and other navy-yard improvements, begun under the preceding régime, was suspended. Gallatin and Jefferson toyed with the idea of closing some of these establishments altogether, and the latter also worked on a plan for concentrating the Navy's shore organization at the capital, where he proposed to build a great covered dock, in which to lay up the Navy, high and dry, to save the ships from decay, and the country from expense and corruption.[24]

Lessons and Consequences of the Tripolitan "War"

Events in the Mediterranean cut short the Administration's raid on the Navy. Federalist naval policy, it is recalled, had originated in a project for overawing the North African Barbary Powers which subsisted largely by levying blackmail on nations whose merchant shipping in the Mediterranean was

[21] Paullin, "Naval Administration under Secretaries Smith, Hamilton, and Jones," p. 1302; Adams, *History*, Vol. I, p. 222, 238–42; D. R. Dewey, *Financial History of the United States* (6th ed., 1918), p. 119*ff*; and *The Writings of Albert Gallatin* (edited by Henry Adams, 1879), Vol. I, pp. 24–6, 63–8.

[22] *A. S. P., Naval Affairs*, Vol. I, pp. 78–80, 83; and Richard Hildreth, *History of the United States* (rev. ed., 1855), Vol. V, p. 439.

[23] Paullin, "Naval Administration under Secretaries Smith, Hamilton, and Jones," pp. 1292–6, 1302.

[24] *ibid.*, pp. 1296–1300.

vulnerable to piracy. In 1795 and 1796, American agents had purchased "peace" with Algiers for $642,500 in cash, a promise of tribute amounting to $21,600 per year, the gift of a naval vessel, and various other presents. After making similar, though somewhat less costly bargains with the rulers of Tunis, Tripoli, and Morocco, American commerce in the Mediterranean had enjoyed an uncertain and uneasy truce during the years when the infant American Navy was occupied in fighting the cruisers and privateers of France. Additional demands and recurrent outrages continued, however, and the Adams administration was about to dispatch a punitive expedition to the Mediterranean, when the elections of 1800 swept the Federalists out and the Jeffersonians in.[25]

While Jeffersonian orators had repeatedly condemned the use of force to protect merchant shipping, President Jefferson himself harbored an hostility to the Barbary Powers more ancient and deeply rooted than his antipathy to the Navy. In May 1801, therefore, he ordered Captain Richard Dale to sail for the Mediterranean with a squadron of four vessels to ascertain the trend of affairs, and to punish aggressions against American shipping. The latter, discovering that the ruler of Tripoli had declared "war" against the United States, commenced operations in accord with his instructions. With so small a force, however, he could not bring the "war" to an issue, and as the year 1801 drew to a close Jefferson found his prestige involved in an enterprise utterly irreconcilable with the fiscal and naval policies to which he and his political supporters were committed.[26]

These developments forced a partial and unwilling retreat from the Administration's initial program for liquidating the Navy. For a year, President and Congress temporized with halfway measures, increasing the number of ships in commission,

[25] R. W. Irwin, *Diplomatic Relations of the United States with the Barbary Powers* (1931), Chaps. V–VII.

[26] *ibid.*, pp. 103–11; and see G. W. Allen, *Our Navy and the Barbary Corsairs* (1905), Chap. VII.

but holding down appropriations, making shift with inadequate materials, and hoping for a lucky turn of events.[27] Another year passed with setbacks and inconclusive victories which advertised the inadequacy of the government's measures. This further involved the prestige of the Administration, and forced a continued retreat from the President's original policy of retrenchment.[28] One may gauge the extent of this retreat from the upward trend of naval expenditures which grew from $915,000 in 1802 to $1,722,000 in 1807, when, after temporarily humbling the Barbary Powers, practically all American forces were withdrawn from the Mediterranean.[29]

The Tripolitan war had still other important results for the United States. It uncovered defective organization and incompetent administration in the Navy Department.[30] It emphasized the difficulties of carrying on naval operations thousands of miles from one's bases of supply and repairs. At the same time, the Navy's spectacular exploits and ultimate success strengthened the morale of officers and men, and demonstrated the utility of armed force in compelling respect from other Powers. And finally, the Tripolitan war provided a plain object lesson in naval strategy, by showing the decisive advantage of seizing command of the home waters of a maritime enemy. Only after the American Navy had established such superiority as enabled it to blockade the coast of Tripoli, was it possible to force the war to a successful conclusion.[31]

[27] *Writings of Gallatin,* Vol. I, pp. 86–90, 98; *Messages and Papers of the Presidents* (Richardson's 1st ed.), Vol. I, p. 327; *Statutes at Large,* Vol. II, pp. 129, 178.

[28] Allen, *Our Navy and the Corsairs,* Chaps. IX–X; *M. & P.* (Richardson), Vol. I, pp. 343, 359, 370, 385; and *Stat. at Large,* Vol. II, pp. 199, 206, 208, 249, 310, 348, 349.

[29] 45 Cong. 1 Sess., *S. Ex. Doc.,* No. 3, p. 156; and Allen, *Our Navy and the Corsairs,* Chaps. XI–XVI.

[30] Allen, *Our Navy and the Corsairs,* pp. 215–17.

[31] For an excellent brief discussion of the operations, strategy, and lessons of the Tripolitan war, see Captain Dudley W. Knox's *History of the United States Navy* (1936), Chaps. VI–VII.

Jefferson's Gunboat Policy

The actual, immediate effect of the Tripolitan war was to foster an unsound line of naval development. The blockade and other operations against Tripoli had quickly revealed a need for small naval vessels to work in conjunction with the frigates, to operate in shallow waters, and to perform various other functions for which the larger vessels were not well adapted. To meet this need, Congress had authorized construction of several armed brigs and schooners,[32] and a larger number of smaller craft described as gunboats. As built, these early gunboats were vessels about fifty feet in length, variously rigged, fitted with oars as well as sails, and armed with one or two small or medium-sized cannon. Each vessel carried a crew of twenty or more. And eight of them, loaded to the gunwales, with their guns stowed below, actually crossed the Atlantic and served with the squadron in the Mediterranean.[33]

These early experimental gunboats gave Jefferson an inspiration. Various European nations, as well as the Barbary Powers, maintained vessels of this type for coast and harbor defense. There was considerable opinion and some actual evidence that, in shallow and protected coastal waters, a flotilla of gunboats could drive off and perhaps capture or destroy hostile frigates and even ships-of-the-line. Gunboats, costing only a few thousand dollars each, appealed strongly to Jefferson as a cheap substitute for a regular sea-going navy.[34] This class of vessel also appealed to the Jeffersonian majorities in Congress, who authorized 25 additional gunboats in 1805, 50 in 1806, and *188 more* in 1807.[35]

[32] *Stat. at Large,* Vol. II, p. 206; and H. I. Chappelle, *History of American Sailing Ships* (1935), pp. 100–2. These vessels were the *Wasp* and *Hornet* of 18 guns rating, the *Argus* and *Syren* of 16 guns, and the *Nautilus* and *Vixen* of 12 guns.

[33] Chappelle, *American Sailing Ships,* pp. 97–8.

[34] *M. & P.* (Richardson), Vol. I, pp. 372, 385, 407, 419.

[35] *Stat. at Large,* Vol. II, pp. 330, 402, 451.

The phraseology of these wholesale authorizations, taken with concurrent appropriations for coastal fortifications and notorious neglect of the regular Navy, clearly indicated the drift of policy.[36] And finally, in February 1807, the President came forward with a detailed statement of the theory underlying the Administration's new system of maritime defense.

This system embraced four elements: stationary fortifications at strategic points on the coast; movable land batteries; floating batteries; and "gunboats which may oppose an enemy at his entrance and cooperate with the batteries for his expulsion." About two hundred gunboats, distributed along the seaboard from Maine to Louisiana, would suffice to give "due protection in times of war. . . ." It was intended to lay up all but six or eight of them in time of peace. During periods of war in Europe, it might be necessary to keep "treble that number afloat" to preserve order in those ports most frequented by foreign vessels. But even these would need only skeleton crews sufficient for navigation, "relying on the seamen and militia of the port if called into action in any sudden emergency." Only when the United States should itself become involved in war, would the "whole number . . . be brought into active service . . . to cooperate with the other means [land forces, fortifications, etc.] for covering . . . our seaports. At all times those unemployed would be withdrawn into places not exposed to sudden enterprise, hauled up under sheds from the sun and weather, and kept in preservation with little expense for repairs or maintenance."

Gunboats were manifestly useless for extended operations upon the high seas. A whole flotilla of them could not keep the open sea against a single frigate or ship-of-the-line, or in fact go to sea at all without first stowing their cannon in the hold. As the President frankly admitted: ". . . this spe-

[36] The gunboat authorizations stipulated that these vessels were for coast and harbor defense. For the legislation relating to fortifications, see *ibid.*, pp. 402, 443, 453.

cies of naval armament is proposed merely for defensive operations. . . ." It was not designed to protect "our commerce in the open seas, even on our own coast. . . ." And it had the great advantage of offering no temptation "to engage in offensive maritime war toward which it would furnish no means."[37]

Here was a frank exposition of the conception of naval defense which had long flourished in the back country. It repudiated the idea of maintaining a navy as a symbol of power to command respect for American interests and policies abroad. It purposely made no provision for protecting shipping upon the high seas. It aimed only to secure the seaboard from actual invasion.

It may seem strange that statesmen as intelligent and well informed as Jefferson and Gallatin[38] should have failed to perceive that the gunboat policy offered no defense against commercial blockade.[39] It is even stranger that prominent captains of the regular Navy, when consulted, should have failed to call this point to the President's attention.[40] Gunboat flotillas might possibly save the country's principal seaports from bombardment or capture. But it was highly doubtful whether they could provide adequate defense for a long coastline. And it should have been obvious that they could not drive off an enemy's blockading squadrons. Jefferson's gunboat policy thus ignored the plain lessons of our own Revolutionary War, as well as of the recent hostilities in the Mediterranean, to say nothing of the British blockade of France which was at that

[37] *M. & P.* (Richardson), Vol. I, pp. 419–21.

[38] For Gallatin's endorsement of the gunboat policy, see *Writings of Gallatin*, Vol. I, pp. 328–31.

[39] While there is little or no direct evidence on this point, it is quite possible that Jefferson and Gallatin minimized the potential consequences of a commercial blockade. At least such an inference would seem to follow from the Administration's willingness to fight European belligerent aggressions with a commercial embargo which had results almost identical with those from a blockade.

[40] Note the opinions of Captains Samuel Barron and Thomas Tingey, in *A. S. P., Naval Affairs*, Vol. I, p. 164. It is possible that these officers hesitated to oppose the President who was known to distrust the regular Navy, and who could do it even greater injury in the future.

very moment in process of starving the Napoleonic Empire into submission.[41]

Naval Power and Neutral Rights

The war in Europe, resumed in 1803 after a breathing spell of less than two years, presented a new challenge to the Administration's gunboat policy. The British blockade and the retaliatory counter-measures of France were producing a rapidly accumulating crop of lawless depredations on American oversea commerce, causing a rising chorus of protests and complaints from the shipping centers of the Atlantic seaboard.

With a view, it would appear, to consolidating recent political gains in New England, traditionally the stronghold of Federalism, Jefferson toyed momentarily, in the spring of 1806, with the idea of strengthening the regular Navy. In a letter to Jacob Crowninshield, a merchant and member of Congress from Salem, Massachusetts, to whom he had previously tendered the Secretaryship of the Navy, Jefferson dwelt on the desirability not only of improving coast and harbor defenses, but also of building some ships-of-the-line. "That we should have a [sea-going] squadron properly composed to prevent the blockading [of] our ports is indispensable," he said. "The Atlantic frontier from numbers, wealth, and exposure to potent enemies," he continued, "have a proportionate right to be defended with the Western frontier, for whom we keep up [an army of] 3,000 men." He would, therefore, support a "moderate" congressional measure for strengthening the regular Navy.[42]

When, however, in June 1807, a British warship attacked the United States frigate *Chesapeake*, disabling the ship and taking off several members of her crew, the Administration veered back to the more congenial policy of passive defense.

[41] Captain A. T. Mahan, *Sea Power in Its Relation to the War of 1812* (1905), Vol. I, p. 298.

[42] May 13, 1806, *Writings of Thomas Jefferson* (Ford's ed., 1892–1899), Vol. VIII, pp. 451, 453.

The President not only gave up any idea of augmenting the sea-going Navy, but even decided, in case of war with Great Britain, to keep the existing frigates in port where they might serve "as receptacles for enlisting Seamen to fill the Gunboats occasionally."[43]

Instead of mobilizing the regular Navy, and otherwise preparing armed protection for American commerce upon the sea—if necessary at the cost of war—Jefferson proposed to take our commerce off the sea altogether. In this way, he would deprive the belligerent countries of American products, of which England in particular was in desperate need, and simultaneously prevent further aggressions on American shipping, which were inflaming public opinion and driving the government toward war.[44] There was no mistaking the trend of the Administration's policy. On October 27, 1807, in a message to Congress largely devoted to the crisis with Great Britain, the President said not one word about manning or increasing the regular Navy.[45] On November 16, the Secretary of the Navy reported only two frigates and four smaller cruising vessels in service.[46] On the 24th, the President signed a bill carrying an appropriation of less than $150,000 for repairs on the vessels of the regular Navy.[47] On December 18, he approved a bill appropriating $852,500 for gunboats.[48] And four days later, he signed the notorious Embargo Act which forbade the sailing of all American vessels with cargoes destined for foreign ports.[49]

Naval Policy and the Approach to War

James Madison, who succeeded to the presidency in March 1809, continued the Jeffersonian policy of starving the regular Navy. Not once prior to the War of 1812 did Madison, in

43 Minute of a Cabinet meeting, Oct. 22, 1807, *ibid.*, Vol. I, p. 330.

44 *M. & P.* (Richardson), Vol. I, p. 433.

45 *ibid.*, pp. 425*ff*.

46 *A. S. P., Naval Affairs,* Vol. I, p. 169.

47 *Stat. at Large,* Vol. II, p. 450.

48 *ibid.*, p. 451.

49 *ibid.*, p. 451; and see L. M. Sears, *Jefferson and the Embargo* (1927).

his messages to Congress, display the slightest interest in that arm of the national defense.[50] In December 1811, with war in the near future a virtual certainty, he dismissed the subject of naval preparation with a suggestion that Congress empower the Executive "to augment the stock of such [naval] materials as are imperishable in their nature, or may not at once be attainable."[51]

However, Madison's Secretary of the Navy, Paul Hamilton,[52] grasped the deficiencies of the Administration's gunboat policy, which, he pointed out in June 1809, restricted the United States to a strategy of inaction. To attack an enemy's ocean shipping or to convoy our own, we must have "well armed, fast sailing frigates and smaller cruisers." Considering their power, such vessels "would be much less costly" to maintain than gunboats. And they would have the additional advantages of providing a school of seamanship and of fostering "improvement in naval science."[53]

The Jeffersonian majorities in Congress were in no mood, however, to foster anything pertaining to the regular Navy. An act, passed in January 1809, restricted use of the cruising vessels to American waters.[54] In 1810, with war sentiment rising within the United States, Congress seriously debated a proposal *to reduce* the Navy.[55] In December 1811, only seven months before declaration of war on Great Britain, the House Naval Affairs Committee turned down a suggestion from the Secretary of the Navy that the government acquire twelve seventy-fours and twenty additional frigates. Recommending only ten frigates, the committee reported to the House that the "objects and operations of any navy which the United States can, or ought to have" should be confined to "defense of your ports and harbors, and the protection of your coasting trade.

50 *M. & P.* (Richardson), Vol. I, pp. 470, 476, 478, 486.

51 *ibid.*, p. 494.

52 See J. G. Van Deusen, "Paul Hamilton," *Dict. Am. Biog.*, Vol. VIII, pp. 189–90.

53 *A. S. P., Naval Affairs*, Vol. I, p. 194.

54 *Stat. at Large*, Vol. II, p. 514; and *A. S. P., Naval Affairs*, Vol. I, p. 195.

55 *Annals, 11th Cong.*, pp. 1933, 1951, 1957, 1989, 2007.

. . ."[56] Even this mild proposal met insuperable obstacles. The most that Congress would do in those final hectic months was to authorize the Executive to repair the old frigates and to purchase timber for new vessels of undetermined specifications to be built at some indefinite time in the future.[57]

The vote on the frigate proposal in the House of Representatives shows the customary sectional alignment, and, when compared with the vote taken less than six months later on the resolution declaring war on Great Britain, reveals an extraordinary situation. The representatives of maritime New England and New York, who stood 31 to 6 for increasing the cruising Navy, were to vote 30 to 12 against war. The Pennsylvania members, who voted down the frigate proposal 17 to 1, were to favor war 16 to 2. The Western Frontier, which stood 12 to 1 against increasing the Navy, was to divide 12 to 1 in favor of war. Altogether, 53 of the 79 members who voted for a declaration of war in June had united in the previous January against preparing a navy upon whose strength and efficiency alone not only protection of ocean shipping, but also defense of the seaboard, must inevitably depend in a war with Great Britain.

What is the explanation of this extraordinary situation? How is one to account for the fact that support for the Navy was strongest in those sections where war sentiment was weakest? Or for the fact that so many of the "War Hawks," as they were called, opposed putting the Navy in readiness for war? It would appear that maritime New England and New York wanted as formidable a navy as possible, both on general principles and as an instrument of protection to their coast and shipping if war should come. But they were bitterly opposed to a war that would almost inevitably destroy their chief source of prosperity. The Western Frontier, on the contrary, while overwhelmingly in favor of war ostensibly to avenge British aggression against American shipping upon

[56] *A. S. P., Naval Affairs,* Vol. I, pp. 247, 248, 249.

[57] *Stat. at Large,* Vol. II, pp. 684, 699.

TABULAR SUMMARY OF ROLL CALLS IN THE HOUSE OF REPRESENTATIVES[58]

ON (1) THE MOTION TO STRIKE OUT THE AUTHORIZATION OF TEN FRIGATES (JAN. 27, 1812), AND
(2) THE RESOLUTION DECLARING WAR ON GREAT BRITAIN (JUNE 4, 1812)

	Vote on (1)			*Vote on (2)*		
	yes	*no*	*n. vtg.*	*yes*	*no*	*n. vtg.*
Maritime New England						
Massachusetts	2	12	2	6	8	2
Rhode Island	0	2	0	0	2	0
Connecticut	0	6	1	0	7	0
New Hampshire	2	0	3	3	2	0
Totals	4	20	6	9	19	2
Middle Atlantic States						
New York	2	11	3	3	11	2
New Jersey	4	2	0	2	4	0
Pennsylvania	17	1	0	16	2	0
Totals	23	14	3	21	17	2
South Atlantic States						
Delaware	0	0	1	0	1	0
Maryland	2	5	2	6	3	0
Virginia	9	10	4	14	5	4
North Carolina	6	3	3	6	3	3
South Carolina	3	5	0	8	0	0
Georgia	2	1	2	3	0	2
Totals	22	24	12	37	12	9
Frontier States						
Vermont	3	1	0	3	1	0
Ohio	1	0	0	1	0	0
Kentucky	5	0	1	5	0	1
Tennessee	3	0	0	3	0	0
Totals	12	1	1	12	1	1
Grand totals	61	59	22	79	49	14

the high seas, really had something quite different in view. As Professor Julius W. Pratt has shown,[59] the Frontier envisaged a war of conquest, waged not upon the ocean but on land; a war in which the supposedly invincible American militia would wrest Canada from Great Britain, and the

[58] *Annals, 12th Cong.*, pp. 999, 1637.
[59] *Expansionists of 1812* (1925).

Floridas from Spain, the weak ally of Britain in the European coalition against the Napoleonic Empire.[60]

The Naval Debate of 1812

The debate which preceded the vote on the frigate proposal throws still further light on the extraordinary state of congressional opinion on the eve of our second war with Great Britain.

Langdon Cheves of South Carolina, Chairman of the House Naval Committee, opened with a speech lasting two days. He prefaced his plea for increasing the regular Navy with a philosophical discourse on the idea of national interest. Special interests, he held, should yield to the general interest, unless protection of the former contributed to the latter. Such he conceived to be the case with commerce. "The interests of agriculture and commerce are inseparable," he declared. A stoppage of foreign commerce would disarrange our whole national economy. It would cut us off from foreign markets, which in turn, would cause a collapse of agricultural prices, and ruin the producers of agricultural commodities. It was manifestly in the national interest, therefore, to provide naval protection to American shipping upon the high seas. And from the expressed determination of his colleagues to treat British aggressions against American commerce as a cause of war, he inferred that they must share his views as to the national interest in maritime commerce.

Cheves next paid his respects to the rapidly crystallizing plan to attack Canada. He had no doubt such an attack would succeed. But how, he inquired, could we continue the war after conquering Canada, unless we had a naval force upon the high seas? Otherwise we should "suffer the evils of war, without inflicting any of them on the enemy." Our land

[60] Many years ago Professor Samuel E. Morison alluded briefly to the contrasting attitudes of each section on the issues of war and naval preparedness. *The Life and Letters of Harrison Gray Otis* (1913), Vol. II, p. 41.

forces could not attack Britain's vulnerable commerce. Only a sea-going navy could do that.

Such a navy, Cheves continued, was equally essential for coast defense. Land fortifications alone were not sufficient. "The experience of modern naval warfare," he declared, "has proved that no fortifications can prevent the passage of ships of war." To fortify our long seaboard was manifestly impracticable for financial and other reasons. "A better defense would be furnished by such a naval force as would give you a mastery of the American seas."

With an elaborate display of financial statistics, Cheves attacked the argument that an adequate navy would be prohibitively expensive. Because of the difficulties of maintaining and operating a fleet far from its home base, it would require a British force at least three times as powerful as that of the United States to defeat the American Navy in its own waters. The manifold demands upon the British Navy in other quarters precluded sending a very formidable detachment against the United States. A cruising force of twelve line-of-battle-ships and twenty frigates would be sufficient to command the maritime approaches to the United States. And such a force was well within the financial capacity of the United States.

He turned next to the argument that we could not man such a navy "without resorting to the odious and tyrannic practice of impressment." There were plenty of idle seamen, he believed, to man a large cruising force. And if a shortage should occur, the government could always restrict privateering, the speculative inducements of which tended to draw men away from the regular Navy in time of war.

Then there were those who opposed our becoming "too great a naval Power" lest our fleets, covering the ocean, "and seeking victory on all the opposite shores of the Atlantic, involve the nation in oppressive expenses, and in wanton and habitual wars." No one, Cheves asserted, had any such object in view. All that was desired was "such a navy as will give to the United States an ascendancy in the American seas, and protect their ports and harbors." The same considerations, which precluded "Great Britain or any other European Power" from stationing "large fleets in our seas" would "equally" prevent us from waging "frequent or habitual wars" in "distant seas."

He also denied that a sea-going navy ran counter to the principles of the Jeffersonian Party. Such an idea had originated in that party's opposition to the Federalist naval program of 1798. Hostility not to a navy *per se,* but rather to the "improper" purposes for which the Federalists had wanted a navy, he contended was the true explanation of Jeffersonian opposition to a navy in those early years.

Finally, he rejected the argument "that navies have ruined every nation that has employed them. . . ." He belittled the menace of a growing public debt incurred because of a navy. Citing the flourishing foreign commerce of various naval Powers, Great Britain in particular, he endorsed the notion that a formidable navy fostered commercial development, and was therefore a source of national prosperity.[61]

This extended plea aroused the opposition which, as on earlier occasions, derived its chief strength from the back country. Samuel McKee of Kentucky, for example, repeated Gallatin's famous argument "that a great proportion of the expense would fall on the agricultural classes . . . and the advantages (if any) to be derived from the protection afforded by it to commerce, would be derived by the mercantile classes."[62] And Richard M. Johnson, another typical opponent, also from Kentucky, declared he was as "ready as any man to keep a small naval force, to be confined to the protection of our maritime frontier," but would not "vote one cent for a system of naval force which is destined to keep foreign nations in check in distant seas, and destined to entail upon this happy

[61] *Annals, 12th Cong.,* pp. 803–22.
[62] *ibid.,* p. 842.

Government perpetual taxes and a perpetually increasing public debt."[63]

When it came to discussing the kind of navy or the type of naval operations best suited to the situation of the United States—whether for protection of ocean shipping or for defense of the coast—there was the same confusion of thought that had been conspicuous on earlier occasions. One or two members apparently had a partial understanding of the basic principle of British naval strategy—namely, that defense of coast or shipping required command of the sea, measured in combat power of massed fleets throughout those areas deemed essential to national security.[64] But the overwhelming majority had only the haziest notions regarding naval warfare and strategy. For example, Josiah Quincy of Massachusetts, a vigorous advocate of a strong navy, would distribute men-of-war along the seaboard—one "ship of war for the harbor of every great city . . . equal, in . . . [power] to the . . . ships-of-the-line of the maritime belligerents." Such a dispersion of force he defended on the ground that it would put "every city and great harbor . . . in a state of security from the insults, and the inhabitants of your seacoast from the depredations of any single ship of war of any nation."[65] Thus, while advocating a cruising fleet of line-of-battle-ships, this eminent Federalist spokesman of maritime New England would have largely nullified their peculiar value by using them merely as isolated floating batteries, thereby endorsing, in effect, the essential principle of the Administration's hated gunboat policy.

A majority of the Administration's congressional supporters were still thoroughly committed to the gunboat policy. When back-country members endorsed a navy for coast defense, they had in mind not a fleet of seventy-fours and frigates, but the two hundred gunboats built by the previous Administration. One of the acts that finally emerged from this debate stipulated

[63] *ibid.*, p. 876.
[64] *ibid.*, pp. 810, 814, 819, 913.
[65] *ibid.*, p. 961.

that the gunboats "be distributed in the several harbors of the maritime frontier which are most exposed to attack, to be carefully kept and used as circumstances may require."[66]

That a fleet of frigates and seventy-fours cruising somewhere beyond the horizon could effectively defend a long seaboard was utterly beyond the comprehension of the men of 1812. William W. Bibb of Georgia voiced a thought probably in the mind of many another, when he scouted a strategic conception which was ultimately to supersede all others. "It is assumed as a fact . . .", he observed, "that our [cruising] navy is not to be separated, while at the same time it is to defend our extensive seacoast; and that the enemy is to be attacked 'in detail, when his vessels may be scattered.' How a few ships are to defend an extent of fifteen hundred or two thousand miles, and always to be kept together, is beyond my limited comprehension; nor do I perceive why the vessels of the enemy should be scattered. It does, indeed, appear to me that the reverse . . . will be found true. If the proposed force is intended to defend our numerous ports and harbors, it must necessarily be divided and apportioned among them. . . . The assailing force has but one object to attain, and that is, to attack the most vulnerable points. While our vessels, therefore, must be scattered, from the necessity of the case, and continually liable to be attacked by a superior force, the enemy will separate, or not, as inducements may present themselves."[67]

When men envisaged larger operations at all, they generally had in mind the cruising warfare employed effectively against France in the undeclared war of 1798. To the argument that there was no use in having any sea-going navy at all unless we could have one as formidable as Britain's, Robert Wright of Maryland blandly replied: "Sir, it is her frigates and lighter ships of war we intend to fight, and her merchantmen we intend to capture. It is not her line-of-battle-ships that capture

[66] Act of March 30, 1812, *Stat. at Large,* Vol. II, p. 699.
[67] *Annals, 12th Cong.,* pp. 981, 988.

our merchantmen; it is her frigates, sloops of war, letters of marque, and privateers."[68]

Thus American opinion in 1812 embraced two strategic theories or doctrines. Broadly speaking, the Jeffersonians generally favored passive and purely local resistance to actual attacks on the coast, whereas the Federalists advocated a sort of guerilla warfare carried on by cruisers and privateers, against the merchant shipping and lighter armed vessels of the enemy. By attacking hostile frigates, smaller men-of-war, and privateers, it was intended to lessen their depredations on American commerce. By raiding hostile merchant shipping, it was thought possible to so harass and cripple the enemy's maritime commerce as to force the war to a successful issue, while at the same time affording American shipowners an opportunity to win fabulous profits from the quasi-piratical business of privateering.

Both the Jeffersonians with their passive-defense policy and the Federalists with their commerce-raiding doctrine ignored the plain lessons of our own Revolutionary War: that naval supremacy throughout a wide zone of open sea was a prerequisite to successful coast defense against the thrusts of a powerful maritime enemy; that a comparable supremacy throughout those lanes of ocean commerce essential to national security was the only sure basis of commercial defense; and that local operations in sheltered coastal waters, guerilla warfare by scattered cruisers upon the high seas, and raids against an enemy's merchant shipping, while useful supplements to larger operations, were not effective substitutes for command of the sea, measured in terms of the combat power of a fleet of seventy-fours.

American failure to grasp these basic principles, especially the failure of the navy-minded Federalists, is all the more remarkable when it is recalled that less than seven years had elapsed since Nelson's great victory over the French and Spanish

[68] *ibid.*, p. 944.

fleets at the Battle of Trafalgar had clinched Britain's command of the Eastern Atlantic and Mediterranean, making possible a continuance and progressive tightening of the blockade which, as the United States entered the struggle, was inexorably strangling the Napoleonic Empire.[69]

[69] Captain A. T. Mahan, *The Influence of Sea Power Upon the French Revolution and Empire, 1793–1812* (1893), Vol. II, pp. 196–8, and Chap. XIX.

CHAPTER SIX

☆ ☆

Strategic Lessons of the War of 1812 (1812–1815)

THE War of 1812 was an important milestone in the rise of American naval power. That conflict abruptly checked the decay and disintegration which were rapidly destroying the sea-going Navy. Its events graphically demonstrated the utter bankruptcy of the dominant agrarian party's system of gunboat defense. These events likewise revealed the fatal deficiencies of the alternative system of commerce-raiding, or cruiser warfare, the cornerstone of Federalist naval policy, and the system most generally favored within the Service itself. And these events, like those of the Revolutionary War, provided a wealth of invaluable if costly experience from which to deduce the fundamental principles of naval power and strategy, and from which to refashion future policy in accord with the situation and needs of the United States.[1]

THE WAR UPON THE INLAND LAKES

Frontier leaders could, and did, clamor for war while simultaneously neglecting the sea-going Navy, because the war they

[1] The standard work on the naval lessons as well as the naval operations of our second war with Great Britain is Admiral A. T. Mahan's scholarly two-volume work, *Sea Power in Its Relations to the War of 1812* (1905). If this chapter does little more than summarize and emphasize Mahan's narrative and conclusions, it is simply a tribute to the thoroughness and excellence of his work.

had in view was not primarily a naval war at all but a war of conquest on land. With a confidence that seems almost incredible today, they believed that a few thousand raw militia could quickly overrun Spanish Florida on the south and British Canada on the north. With a naïveté equally incredible, the "War Hawks" of 1812 belittled the dangers upon the ocean and on the seaboard, and neglected the trunk-line of water communications that supplied the Canadian frontier from Montreal to Lake Superior, and without control of which a successful conquest of the Canadian wilderness would be incalculably difficult if not utterly impossible.

As a few men had foreseen,[2] and as it turned out from first to last in practice, command of the inland lakes (especially Lakes Champlain, Ontario, and Erie) determined the fortunes of war on the northern frontier. The St. Lawrence-Great Lakes water route was the only feasible line of military communications through Upper Canada (Ontario). As long as this line remained intact under British control, the upper Mississippi Valley lay open to invasion at a dozen points.[3] Had the British seized command of Lake Champlain, they might have penetrated into the heart of New York, and might conceivably have split the United States asunder as Burgoyne had attempted without success to do back in 1777.

The St. Lawrence-Great Lakes waterway was likewise the key to successful invasion of Canada. Any break in this line of communications would immediately spell disaster for the British forces farther west. Therefore the strategic objective of American operations on the northern frontier was, or should have been, to break this line as near its source as possible. The focal point was Montreal at the head of navigation on the St. Lawrence, or possibly Kingston, the chief British naval depot, at the foot of Lake Ontario. With the United States forces supreme upon Lake Champlain, Montreal would have been

[2] See J. W. Pratt, *Expansionists of 1812* (1925), Chap. IV.

[3] British naval supremacy upon Lake Erie caused the fall of Detroit at the beginning of the war, and but for the weakness of the British forces in Canada at that time might well have led to successful invasion of the Western States.

within easy reach, while indisputable command over Lake Ontario would have placed the whole of Upper Canada west of Kingston in American hands. Success at either point would have destroyed British military power in the Northwest, and insured the conquest which in frontier eyes was one of the main objects of the war.[4]

American campaign plans, however, largely ignored or at least neglected these strategic principles. Political expediency was undoubtedly a factor contributing to this neglect. War sentiment was strong in the West, weak in the East. It might have been difficult early in the war to raise adequate forces in the East to take Montreal. And the West, terrified by the Indian uprising, would certainly have opposed withdrawal of troops, raised or stationed in that section, no matter how strategically sound the plan.[5] Yet politics alone does not explain the persistence with which American strategists attacked the branches and ignored the trunk of the British imperial tree. Nor does politics explain why they delayed, and then weakened their belated efforts to gain control of the Great Lakes, by dividing attention between Ontario and Erie, when supremacy upon the former would automatically have given command over the latter.

The larger opportunities thus neglected were emphasized by the strategic results of the two decisive naval battles on the lakes. Commodore Oliver H. Perry's famous victory over the British squadron on Lake Erie, in September 1813, compelled immediate retirement of the British land forces from the Detroit frontier, and continued supremacy on Lake Erie kept the country farther to the west in American hands during the rest of the war. Commodore Thomas Macdonough's equally important victory over the British naval forces upon Lake Champlain a year later immediately checked the southward advance of a British army from Canada, and opened the way for a counter-attack on Lower Canada, which might have been

[4] Mahan, *War of 1812*, Vol. I, pp. 300–8, 353–4; Vol. II, pp. 29–30.
[5] Pratt, *Expansionists of 1812*, pp. 167–8.

carried out but for the timely arrival there of strong reinforcements of veteran troops fresh from the European war which had now drawn to a close.[6]

The War Upon the Ocean

Command of the sea likewise determined the fortunes of war upon the ocean and on the Atlantic seaboard. Here, as upon the lakes, the United States was utterly unprepared for war with a strong naval Power. The sea-going Navy included only nineteen vessels, of which not more than fourteen were fit for service. These fourteen included three large frigates rated at 44 guns (but actually carrying a good many more); but eight of the fourteen were only sloops or brigs, rated at less than 20 guns.[7] While British forces in American waters at the outbreak of hostilities were scattered and comparatively weak, the aggregate power of the Royal Navy was immense. In contrast to the handful of American cruisers, it contained more than six hundred fighting ships, nearly one-fourth of which were ships-of-the-line mounting at least 60 guns each.[8]

The American Navy had a fine group of officers, mostly men in the prime of life with war experience acquired in the naval struggle with France (1797–1800) and in the punitive expeditions against the Mediterranean Barbary Powers. But they were too few for the greater work ahead. And their efforts were constantly to suffer from a shortage of seamen trained for service on board men-of-war, a shortage further aggravated by the higher wages offered in the merchant service and by the still more lucrative opportunities on the privateers.[9]

The supporting shore organization was sadly defective. All

[6] Mahan, *War of 1812*, Vol. I, pp. 337–50, and Chap. VII; Vol. II, Chaps. X–XIII, XV, and pp. 355–81.

[7] *American State Papers, Naval Affairs*, Vol. I, pp. 249, 250, 265, 266.

[8] Captain D. W. Knox, *History of the United States Navy* (1936), p. 82.

[9] Mahan, *War of 1812*, Vol. I, pp. 279–80; Vol. II, p. 12; and C. O. Paullin, "Naval Administration under Secretaries of the Navy Smith, Hamilton, and Jones, 1801–1814," *Proceedings of the United States Naval Institute*, Vol. XXXII (1906), pp. 1289, 1320.

navy-yard facilities had deteriorated under the deliberate neglect of ten years' hostile administration. There were still no dry-docks for repairing and cleaning the hulls of naval vessels. Timber stocks were depleted, naval stores were available in limited quantities or not at all. With the long-anticipated war on its hands, the Navy Department had to build from the ground up, securing materials and improvising equipment that should have been ready long before the onset of the emergency.[10]

There was a comparable lack of organization afloat. There was no fleet organization. The highest rank was that of captain. When two or more vessels were in company, the senior captain might become commodore of the squadron. But that was only a temporary designation. Each vessel was generally regarded as an independent entity responsible directly to the Department, rather than as a component of a larger force under a single command.[11]

There was even greater unpreparedness in the sphere of strategy. While the Navy Department was committed to the single-ship commerce-raiding brand of warfare, there was no definite plan of operations. One group within the Administration was said to favor laying up the sea-going vessels altogether in order to save them from capture or destruction. Another group advocated a passive defense that would keep these vessels constantly near the coast. Only a few days before the outbreak of hostilities, the Secretary of the Navy, still undecided, was appealing to certain prominent captains for advice. These all favored offensive action, but disagreed as to where the ships should go, and as to whether they should cruise singly or in squadrons. And in the end, they put to sea before receiving any definite instructions at all.[12]

[10] *A. S. P., Naval Affairs,* Vol. I, pp. 248–9; and Paullin, "Naval Administration, 1801–1814," p. 1317.

[11] Mahan, *War of 1812,* Vol. I, pp. 315–16.

[12] *ibid.,* p. 316; Henry Adams, *History of the United States* (1889–1891), Vol. VI, pp. 363–8; and Thomas Harris, *The Life and Services of Commodore William Bainbridge* (1837), p. 135.

The disparity of naval power, already noted, strictly limited the sphere of American offensive operations upon the ocean. Blockade of the British Isles was manifestly out of the question, as was destruction of the British Navy. American cruisers could, and did, fight numerous single-ship actions with the enemy's smaller naval vessels. And in the majority of these actions the Americans came off victorious. These victories raised the Navy's prestige, probably helped to sustain American morale, and contributed no little to the post-war legend that the United States had again defeated Great Britain. But these naval duels secured no strategic advantage for the United States. On the contrary, every defeat seriously diminished the American Navy's slender resources, while the dozen or so victories had no material effect on the total strength of the enemy. And besides, the loss, or even temporary crippling, of a single American cruiser seriously curtailed the work of commerce raiding which, under existing circumstances, was necessarily the most important function of a navy totally lacking in capital ships.[13]

The commerce raiding of American cruisers and privateers also contributed to the post-war legend of victory. These raiders did inflict serious injury by capturing well over a thousand British merchant vessels in the course of the war, but such losses, while not without political effect in Great Britain, fell far short of paralyzing the economic life, and hence the fighting power of the British Empire.[14]

That American commerce raiding did not achieve larger results was mainly attributable to the effective defensive measures instituted by Great Britain. Several of the American cruisers were captured or destroyed. By a close blockade of American ports, British squadrons imprisoned most of the survivors, and rendered escape difficult for even the smaller privateers. A strict convoy system reduced the number of unaccompanied British merchantmen upon the open sea. The

[13] Mahan, *War of 1812,* Vol. I, pp. 289–90.

[14] *ibid.,* pp. 288, 322–35, Chap. VIII; Vol. II, pp. 1–13, Chap. XIV.

escorting squadrons were usually strong enough to beat off all assailants. And as a result, while the scattered American cruisers and privateers made numerous captures, especially in the vicinity of the British Isles where the convoy system was less rigorously enforced, these raiders could not break the commercial life-lines of the British Empire.[15]

The Royal Navy not only safeguarded the trunk-lines of British oversea commerce but also swept American shipping from the ocean. A steadily tightening blockade of the Atlantic seaboard choked off American commerce at its source; and British cruisers and privateers preyed virtually at will upon the defenseless shipping that broke through. The plight of coastwise shipping was especially serious, for every coaster had to escape through the blockading squadron at the beginning of its voyage, evade hostile raiders en route, and slip through the blockade again on reaching its destination.[16]

The United States Navy, after the first weeks of the war, was unable to give any substantial protection to American commerce. The presence of American cruisers and privateers at large may have afforded some slight indirect protection to American shipping, by forcing the British Admiralty to divert vessels from cruising and blockade duty to service in the merchant convoys. The capture or destruction of a dozen or so British cruisers thinned slightly, but only temporarily, the ranks of enemy raiders, and led eventually to an actual strengthening of the blockading forces on the Atlantic seaboard. And the American Navy lacked the capital ships necessary to drive off the blockading squadrons which normally included at least one ship-of-the-line.

The Blockade and Its Consequences

It would be difficult to exaggerate the damage which this blockade inflicted upon the economy of the United States. In

[15] *ibid.,* Vol. II, p. 130, Chap. XIV.
[16] *ibid.,* pp. 9–27, Chap. XIII.

1812, the ocean was still the main artery of commerce along the seaboard from Maine to Louisiana. There were neither railroads nor improved highways. It took a month and a half to haul freight in wagons from Philadelphia to Charleston, South Carolina, and nearly three weeks from Philadelphia to Boston. Under such conditions interstate commerce was all but paralyzed. Foreign commerce was likewise stricken. Imports which had risen to a peak of $138,500,000 in 1807, totalled only $12,965,000 in 1814. Exports in the same interval dwindled from $108,343,000 to less than $7,000,000. The export of flour, to take but one important commodity, fell within two years from 1,443,492 barrels in 1812, to 193,274 in 1814. As a result of the almost complete stoppage of commerce, regional products which brought famine prices in one locality could scarcely be sold in another a few hundred miles distant. Flour, again for example, is reported to have sold, in August 1813 for $11.87 a barrel in Boston, $8.50 in New York, $7.50 in Philadelphia, $6.00 in Baltimore, $4.00 in Richmond, $10.25 in Wilmington, North Carolina, and $8.00 in Charleston, South Carolina. Imported goods sold at equally fantastic prices which varied from time to time, and from place to place, according to the strength and vigilance of the enemy's blockading squadrons. The marine industries fared perhaps the worst of all. Shipping tonnage engaged in the North Atlantic cod fishery declined approximately 75 per cent. The total export of marine products fell from a peak of more than $3,000,000 to considerably less than $200,000. The ocean carrying trade, which had been one of the chief sources of profit during the European wars, was all but wiped out. And the tonnage of American shipping engaged in foreign commerce dropped from over a million tons in 1807, to less than 60,000 in 1814.[17]

The testimony of contemporary observers fully corroborates

[17] Timothy Pitkin, *A Statistical View of the Commerce of the United States* (1817 ed.), pp. 41, 47, 111, 166, and *passim*; J. H. Frederick, *The Development of American Commerce* (1932), pp. 53, 61; and Mahan, *War of 1812*, Vol. II, pp. 17–18, 177–87, 193–208.

the statistics. In February 1814, Representative Joseph Pearson of North Carolina listed the following consequences of the blockade: ". . . the entire coasting trade destroyed, . . . the planters of the Southern and Middle States, finding no markets for their products at home, are driven to the alternative of wagoning it hundreds of miles in search of a precarious market in the Northern and Eastern States, or permitting it to rot on their hands. Many of those articles which are, or have become by habit, necessary for their comfort, are procured at the most extravagant prices from other sections of the Union. The balance of trade, if trade it may be called, from these and other causes being so entirely against the Southern and Middle States, the whole of our specie is fast travelling to the North and East; our bank paper is thrown back upon the institutions from which it was issued, and as the war expenditures are proportionately inconsiderable in the Southern and Middle States, where the loans have been principally obtained, the bills of those banks are daily returning, and their vaults drained of their specie, to be locked up in the Western and Eastern States, never to return but with the return of peace and commerce."[18]

Francis Wayland, President of Brown University, penned a similar description of conditions in the North: "Our harbors were blockaded; communications coastwise between our ports were cut off; our ships were rotting in every creek and cove where they could find a place of security; our immense annual products were mouldering in our warehouses; the sources of profitable labor were dried up; our currency was reduced to irredeemable paper; the extreme portions of our country were becoming hostile to each other; . . . the credit of the Government was exhausted; no one could predict when the contest would terminate, or discern the means by which it could much longer be protracted."[19]

And to cite but one more contemporary witness, a "distin-

[18] *Annals of the 13th Congress*, p. 1451.

[19] Quoted in *The Memorial History of the City of New York* (edited by J. G. Wilson, 1893), Vol. III, p. 295.

guished naval officer" whose identity was not disclosed, recalled in June 1815, that: "No sooner had the enemy blockaded our harbors and extended his line of cruisers from New Orleans to Maine, than both foreign and domestic commerce came at once to be reduced to a deplorable state of stagnation; producing in its consequences the utter ruin of many respectable merchants, as well as a great multitude besides, connected with them in their mercantile pursuits. But these were not the only consequences. The regular supply of foreign commodities being thereby virtually cut off; many articles, now become necessaries of life, were necessarily raised to an exorbitant price, and bore much upon the finances of the citizen, whose family could not comfortably subsist without them. Add to this, as most of the money loaned to [the] government for the purposes of warfare came from the pockets of the merchants, they were obviously rendered incapable of continuing those disbursements in consequence of the interruption of their trade; and in this manner became in a great measure, the unwilling cause of that impending state of bankruptcy with which the government was at one time threatened. . . . The coasting trade, that most valuable appendage to an extensive mercantile establishment in the United States was entirely annihilated. The southern and northern sections of the Union were unable to exchange their commodities, except upon a contracted scale through the medium of land carriage, and then only at a great loss; so that upon the whole, nothing, in a national point of view, appeared to be more loudly called for by men of all . . . parties than a naval force, adequate to the protection of our commerce and the raising of the blockade of our coast."[20]

The blockade, which had such devastating effects on the internal economy of the United States, also opened the way for invasion of the seaboard. For coast and harbor defense, the Navy Department, under Jeffersonian auspices, had built scores of so-called gunboats whose characteristics were described in

[20] *Niles Weekly Register* (June 17, 1815), Vol. VIII, p. 265.

the preceding chapter.[21] In 1812, these gunboats, 165 in number, were distributed among the principal seaports from Maine to the Mississippi.[22] The gunboat flotillas, supplemented by armed rowing barges and other makeshift floating defenses, were supposed to prevent the enemy's blockading forces from penetrating into the ports, bays, and estuaries of the seaboard. In this they were generally unsuccessful. Detachments from the blockading squadrons plundered the coastal settlements almost at will, especially in the region of Chesapeake Bay where a British force even captured the City of Washington and burned the public buildings.[23]

Lessons for the Future

Looking back over the disasters which had crowded each stage of the war, it was clear, or should have been, that events had invalidated every major postulate of naval policy with which the United States had entered the struggle. It had been widely assumed that the government could quickly and easily improvise sufficient naval forces in an emergency. The war had exposed the fallacy of that assumption. With Great Britain expressly in mind, numberless Americans had argued that commerce raiding, carried on with naval cruisers and privateers, could produce such havoc as to compel a strong maritime enemy to sue for peace. The success of the British convoy system had demonstrated the error of this contention. According to another classic American assumption, protection of commerce would so occupy the enemy's naval forces as to leave none free for operations against the coast of the United States. The blockade had tragically exposed the enormity of this miscalculation. Ignoring or belittling the danger of blockade, the dominant agrarian party had proceeded on the theory that land fortifications could easily repel any actual attack on the seaboard. The plundering

21 See pp. 58*ff.*, *supra.*

22 *A. S. P., Naval Affairs,* Vol. I, p. 252.

23 Mahan, *War of 1812,* Vol. II, Chaps. XIII, XVI.

of that seaboard from Maine to New Orleans left no doubt as to the invalidity of this assumption.

Viewed in the large, the war also taught certain positive lessons. The first was that only a fleet of capital ships could insure security to the coast of the United States in a war with a great naval Power. For strictly defensive purposes, such a fleet need not equal the total force of the enemy. No European Power could send its entire navy across the ocean to attack us. The difficulty of operating in distant waters, as well as the shifting and chronically unstable balance of power in the Old World, were factors of great strategic value to the United States. It was sufficient that the American Navy have a fighting fleet stronger than the force that any probable enemy could detach for service in American waters. Even a considerably less powerful force of capital ships could prevent the blockade of any large part of the seaboard, because the enemy would have to maintain every blockading squadron at a strength greater than that of the entire defending force.[24]

The second positive lesson of the war was that a unified force of capital ships was also essential to the protection of maritime commerce. By forestalling blockades, such a force would prevent the strangling of commerce at its source. Such a fleet would also have a restraining influence upon hostile cruisers and privateers, and under favorable conditions could provide detachments for convoying merchantmen through dangerous seas.

Finally, assuming that commerce destruction was the ultimate objective of offensive naval operations, the war demonstrated the superiority of Great Britain's method of attaining that object. Admitting that commerce raiding, or cruiser warfare, was about the only offensive operation open to the United States in 1812, and that American cruisers and privateers achieved surprising success in the face of terrific obstacles, the fact nevertheless remained that American commerce raiding signally failed to cripple the fighting power of the British Empire. On the other hand, command of the open sea, with its

[24] *ibid.*, Vol. II, pp. 208–11.

blockade corollary, enabled the British Navy to destroy American commerce "root and branch," with utterly demoralizing effects on the economic life, and hence on the military power of the United States.[25]

One important word still remains to be said. The demoralizing effects of the blockade were results not only of the superior naval power of Great Britain, but also of the technological stage which the world had then reached. Railroads and improved highways, not to mention automobiles and aircraft, would have decidedly mitigated those effects. The existence of a diversified, highly developed system of large-scale manufacturing, drawing upon the varied and almost unlimited resources of North America, would have had further decided, and perhaps decisive, mitigating effects.[26] Finally, it should not be overlooked that Great Britain in 1812 possessed naval bases in Canada, Bermuda, and the West Indies, which greatly facilitated operations in American waters. It may be doubted whether the British Navy could have maintained the blockade without these nearby bases. And as will be shown in later chapters, it is even more doubtful whether any non-American Power could duplicate the blockade of 1812, under strategic, technical, and political conditions prevailing in the twentieth century.[27] But the twentieth century was still far away, and the lessons for the immediate future were, or should have been, clear and unmistakable.

[25] *ibid.*, p. 126.

[26] Alexander Hamilton, it is interesting to note, had perceived the obverse side of this problem in his famous Report on Manufactures, back in 1791. "Not only the wealth but the independence and security of a country," he had stated at that time, "appear to be materially connected with the prosperity of manufactures. Every nation, with a view to those great objects, ought to endeavor to possess within itself, all the essentials of national supply. These comprise the means of subsistence, habitation, clothing, and defence."

[27] On the whole question of the present-day situation of the United States as to blockade, see the well supported conclusions set forth in Professor Brooks Emeny's *Strategy of Raw Materials* (1934), p. 16, and *passim.*

CHAPTER SEVEN

☆ ☆

The Neglected Lessons of 1812 (1815–1837)

THE War of 1812 tremendously enhanced the Navy's prestige and temporarily routed its domestic enemies. The disasters of that conflict laid to final rest the long-disputed question as to the desirability of maintaining a sea-going navy. But statesmen, and even military and naval experts, failed in the main to grasp the strategic lessons deducible from the war. The dozen or so victorious naval duels between American and British cruisers upon the ocean, the spectacular exploits of famous privateers, Perry's victory upon Lake Erie, Macdonough's upon Lake Champlain, and the rout of the British Army at the Battle of New Orleans, all contributed to the rise of a legend that the United States had once more defeated the world's greatest naval Power.

This legend of victory, which went virtually unchallenged for nearly a century,[1] blinded men's eyes to the larger lessons of the War of 1812. It ignored the strategic insignificance of the American operations, as well as the blockade which annihilated our maritime commerce, all but paralyzed the economic life of the country, and laid the seaboard open to invasion. Thus, instead of clearing the way for a thorough overhauling of American naval policy, the War of 1812 breathed new life into the cruiser-commerce-raiding and passive-defense doctrines

[1] Admiral Alfred T. Mahan's *Sea Power in Its Relations to the War of 1812,* published in 1905, was the first large work to expose, thoroughly and systematically, this legend of victory.

which continued for three-quarters of a century to dominate American thought and legislation.

Immediate Effects of the War on American Naval Policy

The first effect of the war was to stimulate naval construction. In January 1813, over the protests of a dwindling inland opposition and ostensibly as a war measure, Congress authorized construction of four 74-gun ships-of-the-line and six 44-gun frigates.[2] Another act, two months later, empowered the President to build six sloops of war, to procure armed vessels for service upon the Lakes, and to sell the useless gunboats built during Jefferson's administration.[3] Naval expenditures jumped from less than $2,000,000 in 1811, to more than $8,500,000 in 1815.[4] And while emergency outlays for the war accounted for a large portion of this increase, nearly $3,000,000 went toward new construction under the above acts.[5]

Another effect of the war was to stimulate fresh discussion of the methods and ramifications of naval defense. One especially significant contribution to this discussion was a report, prepared in the fall of 1814 by William Jones, a well-to-do Philadelphia merchant with knowledge of ship-building and seamanship who served as Secretary of the Navy from January 1813 until December 1814.[6] In this report, Jones described the "local [gunboat] service . . . from Louisiana to Maine . . . [as] so weak as readily to be penetrated at almost any point on our maritime frontier by the concentration of a small hostile force. . . ." If, instead of our "ineffective" gunboat flotillas, Jones continued, we had a dozen or more line-of-battle-ships,

[2] *Annals of the 12th Congress, 2nd Session,* pp. 32, 33, 403–30, 436–7, 440–1, 443–50.

[3] *ibid.,* pp. 1011, 1352.

[4] 45 Cong. 1 Sess. *S. Ex. Doc.* No. 3, p. 156.

[5] *American State Papers, Naval Affairs,* Vol. I, pp. 827–8.

[6] C. O. Paullin, "Naval Administration under Secretaries Smith, Hamilton, and Jones, 1801–1814," in *Proceedings of the United States Naval Institute,* Vol. XXXII (1906), pp. 1289, 1308; and J. H. Frederick, "William Jones" in *Dict. Am. Biog.,* Vol. X, p. 205.

"acting in conjunction upon our own coast and waters, or in squadron pursuing the commercial fleets of the enemy on the ocean, or in the harbors of his colonies . . . our waters would be freed from invasion; our coast from blockade; [and the enemy's] . . . military and naval resources intercepted to such a degree as to paralyze his efforts on this continent. . . ." This conclusion, Jones explained, followed from the fact that only the enemy's strongest capital ships could keep the sea against such a fleet, and from the unlikelihood that even the British Navy could "combine such a force [in the Western Atlantic] as would counteract the power and offensive enterprise of an American squadron so truly formidable."[7]

Jones's successor, Benjamin W. Crowninshield, a well known merchant of Salem, Massachusetts,[8] who took office early in 1815, continued the drive for capital ships. With a solicitude for oversea commerce reminiscent of the Federalist régime, Crowninshield recommended a continuing naval program under which the government each year would lay down one seventy-four, two heavy frigates, and two sloops-of-war. But he had little conception of the long training and discipline necessary to weld ships and men into an efficient fighting machine. Like so many of his contemporaries, he would build the ships, and then lay them up, along with a stock of imperishable materials and supplies, "in one or two of the principal ports," where they would remain theoretically available for "active service upon any emergency. . . ."[9]

The idea of a continuing program found favor with Congress. An act, passed in April 1816, for the "gradual increase of the Navy," authorized expenditure of $1,000,000 per year on naval construction for the next six years. Specifically, it authorized nine 74-gun ships-of-the-line, twelve 44-gun frigates,

[7] *A. S. P., Naval Affairs,* Vol. I, pp. 320, 321.

[8] C. O. Paullin, "Naval Administration under the Navy Commissioners, 1815–1842," in *Proc. U. S. Nav. Inst.,* Vol. XXXIII (1907), p. 597; and G. H. Genzmer, "Benjamin Williams Crowninshield" in *Dict. Am. Biog.,* Vol. IV, pp. 577–8.

[9] Dec. 7, 1815. *A. S. P., Naval Affairs,* Vol. I, p. 365.

and three experimental steam-driven "batteries," the latter for "defense of the ports and harbours of the United States. . . ."[10]

This enactment represented the first attempt to lay out in advance a systematic program of naval development. Also for the first time, Congress committed the country to construction of a strong fleet of capital ships. But there is little evidence that the sponsors of this legislation grasped the implications of what they were about. Judging from the brief recorded debate on the bill, there was almost no discussion of strategic principles, and no mention whatever of the inchoate doctrine of command of the sea.[11] The act empowered the President to have the new warships left "on the stocks, and kept in the best state of preservation" until a "public exigency" might "require them."[12] And, so far as we are aware, more than thirty years elapsed before anyone called public attention to the radical implications of the Act of 1816 "for the gradual increase of the Navy."[13]

A third effect of the war was to raise a threat of an Anglo-American naval race upon the Lakes, with prospects so mutually disadvantageous as to bring both nations to an early and, as it turned out, a permanent agreement demilitarizing the maritime frontier between Canada and the United States.[14] At the end of the war, both sides had respectable squadrons upon the inland waters.[15] Especially formidable were those upon Lake

[10] *Statutes at Large,* Vol. III, p. 321.

[11] There is no record of any debate at all in the Senate. For the brief debate in the House, see *Annals, 14th Cong.,* pp. 1367–72.

[12] Section II.

[13] Thomas H. Benton's *Abridgement of the Debates of Congress,* Vol. V, pp. 646n–47n. In this footnote, written about 1850, Senator Benton, who endorsed the strategic fallacies of Jeffersonian naval policy, nevertheless perceived and called public attention to the strategic implications of the Naval Act of 1816.

[14] For the ensuing brief account of the background and conclusion of the Rush-Bagot Agreement, we are deeply indebted to Dr. Charles P. Stacey (Princeton University), who generously permitted us to read two chapters of his forthcoming work on Canadian-American military and naval relations, one of a series of studies on the relations of Canada and the United States sponsored by the Carnegie Endowment for International Peace.

[15] The forces of the United States, as reported by the Navy Department early in 1814, consisted of 16 vessels upon Lake Ontario, with a total rating of 110 guns; 12 vessels upon Lake Erie, with a total rating of 110 guns; and 3 upon Lake Champlain, with 24 guns. Actually, many of these vessels carried guns

Ontario, where each had heavy frigates in service, and was building ships-of-the-line as large as any upon the ocean. The threat of a post-war naval race upon these waters hovered in the background at the peace negotiations, but was left unsettled by the Treaty of Ghent. The United States government, however, immediately began liquidating its squadrons, apparently on the assumption that the British would do likewise.[16] By the end of 1815, the Navy Department had sold or retired all American men-of-war upon the inland waters, save two small vessels upon Lake Ontario, and three upon Lake Erie.[17] The British Command, on the contrary, kept a considerable force on the Lakes. As a result, by the spring of 1816 the British establishment, though considerably reduced, still greatly exceeded that of the United States. And British naval officers in Canada were laying plans for a strong permanent force upon the Lakes.

While the British possessed a decisive superiority for the moment, the ultimate advantage lay just as certainly with the United States. The Lakes constituted for the latter merely a strategic frontier; for Canada, they formed, in addition, a vital line of economic and military communications. Canada was a sparsely populated country—little more, indeed, than a fringe of settlements stretching for more than a thousand miles along the St. Lawrence River and the Great Lakes. Great Britain was far away, while the United States was near at hand. Moreover, the potential strength of the latter in the region of the Lakes would continue to increase with the improvement of overland communications, the settlement of the Mississippi Valley, and the westward migration of industry.

Thus, in 1816, when American statesmen, with a view to the

---

well in excess of their nominal rating. In addition to these vessels, several large frigates were launched during 1814. And still larger vessels were under construction when the war ended. *A. S. P., Naval Affairs,* Vol. I, pp. 308, 380.

[16] On February 27, 1815, only a few days after the arrival of the peace treaty from Europe, the President signed an Act of Congress authorizing the sale or retirement of "all the [United States] armed vessels . . . on the lakes, except such as [were] . . . necessary to enforce . . . the revenue laws. . . ." *Stat. at Large,* Vol. III, p. 217.

[17] *A. S. P., Naval Affairs,* Vol. I, p. 380.

immediate security of their own frontier, proposed a virtual demilitarization of the Lakes, British statesmen were confronted with a choice of evils. They might enter upon a costly naval race with the odds strongly in favor of the United States. Or they might relinquish their existing military advantage, avoid the expense of a naval race, and accept the inevitable supremacy of the United States upon the lake frontier. With Parliament pressing for retrenchment and economy after a long and costly war, the British Cabinet chose the second as the lesser evil, and in 1817 entered into a diplomatic agreement to halt the incipient naval race, thus clearing the way for complete demilitarization of the long water boundary between Canada and the United States.[18]

A fourth effect of the war was to enhance the position and influence of the professional naval bureaucracy (using that term without invidious connotation). Prior to the war, the civilian Secretary had managed the Navy with the aid of a small clerical staff. The commissioned officers had had uncertain tenure, few administrative duties, and a negligible influence on policy. This system placed a heavy burden upon the Secretary, who might or might not have the physical stamina and technical knowledge to carry the load. The system had worked badly even in time of peace. It all but collapsed under the strain of a major war, and gave rise to an insistent demand for reorganization of the Navy Department.[19]

The problem as it appeared to the Service was to secure intelligent and efficient administration, sympathetic to the interests of the professional bureaucracy. Service opinion generally favored some degree of professional control over policy as well

[18] The Rush-Bagot Agreement, as this understanding was known, limited the naval force of each power to one vessel not exceeding 100 tons, with one 18-pounder cannon, upon Lake Ontario; one vessel of the same description upon Lake Champlain; and two upon the upper Great Lakes. *A. S. P., Foreign Relations,* Vol. IV, pp. 205–6.

[19] Paullin, "Early Naval Administration under the Constitution" in *Proc. U. S. Nav. Inst.,* Vol. XXXII (1906), pp. 1001, 1016; *idem,* "Naval Administration, 1801–1814," *ibid.,* pp. 1289, 1309; and *idem,* "Naval Administration, 1815–1842," *op. cit.,* Vol. XXXIII, pp. 597, 602.

as administration.[20] And one "distinguished naval officer" went so far as to advocate abolishing the Navy Department altogether. He would then transfer its duties to a board of three naval officers, and "give it, in conjunction with the president of the United States, the complete management and control of our naval establishment." For the Secretary of the Navy, he maintained, "although in all other respects a man of uncommon probity and talents, can never, from his ignorance of naval architecture and practical seamanship, conduct its [Navy's] concerns as they ought to be conducted."[21]

The problem, as more or less clearly envisaged in civilian political circles, was to devolve technical detail with a measure of administrative responsibility on selected officers, without at the same time relinquishing civilian control over policy. The plan which Congress finally enacted in 1815, after weighing professional as well as civilian opinion,[22] sought the desired end through a Board of Navy Commissioners. This body was to consist of three captains (then the highest rank in the Service), appointed by the President with the consent of the Senate. These Commissioners, under the "superintendence" of the Secretary of the Navy, were "to discharge all the ministerial duties" of the latter's office "relative to the procurement of naval stores and materials, and the construction, armament, equipment, and employment, of vessels of war, as well as all other matters connected with the naval establishment. . . ." In addition, they were "to furnish all the estimates of expenditure, which the several branches of the service may require, and such other information and statements as" the Secretary "may deem necessary." But nothing in the act was to "be construed" as taking "from the Secretary of the Navy his control and direction of the naval forces . . . as now by law possessed."[23]

[20] See *A. S. P., Naval Affairs,* Vol. I, pp. 354–9.
[21] Quoted in *Niles Weekly Register* (June 17, 1815), Vol. VIII, pp. 265, 267.
[22] *A. S. P., Naval Affairs,* Vol. I, pp. 285, 305, 320–4, 354–9.
[23] *Stat. at Large,* Vol. III, pp. 202–3.

The legislative intent was clear. Distrust of the military, which in those days was still strong, especially within the ranks of the dominant Jeffersonian Party, forbade any delegation of policy-determination to the officers of the Navy. The Commissioners were to supervise administration and advise the Secretary, but control of policy was to remain where the Constitution placed it in civilian hands.[24]

It was easy enough to decree complete separation of administration and policy-determination, but it was difficult to enforce such a separation in practice. The capable officers appointed to the Board of Commissioners had ideas of their own, not only with regard to the design and construction of ships and the management of navy yards and personnel, but also with regard to the strength and disposition of the Navy and its relation to the diplomacy and foreign policy of the United States. As the professional naval bureaucracy grew in numbers and solidarity, its efforts to influence policy tended progressively to increase. These efforts were to produce recurrent friction with the civilian executive and especially with Congress. This friction, varying in intensity and results from year to year, depending upon the party in power, the personalities of dominant leaders, the drift of public opinion, and the state of foreign relations, constituted a continuing problem, not merely of administration, but also of policy-determination. The essence of this problem was how to combine the expert knowledge of the professional naval bureaucracy, the political leadership of the civilian executive, and the representative function and legislative power of Congress. This problem, which will recur again and again in the pages of this study, and for which, to this day, no wholly satisfactory solution has been found, was squarely faced for the first time in the Act of 1815 creating the Board of Navy Commissioners.

[24] The Constitution, it is recalled, vested in Congress the power "to provide and maintain a navy" [Art. I, Sec. 8, Par. 13], and made the President "commander-in-chief of the army and navy . . ." [Art. II, Sec. 2, Par. 1].

Post-War Functions and Reorganization

The transition from war to peace raised fundamental problems as to future disposition and administration of forces afloat. For more than a generation, the Navy was exclusively preoccupied with a wide variety of functions growing out of the revival and expansion of foreign commerce and the marine industries following the war with Great Britain. These functions, which included displaying the flag abroad, opening new markets to American commerce, protecting merchantmen from discriminatory or other unjust treatment in foreign ports, clearing the seas of pirates and slave traders, aiding vessels in distress, and extending the boundaries of oceanography, all involved problems of disposition and organization radically different from those of wartime strategy and operations.[25]

In the performance of these peacetime functions, the Navy Department, with few applicable precedents, felt its way step by step, generally following the line of least resistance. The practice at first was to send out one or more ships to deal with particular situations as they arose. But this had manifest disadvantages, especially in those lawless days of slow and uncertain communication. The recurrent or constant need for naval forces in certain localities led gradually to the establishment of permanent "squadrons" on a number of "stations." Each station was simply a more or less well defined area within which several naval vessels cruised all the time. And the vessels assigned to each station at any given time comprised a squadron.

The Mediterranean Squadron was the first one established. In 1815 a strong force was sent out to punish and overawe the Barbary Powers, which had renewed their piratical depredations while the United States was preoccupied in the war with

[25] See, in general, Captain D. W. Knox, *History of the United States Navy* (1936), Chaps. XIII–XV; and Paullin, "Naval Administration, 1815–1842," pp. 597, 623*ff*.

Great Britain. This task was successfully completed in a few months. The force was then considerably reduced but not entirely withdrawn. And for several decades the Mediterranean Squadron, permanent as an institution though frequently changing in strength and composition, symbolized the power of the United States in the recurrently troubled waters of that sea.[26]

The next two regular squadrons were established about 1822. One of these, the West India Squadron, was organized to police the Gulf of Mexico and the Caribbean Sea against the pirates and irregular "privateers" which preyed on the lucrative traffic radiating from New Orleans, the commercial outlet of the Mississippi Valley.[27] Simultaneously, the post-war revival of the Pacific whaling industry, the civil disturbances which accompanied the disintegration of Spanish sovereignty on the West Coast of North and South America, and the growth of United States commerce with these countries and with the islands of the South Seas, all required the presence of a naval force in the Pacific. A man-of-war was dispatched to that ocean in 1817; others followed, and in 1821 all forces in this area were organized under one command which came to be known as the Pacific Squadron.[28]

The Brazil, or South Atlantic, Squadron was organized in 1826, for reasons comparable to those which produced its counterpart in the Eastern Pacific. The growing volume of commerce with the Far East led to the establishment of the East India Squadron in 1835. A so-called Home Squadron was organized in 1841, and a regular slave trade patrol, or African Squadron, in 1843.[29]

[26] See G. W. Allen, *Our Navy and the Barbary Corsairs* (1905), Chaps. XVI–XVII; *Papers of Isaac Hull* (edited by G. W. Allen, 1929), Chaps. X–XIX; and C. S. Alden, *Lawrence Kearny, Sailor Diplomat* (1936), Chap. IV.

[27] See G. W. Allen, *Our Navy and the West Indian Pirates* (1929); and Alden, *Kearny*, Chap. III.

[28] See Paullin, "Naval Administration, 1815–1842," p. 624; and *Papers of Isaac Hull*, Chap. V.

[29] See Paullin, "Naval Administration, 1815–1842," pp. 624–5; and *idem*, "Early Voyages of American Naval Vessels to the Orient," *Proc. U. S. Nav. Inst.*, Vol. XXXVI (1910), pp. 429*ff.*, 707*ff.*, 1074*ff.*

Dispersion of the ships in commission among these regular cruising stations,[30] not to mention the frequent detachment of vessels for various special services,[31] unquestionably retarded the development of the Navy into a synchronized fighting machine. The designation "squadron" was often if not usually misleading. The different units, it is true, were under the command of a single officer, generally the senior captain who carried the courtesy title of commodore. But the vessels usually cruised separately, or at most in groups of two or three. In consequence, there was little opportunity for the larger group operations necessary to weld the individual ships into squadrons in fact as well as in name. And it is no exaggeration to say that the United States lacked even the rudiments of a fleet organization in the generation following the War of 1812.

The Post-War Reaction

The post-war reaction against progressive naval expansion, which set in before 1820, likewise retarded development of an efficient fighting machine. This reaction was foreshadowed in certain sections of the 1816 Act for the "gradual increase of the Navy" and in the prompt liquidation of the naval forces upon the inland lakes. It developed rapidly as the country slid into the trough of the business recession which abruptly ter-

[30] In 1835, for example, the disposition of the forces in commission was as follows:

- Mediterranean: Frigate *Constitution*, Frigate *Potomac*, Sloop *John Adams*, Schooner *Shark*.
- West Indies: Frigate *Constellation*, Sloop *St. Louis*, Sloop *Vandalia*, Sloop *Warren*, Schooner *Grampus*.
- Coast of Brazil: Sloop *Erie*, Sloop *Ontario*.
- Pacific: Frigate *Brandywine*, Sloop *Vincennes*, Sloop *Fairfield*, Schooner *Dolphin*, Schooner *Boxer*.
- East Indies: Sloop *Peacock*, Schooner *Enterprise*.

[31] ". . . Such as surveying the coast of the United States, guarding the live oak reservations, protecting Newfoundland fisheries, and conveying our diplomatic representatives abroad." Paullin, "Naval Administration, 1815–1842," p. 625.

minated a brief post-war prosperity and led to a decline in customs receipts from $36,000,000 in 1816 to only $13,000,000 in 1821.

One of the first symptoms of the reaction against continued naval expansion was a movement to suspend further operations under the 1816 building program.[32] It was proposed, in January 1821, to retire one-half of the naval force still in active service, and to spread over a longer period the appropriations necessary to complete the ships under construction.[33] A few weeks later, a motion that would have prevented putting any of the new vessels into commission was defeated in the House by the close division of 67 to 66, with most of the anti-navy votes coming from inland representatives.[34] A bill reducing from $1,000,000 to $500,000 the annual outlay for new construction and authorizing the smaller expenditure for six more years, was passed, over the protest of the Navy Department, without a record vote in either chamber.[35] Annual appropriations for the Navy reflected the same trend, declining from a yearly average of nearly $3,700,000 during the first administration of President Monroe (1817–1821) to $2,900,000 per year for the period of his second administration (1821–1825).[36]

The necessity for economy, coinciding with a growing demand for naval forces to perform a wide variety of peace-time functions in all parts of the world, fostered a trend toward smaller vessels. Heavy frigates and ships-of-the-line required large crews and were otherwise expensive to maintain in active service. Sloops, brigs, and schooners, supported by a few of the larger ships, could police the seas and display the flag abroad nearly as well and at considerably less expense. Accordingly, the Navy Department sought and secured additional small

[32] See, for example, *A. S. P., Naval Affairs,* Vol. I, pp. 648*ff.*

[33] *Annals, 16th Cong., 2nd Sess.,* p. 716.

[34] *ibid.,* p. 1287.

[35] *A. S. P., Naval Affairs,* Vol. I, pp. 649, 651; *Annals, 16th Cong., 2nd Sess.,* pp. 401, 1292; *Stat. at Large,* Vol. III, p. 642.

[36] Averages computed from statistics compiled in 45 Cong. 1 Sess., *S. Ex. Doc.,* No. 3, p. 156.

men-of-war, laid up most of the larger vessels, and retarded or suspended work on those still under construction.[37]

The post-war reaction found still further expression in a congressional assault upon the Navy's personnel. Between 1801 and 1812, Congress had passed several acts limiting the number of officers and seamen. A war measure, voted in 1813, repealed these limitations and empowered the President to employ as many officers and men as required for the vessels in commission. Presidential discretion was limited, of course, by congressional control over appropriations, a control clearly reflected in the reduction of naval personnel from about 5,500 in 1816 to 4,000 in 1822. But such indirect control did not satisfy the anti-navy element in Congress, who demanded that the national legislature itself set the "peace establishment," and set it low.[38]

Although this agitation failed to produce legislative results at the time, it did stimulate fresh discussion which culminated in an important report on the objectives and fundamental principles of naval policy.[39] This report, submitted to Congress in January 1824 over the signatures of President Monroe and his Secretary of the Navy, Samuel L. Southard, opened with a sur-

[37] *A. S. P., Naval Affairs,* Vol. I, pp. 676, 787, 803, 804, 805, 1015, 1049, 1093; Vol. II, pp. 103, 126. The following table shows the disposition of the Navy, as reported by the Navy Department in March 1822 and Nov. 1823.

	1822	*1823*
In service:		
74-gun ships	1	1
44-gun ships	1	1
36-gun ships	1	1
12 to 30-gun ships	13	12
Ships rating less than 12 guns	1	15
Laid up "in ordinary":		
74-gun ships	2	6
44-gun ships	3	2
36-gun ships	2	2
Ships rating less than 36 guns	2	3
Under construction:		
74-gun ships	9	5
44-gun ships	5	5

[38] See *A. S. P., Naval Affairs,* Vol. I, pp. 732*ff.*; and Paullin, "Naval Administration, 1815–1842," pp. 626–7.

[39] See *A. S. P., Naval Affairs,* Vol. I, pp. 815*ff.*, 870, 906, 933.

vey of the fatal consequences of our naval impotence prior to the late war, and a review of the disasters suffered in that conflict. Geographic remoteness and a strict neutrality had not saved American property from lawless aggression at the hands of all the principal belligerents. And when at length we entered the struggle our whole coast from the St. Croix River in Maine to the Mississippi "was either invaded or menaced with invasion . . . there was scarcely an harbor or city . . . which could be considered secure. . . . In whatever direction the enemy chose to move with their squadrons and to land their troops, our fortifications, where any existed, presented but little obstacle to them. . . ."

By way of practical suggestions, however, the President and his naval advisers had relatively little to offer, and most of what they did offer ignored the lessons of the recent struggle. It was recognized that only "adequate fortifications and a suitable naval force" could save us, in a future war "with a strong naval Power," from the "calamities" suffered in the last war; and that the Navy should be so organized in peace as to facilitate its mobilization for war. It was further recommended that enough vessels be kept in commission not only to "protect all our scattered interests [and] secure the respect of other Powers" in peace, but also to "give active service sufficient to qualify as many officers as will be required to command and manage the whole of our vessels, when necessity shall call for their use. . . . It were better to have no ships than to have them filled with incompetent and unskilled officers." While it was urged that Congress create the rank of admiral, there was little apparent conception of the squadron and fleet organization logically associated with ranks higher than that of captain. In the realm of strategy, the report had even less to offer. Ignoring the blockade in the late conflict with Great Britain, it was positively laid down that "the great object in the event of war is to stop the enemy at the coast." This achieved, "our cities and whole interior" would "be secure." For this purpose we should rely on fortifications and floating batteries, leaving the sea-going Navy free to raid the coast and commerce of the enemy, and thereby compel withdrawal of hostile forces from our own seaboard.[40]

The same trend of thought was further developed in a series of reports on coast defense, prepared mainly by two famous military engineers, Simon Bernard[41] and Joseph G. Totten.[42] These authorities based their recommendations upon the sound proposition that a comprehensive system of defense for the maritime frontier of the United States should embrace a navy, coastal fortifications, interior communications, and an army. But their discussion of the special function and relative importance of each element of their system reflected not only the natural bias of the army engineer, but also the strategic fallacies that had survived the War of 1812.[43]

The only way that a naval force could contribute directly to the defense of a maritime frontier, in the opinion of these famous experts, was through a distribution of the vessels along the seaboard. Any concentration of the defending navy's units, they argued, would leave the enemy's squadrons free to strike at every unguarded point. Well planned fortifications could provide a far more efficient system of defense. Such works, supported by adequate interior communications and an army, could not only stop an invader at the coast and provide havens of refuge for the Navy, but also prevent close blockades of our seaports and free the Navy's cruisers for their natural function of raiding the enemy's coast and shipping, and attacking scattered detachments of the enemy's naval forces.[44]

These various reports, from both military and naval sources, appear to have reflected the best available expert opinion of the post-war generation. While they certainly showed some ad-

[40] See *ibid.*, Vol. I, pp. 906*ff*.

[41] T. M. Spaulding, "Simon Bernard," *Dict. Am. Biog.*, Vol. II, p. 223.

[42] W. A. Ganoe, "Joseph Gilbert Totten," *ibid.*, Vol. XVIII, pp. 598–9.

[43] For a summary of their earlier reports, submitted in 1818, 1819, 1820, and 1821, see *A. S. P., Military Affairs,* Vol. II, pp. 305*ff*.

[44] Revised Report of the Board of Engineers on the Defense of the Seaboard, March 24, 1826, *ibid.*, Vol. III, pp. 283*ff*.

vance over earlier thinking, one may search in vain for any clear-cut recognition of the great strategic principles, deducible from our own Revolutionary War and every subsequent maritime conflict: that it was not sufficient merely to stop an invader at the water's edge; that a guerilla warfare against an enemy's coast and shipping might harass but could not cripple a strong maritime Power; that the first object of naval strategy was to prevent a blockade of one's own seaboard; that the only way to achieve this object was to maintain a fleet of capital ships strong enough to defeat any force that a potential enemy could send into a wide zone of open sea beyond the coastline, or, at the very least, strong enough to prevent a dispersion of the enemy's forces within that area.

There was an equally general failure to grasp the further principles, likewise deducible from the wars of the preceding generation, that the second object of naval strategy was to blockade the enemy's ports, and thereby destroy their commerce root and branch; that the only way to achieve that object was to imprison or destroy the enemy's fleet; and that the only force that could execute such an enterprise was a fleet of capital ships strong enough to meet the enemy's fleet within its own waters. While it might prove strategically impossible or politically impracticable to maintain a navy capable of attaining the second objective against any and all possible enemies, the War of 1812 had provided a recent and conclusive demonstration that failure to achieve the first objective might end in a stoppage of maritime commerce, military defeat, and national humiliation and disaster.

Naval Policy and the Political Realignment of the Later 'Twenties

The presidential election of 1824 foreshadowed a trend back toward the ideas and policies formerly associated with the now defunct Federalist Party. John Quincy Adams, who succeeded to the presidency in March 1825, was a son of John Adams, during whose Administration (1797–1801) the Navy had experienced its initial rapid development. The younger Adams, like his father, was a maritime New Englander, with that region's typical attitude toward the Navy. He favored its progressive improvement, and viewed with satisfaction the fleet of formidable warships which, as he put it, "with a few months of preparation" could "present a line of floating fortifications along the whole range of our coast." He fully approved the policy embodied in the Act of 1816 which was continued in qualified form in the supplementary Act of 1821. This legislation was, in his view, "a declaration . . . that it was the destiny and the duty of these confederated States to become in regular process of time and by no petty advances a great naval power." And as the period of the supplementary statute was about to expire, he strongly urged fresh legislation to carry us further toward our destined national objective.[45]

In response to this recommendation, a bill was introduced continuing the policy of progressive expansion, and authorizing an annual expenditure of $500,000 for another six years. In its details, however, this bill reflected a compromise with the policy set forth in the Act of 1816. The 1827 bill was for "the gradual improvement [not 'increase'] of the Navy." It authorized the Navy Department to build two dry-docks, to improve the existing navy yards, and to institute an "academy" for training naval officers. But it authorized no new ships, directing the Executive merely to procure stocks of ship timber and to reserve standing timber for use in the future.[46]

There was little opposition to the accumulation of raw materials, and comparatively little to building dry-docks, of which the Navy Department, even at this late date, still had none. But there was a great outcry against setting up a naval academy. It was argued that such an institution would cost too much;

[45] Annual Message, Dec. 5, 1826, *Messages and Papers of the Presidents* (Richardson's 1st ed.), Vol. II, pp. 361–2.

[46] *Register of Debates,* 19 Cong. 2 Sess., p. 348.

that it would foster a military class whose members would monopolize all the higher positions in the Navy, contrary to the spirit of democracy; that it would place in the hands of the Executive one more instrument of political patronage; that such a school was wholly unnecessary, since the merchant service already provided the best possible training for a naval career. Besides, it was maintained that the Navy already had more officers than it needed in time of peace. And it was feared that a large corps of unemployed officers would wield a dangerous influence, working persistently for the construction of additional vessels, and for a larger number in commission in time of peace.[47]

This controversy over a naval academy led easily to a discussion of naval preparedness in general. On the larger question, Senator Robert Y. Hayne of South Carolina, Chairman of the Senate's Naval Committee, declared "that a Navy was not only the safest, but the cheapest defence of this nation"; "that it was the true policy of the United States to become a great Naval Power"; and that our progress toward that goal "should depend, not upon irregular and varying acts of legislation, but should proceed on some regular plan, from which there ought to be no departure, except in some great emergency."[48]

While this was perhaps the prevailing opinion, there were dissenting voices. Representative Lemuel Sawyer of North Carolina, for example, thought "we ought to be satisfied with the present number of ships," until there was some prospect of actually using them.[49] And Senator Nathaniel Macon of the same State was another who bluntly stated his opposition to the plan of "preparing for war in peace. . . . The moment we get through one war, we prepare for another. . . . Can you expect to keep the country at peace, when it is full of soldiers?" He thought not, for ". . . when People are ready"

[47] For the debate in the Senate, see *ibid.*, pp. 345–76, 505–24; for the debate in the House, *ibid.*, pp. 1496–1500, 1507–9, 1512–14.

[48] *ibid.*, pp. 351, 353.

[49] *ibid.*, p. 1499.

for war, "they are sure always to fight." A navy was useful only "for conquest," and he did not "wish to conquer other nations."[50]

After defeating a motion to strike out the sections providing for a naval academy, the Senate passed the bill by a vote of 28 to 18. The House of Representatives, however, rejected the controverted sections, and the bill was finally enacted without provision for a naval academy.[51] Unfortunately, there is no record of the divisions in the House. But we do have the roll calls in the Senate, both on the motion to strike out the naval academy sections, and on the bill's final passage. Analysis of these votes reveals that the sectional cleavage was no longer as clear-cut as it had been before the war. Maritime New England and New York still presented an almost solid pro-navy front. The anti-navy tradition persisted in Pennsylvania, Virginia, Kentucky, Tennessee, and a few other localities. But elsewhere the sectional cleavage was blurred, and nowhere more so than in the frontier States of Ohio, Indiana, Illinois, and Missouri.

While various factors probably contributed to this result, perhaps the most important was the realignment in American politics which was then taking place. A large majority of those who opposed the 1827 bill for the "gradual improvement of the Navy" were followers of General Andrew Jackson, who was leading a new agrarian movement. The group supporting the bill, on the other hand, included relatively few Jacksonians, but many who were then, or were soon to become, associated with the new Whig Party which was rising from the ruins of Federalism. While the cleavage was not too clear-cut, and was to shift somewhat from time to time, the Whigs tended to carry on the Federalist naval tradition, while the Jacksonians evolved a modified version of the naval policy originally identified with the party of Jefferson.[52]

[50] *ibid.*, pp. 521, 522.
[51] *Stat. at Large,* Vol. IV, pp. 206–8.
[52] See Paullin, "Naval Administration, 1815–1842," pp. 597, 613–14.

Jacksonian Naval Policy

One could have forecast the naval policy of the new agrarian party from the statements on national defense made by its founder. In his Inaugural Address on March 4, 1829, President Jackson denounced standing armies as "dangerous to free governments in time of peace. . . ." A navy, he allowed, was less dangerous, "but the bulwark of our defense is the national militia, which in the present state of our intelligence and population must render us invincible."[53]

This philosophy of national defense led Jackson to the belief that in time of peace the United States had "need of no more ships of war [in commission] than are requisite to the protection of commerce [against pirates, etc.]"; and that the government should stop building warships "of the first and second class," confining its naval preparations to laying in materials with which to build or fit out additional vessels in case of war.[54]

The President found further grounds for such a policy in the geographical isolation of the United States. Our great distance "from all those governments whose power we might have reason to dread" left us "nothing to apprehend from attempts at conquest. . . ."[55] Jackson's Secretary of the Navy believed, in 1832, that the United States, "though nominally, as to vessels in commission, only the fifth or sixth naval Power in the world," had no cause for anxiety, with "an ocean rolling between us and most of the governments with whom we are likely to have collision. . . ." In an emergency we could always improvise a naval force from vessels in course of construction, from the merchant marine, and from accumulated stocks of timber and other materials.[56]

53 *M. & P.* (Richardson), Vol. II, pp. 436, 437–8.

54 Annual Message, Dec. 8, 1829, *ibid.*, p. 459.

55 Second Annual Message, Dec. 6, 1830, *ibid.*, p. 526; and see Annual Report of the Secretary of the Navy for 1830, *A. S. P., Naval Affairs,* Vol. III, pp. 753–9.

56 Annual Report, 1832, *A. S. P., Naval Affairs,* Vol. IV, pp. 158, 160. Naval

The Jackson administration was still following this line of policy when in 1835 a long-standing dispute with France, over claims dating from the French Revolutionary War, flared up into a serious crisis. Following a rupture of diplomatic relations, it was reported that the French government was sending a formidable fleet across the Atlantic on an "observation" cruise, manifestly designed to intimidate the United States government, and to be in a position to strike in case of war.[57]

These events fortuitously coincided with the extinction of the public debt and the extraordinary phenomenon of a large and rapidly increasing surplus revenue pouring into the Federal Treasury. Viewing with alarm the ominous trend in our foreign relations and the neglected state of our national defenses, certain Administration leaders, Senator Thomas Hart Benton of Missouri in particular, contrary to their party's declared policy of cutting naval expenditures to the limit, advocated use of the surplus to put the country in a position to resist an attack from overseas.[58]

This proposal, however, loosed a storm of protest from a host of politically minded Senators and Representatives who preferred, on the eve of a national election, to distribute the surplus among the States. And this opposition to strengthening the country's defenses, it should be noted, came chiefly from the Whigs, whose party had been hitherto, and was again to become, the champion of a strong navy.[59]

This anomalous situation continued to the end of Jackson's term. In 1836, the War and Navy Departments recommended greatly increased expenditures on naval defense.[60] And the

---

expenditures clearly reflected the trend of policy. From an annual average of nearly $4,000,000 during John Quincy Adams's administration (1825–1829), they declined to a yearly average of slightly over $3,500,000 during Jackson's first administration.

[57] See T. H. Benton, *Thirty Years View* (1854), Vol. I, p. 593.

[58] *Reg. of Debates,* 24 Cong. 1 Sess., p. 106; and 26 Cong. 2 Sess. *S. Doc.,* No. 227, p. 2.

[59] *Reg. of Debates,* 24 Cong. 1 Sess., pp. 106–14; 130–63, 211–81, 291–300, 304–323, 325–66, 367–83, 392–464, 534–63, 566–77.

[60] *A. S. P., Military Affairs,* Vol. VI, p. 365; and *ibid., Naval Affairs,* Vol. IV, pp. 883, 953.

President himself, on the day of his retirement (March 4, 1837), solemnly renounced the naval policy which he had strongly endorsed during the first six years, and ignored during the last two years, of his Administration.

Fortifications, he held, were useful and necessary "to protect cities from bombardment, dockyards and naval arsenals from destruction, to give shelter to merchant vessels in time of war and to single ships or weaker squadrons when pressed by superior force." But it would be "impossible by any line of fortifications to guard every point from attack against a hostile force advancing from the ocean. . . ." Only a navy could afford such complete protection. "Now is the time," he declared, "in a season of peace and with an overflowing revenue, that we can year after year add" to the Navy's "strength without increasing the burdens of the people. It is your true policy, for your Navy will not only protect your rich and flourishing commerce in distant seas, but it will enable you to reach and annoy the enemy and will give to defense its greatest efficiency by meeting danger at a distance from home."[61]

It is a question how much to read into these words of the old warrior-statesman. He manifestly perceived the limitations of a purely passive coast defense. He was just as certainly familiar with the military maxim that offense is the best defense. And it is possible that he had some conception of the strategic doctrine which is summed up in the phrase, command of the sea. If so, he had clearly outstripped even the professional naval opinion of his day.

One may judge the state of that opinion from a report of the Board of Navy Commissioners, submitted to the Secretary of the Navy, March 2, 1836, over the signature of Commodore John Rodgers, the highest ranking officer in the Service at that time. This report, which the Secretary passed on to the President and Congress with the endorsement that it contained the "best information . . . in [the Department's] possession,"[62] em-

[61] *M. & P.* (Richardson), Vol. III, pp. 306–7.
[62] *A. S. P., Military Affairs,* Vol. VI, p. 399.

bodied the results of the Board's study "of the nature and extent of the naval force which is 'necessary to place the naval defences of the United States upon the footing of strength and respectability which is due to the security and welfare of the Union.' . . ."[63]

In framing their answer to this question, the Commissioners noted certain "geographical" features of our situation—the "position of the United States with reference to other nations with whom we are most likely to be brought into future collision; the great extent of our maritime frontier. . . ." They also noted certain obvious strategic objectives—"the extreme importance of securing the communications of the whole Mississippi Valley through the Gulf of Mexico, and the intercourse between all parts of the coast; the efficient protection of our widely-extended and extremely valuable commerce under all circumstances. . . ."

In fixing the proper "extent" of the Navy, however, they completely ignored these fundamental facts and conditions, and simply advocated as large a navy as the government could find seamen to man in time of war. And in calculating the probable number available in such a contingency, they proceeded upon the assumption that our maritime commerce would inevitably be disrupted as it had been in previous wars, thus throwing out of private employment, and making available for government service at least 30,000 out of a total of approximately 90,000 seamen.

With respect to the number and types of warships, the Commissioners admitted that there would "undoubtedly be differences of opinion." Even so, they did not deem it necessary to discuss the distinctive functions of different classes of war vessels, and gave no reasons for their own program which included 25 ships-of-the-line,[64] 35 frigates,[65] 25 sloops-of-war, 25 steamers, and 25 smaller vessels.

[63] *ibid.*, p. 400.

[64] Fifteen to be completely built, and ten more laid down, with timber to complete them available.

[65] Twenty-five built, and ten more laid down.

They did not, of course, advocate keeping such a huge force in commission in time of peace. But they did recommend maintaining enough vessels in active service at all times to command respect for "our commercial interests, and to prepare the officers and others for the efficient management of the force proposed for a state of war." But the training which they contemplated, clearly extended little, if at all, beyond the handling of individual vessels. For they unqualifiedly endorsed the practice of distributing the peacetime force among half a dozen or more widely separated stations, ignoring the difficulty, or even impossibility under such conditions, of developing individual ships and their operating personnel into a unified, efficient, large-scale fighting machine. And the failure of these eminent captains of the Old Navy to envisage a highly organized fighting fleet, was further indicated by their proposal to keep only five capital ships in commission, and to maintain only two of these in active service.[66]

Taking a broad view of this official statement by the highest naval authority in the United States, it is difficult to resist the conclusion that professional opinion, in 1836 as in 1826, was still groping for sound principles of naval strategy and organization. While the leading spirits of the Old Navy were thoroughly committed to building capital ships, they still failed, by either word or act, to show any grasp of the organization or use of massed power to secure and hold the regional command of the sea necessary to defend the coastline and to keep open the ports of the United States in case of war with a strong naval Power.

[66] *A. S. P., Military Affairs,* Vol. VI, pp. 400–3; for a supplementary report, equally vague on those important questions, see *ibid., Naval Affairs,* Vol. IV, pp. 954–6.

CHAPTER EIGHT

☆ ☆

From Sails to Steam: The First Phase (1837–1845)

THE eight years spanned by the Democratic administration of Martin Van Buren (1837–1841) and the Whig administration of William Henry Harrison and John Tyler (1841–1845), was a period of transition in naval technology, and, save for a brief interval in 1841 and 1842, one of drift in the realm of naval policy.

When President Van Buren entered the White House, naval science was passing through the early stages of a technological revolution. Save for minor refinements from time to time, naval ordnance and architecture had undergone little change during the preceding century. Naval vessels of the 'thirties differed little in appearance, structure, and armament from those of the days of Rodney and Nelson. The two- or three-deck ship-of-the-line, a massive wooden sailing vessel, was still the symbol and embodiment of naval power. Smooth-bore cannon and solid shot were still the prevailing characteristics of naval ordnance. And seamanship was still the highest qualification of a naval officer.

Revolutionary developments, however, were in process. Sails were beginning to give way to steam. The submerged screw propeller was soon to supersede the amidship paddle wheels of the first steamers. Introduction of explosive shells was turning the unprotected wooden warship into a potential shambles.

And further developments in naval ordnance were destined within a generation to force a revolution in naval architecture that would make the unarmored wooden warship as obsolete as the war galleys of ancient Rome.[1]

Civilian leadership and imagination, always important, were to prove indispensable in this initial stage of the technological revolution, for the professional bureaucracy tended to resist change. Only the superior authority of the civilian political Executive (the President, Secretary of the Navy, etc.) could compel a hearing and trial for new ideas offered by professional or civilian inventors. Likewise, only the political Executive could prevent the Navy from becoming a football of party politics and a victim of political patronage and the spoils system. This importance of executive leadership was not something new. We have traced the results of such leadership, or the lack of it, from the founding of the Navy. It was to assume a new importance, however, as the Navy entered the technological revolution. And through a fortuitous concurrence of events, this initial period of transition was to throw new light on the potentialities both of intelligent and sympathetic executive support and of executive indifference and hostility.

Beginnings of the Steam Navy

Experiments with steam were the first portents, within the United States, of the impending revolution in naval technology. These experiments began during the War of 1812, when the government built a steam-driven war vessel generally described as a "steam battery." This craft, known both as the *Fulton* and the *Demologos,* was little more than a huge unwieldy hull with a primitive engine and water wheel. It was 156 feet long, 56 feet wide, and displaced 2,475 tons—a tremendous vessel for that period. Fully equipped, it proved capable of an average

[1] The standard work on this revolution of naval architecture is Dr. James Phinney Baxter's excellent monograph entitled *The Introduction of the Ironclad Warship* (1933).

speed, under steam alone, of about five and a half miles an hour. And it had the further distinction of being the first steam-driven warship ever constructed for any navy.[2]

After the war, the *Fulton* was laid up at the Brooklyn Navy Yard where it remained until accidentally destroyed by an explosion in 1829. Meanwhile, though the Act of 1816 for the "gradual increase of the Navy" authorized three more "steam batteries," no steps were actually taken beyond purchasing some machinery which grew obsolete long before there was any hull in which to place it. From time to time, Secretaries of the Navy noted the progress of steam navigation abroad, and discussed the desirability of reintroducing it into the United States Navy. In 1826, for example, Congress was mildly urged to support further experiments with a view to ascertaining the value of steam-driven batteries as adjuncts to land fortifications for coast and harbor defense.[3] Five years later, another Secretary thought "it would be improvident to overlook" the "probable importance" of steam power in "maritime warfare," and recommended building "two steam batteries of twelve heavy guns each, on the most modern and improved models."[4] But the matter was not pressed, and neither Congress nor the Navy Department took any action.

The question was again raised in 1834, by Mahlon Dickerson of New Jersey, who had just entered the office of Secretary of the Navy. Dickerson, like his predecessors, viewed steam warships as "floating batteries" useful mainly for coast defense. But for this purpose, he thought them indispensable. In their home waters, steam batteries could drive back any attacking force of sailing vessels. And that was the only kind of force that need be considered, for "the heavy and cumbrous steam vessels and batteries, with their necessary apparatus and supplies, which may be brought into action with the most power-

[2] For further details and drawings of this vessel, see F. M. Bennett, *The Steam Navy of the United States* (1896). Chap. II.

[3] *American State Papers, Naval Affairs,* Vol. II, p. 727.

[4] *op. cit.,* Vol. IV, p. 8.

ful effect by a nation near its own shores and harbors, cannot be transported over distant seas and oceans for the purpose of attacking its enemies." Possession of steam batteries would accordingly "diminish the frequency" of wars by taking from the "aggressor . . . his hope of success, and, of course, his motive for action."[5]

Dickerson, unlike his predecessors, did not stop with recommendations. Proceeding under the unrepealed Act of 1816, he laid down a war steamer, and then went to Congress for funds with which to complete it.[6] This vessel, also named the *Fulton*, was launched in 1837, and marked the real beginning of the steam navy of the United States.[7]

But it was only a beginning. Adjustment of the crisis with France,[8] relieved the pressure which had temporarily forced the agrarian party from its traditional position of hostility to naval expansion. The financial panic of 1837, resulting in diminished revenue and a series of annual deficits, necessitated a policy of retrenchment. President Van Buren who took office March 4, 1837, showed little interest in, or comprehension of, the potentialities of steam warships. On several occasions he referred complacently to the manner in which the government's existing men-of-war were performing their routine peacetime functions.[9] He was even quoted as saying "that this country required no navy at all, much less a steam navy."[10]

The older generation of naval officers, with few exceptions, resisted the trend toward steam.[11] Naval architecture, in their opinion, had reached the final stage of perfection. They had no use for the noisy and dirty steamer.[12] And during Van Buren's administration, they had an outspoken champion in

[5] *ibid.*, p. 590.
[6] *ibid.*, p. 748; Bennett, *Steam Navy*, p. 16.
[7] Bennett, *Steam Navy*, Chap. II.
[8] See Chap. VII, esp. p. 106, *supra*.
[9] *Messages and Papers of the Presidents* (Richardson's 1st ed.), Vol. III, pp. 392, 502, 537, 618.
[10] *New York Herald*, Jan. 23, 1878, p. 10.
[11] See Bennett, *Steam Navy*, Chaps. II–III.
[12] W. R. Griffis, *Matthew Calbraith Perry* (1887), p. 140.

the Secretary of the Navy, James K. Paulding, more widely known to posterity as a man of letters and an intimate friend of Washington Irving. Declaring that he would "never consent to let our old ships perish, and transform our navy into a fleet of [steam] sea monsters,"[13] Paulding planted himself firmly in the path of progress.[14]

There would have been no progress at all but for the initiative which unexpectedly developed in Congress at this juncture. The increasing use of steam power in the French and British Navies was noted with some apprehension. Secretary Paulding was criticized for ignoring this question in his annual report the previous year (1838). Resolutions from both chambers demanded information. And a bill was passed in March 1839 authorizing construction of three additional steam warships.[15]

It was one thing to authorize the ships; another to build them successfully at this transitional stage in the evolution of naval architecture. Credit for the latter is due chiefly to the imagination, enterprise, and expert knowledge of Captain Matthew C. Perry. Although better remembered as commander-in-chief of the famous naval expedition to Japan in the 'fifties, Perry was also a pioneer in steam navigation. He had previously commanded the second *Fulton*, and in 1839 had just returned from a European tour devoted to study of steam engineering in the Navies of France and Great Britain. And it was largely because of Perry's efforts that the first two of the authorized steamers, laid down in 1839 and completed in 1842, proved to be highly creditable specimens of naval architecture for their day.[16]

[13] W. L. Paulding, *Literary Life of James Kirke Paulding* (1867), p. 278.

[14] See Paulding's report to the Senate, Jan. 6, 1839, 25 Cong. 3 Sess. *S. Doc.* No. 267.

[15] *Congressional Globe*, 25 Cong. 2 Sess., pp. 48–9, 87, 89, 195, 221; *Statutes at Large*, Vol. V, pp. 362, 364; and A. L. Herold, *James Kirke Paulding, Versatile American* (1926), p. 130.

[16] Griffis, *Perry*, p. 158. These vessels, named the *Mississippi* and *Missouri*, were bark-rigged frigates, 229 feet long, 40 feet beam, 19 feet mean draft, and 3,220 tons displacement. Their rather small engines drove amidship paddle

In the meantime, the commotion in Congress had not moved the Administration in the slightest. Van Buren completely ignored the subject of naval expansion in his last two annual messages.[17] And in his final annual report, Paulding, while showing deep concern over the state of seamanship in the Navy, dismissed the subject of steam with one brief paragraph reporting progress on the two vessels under construction.[18]

More revealing, if scarcely more enlightening, were the professional reports submitted in 1840 in response to the congressional demands of the preceding year. The first, prepared by the Board of Navy Commissioners, showed partial resignation to the encroachment of steam, but scarcely any appreciation of the importance which steam warships were assuming abroad.[19] The second report, though prepared by a board of army engineers, dealt more comprehensively with naval defense. These engineers perceived that passive coast and harbor defense was properly the function of fortifications, not of a seagoing navy. But, like so many of their contemporaries, they improperly classified steam warships as "floating batteries," movable adjuncts to land fortifications. They would leave the "sea-going vessels" (ships-of-the-line, frigates, sloops, etc.) free for "destroying the enemy's commerce, carrying the war into the enemy's seas, and contending for the mastery of the ocean." But they apparently had no conception of fleet operations. On the contrary, they expressly envisaged the types of operations used in the War of 1812, when American men-of-war "scattered themselves over the wide surface of the ocean, penetrated to the most remote seas, everywhere acting with the most brilliant success against the enemy's navigation."[20]

---

wheels. Each was armed with two 10-inch and eight 6-inch shell guns. Bennett, *Steam Navy,* Chap. III.

[17] *M & P* (Richardson), Vol. III, pp. 537, 618.

[18] 26 Cong. 2 Sess., *S. Doc.* No. 1, p. 406.

[19] 26 Cong. 1 Sess. *S. Doc.* No. 120.

[20] 26 Cong., 1 Sess. *S. Doc.* No. 451, pp. 5, 6, 8.

Naval Policy and the Anglo-American Crisis of 1840–1841. Establishment of the "Home Squadron"

Events during the year 1840 foreshadowed an early stiffening of American naval policy. The Whig victory in the presidential and congressional elections of that year, once more brought into power those groups in American politics which had traditionally advocated a strong navy. And a diplomatic crisis with Great Britain raised another war scare which immediately refocused attention on the state of the Navy.

The immediate cause of the trouble with Great Britain was the arrest, within the State of New York, of one Alexander McLeod, a British subject, charged with murdering an American citizen upon United States soil in the abortive Canadian rebellion of 1837. Lord Palmerston's demand for his release, and President Van Buren's refusal to interfere with proceedings in the State courts, brought the two countries to the verge of war in the winter and spring of 1840–1841.

The crisis was aggravated and complicated by several other issues. One was the long-standing dispute over the Maine-New Brunswick boundary. Another related to suppression of the African slave trade. A third arose from reported British efforts to prevent the annexation of the Texan republic; and a fourth from the impending struggle for possession of the Columbia River valley in the Oregon wilderness of the Pacific Northwest.

The change of administration in the United States (March 1841), followed within a few months by a cabinet change in England (September 1841), opened the way for peaceful negotiations which culminated in the Webster-Ashburton Treaty of 1842. But the tension and alarm which continued through the summer of 1841 produced two immediate effects on American naval policy. Acting under an early statute which granted the President large discretion over naval personnel, the number of officers was increased nearly as much in the one year 1841 as in the entire preceding twenty years.[21] And the Administration started a movement which led to establishment of a permanent "home squadron."

In recommending this step, the Secretary of the Navy emphasized the world-wide dispersion of American naval forces. Assignment of practically all the ships in commission to the oversea squadrons had left our own shores "without any adequate protection." Had war occurred, British squadrons could have invaded American waters before our scattered forces were brought home and organized for defense. To guard against such a disaster in the future, it was "necessary that a powerful squadron should be kept afloat at home."[22]

The House Naval Committee, to which this proposal was referred, found additional grounds for creating a home squadron. One of these was the reported increase of British armed forces in the West Indies. Another was the rapid development of steam navigation in the French and British Navies and merchant marines. "Under the old system of maritime war," the Committee argued, "our squadrons could be employed in the protection of our commerce and our flag abroad, without danger of aggression on our own coast, because the fleets of an enemy could no sooner approach to assail than our own return to defend us." But the "introduction of steam power" had so increased the mobility of naval power that only a permanent home squadron could insure the defense of our seaboard in the future.[23]

A bill appropriating a special fund for such a squadron passed the House after a brief debate, by the decisive vote of 184 to 8.[24] It passed the Senate without either a debate or a record vote.[25] And its enactment into law[26] was an event of far

[21] *Cong. Globe,* 27 Cong. 2 Sess., p. 638.
[22] May 31, 1841, 27 Cong. 1 Sess. *S. Doc.* No. 1, p. 61.
[23] 27 Cong. 1 Sess. *H. Rept..* No. 3, July 7, 1841.
[24] *Cong. Globe,* 27 Cong. 1 Sess., pp. 238–40.
[25] *ibid.,* p. 270.
[26] *Stat. at Large,* Vol. V, p. 438.

reaching importance in the rise of American naval power. For it resulted in the establishment of an organization which was to evolve through successive stages into the North Atlantic Squadron of the 1890's, the Atlantic Fleet of the 1900's, and finally the United States Fleet of today—the supreme embodiment of the now universally recognized strategic principle of concentration of power.

THE WHIG NAVAL PROGRAM AND DOMESTIC POLITICS

In December 1841, although the war scare was now well over, the Whig Administration came forward with a naval program which surpassed anything hitherto attempted. The naval estimates for 1842 exceeded $8,500,000, an increase of more than 50 per cent over the preceding year.[27] This program included new construction, more ships in commission, and greatly enlarged personnel. And it was strongly supported (and possibly formulated in large measure) by the professional Board of Navy Commissioners,[28] whose increasing influence over policy seems to have contributed to the growing dissatisfaction which culminated the following year in legislation abolishing that body and reorganizing the Navy Department into separate bureaus without collective functions or responsibility.[29]

The proposed naval program was publicly justified and defended in a long report signed by Abel P. Upshur, an aristocratic Virginia planter who had just succeeded to the Secretaryship of the Navy. The Administration's naval policy, according to Upshur, envisaged two objectives: promotion and protection of commerce, and defense of the coastline. With respect to the first, he contended that every section, class, and economic group in the country, should regard foreign

[27] 27 Cong. 2 Sess., *H. Rept.* No. 673, p. 1.

[28] *ibid.*, p. 5.

[29] See, for example, *Cong. Globe*, 25 Cong. 3 Sess., p. 195; *op. cit.*, *Appendix*, pp. 160*ff.*, 217*ff.*; *Globe*, 26 Cong. 2 Sess., *Appendix*, pp. 222, 315.

commerce and the coasting trade as "our principal [national] interest. . . ." The farmer, the planter, the mechanic, the manufacturer, and even the day laborer, all "depend[ed] in a greater or less degree" on maritime commerce "for the success of his own peculiar branch of industry. . . ." It was therefore imperative to maintain a navy strong enough to command respect for American commercial interests in peace and to defend them in war. "Any other course," he declared, "will only invite aggressions . . . which must ultimately force us to resistance, at the precise time when we are least prepared to make it successfully."[30]

The situation in the Pacific called for special attention in this connection. There was a large American whaling industry in that ocean. There were growing American settlements in the Mexican province of California. American commercial enterprise extended from Chile to the Columbia River, and out across the Pacific to the Orient. To safeguard these remote and widely scattered interests, Upshur held that we should maintain at least "twice the number of vessels now employed" in the Pacific, and that we should establish a naval base either upon the West Coast of America or in the Sandwich (Hawaiian) Islands.[31]

Turning to his second point, defense of our coastline, Upshur noted that we had formerly derived a strategic advantage from the shallowness of our coastal waters, which had precluded the approach of deep-draft sailing vessels, save at a few points which could be strongly fortified. The introduction of shallow-draft steam warships into European navies exposed our entire seaboard to attack from the sea. From now on, therefore, we must meet "the enemy upon the ocean."[32]

It was "worse than idle," he said, to suppose that our existing naval force was adequate to protect "all these high interests." While it was arguable that no foreign Power would be able

[30] 27 Cong. 2 Sess., *S. Doc.* No. 1, pp. 379, 380.
[31] *ibid.*, p. 369.
[32] *ibid.*, pp. 380, 381.

to attack us with more than one-fourth of its total force at any time, it was also unlikely that we could ever concentrate more than one-half of our Navy at one point. We could not, therefore, "safely stop short of half the naval power of the strongest maritime Power in the world." (This, we may note parenthetically, seems to have been the first attempt to establish a standard of naval power relative to that of other states. It contrasted sharply with the standard hitherto recommended by the professional Navy Commissioners, who had ignored international political relations, and simply advocated as large a navy as "could be properly manned" in an emergency.[33] And it is to be noted that the standard now proposed was to be based upon the naval power of Great Britain, at that time deemed the most probable maritime enemy of the United States.)[34]

In the matter of naval construction, it was clear to Upshur that we should proceed "with reference to the practice of other countries" where sails were rapidly giving way to steam. While we might postpone building steam warships of the "largest class," we should immediately build additional steamers for coast and harbor defense. Such vessels should be constructed of iron. We would thereby secure "a cheap and almost an imperishable naval force," and at the same time foster the domestic iron industry[35]—and incidentally, be it noted, raise up another vested interest in continuous and progressive naval expansion.

Ships, however, were not the only consideration. It was possible to build a warship "in a few weeks," but it required "twenty years of arduous service, of active instruction, and of strict discipline, to qualify an officer to command her." We should institute a naval training school, enlarge the corps of officers, and maintain enough ships in commission to keep these officers actively employed and abreast of progress in naval

[33] See 26 Cong. 1 Sess., *S. Doc.* No. 120, p. 2; and also p. 108, *supra*.
[34] 27 Cong. 2 Sess., *S. Doc.* No. 1, p. 381.
[35] *ibid.*, pp. 381, 382; and see 27 Cong. 2 Sess. *S. Doc.* No. 98.

art and science. And Congress was again urged to establish ranks above that of captain, in order to improve morale and to sustain the Navy's prestige abroad.[36]

Upshur's long and persuasive plea, and the naval estimates which accompanied it, precipitated one of the most enlightening parliamentary struggles in the history of American naval legislation. Once more the ancient sectional cleavage was revealed. Typical of the inland opposition was the speech of Senator Thomas Hart Benton of Missouri. Noting that the Navy was now costing more than it had during the War of 1812, he called upon Congress "to arrest the present state of things. . . ." While "a navy of some degree, and of some kind" was probably necessary, it was the duty of Congress to decide whether it was to be a navy "to defend our homes, or to carry war abroad. . . ." Leaving no doubt as to his aversion to the latter, he insisted that our "coast and cities could be defended without great fleets at sea."[37]

Typical also was the attitude of Representative John Reynolds of Illinois, who pronounced the recently established "home squadron" to be the "most unreasonable humbug ever practiced upon the people." With war no longer in prospect, and with no pirates threatening our seaboard, this home squadron reminded him of Don Quixote, except that it did not even have a windmill "to combat."[38] Another westerner, Cave Johnson of Tennessee, wanted to know why we should keep fifty-four large men-of-war in active service, most of them in foreign waters. He had been told that such a force was needed for the protection of commerce; but against whom? We were at peace with all the Powers, and piracy had practically ceased. This argument, he believed, was a "mere pretext—a plausible excuse" for enlarging the Navy.[39]

Local rivalries, patronage considerations, and the demand

[36] 27 Cong. 2 Sess., *S. Doc.* No. 1, pp. 383–8.
[37] *Cong. Globe,* 27 Cong. 2 Sess., p. 639.
[38] *op. cit., Appendix,* p. 388.
[39] *ibid.,* pp. 655, 656.

for political spoils, also figured conspicuously in this debate. There was a loud complaint, backed up by an impressive show of statistics, that a group of seaboard States were monopolizing naval patronage.[40] It was argued that naval appointments should be apportioned among the States in order to "attach the [whole] country to the navy. . . ."[41] It was charged that the House Naval Committee shamelessly divided naval spoils among the six Atlantic seaboard States represented upon that committee.[42] Members from Philadelphia and Norfolk quarreled over the merits of their respective navy yards,[43] until "it struck" a disgusted onlooker as "not improbable, that while they were fighting over the bone, the taxpayers . . . might come in and take it from both of them."[44] Meanwhile, spokesmen of the South Atlantic States were demanding additional defenses and navy yards for their section, raising up a specter of naval attack from Bermuda, Britain's "Gibraltar" in this hemisphere.[45] And Millard Fillmore of Buffalo was claiming a share of the spoils for the Great Lakes region, since "the first shock of war would be felt in that quarter."[46]

This was not the first time that local interests had entered into the discussion of naval policy, but this particular debate graphically illustrated the extent to which conceptions of national interest might give way to a mercenary scramble for spoils. This tendency to sacrifice national interest for the sake of local politics was destined to increase with the years. A wide geographical distribution of naval patronage and other spoils was to become the established and accepted method of securing the majorities necessary to pass naval bills. Selecting naval personnel on a geographical basis, pouring public funds into

[40] Charles Brown, Pa., *ibid.*, pp. 393, 396.

[41] Horave Everett, Vt., *Cong. Globe,* 27 Cong. 2 Sess., p. 498.

[42] John Reynolds, Ill., *op. cit., Appendix,* pp. 388, 390.

[43] Charles Brown and Francis Mallory, *Cong. Globe,* 27 Cong. 2 Sess., pp. 508, 519, 520; *op. cit., Appendix,* p. 393.

[44] William Gwin, Miss., *ibid.*, p. 442.

[45] Henry Wise, Va., Richard Habersham, Ga., and Roger Gamble, Ga., *Cong. Globe,* 27 Cong. 2 Sess., pp. 500, 505, 513.

[46] *ibid.*, p. 524.

superfluous or poorly located navy yards and other equipment, often paying exorbitant prices for inferior labor and materials, all for the purpose of promoting the political fortunes of Senators and Representatives, were to become distinguishing characteristics of the process of naval legislation—characteristics which have persisted down to the present day. With large sections of the country indifferent or hostile to the Navy, and with Congressmen often at the mercy of local party machines, it was perhaps inevitable that the Navy should become a football not only of national politics but also of local politics. As a result, however, the Navy was to cost a great deal more than it should, and was rarely, if ever, to attain the power and efficiency that the country had a right to expect from the progressively rising outlays voted for this arm of the national defense.

Returning from this digression to the 1842 naval bill, we find, as on earlier occasions, that the critical votes in Congress, are as enlightening as the debates which preceded them. In this instance, Whig members from seaboard constituencies voted almost solidly for a larger Navy. Inland Democrats were almost as solidly against it. Party lines held firmly in the Senate, with several western Whigs, including members from the traditional anti-navy stronghold of Kentucky, joining their seaboard colleagues in support of the Administration's program. Sectional influence proved stronger in the House, where Whig leaders were unable to prevent wholesale defections among their western members. The Kentucky and Tennessee delegations, though predominantly Whig, stood solidly against increasing the Navy. Representatives from the frontier States of Michigan, Illinois, and Missouri, all voted anti-navy regardless of party affiliation.[47] And in the end a combination of partisan, sectional, and local influences, as well as dissipation of the international crisis, forced the Administration to accept a com-

[47] These conclusions are derived from analysis of several critical divisions in the Senate and House. See *Cong. Globe,* 27 Cong. 2 Sess., pp. 525, 639; and 27 Cong. 2 Sess. *H. Jour.,* pp. 846–8.

promise which fell far short of the program originally proposed and so vigorously pressed.[48]

Technological Progress under Whig Leadership

Despite the drag of sectional and partisan opposition, and the raids of the spoilsmen, the Navy prospered during the remainder of the Tyler administration (1841–1845), especially during its first two years while Upshur remained at the head of the Navy Department and the Whigs controlled both branches of Congress. Strong political support, always desirable from the standpoint of naval progress, was especially important at this time when naval science and technology were passing through the critical transition described in the opening pages of this chapter. When the reformers, rarely more than a handful of civilian inventors and engineers and forward-looking naval officers, had to overcome executive indifference or hostility, in addition to congressional inertia and bureaucratic conservatism, progress became practically impossible. But when, as during the brief period of Upshur's leadership, the reformers had strong support from the political Executive, it was sometimes possible to move forward against the inertia of Congress and the resistance of reactionary Service opinion.

One forward step taken under Whig leadership was the introduction of the screw propeller. Under the Act of 1839, it is recalled, the Navy Department had constructed two large wooden frigates, with auxiliary engines to drive paddle wheels placed amidships.[49] As specimens of contemporary naval architecture these ships were a success, but as fighting machines they were a failure. Their inefficient engines rendered them

[48] The House Committee on Ways and Means reduced the Administration's bill nearly 25% [27 Cong. 2 Sess., *H. Rept.* No. 673, p. 10]. And the appropriation which finally passed both chambers only slightly exceeded $6,000,000 [*Stat. at Large,* Vol. V, p. 500], more than a million less than was appropriated by several acts passed during the crisis year of 1841 [45 Cong. 1 Sess., *S. Ex. Doc.* No. 3, p. 156].

[49] See F. M. Bennett, *Steam Navy,* Chap. III.

"unsuited to cruising in time of peace."[50] Their machinery, which had to be placed above the waterline because of the side-wheel drive, made them so vulnerable as to raise serious doubts as to their potential value in war. These results seemed to vindicate the prevailing expert opinion that steam could never supersede sails in men-of-war.[51]

At this moment, however, the Navy was at the threshold of a technological development destined to overcome the fatal vulnerability of side-wheelers. In 1841, an enterprising officer, Captain Robert F. Stockton of Princeton, New Jersey, persuaded Secretary Upshur to construct along radically different lines the third steamer authorized by the 1839 Act. The new vessel was to have a submerged screw propeller placed at the stern. And this type of drive enabled the designer to place the ship's vital machinery below the waterline, comparatively safe from shot and shell.[52]

Stockton's vessel, named the *Princeton,* was the first screw-driven warship in any navy. In demonstrating the practicability of this method of propelling a war vessel, Stockton not only invalidated one of the strongest arguments hitherto raised against steam warships, but also gave the United States Navy a potential advantage over all others. But this advantage was not exploited. The Navy Department under succeeding Administrations not only clung for several years longer to the side-wheel principle, but even completed a number of sailing vessels with no auxiliary steam power at all.[53]

Another forward step taken under Whig leadership had to do with naval armor. The wooden hulls of the old ships-of-the-line "could withstand a terrific hammering from solid shot,"

[50] Annual Report, Secretary of the Navy, 1842, 27 Cong. 3 Sess., *S. Doc.* No. 1, p. 535.

[51] See S. J. Bayard, *A Sketch of the Life of Commodore Robert F. Stockton* (1856), pp. 80–1.

[52] The designer of this machinery was an engineer, named John Ericsson, who was to win still greater laurels in the realm of naval architecture. See W. C. Church, *Life of John Ericsson* (1890), Vol. I, Chap. VII–VIII.

[53] See Bennett, *Steam Navy,* Chap. V, and Appendix B; and G. F. Emmons, *The Navy of the United States, 1775–1853* (1853), p. 24.

but they could not stand up under the destructive bombardment of explosive shells which were undergoing a rapid development during these years. This development "upset the balance between offense and defense," resulting eventually in the introduction of armored, or iron-clad, warships.[54] As in the utilization of steam power and in the use of the screw propeller, so in the matter of naval armor, the United States momentarily led the way. Taking advantage of the recent Anglo-American crisis, the Secretary of the Navy, various private interests, and Whig leaders in Congress pushed through a bill in 1842, appropriating $250,000 toward the first ironclad warship ever authorized for any navy.[55] But this also proved to be a false start. Work on the Stevens Battery, as this vessel came to be known, dragged along from year to year, and finally came to a stop. While European admiralties were feverishly "revolutionizing naval architecture," the United States government continued to build unprotected wooden warships, completing not even one armored vessel prior to the Civil War.[56]

[54] Baxter, *Ironclad Warship*, pp. 17*ff*.

[55] *ibid.*, pp. 48*ff*.; 27 Cong. 2 Sess., *H. Rept.* No. 448; *Cong. Globe*, 27 Cong. 2 Sess., pp. 399–400.

[56] Baxter, *Ironclad Warship*, pp. 211*ff*.

CHAPTER NINE

☆ ☆

Naval Policy, Manifest Destiny, and Slave Politics (1845–1861)

THE Democratic Party's return to power in 1845 inaugurated a period in which territorial expansion and the approaching slavery crisis were the chief factors conditioning American naval policy and development. The flamboyant presidential campaign of 1844 had turned on the issue of westward expansion, with the Democratic platform and campaigners promising annexation of Texas and occupation of the whole wilderness embracing the present States of Oregon and Washington and the Canadian Province of British Columbia. Consummation of the former led indirectly to the Mexican War and the resulting conquest of California. Prospect of the latter precipitated another crisis with Great Britain, whose claim to the Oregon country conflicted with that of the United States. The Oregon crisis, with the possibility of war in the background, gave a decided impetus to naval development. The peaceful partition of Oregon and the military conquest of California extended the United States to the Pacific, and raised the problem of defending two widely separated seaboards fronting on different oceans. This in turn stimulated demand for a still larger navy and agitation for a trans-isthmian canal.

This canal agitation, in conjunction with other developments, made the Caribbean a focus of American interest and of international rivalry in the 'fifties. The resulting intrigues, maneuvers, abortive aggressions, and incipient expansionism which characterized American activities in this region produced fresh collisions with the vested interests and entrenched power of the British Empire. These activities and collisions, together with a rapid growth of oversea commerce and ocean shipping, gave a still further impetus to naval expansion during the final decade before the Civil War.

Such expansion was contrary, of course, to the agrarian party's traditional attitude toward the Navy. This reversal was the logical consequence of that party's territorial ambitions and foreign policy, which had periodically brought the United States into diplomatic or armed conflict with Great Britain. Yet the logic of foreign policy and recurrent international crises failed signally to destroy either the inlander's pervading sense of security from external danger or his habitual receptivity to the classic arguments against naval expansion. The consequent inconsistencies were accentuated by the steadily encroaching slavery crisis which destroyed the Whig Party and in the end all but paralyzed the Federal Government. And the Navy still suffered from the failure of statesmen and professional experts to apply some of the fundamental principles deducible from past wars, as well as from their neglect of some of the technological advances of their own day. As a result, American naval development from 1845 to 1861 was a record of spasmodic expansion in response to varied, shifting, and often conflicting influences.

Naval Policy and the Oregon Crisis

The Oregon crisis of 1845–1846 originated in the conflicting claims of the United States and Great Britain to the immense territory extending inland from the Pacific to the Rocky Mountain divide between 42° and 54° 40′ N.L. These claims, reaching far back into the colonial period, caused no serious difficulty as long as the Oregon country remained a vast wilderness inhabited by Indians, itinerant trappers, and agents of the Hudson's Bay Company. By a treaty concluded in 1818, the British and United States Governments carried the international boundary westward along the 49th parallel as far as the Rocky Mountains, leaving the line unsettled from there to the Pacific. Further negotiations during the 'twenties failed to reach a settlement. In the ensuing decade American traders, missionaries, and farmers began to filter into this region, especially into the fertile valley of the Willamette River. The impending struggle for possession lurked in the background during the Webster-Ashburton negotiations of 1842. Emigrants from the States poured into Oregon in a rising flood during the remaining years of the Tyler administration (1842–1845). Oregon and Texas were the crucial issues of the political campaign of 1844, with the country resounding to the popular slogan, "54–40 or fight." The election of James K. Polk, leader of the militant expansionists, foreshadowed a crisis with Great Britain. And Polk's defiant public utterances, together with unmistakable signs of resistance in Great Britain, precipitated the crisis which once more raised the specter of war with the world's greatest sea Power.

Throughout this crisis, the Administration pursued a decidedly anomalous course. While publicly defying the British Empire, the President took no positive steps in preparation for war.[1] And although war was widely regarded as imminent throughout the autumn of 1845,[2] the naval estimates for 1846–1847, sent to Congress in December 1845, were only two-thirds as large as those submitted the preceding year by the Tyler administration.[3] The Secretary of the Navy noted in his annual report that, "in comparison with other nations, our

[1] Such preparations as were made are exhaustively covered in a forthcoming work on Canadian-American military and naval relations, by Dr. Charles P. Stacey of Princeton University.

[2] A very fair impression of the state of public feeling can be derived from the columns of *Niles National Register*. Vols. LXVIII–LXIX.

[3] 29 Cong. 1 Sess., *H. Ex. Doc.* No. 2, p. 661.

navy is poorly equipped with sea going steamers," but he studiedly avoided any recommendation for overcoming this deficiency.[4] And the President, while hurling fresh defiances at Europe in general and Great Britain in particular, simultaneously endorsed the distribution of American warships along the "great highways of trade throughout the world," and expressly stated that "no additional appropriations are required" at this time.[5]

There is reason, however, to question the sincerity of the position thus assumed. It may be doubted that the Administration had any intention of resorting to arms in the Oregon dispute.[6] Yet the President, while publicly advocating retrenchment along lines popular with the inland agrarian wing of the Democratic Party, was quietly supporting a congressional movement for naval expansion originating chiefly among the Whigs and Eastern Democrats. These latter groups carried on a noisy agitation during the winter of 1845–1846. They forced through resolutions inquiring as to the condition of the naval establishment.[7] They obtained public assurances (one suspects, without great difficulty), that the President was not opposed to strengthening the Navy.[8] And they secured and published several reports from the Navy Department, which presented an alarming picture of the country's defenseless condition upon the sea.

The first of these, published early in March 1846, consisted of a detailed statistical summary of the principal navies of the world. In this comparison, the American Navy made a poor showing, especially in the category of steam warships. Of such vessels, built or building, the United States possessed only seven, mounting a total of 39 guns. Great Britain, on the other

[4] 29 Cong. 1 Sess., *S. Doc.* No. 1, p. 649.

[5] *Messages and Papers of the Presidents* (Richardson's 1st ed.). Vol. IV, p. 412.

[6] Such at least is a possible inference from the actual disposition of the land and naval forces, as well as the Administration's preoccupation with the impending war with Mexico.

[7] See, for example, 29 Cong. 1 Sess., *S. Jour.*, pp. 39, 49, 171, 200.

[8] *M. & P.* (Richardson), Vol. IV, p. 426.

hand, had 141 war steamers with a total of 698 guns, and France had 68 ships with 430 guns.[9]

This was followed by a letter from the bureau chiefs of the Navy Department (dated December 30, 1845, but not published until March 30, 1846), which listed the Navy's deficiencies, and discussed the strategic operations open to the United States in case of war with Great Britain.[10] These points were canvassed even more frankly in a companion report from the same source (also dated December 30, 1845, but held strictly confidential until the following April).[11]

These two documents presented a most discouraging picture of the outlook upon the ocean. With Great Britain "at peace with other nations," the United States could neither "contend directly" with the British "fleets or squadrons, nor . . . protect our commerce by adequate convoys." And under these circumstances, the authors of the reports doubted the wisdom of continuing "our force in considerable numbers [i.e., in squadrons]. . . ." Commerce raiding by solitary cruisers was still the only offensive operation open to the United States. For this purpose, it was proposed to augment the number of frigates and sloops, as well as of sea-going vessels with auxiliary steam power. The object of such operations was to "harass or destroy" the enemy's shipping, "and, by operating in different and distant places, to give employment to as large a portion of their naval force as practicable, and thus diminish their available force for operations on our own coasts whilst we are gaining the additional advantage of inflicting injury on them."

The outlook in our coastal waters was even more unfavorable. "The possession of convenient and strongly defended ports in Nova Scotia, New Brunswick, Bermuda, Jamaica, with others of less importance in the Bahamas, from which supplies may be readily drawn, where armaments may be organized, place it in the power of Great Britain to use her exten-

[9] 29 Cong. 1 Sess., *S. Doc.* No. 187. This report was also circulated through the press. See *Niles Register*, Vol. LXX (March 14, 1846), p. 18.

[10] 29 Cong. 1 Sess., *S. Doc.* No. 263.

[11] Published in *Niles Register*, Vol. LXX (April 11, 1846), p. 83.

sive naval means with great facility, against the Atlantic and Gulf coasts of the United States."

These revelations naturally fostered a demand for legislation, which resulted in the introduction of bills in both branches of Congress. Those in the House did not even come to debate.[12] And in the Senate, a bill from the Committee on Naval Affairs to authorize construction of ten sea-going steam warships aroused so much opposition, especially among the Westerners, that its sponsors never forced it to a vote.[13]

One may profitably compare this outcome, or indeed the whole Oregon episode, with the earlier crisis of 1812. The events leading up to war on that occasion, had advertised the inconsistency between the territorial and naval policies of the dominant agrarian party.[14] And the resulting conflict had temporarily forced that party from its traditional opposition to a sea-going navy.[15] The Democratic campaign of 1844, Polk's defiance of Great Britain, and the slogan, "54–40 or fight," strikingly resembled the noisy clamor of the "War Hawks" of 1812. The Polk administration's delay in strengthening the Navy differed only in degree from the dominant party's hostility to naval preparations on the eve of the earlier war. The belated agitation and inquiry into the state of the Navy bore at least a superficial resemblance to the flurry of activity which followed the outbreak of war in 1812. But the parallel ends here, for the peaceful compromise of the Oregon dispute in 1846 saved the United States from a repetition of the disasters which characterized our second war with Great Britain. And for that very reason, the later crisis, while it aroused fresh interest in the Navy and produced several revealing documents on the state of our naval power, failed to provide the stimulus necessary to force the Democratic ad-

[12] 29 Cong. 1 Sess., *H. Jour.*, pp. 403, 1349; *Cong. Globe*, 29 Cong., 1 Sess., pp. 846, 1135.

[13] *Congressional Globe*, 29 Cong., 1 Sess., pp. 182, 226–9, 251–6, 263–8, 337, 850, 871.

[14] See pp. 62*ff.*, *supra*.

[15] See pp. 87*ff.*, *supra*.

ministration and the Democratic majorities in Congress to carry through a program of naval rejuvenation.[16]

Naval Policy and Steamship Subsidies

While the Oregon crisis failed to force the Democrats into a systematic and comprehensive strengthening of the regular Navy, the agitation aroused by that episode fostered an alternative scheme of naval defense. This was a proposal to subsidize private construction of merchant steamers theoretically convertible into efficient warships in case of need.

This project considerably antedated the Polk administration. The British government's subsidies to the Cunard Line had figured slightly in the discussions of naval policy during the Anglo-American crisis of 1840–1841. In July 1841, the House Naval Committee recommended study of means for founding commercial steamship lines to compete with foreign lines in peace and provide naval auxiliaries in war.[17] It now appears that some, if not most, of this agitation originated in the lobbying of Edward K. Collins, a New York shipowner who was active in Washington from the early 'forties on.[18] In his last annual message (December 1844), Tyler endorsed the steamship subsidy plan as a cheap method of securing an auxiliary naval

[16] Another event of the year 1845 was the founding of the United States Naval Academy. This was a step which Secretaries of the Navy had been urging for thirty years or more. Every proposal to this end had encountered the stubborn and unyielding opposition of the anti-navalists, especially the Jacksonian Democrats of the Central and Western States. Now, however, a Democratic Secretary of the Navy, George Bancroft, who served for a few months at the beginning of the Polk administration, started a school on his own initiative and responsibility, using funds already assigned to his department. And Congress, confronted with this *fait accompli* at a moment when the Oregon crisis and the impending war with Mexico had weakened the opposition, appropriated the necessary funds to continue the new institution. See J. R. Soley, *Historical Sketch of the United States Naval Academy* (1876), pp. 7–62; and *Statutes at Large*, Vol. IX, p. 97.

[17] 27 Cong. 1 Sess., *H. Rept.* No. 3.

[18] R. G. Albion, "Edward Knight Collins," *Dict. Am. Biog.*, Vol. IV, p. 305; *idem*, *Square-Riggers on Schedule* (1938), p. 263; *idem*, *The Rise of New York Port* (1939), pp. 323*ff*.

force.[19] A congressional act passed in March 1845 made an ineffective gesture in this direction.[20] And the following year, Collins revived the project with a fresh plea for a subsidy to enable his concern to establish first-class steamship service to Europe.[21]

This scheme immediately appealed to the small-navy majority in Congress. The House Naval Committee whose chairman, Thomas B. King of Georgia, was opposed to a "large and expensive naval establishment in time of peace," favored the idea of combining a small regular navy with a fleet of private merchant steamers so constructed as to be convertible into fighting ships in case of war.[22] When the Administration came forward in December 1846 with a tardy request for additional steam warships,[23] the congressional opponents of naval expansion countered with a flank movement in which they accepted the proposal in principle but recommended subsidy legislation as the cheapest means to this end.[24] This led to a compromise in which the Navy got four steam warships, the shipping companies won a generous subsidy for vessels theoretically "convertible . . . into war steamers of the first class,"[25] and the small-navy groups secured recognition of the fallacious principle that an effective naval force could be quickly improvised in an emergency from the country's merchant marine.

This unsound principle, we may note briefly in anticipation of later events, was to become a serious incubus upon American naval development. Within narrow limitations, the merchant marine might provide officers and seamen to expand the regular Navy in an emergency. Merchant vessels, if properly designed, might perform useful auxiliary functions as transports

19 *M. & P.* (Richardson), Vol. IV, p. 350.
20 *Stat. at Large,* Vol. V, p. 749.
21 29 Cong. 1 Sess., *S. Doc.* No. 237, p. 28.
22 29 Cong. 1 Sess., *H. Rept.* No. 685.
23 *M. & P.* (Richardson), Vol. IV, p. 505; 29 Cong. 2 Sess., *S. Doc.* No. 1, p. 383.
24 *Cong. Globe,* 29 Cong. 2 Sess., p. 423.
25 29 Cong. 2 Sess., *H. Jour.*, pp. 521, 523; *Cong. Globe,* 29 Cong. 2 Sess., p. 572; *Stat. at Large,* Vol. IX, p. 187.

and cargo carriers in connection with a fleet. Construction and maintenance of a merchant marine might stimulate the shipbuilding and related industries, with some benefit to the Navy. But converted merchant vessels were no substitute for regular warships. The idea of converting such vessels into men-of-war was a survival from the days of sail and the practice of privateering. Even in those days, as we have seen, converted merchantmen were no match for sloops and frigates, to say nothing of ships-of-the-line. With the advent of steam navigation, with the development of the iron-clad warship, with the increasing power of naval ordnance, and with the growing complexity of naval technology, the sphere of converted merchantmen progressively narrowed until in the twentieth century it all but vanished.

Lessons and Consequences of the Mexican War

The Mexican War (1846–1848), fought mainly on land, afforded little opportunity for testing the strategic principles and naval technology still in vogue within the United States. But that conflict nevertheless had some naval implications. In particular, it demonstrated the importance of superior naval power as an adjunct to oversea military operations. As John Y. Mason of Virginia, who succeeded to the office of Secretary of the Navy in 1846, pointed out at the close of the war: The Navy had rendered its most important service in "holding a constant command of the sea," which had made possible the transportation of the Army to Mexico, covered its landing upon a hostile coast, and above all, cut off the enemy from foreign munitions and other supplies necessary to carrying on the war.[26]

This practical demonstration of the importance of naval

[26] 30 Cong. 2 Sess., *H. Ex. Doc.* No. 1, p. 609. The Navy also performed numerous important services in the Pacific in connection with the conquest of California. See Captain D. W. Knox, *History of the United States Navy* (1936), Chap. XVI.

power did not move the Polk administration, however, to advocate a stronger navy. All that we needed in peacetime, Secretary Mason declared in 1848, were a "few ships of war" to display the flag abroad, and "to serve as a nucleus, capable of any degree" of expansion in the event of war. The government might better devote its energies, he continued, to providing docks, munitions, and materials, for use if the need should ever arise.[27] And with this valedictory, the Polk administration folded its tents and marched away,[28] leaving to its successors the complicated strategic problem created by the partition of Oregon and the conquest of California.

This problem arose from the geographical configuration of North and South America. From the standpoint of national defense, California and Oregon were distant oversea colonies. Pending construction of a trans-continental railroad, there could be little overland communication between the Mississippi Valley and the Pacific Coast. The shortest line of communications, via Central America, traversed alien territory over which Great Britain exercised large, if not paramount, influence. The sea route around Cape Horn, notorious for its length, perils, and hardships, passed on its Atlantic stretch through an expanse of ocean which was indisputably under the domination of the British Navy. Although there was at that time slight prospect of war in the Eastern Pacific, the annexation of California and Oregon nevertheless stimulated a demand for increasing the Navy. For it was now argued that the only practicable way to defend our western seaboard under existing conditions was to station permanently in the Pacific a self-sufficient naval force strong enough to cope with any enemy that might be encountered in that ocean.[29]

[27] 30 Cong. 2 Sess., *H. Ex. Doc.* No. 1, p. 610.

[28] In his last annual message, December 1848, President Polk dismissed the subject of naval policy with a brief endorsement of the annual report of the Secretary of the Navy, from which we have quoted in the text. See *M. & P.* (Richardson), Vol. IV, p. 651.

[29] 31 Cong. 2 Sess., *H. Rept.* No. 35.

The Navy Adrift, 1849–1853

Election of a Whig President in 1848 seemed to foreshadow a prompt and vigorous attack on this enlarged problem of naval defense. The Whig Party, it is recalled, was traditionally identified with a strong-navy policy. From a financial standpoint, the outlook was propitious for naval expansion. The country was prosperous, and, beginning with the year 1850, the Federal Treasury had a large and increasing surplus revenue. But the general political outlook was less favorable. The intersectional struggle over the extension of slavery, which reached another crisis in 1850, pushed other interests temporarily into the background. The Whig Party, fatally divided on the slavery issue, was already disintegrating. The Whig administration could command a majority in neither branch of Congress. The death of President Taylor in 1850, and the succession of Vice President Fillmore, brought to the White House a Chief Executive with a cautious foreign policy and a disposition to compromise rather than fight over controversial issues.

While the views of the Taylor-Fillmore administration on naval policy conformed in the main to the pattern previously associated with the Whig Party, they were put forward timidly, without reference to a specific program of development. It was asserted that we needed a larger navy not only to defend our widely separated ocean frontiers but also to support our rapidly expanding commerce and to sustain our national prestige abroad. While it was believed unnecessary to maintain a navy in any fixed ratio to those of European Powers, it was suggested that we could improve on the haphazard method of formulating naval policy hitherto in vogue. Without moving to abandon the use of sailing vessels, it was suggested that we should have additional war steamers. But, with steam navigation still in its infancy, it was thought that we might well confine our efforts, for the time being, to small steamers, each the best of its type. Also, it was regarded as a mistake to place too much reliance upon merchant steamers, in theory convertible into efficient fighting ships. Such vessels would doubtless make good commerce raiders, but they could never take the place of regular warships. There the Administration rested, leaving the initiative to Congress.[30]

This abdication of executive leadership could lead to but one result—a sordid scramble for spoils. Congress continued to dole out subsidies to private steamship companies, justifying such action on grounds of national defense, despite accumulating evidence that this form of defensive preparation had little to commend it on purely naval grounds.[31] Senators and Representatives agitated for and voted additional navy yards and other spoils for their respective constituencies with slight regard for larger considerations of national interest.[32] As a result, though individual members attempted to grapple seriously with the problem of naval defense,[33] and though naval appropriations during this period averaged larger than ever before in peace,[34] the power and efficiency of the Navy steadily declined until, in 1853, the United States possessed not one vessel that could have given battle with prospect of victory against any first-class warship of the major European Powers.[35]

[30] See annual reports of the Secretary of the Navy for the years 1849–1852. 31 Cong. 1 Sess., *S. Ex. Doc.* No. 1, pp. 425, 432, 433, 438; 31 Cong. 2 Sess., *S. Doc.* No. 1, pp. 193, 198, 199, 204; 32 Cong. 2 Sess., *S. Doc.* No. 1, Vol. II, pp. 291, 319, 320.

[31] See 32 Cong. 1 Sess., *S. Doc.* No. 50, pp. 114–28, 136, 138, 143, 153, 155; 32 Cong. 1 Sess., *S. Rept.* No. 267; and Royal Meeker, "History of Shipping Subsidies," *Publications of Am. Econ. Assoc.*, Sec. III, Vol. VI, No. 3 (1905), p. 155.

[32] See, for example, the debates on naval appropriation bills in the 31st and 32nd Congresses, as reported in the *Congressional Globe.*

[33] See, for example, the special report of the House Naval Committee, February 20, 1851, 31 Cong. 2 Sess., *H. Rept.* No. 35. And see also *Cong. Globe,* 32 Cong. 1 Sess., pp. 2237*ff*.

[34] 45 Cong. 1 Sess., *S. Doc.* No. 3, p. 156.

[35] See 33 Cong. 1 Sess., *S. Doc.* No. 1, Vol. III, pp. 545–553.

Dynamics of Naval Policy in the 'Fifties

While the Executive drifted and Congress divided the spoils, the Navy's responsibilities were steadily growing. The strategic importance of the Caribbean Sea and the Gulf of Mexico, dating from the purchase of Louisiana in 1803, had increased rapidly with the settlement of the Mississippi Valley, and the consequent growth of commerce through New Orleans. These waters acquired a still greater strategic importance following the Mexican War, for the shortest line of communication to the Pacific Coast lay across the isthmus connecting North and South America. The strategic isolation of the Pacific frontier, together with a growing interest in the commercial potentialities of the Far East, fostered agitation for a trans-isthmian canal. But serious political obstacles stood in the way of such an undertaking. The British aspired, for commercial and political reasons, to control the transit routes across the Isthmus. They had territorial footholds in Central America and the West Indies. And they showed no disposition to withdraw in favor of the United States. In the resulting scramble for transit concessions and political control over the Isthmus, the possibility of an Anglo-American war, always in the background, provided a continuing incentive for naval development during the 'fifties.

The territorial ambitions of the South provided another incentive. The admission of California as a "free" State in 1850, with the prospect of others soon to follow, left the slaveholding section with a minority in both branches of Congress. To restore the Federal balance of power between North and South, certain Southern leaders agitated for additional territory to erect into "slave" States. Their schemes, embracing portions of Mexico, Central America, and, in particular, the Island of Cuba, clearly envisaged the possibility of war with Spain, and even with France and Great Britain. This possibility of a war in Southern waters fostered a sense of insecurity within the Gulf States, and tended to overcome the traditional indifference or hostility of that region toward the Navy.

Still other developments favored naval expansion in the 'fifties. Discovery of gold in California in 1848 inaugurated a brief period of abnormal prosperity in the United States. Political unrest in Europe and other causes fostered a trans-Atlantic migration which greatly increased the demand for ocean shipping services. The Crimean War (1854–1856) further stimulated trans-Atlantic commerce and navigation, under conditions especially favorable to naval development. Meanwhile, the California gold rush and a similar migration to Australia, following discovery of gold there in 1851, were giving a tremendous impetus to shipping in the Pacific. And these events coincided with a boom in the Far Eastern carrying trade, resulting in part from development of the famous clipper ships which enabled Americans for a brief time to skim the cream of the China tea trade. More intangible, but probably none the less important, was the influence of the Mexican War, of the gold rush, and of the rapid expansion of industry and commerce, on the American outlook on the world at large. These events contributed to a general atmosphere of militant nationalism highly favorable to naval development, despite the paralyzing influence of the great intersectional struggle now hurrying on toward its fatal climax.

Naval Expansion under Pierce

The election of 1852 opened the way for naval rejuvenation. The Democrats recaptured the presidency and increased their majorities in the House and Senate. But the Democratic Party of the 'fifties bore slight resemblance to the party of Jackson or of Jefferson. It was now the dominant party in every section of the country; and with its broader geographical appeal, the influence of the frontier had proportionately declined. Indeed, with the rapid settlement of the Middle West, particularly the influx of immigrants from Europe and the growth of towns and cities, regions which had only recently been frontier country were now taking on the habits and ideas of the older, more cosmopolitan centers. A group within the Democratic Party, drawn from all sections and known as "Young America," was vigorously contesting the primacy of the "Old Guard." These younger men, catching the spirit of the times, were agitating a threefold program of national expansion—territory, commerce, and republican institutions.[36] And with inauguration of Franklin Pierce in March 1853, the doctrines of "Young America" entered the White House. Nominated through Southern influence, this son of New Hampshire ascended to the presidency with a determination to restore internal unity by a prudently aggressive assertion of American claims and interests abroad. And with this program in view, he turned at once to the long-overdue task of modernizing the Navy.[37]

When Congress met in December 1853, Secretary of the Navy Dobbin was ready with a comprehensive reform program and a supporting theory of naval policy. We should have a modern naval force adequate to maintain "our proper and elevated rank among the great powers of the world," to protect the interests of American shipping in peace and in war, and to defend our widely separated ocean frontiers. Profiting from the lessons of earlier wars, Dobbin held "that our navy should, at least, be large enough to command our own seas and coast," for coastal fortifications "without a navy" were like a "shield without a sword." At present we had about seventy naval vessels. Many of these were out of repair and not worth repairing. The remainder were obsolete sailing vessels or vulnerable side-wheel steamers. There was not one first-class steam warship in the lot. And the personnel situation was not much better. The Department had already undertaken, on its own initiative, to convert one of the old line-of-battle-ships into an efficient steam

[36] M. E. Curti, "Young America," *American Historical Review* (1926), Vol. XXXII, pp. 34–55.

[37] R. F. Nichols, *Franklin Pierce, Young Hickory of the Granite Hills* (1931), p. 220.

frigate. The Administration now called upon Congress for legislation authorizing sweeping personnel reforms and immediate construction of six first-class, screw-driven, steam frigates.[38]

A bill embodying the steam frigate proposal was rushed through the Senate without debate, but provoked a spirited discussion in the House.[39] Its chief sponsor, Thomas S. Bocock of Virginia, Chairman of the Naval Affairs Committee, opened his plea with a review of our extraordinary territorial and commercial expansion. Within ten years we had extended our coastline "more than two thousand miles," expanded our foreign commerce "more than 100 per cent," and increased our merchant tonnage "about 100 per cent." But the Navy had not kept pace with these developments. Indeed, it had "actually decreased, . . . both in ships and . . . guns." And the ships still available were rapidly becoming obsolete. We had made practically no use of the screw propeller. We had no steamers with more than ten guns, whereas many in European navies mounted one hundred or more. We did not need a navy as large as those of certain European Powers; but we should remember that "with them is our competition, and with them are to be our contests, if any shall shortly befall us." We should therefore formulate our naval policy with reference to the navies of those Powers.

Passing from the general to the specific, Bocock urged immediate modernization of the Navy. Europe was on the verge of another great war.[40] We needed a stronger navy to forestall belligerent aggression against our neutral commerce. Furthermore, an impressive display of power, in conjunction with the European war, would facilitate both further expansion of American commercial interests in the Far East, and acquisition of the Island of Cuba. With respect to the latter, the outlook was especially favorable, for a pending dispute with Spain,

[38] 33 Cong. 1 Sess., *H. Ex. Doc.* No. 1, Vol. III, pp. 297, 307–17.

[39] *Cong. Globe,* 33 Cong. 1 Sess., pp. 69, 455, 465, 477, 488, 758, 772, 788, 803, 825, 849.

[40] He had reference to the Russo-Turkish crisis which led to the Crimean War. By the purest coincidence his plea for a larger navy was delivered on the very day that Great Britain and France declared war on Russia.

arising over indignities to an American merchant vessel, the *Black Warrior*, in Havana harbor, might yet afford an opportunity "to take redress into our own hands." With sufficient naval power, we could safely defy British opposition to our acquiring Cuba, oust Great Britain from the Mosquito Coast in Central America, and, overriding all resistance, carry our flag southward in fulfillment of our manifest destiny.

In conclusion, he deplored prevailing sectional opposition to the Navy. The interests of the seaboard were more apparent, but the interests of the interior were equally real. The people of the interior sold their products abroad, and depended heavily upon articles procured from foreign countries. A blockade of the Gulf, for example, would paralyze the life of the whole Mississippi Valley. There was "yet a higher ground of common interests." The "glory of the navy" was the "glory of the whole country," which should unite all sections, however "discordant" on domestic questions (such as slavery), in "one common brotherhood of patriotism. . . ."[41]

The aged Thomas Hart Benton of Missouri, now in his seventy-third year, and one of the few surviving representatives of the Jacksonian faith, led a spirited assault on this prospectus of oversea "aggression" and "conquest."[42] But without the slightest success! By the decisive vote of 112 to 43, the House joined the Senate in authorizing the Administration to proceed with its naval program.[43]

This vote revealed important shifts in both the sectional and partisan alignment. New England Representatives, as usual, stood almost unanimously for strengthening the Navy. Northern and western Pennsylvania, formerly an anti-navy stronghold, contributed only three negative votes, a result perhaps of the growing influence of the iron, coal, and other industries in this region. Equally marked was the increase of support in the South Atlantic and Gulf States, whose Representatives voted

[41] *Cong. Globe*, 33 Cong. 1 Sess., *Appendix*, pp. 422–5.
[42] *Cong. Globe*, 33 Cong. 1 Sess., p. 803.
[43] 33 Cong. 1 Sess., *H. Jour.*, p. 587.

37 to 5 for the steam frigate bill. Even the traditionally anti-navy States of Kentucky and Tennessee stood 9 to 5 for the bill. Only in the North Central States and Trans-Mississippi Frontier was there any substantial opposition, the members from these regions dividing 11 to 25 against the bill. The partisan cleavage was even more remarkable. Taking the House as a whole, the Democratic members stood in the ratio of 3 to 1 for increasing the Navy, while the pro-navy ratio of the Whig votes was only 2 to 1. With maritime New England and New York, industrial Pennsylvania, and the slave States lined up behind a big-navy policy, the Democratic Party, contrary to the Jeffersonian and Jacksonian traditions, seemed fairly launched upon a program of naval expansion.

But this was only a beginning. In 1854, Secretary Dobbin noted with manifest approval the display of force used by Commodore Matthew C. Perry in opening the ports of Japan.[44] Dobbin next renewed his drive for additional warships, urging immediate construction of seven screw-driven sloops-of-war, heavily armed craft somewhat smaller than the steam frigates, with a draft shallow enough to permit use in the shoal waters of the South Atlantic and Gulf ports.[45] When Congress took no action, Dobbin and Pierce reiterated the imperative need of continuing the work of naval rejuvenation, insisting that naval power could not be improvised in an emergency, and declaring that our Navy was still "too feeble to command the waters of our own coast."[46]

Another Anglo-American crisis, in the winter of 1855–1856, called special attention to the unpreparedness of the Navy. The possibility of a war with Great Britain for control of the Isthmus, and a rumor that the British Admiralty was sending a fleet to American waters, provided the stimulus necessary to force through the Senate a bill in accord with the Administra-

[44] 33 Cong. 2 Sess., *S. Doc.* No. 1, Vol. II, pp. 383, 387–8.

[45] See 33 Cong. 2 Sess., *H. Misc. Doc.* No. 10.

[46] 34 Cong. 1 Sess., *S. Doc.* No. 1, Vol. III, pp. 1, 14; and *M. & P.* (Richardson), Vol. V, p. 339.

tion's recommendations.[47] This bill failed to pass the House, however, and the Pierce administration entered its final year with slight prospect of further constructive legislation. Secretary Dobbin, nevertheless, returned to the attack in his last report, December 1856;[48] and the following March, in the final hectic hours of the short session, Southern leaders jammed through an amendment to the naval appropriation bill, authorizing five shallow-draft steam sloops-of-war.[49]

Thus the naval policy of the Pierce administration was a blend of progressive and narrowly conservative views. Not since the days of Upshur[50] had there been such aggressive executive leadership, or such intelligent discussion of naval policy. Yet in 1854, when Commander (later Admiral) David G. Farragut asked leave to observe the naval operations of the Crimean War, he was ordered instead to the Mare Island Navy Yard in California.[51] The steam frigates authorized that year, while beautiful specimens of the shipbuilder's art, and armed with powerful ordnance, were essentially sailing vessels with small auxiliary engines. They were constructed of wood. Their highest speed under steam was only eight to ten knots.[52] The Administration which built these vessels showed no more than casual interest in the feverish activity in European naval circles following the Crimean War, in which had been demonstrated the fatal vulnerability of unarmored wooden ships under shellfire. Some further work was done on the unfinished Stevens Battery laid down in the early 'forties. But neither civilian statesmen nor the professional experts showed any real understanding of the revolutionary changes in naval architecture which were then taking place across the Atlantic.[53]

[47] R. F. Nichols, *Franklin Pierce* (1931), pp. 457, 458; and *Cong. Globe,* 34 Cong. 1 Sess., pp. 501, 544–7.

[48] 34 Cong. 3 Sess., *S. Doc.* No. 1, Vol. III, pp. 405, 414.

[49] *Cong. Globe,* 34 Cong. 3 Sess., pp. 990, 1067.

[50] Secretary of the Navy, 1841–1842.

[51] Captain A. T. Mahan, *Admiral Farragut* (1892), pp. 98–9.

[52] The best description of these vessels is that in F. M. Bennett, *Steam Navy of the United States* (1896), Chap. X.

[53] See J. P. Baxter, *Introduction of the Ironclad Warship* (1933), Chap. XI.

Naval Expansion under Buchanan

Southern influence on naval development, which began to be conspicuous in the Pierce administration, increased with the succession of James Buchanan to the presidency in March 1857. Buchanan was willing, apparently, to make any concession to save the Union. His Secretary of the Navy, Isaac Toucey of Connecticut, while a loyal Unionist, nevertheless had Southern sympathies and took his cue on naval questions from the South. Thomas S. Bocock of Virginia, destined to become Speaker of the Confederate House of Representatives, was still Chairman of the House Naval Affairs Committee. And Stephen R. Mallory of Florida, soon to become Secretary of the Confederate Navy, held the chairmanship of the powerful Senate Committee on Naval Affairs.

Toucey's first annual report (December 1857) revealed the drift of the Administration's naval policy. It was not "to maintain a great navy in time of peace . . . or to compete with other great commercial powers in the magnitude of their naval preparations." It was rather our "true policy" to maintain a small navy which, "within its limited extent, should be unsurpassed in its efficiency and its completeness. . . ." To attain this object, certain additions were still necessary, in particular smaller naval vessels that could freely enter the shallow waters of Southern ports. Such vessels, combining "great speed and heavy guns, would be formidable in coast defense," and he recommended building at least ten of them.[54]

Another crisis with Great Britain, this time over British visitation and detention of American vessels engaging in the illegal African slave trade, aroused a storm of anger in the South, and afforded a plausible excuse for a legislative drive to secure the vessels recommended by the Navy Department. In June 1858, with a great hue and cry, and even open agitation

[54] 35 Cong. 1 Sess., *S. Doc.* No. 11, pp. 573, 585, 586.

for war on Great Britain, Southern Senators and Representatives under the leadership of Mallory and Bocock labored to drive through Congress an amendment to the naval appropriation bill, authorizing ten additional sloops-of-war. This proposal encountered great opposition in the North, with even the New England Representatives voting in a ratio of 4 to 1 against it. In the end, the South compromised on seven, the act stipulating that these gunboats should draw not over fourteen feet, that they should have screw propellers and "full steam power," and that they should "combine the heaviest armament and greatest speed compatible with their character and tonnage. . . ."[55]

In December 1858, Secretary Toucey advocated a still larger force of shallow-draft vessels. They were needed, he held, to protect American lives and property abroad, especially in Mexico and Central and South America "where the existing governments lack stability. . . ." Then there was the larger problem of coast defense. This required guarding the Gulf and adjoining waters "like inland seas" and acquiring "a predominating influence over [this] continent. . . ." To attain these objects we should build at least ten more heavily-armed, shallow-draft warships.[56]

Despite an emphatically favorable report from the Senate Naval Committee,[57] and continued pressure from the Navy Department,[58] Congress took no further action at this time. There was no serious foreign crisis with which to overawe the opposition. And the Federal Treasury was in serious straits following the Panic of 1857.

In 1860, however, the question of further naval expansion arose in a form nicely, if fortuitously, calculated to turn the tables on the South. Early in the congressional session of 1859–1860, Senator Henry Wilson of Massachusetts introduced a bill

[55] *Stat. at Large,* Vol. XI, p. 314; and see *Cong. Globe,* 35 Cong. 1 Sess., index (for both Senate and House), title: "bill making appropriations for the Navy for the year ending June 30, 1859."

[56] 35 Cong. 2 Sess., *S. Doc.* No. 1, Vol. IV, pp. 1, 7–9.

[57] 35 Cong. 2 Sess., *S. Rept.* No. 363.

[58] 36 Cong. 1 Sess., *S. Doc.* No. 2, pp. 1137, 1139.

to construct five steam war-sloops for use in suppressing the African slave trade. The Naval Committee, still under the direction of Senator Mallory, amended this bill, changing the number to seven, specifying shallow draft, and deleting all mention of the slave trade. Thus amended, it simply authorized further vessels to patronize Southern harbors. Whereupon Wilson lost interest in it. In its place he moved an amendment to the regular naval appropriation bill, authorizing the Secretary of the Navy to purchase three steamers for the express purpose of suppressing the slave trade. To head off this plan, Mallory moved to substitute his own amended version of Wilson's original bill. This proposal brought on a three-sided struggle. Anti-navy Senators denounced the whole scheme, regarding suppression of the slave trade as a mere pretext for increasing the Navy. Advocates of naval expansion welcomed this opportunity further to strengthen the Navy. And the Southerners, thoroughly alarmed at the prospect of a real drive to suppress the illegal slave traffic, opposed not only the Wilson amendment, but also Mallory's substitute, which proposed to carry on exactly the kind of naval expansion which the South had so enthusiastically supported only two years before.[59]

But this was only the beginning of the rout. The shallow-draft warships, for which Southern leaders had so successfully clamored in the middle 'fifties, would prove just as useful against the South as in its defense. And in February 1861, with one Southern State after another leaving the Union, and a Republican President about to enter the White House, Northern statesmen who had hitherto opposed this type of naval force lined up behind a proposal to add seven more shallow-draft war-sloops. In vain did the remaining Southern Senators and Representatives denounce this plan to organize force against the seceding States. With their ranks depleted by those already departed, they could not stave off this legislation which passed 30 to 18 in the Senate, and 113 to 38 in the House, with

[59] *Cong. Globe*, 36 Cong. 1 Sess., pp. 3067, 3068, 3108, 3110.

a sectional alignment almost exactly the reverse of that on the similar measure passed in 1858.[60]

On the Eve of the Civil War

Retirement of President Buchanan (March 4, 1861), closed another chapter in the rise of American naval power. It had been a chapter of change and transition. Sails were giving way to steam, and the screw propeller had largely overcome the vulnerability of the early side-wheelers. Naval ordnance was undergoing equally important developments—explosive shells, rifled bores, heavier projectiles, greater range and fire control. These developments, especially the introduction of shells and of guns constructed to fire them, were forcing still greater changes in naval architecture.

In this last respect, the United States was lagging far behind. Despite the enormously destructive potentialities of shellfire, revealed as far back as the Crimean War of 1854–1856, the American Navy clung tenaciously to its wooden walls. The steam frigates and sloops, built in the 'fifties, represented a high development of the shipbuilder's art, but the entire fleet could scarcely have offered battle to a single one of the sea-going iron-clad warships which were beginning to appear in European navies on the eve of the American Civil War.[61]

There is little indication that American experts perceived the gravity of the situation, and it is probable that, if they had, they would have filed a demurrer. They saw no reason for building heavy ironclads, or indeed any capital ships at all.[62] Once more the American trend was toward smaller warships. The steam frigates and sloops were the heavy and light cruisers

[60] *Cong. Globe,* 36 Cong. 2 Sess., pp. 845–6, 1067–75; and *Stat. at Large,* Vol. XII, p. 147.

[61] Baxter, *Ironclad Warship,* Chaps. VI–X. The "wooden walls" also died hard in Great Britain. See R. G. Albion, *Forests and Sea Power* (1926), pp. 403*ff*.

[62] The ships-of-the-line laid down after the War of 1812 were still unfinished or laid up to rot at their moorings. See 36 Cong. 2 Sess., *S. Doc.* No. 1, Vol. III, p. 3.

of their day. With sufficient speed, it was argued, they could flee from an enemy's heavy ships, overhaul his weaker ships, and give battle at will. By equipping these cruisers with the most powerful guns,[63] American naval authorities aimed to possess, type for type, ship for ship, the most formidable armaments afloat. Utterly sceptical of the possibility of building seaworthy armored warships with sufficient speed to overtake their own heavily armed wooden cruisers, American statesmen and their professional advisers complacently marked time while European admiralties carried on the experiments which were revolutionizing naval architecture.[64]

Taking a still larger view, it is fairly clear that the United States, after a long period of confusion and vacillation, had returned on the eve of the Civil War to the theory of naval power and warfare in vogue during the War of 1812. While Great Britain, still generally regarded as the most likely enemy, was the stated or implicit object of American naval preparations, it was not deemed necessary to build a great fleet of capital ships to rival Britain's. Instead, as Senator Mallory tersely put it, we should adhere to the policy which enabled our Navy to win such glory in the War of 1812, "in which frigate was matched against frigate, sloop against sloop, and brig against brig."[65] Thus, American statesmen in the 'fifties were pointing their preparations toward the strategy which in 1812, despite the subsequent legend of victory, destroyed the foreign commerce of the United States, disrupted its internal economy, and opened the way for armed invasion from the sea.

[63] See *Memoir of John A. Dahlgren* (edited by M. V. Dahlgren, 1882), Chaps. VI-VII.

[64] See 35 Cong. 2 Sess., *S. Rept.* No. 363.

[65] Debate in Senate, June 7, 1858, *Cong. Globe,* 35 Cong. 1 Sess., p. 2732.

CHAPTER TEN

☆ ☆

The Civil War: Strategic Lessons and Technical Progress (1861–1865)

THE Civil War, like the War of 1812, was an episode of great importance in the rise of American naval power. The experience of the Confederacy, and to some extent that of the North as well, again emphasized the difficulties of improvising a naval force after the outbreak of war. The contrasting methods and results of Confederate and Union naval operations dramatized the strategic lessons which naval officers and civilian statesmen had failed in the main to deduce from earlier conflicts upon the water. Finally, coming when it did, the Civil War not only emphasized and popularized recent revolutionary developments in ship propulsion, ordnance, and naval architecture, but also gave a tremendous impetus to further progress in naval technology.

Naval Background of the Civil War

A survey of the naval resources of the United States in 1861 would have revealed elements both of strength and of weakness. Thanks to the building programs of the Pierce and Buchanan administrations, the Navy was unquestionably stronger than at any previous period. Although the Navy Department still listed more than thirty old sailing vessels as available for active service, there were also a dozen comparatively new steam cruisers, and several more under construction.

Judged by prevailing standards, these were first-class vessels armed with guns unsurpassed in any navy. There were, it is true, no armored warships such as were beginning to displace wooden vessels in European navies. But this deficiency, which might have proved fatal in a war with France or Great Britain, was to have less serious immediate consequences in a conflict with an adversary possessing at the outset no navy at all.[1]

Turning to personnel, the United States had a fine group of officers. But the Service had suffered both from the long period of routine employment and from a narrow bureaucratic administration that too often had tended to reward conformity and to penalize enterprise and originality. Caught in a system which gave limited play for individual talent, and which held out little promise of promotion, many capable officers had resigned. And now, in the great crisis, still others were to withdraw to enter the service of the Confederacy.[2]

As a result of President Buchanan's policy of non-coercion and inaction, continued for political reasons in the first weeks of Lincoln's administration, the outbreak of war caught the Navy wholly unprepared. The vessels in commission were scattered over the world at their peacetime cruising stations. Others were laid up undergoing repairs. The home squadron numbered only twelve vessels, only four of which were in Northern ports ready for immediate service.[3]

The ultimate triumph of Union arms, as well as the scale of Union naval operations, gave new life to the classic dogma that an adequate naval force could always be improvised in an

[1] See Special Report of the Secretary of the Navy, July 4, 1861. 37 Cong. 1 Sess., *S. Ex. Doc.* No. 1, pp. 85*ff*.; C. O. Paullin, "Naval Administration, 1842–1861" in *Proceedings of the United States Naval Institute*, Vol. XXXIII (1907), pp. 1435, 1448–55; and F. M. Bennett, *Steam Navy of the United States* (1896), Chaps. X, XII.

[2] Paullin, "Naval Administration, 1842–1861," pp. 1455–77; and *idem*, "A Half Century of Naval Administration in America," Part I, in *Proc. U. S. Nav. Inst.*, Vol. XXXVIII (1912), pp. 1309, 1328.

[3] Annual Report of the Secretary of the Navy, 1861, 37 Cong. 2 Sess., *S. Ex. Doc.* No. 1, Vol. III, pp. 10*ff*.; and Paullin, "Naval Administration, 1842–1861," pp. 1446–7.

emergency, and that it was therefore permissible to neglect the regular standing Navy in time of peace. The war did emphasize the industrial strength and versatility of the American people. Thanks to the mines, ironworks, factories, shipyards, railroads, merchant marine, and fairly abundant liquid capital of the North, the Union Government succeeded in expanding the Navy to meet the extraordinary demands of the war. But the process of expansion, achieved at terrific cost, revealed appalling and unsuspected obstacles in the way of hastily improvising a naval force with a war already in progress.

All but insuperable difficulties were encountered at every stage. The Navy Department had no prearranged plans for meeting a great war emergency. First there was the problem of ships. The oversea squadrons were abolished or drastically cut down; vessels upon the stocks were hurried to completion; new ones were laid down by the dozen; and scores were transferred from the merchant marine and hastily equipped for war service. Then there was the problem of finding officers and seamen to man the vessels, and the equally difficult problem of creating a shore organization to supply and direct the forces afloat.[4]

The results achieved pointed plainly to the need of better preparation at the outset. Hastily built warships developed serious defects and frequently broke down in emergencies. It proved utterly impossible to convert merchant vessels into efficient men-of-war.[5] There was a chronic shortage of personnel.[6]

[4] See annual reports of the Secretary of the Navy for 1861–1865, *passim.*

[5] In 1866, John Lenthall, Chief of the Bureau of Construction and Repair, declared that the converted merchantmen had proved unsatisfactory as to speed and other essential qualities. Benjamin F. Isherwood, Chief of the Bureau of Steam Engineering, testified that the machinery of these vessels "was entirely unadapted for war purposes, and was much inferior in durability and power to the machinery built especially for the Navy Department." 39 Cong. 2 Sess., *H. Ex. Doc.* No. 1, Vol. IV, pp. 159, 177. And to the same effect, see Bennett, *Steam Navy*, pp. 503*ff.*

[6] See *Diary of Gideon Welles, Secretary of the Navy under Lincoln and Johnson* (edited by J. T. Morse, Jr., 1911), Vol. I, p. 546; and 38 Cong. 1 Sess., *H. Ex. Doc.* No. 1, Vol. IV, pp. xxiv–xxvii.

Waste, confusion, mismanagement, and corruption each took its toll.[7] Only the naval weakness of the Confederacy, it would appear, saved this jerry-built navy from a greater number of minor setbacks, and possibly major disasters which might have decisively affected the outcome of the war.[8]

Objectives and Strategy of the Union

Blockade of the Confederate seaboard was unquestionably the Navy's greatest contribution to the victory of the North. To close this seaboard throughout its full extent of more than 3,500 miles, from Chesapeake Bay to the Mexican border, was a colossal undertaking, but one based upon thoroughly sound strategic principles.

Deficient in industrial resources and equipment, the South could not continue its resistance indefinitely when cut off from the outside world. The Southern armies needed guns, ammunition, medical supplies, clothing, and the thousand other articles absolutely necessary to the business of waging war. All these things were procurable in Europe. And European manufacturers desperately needed the cotton which the South had for exchange. But despite the remarkable success of blockade runners early in the war,[9] the steadily growing strength of the Union squadrons rendered the blockade more and more effective with the passage of every month. It would be difficult to measure with any precision the effects of the blockade on the fighting power of the Confederate armies, or on the health and morale of the civilian population. But the testimony of those who lived through those four years of progressive deprivation, as well as the conclusions of those who have studied the avail-

[7] Paullin, "Half Century of Naval Administration," Part II, in *Proc. U. S. Nav. Inst.*, Vol. XXXIX (1913), pp. 165*ff.*; and *Diary of Gideon Welles*, Vol. I, pp. 546–7.

[8] Captain A. T. Mahan, *The Influence of Sea Power upon History, 1660–1783* (1890), pp. 43-4.

[9] See F. L. Owsley, *King Cotton Diplomacy* (1931), Chap. VIII.

able evidence, tend to show that the blockade at least hastened the downfall of the Confederacy.[10]

Union naval operations upon the Western rivers also contributed vitally to the defeat of the Confederacy. The occupation of the Mississippi and its main tributaries had a strategic significance second only to that of the seaboard blockade. These operations isolated the Trans-Mississippi Confederate States, extended the blockade along a third side of the military frontier, and seriously disrupted the internal communications of the Confederacy.[11]

These operations raised unique problems as difficult as those upon the seaboard. Suitable gunboats had to be improvised; operating principles had to be adapted to the peculiar conditions of river warfare. Much of this experience manifestly had little significance for future policy. But these operations nevertheless had a broad strategic significance in showing the vital importance of controlling water communications giving access to the enemy country.

Union naval operations upon Chesapeake Bay and the Virginia rivers had a comparable significance. This was especially the case with the Navy's cooperation with the Army of the Potomac, in McClellan's Peninsula Campaign of 1862, and again in Grant's victorious offensive against Richmond in 1864–1865. Union naval forces covered the movement of the Army across waters otherwise strategically impassable, and guarded the vital line of water communications to that Army's ultimate source of supplies.[12]

[10] See, for example, Captain D. W. Knox, *History of the United States Navy* (1936), Chap. XXV; J. C. Schwab, *The Confederate States of America, 1861–1865* (1901), pp. 311 and *passim*; J. F. Rhodes, *History of the United States from the Compromise of 1850* (1904), Vol. V, Chap. XXVIII; J. B. McMaster, *History of the People of the United States During Lincoln's Administration* (1927), Chap. XIX; and Edward Channing, *History of the United States*, Vol. VI (1925), pp. 488*ff*., 511*ff*.

[11] See Knox, *United States Navy*, Chaps. XXI, XXIII.

[12] J. W. Pratt, "Naval Operations on the Virginia Rivers in the Civil War," in *Proc. U.S. Nav. Inst.*, Vol. XLV (Feb. 1919), pp. 185*ff*.; Knox, *United States Navy*, Chap. XXII.

Objectives and Strategy of the Confederacy

Southern naval objectives, in contrast to those of the North, were primarily defensive. But the Secretary of the Confederate Navy, Stephen R. Mallory of Florida,[13] well understood that offense is the best defense.[14] To throw the North back upon the defensive, he proposed an aggressive commerce-raiding campaign upon the ocean, with "vessels built exclusively for speed," armed "with a battery of one or two accurate guns of long range," equipped to remain at sea for long periods, and able "to engage or avoid an enemy at will."[15] Such cruisers, he hoped, would raise havoc with Northern commerce and compel sending in pursuit warships that would otherwise be used to blockade Southern ports.[16]

To break up the blockade, and if possible to carry the war to the Northern seaboard, Mallory advocated acquiring a few powerful ironclads. By "fighting with iron against wood," he aimed to compensate for "inequality of numbers. . . ." One armored vessel, he contended in 1861, "could traverse the entire coast of the United States, prevent all blockades, and encounter with a fair prospect of success," the "entire [Union] Navy."[17]

Transfer of the capital from Montgomery, Alabama, to Richmond, Virginia, led to a further development of Confederate naval strategy. Both Richmond and Washington lay on navigable rivers emptying into Chesapeake Bay. If the Confederate Navy could seize command of this great estuary, it would open Richmond to the ocean, seriously hamper Union

[13] As Chairman of the Senate Naval Affairs Committee in the 'fifties, Mallory had acquired a broad knowledge of naval strategy and technical naval progress both abroad and in the United States.

[14] See Owsley, *King Cotton Diplomacy,* Chap. XIII.

[15] *Official Records of the Union and Confederate Navies,* Ser. II, Vol. II, p. 51.

[16] See J. D. Bulloch, *The Secret Service of the Confederate States in Europe* (1884), Vol. I, p. 46.

[17] *Official Records of U. and Conf. Navies,* Ser. II, Vol. II, pp. 67, 69; and see the approving comment on this plan in J. P. Baxter's *Introduction of the Ironclad Warship* (1933), p. 237.

military campaigns in Northern Virginia, perhaps win Maryland over to the Confederacy, and even menace the Federal capital.[18]

The Ironclad Problem

The industrial resources of the South, however, were utterly inadequate to carry out the naval program of the Confederacy.[19] In the face of all but insuperable obstacles, the South did succeed in building several primitive armored vessels which, at different times and places, threatened but failed to break the blockade.[20] The first and most famous of these was the *Virginia*, reconstructed from the steam frigate *Merrimac* which fell into Confederate hands at the beginning of the war. With a view to seizing command of the Chesapeake, the Confederates converted this vessel into a crude floating fortress, erecting upon the lower hull an iron-covered superstructure the sloping sides of which resembled a shed upon a raft. On a fateful day in March 1862, this formidable if clumsy craft steamed out of Norfolk, sank two large wooden warships in Hampton Roads, and terrorized the Atlantic seaboard, where it was feared that the ugly monster would destroy all Union naval forces in the Chesapeake and even steam up the Atlantic coast to attack New York.

Such fears were actually groundless, for the *Virginia* drew too much water to operate in the upper reaches of Chesapeake Bay, and was too unseaworthy and otherwise decrepit to venture out upon the ocean.[21] But the alarm was none the less effective in dramatizing the obsolescence of the unprotected wooden warship.

[18] *Official Records of U. and Conf. Navies,* Ser. II, Vol. II, pp. 77, 99, 117; Channing, *History of the United States,* Vol. VI, p. 499; and Pratt, "Naval Operations on Virginia Rivers."

[19] Bulloch, *Secret Service,* Vol. I, pp. 46, 380.

[20] J. R. Soley, "The Union and Confederate Navies" in *Battles and Leaders of the Civil War* (edited by R. N. Johnson and C. C. Buell, 1887), Vol. I, pp. 611, 624–31.

[21] T. J. Wertenbaker, *Norfolk, Historic Southern Port* (1931), Chap. X.

During the year these events were in preparation, Union naval authorities had also been struggling with the ironclad problem. Plans for armored warships had poured in upon the Navy Department. Many of these had received serious consideration, but there was a great deal of uncertainty and confusion, partly because naval architecture was everywhere in a state of transition, but also because American naval authorities had previously failed to keep abreast of naval progress abroad.[22]

After considerable delay, a committee of naval officers was appointed to formulate an ironclad policy. This committee's report showed a deep-seated prejudice against armored warships and little grasp of their potentialities.[23] Frankly admitting "no experience and but scanty knowledge in this branch of naval architecture," the committee thought armored "floating batteries" might have value as "adjuncts to fortifications on land," but was "sceptical" as to the "advantages and ultimate adoption" of armor on cruising vessels. Ironclads could never attain the speed of wooden vessels. The latter could therefore "choose their position, and keep out of harm's way entirely." Shell guns, which had foreshadowed the passing of the wooden warship, were lightly dismissed with the comment that the committee knew "of nothing superior to the large and heavy spherical shot in its destructive effects on vessels, whether plated or not." Passing from the general to the specific, the committee, without expressly noticing the naval program of the Confederacy, correctly perceived that the immediate need was for shallow-draft armored vessels that could operate in the harbors and other coastal waters of the South. And, as a result of their recommendations, three experimental ironclads were authorized, one of which was to become the famous *Monitor*.[24]

This vessel consisting of a submerged hull, covered with a flat iron-plated deck upon which was erected an armored revolving turret housing two heavy cannon, was popularly known

[22] See Baxter, *Ironclad Warship*, Chap. XII, and authorities cited therein.
[23] 37 Cong. 2 Sess., *S. Ex. Doc.* No. 1, Vol. III, pp. 152*ff*.
[24] See Baxter, *Ironclad Warship*, Chap. XII, and authorities cited therein.

as the "cheese box on a raft." It was rushed to completion and towed to Hampton Roads, where it arrived the evening after the *Virginia's* destructive raid on the Union squadron there. A clumsy, unseaworthy vessel, the *Monitor* nevertheless saved the day, for the Confederate ironclad, after an indecisive engagement, steamed back to Norfolk and stayed there.[25]

These events transferred to the public forum a debate on naval architecture previously confined to technical circles. This debate focused chiefly on two issues: wooden vessels versus ironclads; and the monitor type versus sea-going armored cruising vessels. Discussion of these technical issues led straight into the sphere of strategy, for one's views on the latter inevitably colored one's conclusions as to the former.

One group, represented by the eminent marine engineers, John Lenthall and Benjamin F. Isherwood,[26] viewed the introduction of naval armor as the occasion for reforming our system of naval strategy. The development of ironclad warships, by rendering "nearly useless" the wooden vessels hitherto "composing the navies of Europe," afforded us an opportunity to "start equal with the first powers of the world in a new race for the supremacy of the ocean." To improve this opportunity, they urged building a fleet of sea-going "iron steamships . . . clad with invulnerable armor plates, furnished with maximum steam-power, and . . . larger than any vessel we now possess." We could then "preserve our coasts from the presence of an enemy's naval force by keeping command of the open sea, with all the power" such a command would give "of aggression" upon the enemy's "own shores and commerce." This strategy, they contended, would be "cheaper" and "more effective" than "any system of harbor defense which requires every point to be protected that may be assailed," leaving the enemy "choice of the time and place, and the advantages of perfect security for his own ports and commerce. Harbor defenses were "indeed valu-

[25] See *ibid.*, Chap. XIII, and authorities cited.

[26] Lenthall was Chief of the Bureau of Construction and Repair, and Isherwood was Chief of the Bureau of Steam Engineering, both in the Navy Department.

able adjuncts"; they "might prevent the enemy's entrance to a port, [but] they could not drive him from its gates. . . ." It was "better to fight at the threshold than upon the hearthstone."[27]

This view, which anticipated Mahan by nearly thirty years, won few supporters in the 'sixties. The prevailing opinion was that it would be difficult, if not utterly impossible, to design a satisfactory sea-going ironclad; and that fast wooden cruisers, armed with long-range guns, could either escape or else keep ironclads at a distance.[28] The victory of the *Monitor* over the *Virginia* was widely interpreted as proving the superiority of that type over all other ironclads, and, as a result of this conclusion, thirty-five vessels of the monitor type were added to the Navy.[29] These monitors, as they were called, were admittedly unsuited to extensive cruising upon the open sea, but they were useful for operations in the sheltered waters of the Southern seaboard, and it was believed that they would provide adequate means of coast and harbor defense in case of future wars with foreign Powers.

This view ignored contemporary war experience. Command of the open sea was enabling the Union Navy to blockade Southern ports. The inability of the South to contest that command frustrated not only their efforts to break up the blockade but also to prevent Union forces from occupying one strategic shore point after another. Yet Northern statesmen and naval experts, in the face of this demonstration, plotted a course for the future that was indistinguishable in principle from that which circumstances had forced upon the Confederacy. By unqualifiedly endorsing the shallow-draft, unseaworthy monitor-type to the exclusion of sea-going ironclads, not merely as a temporary wartime expedient, but also as a permanent policy,

[27] Memorandum to the Secretary of the Navy, dated March 17, 1862. 38 Cong. 2 Sess., *S. Rept.* No. 142, pp. 110, 111, 112. Two and a half years later Lenthall reiterated this view in his annual report as Chief of the Bureau of Construction and Repair. 38 Cong. 2 Sess., *H. Ex. Doc.* No. 1, Vol. VI, pp. 1000, 1003.

[28] See, for example, *The United States Army and Navy Journal*, Vol. I (1863–1864), pp. 3, 36, 67, 330, 374, 390, 562, 650.

[29] See Baxter, *Ironclad Warship*, p. 302; and Bennett, *Steam Navy*, Chap. XX.

the United States was perpetuating the strategy of passive coast and harbor defense, which had contributed so largely to the disasters of the War of 1812, and which was now failing to save the Confederate seaboard either from blockade or occupation by the Union forces.

Another important result of the *Monitor-Virginia* action was to force improvements in naval ordnance. The real victory on that occasion was that of armor-plate over guns. This resulted in the design and manufacture of larger guns, and, still more important, the rapid improvement of rifled cannon with higher muzzle velocities and correspondingly greater penetrating power. With an eye to the future, Assistant Secretary of the Navy Fox, a man of extensive naval training and experience, held that the United States must develop ordnance that could destroy the most formidable ironclad any foreign Power could send across the ocean.[30] And largely, it would appear, as a result of this line of reasoning and activity, a dogma was soon to arise in American naval circles, and to persist for many years, that it was unnecessary and unwise to build sea-going ironclad warships, because of the inevitable ultimate victory of ordnance over armor.

Emergence of the ironclad completed the triumph of steam over sails. Unable either to escape or to withstand shellfire, the wooden sailing vessels of the Old Navy had been helpless before the onslaught of the ironclad *Virginia*. Only steam could provide adequate motive power for the heavy ironclad. Only steam could assure the certainty of movement essential to enable the unarmored cruiser to escape destruction. And that was not all. Steam alone made possible the close blockade of the Southern seaboard through summer and winter, fair weather and foul. And when, confronted with the menace of possible European intervention on the side of the Confederacy, the Navy Department set about preparing a naval force to meet this greater emergency, it was found that steam afforded potential-

[30] Baxter, *Ironclad Warship*, pp. 309–10.

ities of high and sustained speed never attainable under canvas.[31]

Commerce Raiding and the Blockade

Not only the ironclad but also the commerce-raiding phase of Southern naval policy contributed its quota of naval lessons. In the face of immense obstacles, the Confederate Government improvised or purchased a motley array of cruisers, the most famous and destructive of which was the English-built *Alabama.* These cruisers raided shipping lanes, visited the fishing and whaling grounds, and even lurked in the vicinity of Northern ports. These raiders captured or destroyed nearly three hundred Northern vessels aggregating considerably more than one hundred thousand tons. The direct losses in ships and cargoes is estimated to have reached $25,000,000. The indirect losses, resulting from prohibitive insurance rates, diversion of business to neutral shipping, and other factors, probably amounted to a great deal more. Altogether, the depredations of the Confederate raiders were directly and indirectly responsible for the capture, destruction, or sale to foreign owners, of nearly a million tons of American merchant shipping.[32]

These depredations raised great clamor in the commercial centers of the Northern seaboard. When it was learned that the Confederates had contracted with English shipbuilders for seagoing ironclads designed to break up the blockade and carry the war into Northern waters, the alarm verged on panic. Merchants, shipowners, boards of trade, metropolitan editors, mayors of port cities, governors of seaboard States, and members of Congress descended upon the President and Navy Department, demanding warships to defend Northern harbors, to

[31] Bennett, *Steam Navy*, pp. 501*ff.*, and Chaps. XXVIII–XXIX.

[32] See 41 Cong. 2 Sess., *H. Rept.* No. 28, p. ix; *Official Records of U. and Conf. Navies*, Ser. I, Vol. I, pp. 613*ff.*; Vol. II, pp. 639*ff.*; Vol. III, pp. 609*ff.*; E. D. Fite, *Social and Industrial Conditions in the North During the Civil War* (1910), pp. 147–8; and Owsley, *King Cotton Diplomacy*, pp. 574*ff.*

patrol the coast, to guard the fishing grounds and shipping lanes, and to run down the Confederate raiders.[33]

Secretary of the Navy Welles resisted this pressure to the best of his ability. He stubbornly opposed withdrawing vessels from the blockading squadrons either to guard the Northern seaboard against largely imaginary perils,[34] or to scour the seas for the elusive raiders.[35] For this stand, Welles was intemperately denounced,[36] and, on several occasions, he yielded sufficiently to dispatch vessels to run down the Confederate cruisers.[37]

Failure of these expeditions testified both to the soundness of Welles's judgment and to the skill with which the Confederate cruiser captains evaded their pursuers. In this respect, Confederate strategy contrasted sharply with that of the United States in the War of 1812. In the earlier conflict, American naval commanders rarely avoided combat with the enemy's smaller naval vessels. On the whole, it would seem that the Confederate strategy was the sounder. Loss of a few naval vessels would not materially weaken the stronger naval Power. On the other hand, loss of even one cruiser might seriously cripple the commerce-destroying ability of the weaker. And commerce destruction, not victorious naval duels, was the paramount object of cruiser warfare.[38]

Viewed in the large it would seem that Welles's stubborn

[33] 38 Cong. 1 Sess., *H. Ex. Doc.* No. 69, pp. 595–8; J. D. Bulloch, *Secret Service,* Vol. I, Chap. VII; Vol. II, pp. 59*ff*.; and *Diary of Gideon Welles,* Vol. I, pp. 123, 288, 347, 364, 375, 380, 435; and Vol. II, p. 256.

[34] *Diary of Gideon Welles,* Vol. I, pp. 347, 380, 435; and Vol. II, p. 256.

[35] *ibid.,* Vol. I, pp. 207, 497; and Annual Report of the Secretary of the Navy for 1863, 38 Cong. 1 Sess., *H. Ex. Doc.* No. 1, Vol. IV, p. xxiv.

[36] *Diary of Gideon Welles,* Vol. I, pp. 123, 380, 435, 448; and for a sample of press opinion, see editorials in the *New York Herald,* Oct. 28, 31, Nov. 3, 7, Dec. 1, 2, 29, 1862.

[37] *Diary of Gideon Welles,* Vol. I, pp. 109, 111, 122, 123, 134, 224, 304, 327, 333, 342, 497; Vol. II, pp. 39, 102, 105, 111, 113, 119.

[38] The consequences of fighting the warships of the stronger Power were tragically demonstrated when the action of the French government forced the Confederate cruiser *Alabama* to leave the port of Cherbourg, and to give battle to the superior Union cruiser *Kearsarge* waiting outside. The resulting loss of the *Alabama* was a terrible blow to the naval power of the Confederacy. Destruction of the *Kearsarge* would not have materially weakened the vastly superior power of the North.

resistance to any course calculated to weaken the blockade rested upon solid ground. The Union Government's supreme military objective was to crush the Confederacy, and the Navy's main contribution was to draw ever more tightly the blockade that was strangling the South. Any diversion of force from this purpose would be strategically justified only on the ground of grave peril to some vital interest of the North.

Such a peril did not materialize. None of the Southern-built ironclads proved seaworthy enough to venture out upon the ocean. The tardy decision of the British Government to enforce its neutral obligations prevented delivery of the more formidable sea-going ironclads constructed for the Confederacy in England. And the Confederate cruisers failed to menace seriously either the coast or the commerce of the North. Their depredations on shipping, which in conjunction with other factors did cripple the American merchant marine, simply diverted the ocean carrying trade to British and other neutral shipping, without diminishing in the slightest the flow of munitions and other goods into the Northern States.

Viewed in retrospect, the naval lessons and consequences of the Civil War seem clear and unmistakable. A navy could not be quickly and readily improvised in an emergency. Merchant vessels could not be converted into efficient men-of-war. In the realm of technology, steam had conclusively triumphed over sails, and the ironclad over the unprotected wooden warship, while improvements in ordnance had rendered the latter completely obsolete. In the realm of strategy, the war had but repeated the lessons of earlier conflicts. Confederate commerce-raiding, though well planned and skilfully executed, had not affected the outcome in the slightest. On the other hand, the Union blockade had contributed largely to that outcome. And the Union Navy's indisputable command of the open sea in the theater of operations had alone made possible that blockade which relentlessly sapped the military strength and morale of the Confederacy.

CHAPTER ELEVEN

☆ ☆

Last Years of the Old Navy (1865–1881)

THE naval lessons of the Civil War, like those of earlier conflicts, were largely ignored during the generation following the war. The public suffered the inevitable post-war reaction against all things military. The Service drifted back into the habits and routine of the pre-war period. And so complete was the restoration that a visitor returning in 1870 after ten years' absence, might never have guessed that the Navy had passed through any war at all, much less a war that had hastened a revolution in naval architecture and thoroughly demonstrated the inadequacy of the strategic theories in vogue on the eve of the conflict.

Post-War Reorganization and Stagnation

Demobilization proceeded rapidly following the cessation of hostilities. The shore establishments were closed or greatly curtailed. The auxiliary warships, improvised from the merchant marine, were sold or scrapped. The ironclad monitors were laid up, ostensibly for safe keeping against some future emergency. The regular cruisers, the best of which antedated the war, were likewise laid up or refitted for routine peacetime service on the oversea stations. In December 1864, the Navy List included nearly 700 vessels, aggregating half a million tons, and mounting almost 5,000 guns.[1] By the end of 1870,

[1] Ann. Rept., Sec. of the Navy, 1864, 38 Cong. 2 Sess., *H. Ex. Doc.* No. 1, Vol. VI, p. xxiii.

this force had shrunk to less than 200 vessels, aggregating less than 200,000 tons, and capable of mounting only about 1,300 guns. In reality, the shrinkage was even greater, for many of these vessels were worn out or otherwise unfit for service. The total number in commission, including store-ships and hospital ships, was only 52, mounting altogether less than 500 guns, most of which were now obsolete.[2]

On the return of peace, the Navy Department had at once set about restoring its traditional oversea cruising squadrons, some of which had been withdrawn and the remainder depleted to strengthen the blockade of Southern ports. This practice of dividing the Navy's cruising vessels into several small squadrons assigned respectively to particular geographical areas in the Atlantic, Pacific, and elsewhere, it is recalled, had grown up following the War of 1812 as a means of policing certain seas overrun by pirates, of suppressing the slave trade, and of extending protection to American commerce in foreign ports. Throughout the long period from 1815 to the Civil War, this routine cruising had constituted the chief function of the Navy. Universally regarded as the Navy's normal occupation in time of peace, it was assumed that the government would restore its oversea stations just as soon as the war was over. And Secretary of the Navy Welles was merely voicing the sentiment prevailing in professional naval circles when, in 1865, he justified this course on the ground that "one or more of our naval vessels ought annually to display the flag . . . in every port where our ships may trade."[3]

The Navy Department had maintained these oversea squadrons with little difficulty before the advent of steam. Sailing vessels were practically self-sufficient so long as their provisions lasted. The introduction of steam seriously complicated the problem, because the United States lacked oversea colonies where stores of coal could be accumulated. Without such coal-

[2] Ann. Rept., Sec. of the Navy, 1869, 41 Cong. 2 Sess., *H. Ex. Doc.* No. 1, Vol. I, p. 34; and Ann. Rept., 1870, 41 Cong. 3 Sess., *H. Ex. Doc.* No. 1, Vol. III, pp. 3 and 55*ff*.

[3] 39 Cong. 1 Sess., *H. Ex. Doc.* No. 1, Vol. V, p. xv.

ing stations, the Navy's cruising vessels had to depend either upon sails or upon expensive and uncertain coal supplies obtainable in foreign ports. To avoid this dependence, and at the same time to maintain cruising squadrons in distant seas, it was necessary for American naval vessels to have fuel capacity for long voyages, and also good maneuvering and sailing qualities under canvas.[4]

Prior to the Civil War, everyone had taken for granted the desirability of fitting our naval vessels with full sail power. Steam was regarded merely as an auxiliary power for use in battle, in calms, or on entering and leaving port. The war, however, had begun to open men's eyes to the real potentialities of steam. Wartime experience had taught not only the superiority of steam over sails as a motive power, but also the further fact that sails and rigging retarded a vessel's speed under steam. Despite great progress in steam machinery and the demonstrated advantages of steam propulsion in naval vessels, "the moment the Civil War was over . . . the Navy went back to canvas. . . ."[5] Propellers were altered to improve the sailing qualities of the Navy's cruising vessels, and boilers were cut down to enlarge the storage space for coal and provisions.[6] A general order, issued in 1869, directed that all naval vessels should thereafter have "full sail power."[7] The Navy Regulations of 1870 expressly forbade using steam at all, except when absolutely necessary.[8] "To burn coal was so grievous an offense in the eyes of the authorities that for years the captain was obliged to enter in the logbook in *red ink* his reasons for getting up steam and starting the engines."[9] It was even sug-

[4] See Report of John Lenthall, Chief of Bureau of Construction and Repair, Nov. 1, 1866, 39 Cong. 2 Sess., *H. Ex. Doc.* No. 1, Vol. IV, p. 160; Report of the Board on Steam Machinery Afloat [Goldsborough Board], Sept. 29, 1869, 41 Cong. 2 Sess., *H. Ex. Doc.* No. 1, p. 145; Ann. Rept., Sec. of the Navy, 1869, *ibid.*, p. 6.

[5] Admiral C. F. Goodrich, *Rope Yarns from the Old Navy* (1931), p. 65.

[6] See Report on Steam Machinery Afloat, pp. 142–209; and F. M. Bennett, *Steam Navy of the United States* (1896), Chap. XXXI.

[7] Quoted in Bennett, *Steam Navy*, p. 614.

[8] United States Navy Department, *Regulations for the Government of the United States Navy, 1870*, pp. 36–7.

[9] Goodrich, *Rope Yarns from the Old Navy*, p. 65.

gested that the government might, as a means of enforcing the Regulations, charge the cost of coal consumed against each commanding officer's pay.[10]

Division of the Navy into small groups of cruising vessels thousands of miles apart precluded any possibility of developing an efficient fleet organization. Indeed, as before the war, the dispersion of the Navy's sea-going forces was carried even further. In theory, the vessels assigned to each station comprised a squadron under a single command. As a rule, however, each ship cruised by itself. Even when in company, the ships rarely engaged in group maneuvers. Such exercises for acquiring skill in "handling vessels in rapid and close proximity," had little value in the eyes of men accustomed to think of each ship rather as a potential solitary raider than as a unit of a fighting fleet.[11] While a professional minority contended that the United States should have a fleet so organized and "drilled" as to be *"a unit of force acting under one head,"*[12] the Service as a whole remained thoroughly committed to the "cut and run," single-ship strategy which, both for the United States in the War of 1812, and for the Confederacy in the Civil War, had inflicted great injury on the enemy's commerce without, however, affecting the war's outcome in the slightest.

At this point, one discovers still another serious weakness in the naval policy of this period. The first essential of a successful raider was high speed. Such a vessel must be fast enough to overhaul an enemy's merchantmen and weaker naval vessels, as well as to escape from his heavy capital ships. During the Civil War, when there seemed to be danger of European complications, the Navy Department had labored to build a group of fast cruisers with which to meet such a contingency. These

[10] See Report of Admiral D. D. Porter, Oct. 2, 1871, 42 Cong. 2 Sess., *H. Ex. Doc.* No. 2, Vol. IV, p. 63.

[11] Admiral A. T. Mahan, *From Sail to Steam* (1906), p. 270.

[12] Quoted from an address by Commodore F. A. Parker, before the United States Naval Institute, Dec. 10, 1874. 44 Cong. 1 Sess., *H. Misc. Doc.* No. 170, Pt. 8, p. 80.

vessels, not finished until after the war, were for their day beautiful specimens of cruiser design. One of them, the U.S.S. *Wampanoag*, proved to be the fastest ship afloat, steaming nearly eighteen knots, or better than twenty statute miles per hour, a speed not equalled by any other vessel of the United States Navy for twenty-one years.[13]

The logical course for a government thus committed to commerce raiding as its principal offensive operation would have been to continue this line of development.[14] The highest naval authorities, however, took precisely the opposite view. A board appointed to observe the trials of the *Wampanoag* agreed that there was "probably . . . no vessel afloat" that could either "overtake" or "escape from" this cruiser; and that she could carry a battery "affording ample offensive and defensive means to a vessel of her speed. . . ." But "inasmuch as the main and special purpose for which this vessel was built no longer exists for a navy in time of peace," the board recommended radical alterations to adapt the ship to economical routine cruising on foreign stations.[15]

Another and even more imposing board, headed by Rear Admiral L. M. Goldsborough, to inspect and report on "steam machinery afloat," recommended still more drastic alterations in the Navy's steam cruisers. As a result of this report the department had these rerigged for full sail power, their boiler capacity radically cut down, two-bladed propellers substituted for the original four-bladed ones, and their machinery otherwise changed to adapt them to economical cruising under canvas.[16]

Such a policy could, of course, lead to but one result. Com-

[13] See Bennett, *Steam Navy*, Chap. XXIX.

[14] See advice to this effect from John Lenthall, Chief of the Bureau of Construction and Repair, Oct. 17, 1864, and Oct. 21, 1868, 38 Cong. 2 Sess., *H. Ex. Doc.* No. 1, Vol. VI, p. 1003; 40 Cong. 3 Sess., *H. Ex. Doc.* No. 1, Vol. IV, p. 95. And see B. F. Isherwood, Chief of the Bureau of Steam Engineering, to the same effect, May 15, 1868. 40 Cong. 2 Sess., *H. Ex. Doc.* No. 339, p. 10.

[15] 40 Cong. 2 Sess., *H. Ex. Doc.* No. 339, pp. 7–8.

[16] Report of Board on Steam Machinery Afloat; and Bennett, *Steam Navy*, Chap. XXIX.

manding officers complained of the unsatisfactory steaming qualities of their respective vessels.[17] Admiral David D. Porter, who was at the same time a leader in the reaction against steam, noted bitterly that our cruising vessels could do little more than eight knots on the average as compared with fourteen or fifteen knots in the French and British Navies.[18] And a large number of line officers, in reply to a circular letter from the House Naval Affairs Committee, were practically unanimous that lack of speed was one of the gravest deficiencies of our cruising vessels.[19]

Not only were the Navy's vessels deficient in the speed essential to a cruiser; they also lacked modern ordnance with which to fight battles or to keep enemy ironclads at a distance. While European admiralties were equipping their warships with high-power breech-loading rifles, our Navy continued to rely on obsolete muzzle-loading smooth-bore guns, or makeshift rifled pieces improvised from old smooth-bores.[20]

Equally notable was the Navy's failure to keep abreast of progress in ship armor. Wartime experience had clearly shown the fatal vulnerability of wooden ships, especially when pitted against ironclads equipped with shell-guns. Yet American naval authorities ignored this experience, prolonging the life of the wooden warships launched before the war, and reconstructing several of the jerry-built wooden cruisers of the war period.[21] In 1872, the Navy Department requested authority to build several additional vessels of this same obsolete type.[22] And

[17] Bennett, *Steam Navy,* Chap. XXXII.

[18] Report of the Admiral of the Navy, Oct. 2, 1871. 42 Cong. 2 Sess., *H. Ex. Doc.* No. 1, Pt. III, Vol. IV, p. 37.

[19] 44 Cong. 1 Sess., *H. Misc. Doc.* No. 170, Pt. VIII, pp. 2, 5, 9, 46, 57, 66, 74, 83, 87, 89, 96, 98, 100, 102, 104, 109, 111, 114, 115, 117, 120, 123, 126.

[20] See reports of Bureau of Ordnance appended to the annual reports of the Secretary of the Navy; also Report of the Admiral of the Navy, Nov. 6, 1874. 43 Cong. 2 Sess., *H. Ex. Doc.* No. 1, Pt. III, Vol. V, pp. 212*ff*.; also replies to circular letter, 44 Cong. 1 Sess., *H. Misc. Doc.* No. 170, Pt. VIII, pp. 9, 19, 46, 57, 66, 109, 114, 115, 117; and 47 Cong. 1 Sess., *H. Rept.* No. 653.

[21] Bennett, *Steam Navy,* pp. 632–48.

[22] Ann. Rept., Sec. of the Navy, 1872. 42 Cong. 3 Sess., *H. Ex. Doc.* No. 1, Pt. III, Vol. I, p. 5.

Congress complied after a debate which disclosed little interest in, and practically no understanding of, the revolution in naval architecture which had rendered unprotected wooden ships utterly useless as engines of actual warfare. Indeed, that question figured scarcely at all in the debate. As Senator Lot M. Morrill of Maine frankly admitted: we were not trying to build up a fighting force to rival those of France and Great Britain, but "simply . . . to provide . . . a naval police force" to guard the country's peacetime commerce.[23]

Failure to keep abreast of progress in ordnance and armor magnified the potential consequences of the failure to maintain fast steam cruisers. For many years the United States did not possess a single vessel that could have either repelled or escaped the faster sea-going armored ships of several European Powers.[24]

American naval authorities in this period not only clung tenaciously to the commerce-raiding system of naval warfare (without providing a single ship suited to that type of warfare), but also revived and adapted the strategy of passive coast defense, which had had such vogue under Thomas Jefferson, and which had figured recurrently in naval discussions down to the Civil War.

In 1865, the Navy had, in commission or under construction, a large number of so-called monitors. These large, shallow-draft ironclads, with low freeboard and two or four guns mounted in one or two revolving turrets, were refinements on the original *Monitor* which had won such renown in the battle of Hampton Roads. While these vessels had proved more or less useful for the coast and harbor operations of the

[23] *Congressional Globe,* 42 Cong. 3 Sess., p. 712. For the rest of the debate, see *ibid.*, pp. 16, 17, 34, 44, 703, 735, 766. The House passed the bill (p. 55) by a vote of 86–42, without yeas and nays; the Senate passed it in slightly amended form (p. 771) by a record vote of 39–8. For the Act as finally adopted, see *Statutes at Large,* Vol. XVII, p. 553.

[24] Report of the Admiral of the Navy, Nov. 6, 1874. 43 Cong. 2 Sess., *H. Ex. Doc.* No. 1, Pt. III, Vol. V, pp. 198, 201; and also 46 Cong. 2 Sess., *H. Rept.* No. 169.

Civil War, they were too slow and too unseaworthy for extensive cruising upon the open sea.[25] And they soon became worthless even as adjuncts to land fortifications, through failure both to keep them in repair and to arm them with high-power rifled guns comparable to those used in the leading European navies.[26] In 1881, Admiral Porter declared them to be "simply useless," because they could "not go to sea without being towed"; because "their armor would not withstand even small rifled guns"; because their average speed was not more than six knots per hour; and because their guns could "not penetrate four-inch armor at a distance of 500 yards."[27]

While admitting the structural defects and inferior equipment of particular monitors, the majority of American naval authorities in this period complacently ignored their deficiencies as a class. It was frequently urged that the government should rebuild these coast-defense ironclads, and arm them with modern ordnance.[28] But scarcely anyone advocated scrapping the monitors and abandoning this type of warship altogether. On the contrary, it was repeatedly argued, in disregard of readily available facts, that our monitors were equal or superior to any warships afloat.[29] One or more of these floating fortifications stationed within the harbor of each of our great

[25] After the war, the monitors *Miantonomoh* and *Monadnock* made successful voyages to Europe and to California respectively. These voyages were cited as disproving the alleged unsuitability of monitors for ocean service. Report of the Secretary of the Navy, Dec. 3, 1866, 39 Cong. 2 Sess., *H. Ex. Doc.* No. 1, Vol. IV, p. 23; and Bennett, *Steam Navy,* pp. 584–92. Actually, these voyages demonstrated little more than the ability of this type of warship to cross the ocean under favorable conditions in time of peace.

[26] 44 Cong. 2 Sess., *H. Ex. Doc.* No. 1, Pt. IV, p. 6; and 47 Cong. 1 Sess., *H. Rept.* No. 653, pp. iv, viii.

[27] 47 Cong. 1 Sess., *H. Ex. Doc.,* No. 1, Pt. III, Vol. VIII, p. 96.

[28] For a representative cross-section of professional opinion on this question, see 44 Cong. 1 Sess., *H. Misc. Doc.* No. 170, Pt. VIII, pp. 32, 46, 49, 66, 74, 94, 100, 111, 120. For representative samples of official civilian opinion, see 43 Cong. 1 Sess., *H. Ex. Doc.* No. 1, Pt. III, pp. 4, 132: 44 Cong. 2 Sess., *H. Ex. Doc.* No. 1, Pt. IV, p. 7; and *Messages and Papers of the Presidents* (Richardson's 1st ed.), Vol. VIII, p. 350.

[29] See, for example, 39 Cong. 2 Sess., *H. Ex. Doc.* No. 1, Vol. IV, pp. 23–4; 44 Cong. 1 Sess., *H. Misc. Doc.* No. 170, Pt. VIII, pp. 15, 74, 94, 100, 111, 120; and 44 Cong. 1 Sess., *H. Ex. Doc.* No. 1, Pt. III, Vol. III, p. 180.

seaports was sufficient, it was contended, to repel any force that a maritime enemy could send across the ocean.[30]

While there was some difference of opinion, it is true, as to the defensive potentialities of the monitor type of warship, there was almost none as to the strategy of passive coast and harbor defense. Some experts who doubted whether monitors alone were sufficient argued that we should also guard our harbors with submarine mines and torpedoes.[31] And there were a considerable number who pinned their faith on "marine rams"—swift vessels with a heavy iron shoe or beak attached to the prow. Admiral Daniel Ammen ventured the opinion "that the time is not distant when the marine ram will take the place of the enormously expensive armor-plated gun-bearing ships of today. . . ."[32] Marine rams, it was argued, could annihilate a fleet of cruising ironclads and thereby break up any blockade of our ports.[33] Even if they failed to do so, we had little to apprehend from blockades. With dogmatic finality, it was declared that a blockade could not materially injure the United States; indeed, that it would have no effect other than to "increase railroad transportation" within the country.[34]

It was admitted that a navy consisting of wooden cruisers, shallow-draft monitors, torpedo boats, and rams could neither blockade an enemy's ports nor engage hostile fleets of armored ships. Such a blockade, according to one distinguished officer, would not give us any important advantage, since it would simply divert trade from the enemy's ports to those of adjoin-

[30] See, for example, 39 Cong. 2 Sess., *H. Ex. Doc.* No. 1, Vol. IV, pp. 23–4, 30; 43 Cong. 2 Sess., *H. Ex. Doc.* No. 1, Pt. III, Vol. V, p. 209; and 44 Cong. 2 Sess., *H. Ex. Doc.,* No. 1, Pt. IV, Vol. III, pp. 5–7.

[31] See, for example, 44 Cong. 1 Sess., *H. Misc. Doc.* No. 170, Pt. VIII, pp. 32, 45, 120; and 41 Cong. 3 Sess., *H. Ex. Doc.* No. 1, Vol. III, p. 11.

[32] "The Purposes of a Navy and the Best Methods of Rendering It Effective," *The United Service,* Vol. I (April 1879), pp. 245, 253.

[33] Daniel Ammen, "The Marine Ram as a Naval Economy," *op. cit.,* Vol. II (April 1880), pp. 397, 399. For other opinions to much the same effect by various naval officers, see 44 Cong. 1 Sess., *H. Misc. Doc.* No. 170, Pt. VIII, pp. 3, 45, 58, 66, 74, 100, 120.

[34] Ammen, "The Purposes of a Navy," p. 253.

ing neutral countries.[35] And fleet actions, it was argued, would be just as futile. Another prominent officer informed a congressional committee, in 1876, that "few, if any, of the experienced officers of the Navy . . . would advocate . . . building . . . heavily iron-plated ships for cruising or fleet operations. . . . We have no near naval neighbors," he explained, "nor is it probable that we will have for a century to come, or that there will be fleet-fights when we do."[36] And Admiral David D. Porter, the highest ranking officer in the Navy, was on record to the same effect, having declared in 1874 that engagements between "powerful ironclad fleets" would never decide wars. It was only "by destroying the commerce of a great nation that we could bring her to terms; hence, one vessel like the [Confederate] *Alabama* roaming the ocean, sinking and destroying, would do more to bring about peace than a dozen unwieldy ironclads cruising in search of an enemy of like character."[37]

If the foregoing summary fairly represents the drift of professional naval opinion in the 'seventies, it indicates another failure to reshape naval policy in the light of actual wartime experience. As in the years following our second war with Great Britain, civilian statesmen and naval officers again ignored the lessons of the recent blockade of the South, and reverted to their traditional endorsement of commerce raiding and passive coast defense, useful enough as adjuncts to larger operations, but utterly inadequate as substitutes for command of the marine approaches to the United States.

Meanwhile, rust and decay were gradually but inexorably destroying such vessels as the government actually possessed. The ships of the war period, built of inferior and unseasoned materials, deteriorated rapidly. Those constructed in the 'fifties,

[35] *loc. cit.*

[36] Admiral A. L. Case, 44 Cong. 1 Sess., *H. Misc. Doc.* No. 170, Pt. VIII, p. 49. In an article entitled, "Reform in the Navy," *The United Service,* Vol. II (April 1880), p. 450, Captain W. T. Truxton declared that "the days of ships-of-the-line are past; fleet engagements are no more, certainly for this country."

[37] 43 Cong. 2 Sess., *H. Ex. Doc.* No. 1, Pt. III, Vol. V, p. 209.

while excellent ships in their day, had seen hard service during the war and required frequent and extensive repairs to keep them in commission. An attempt to mobilize a fighting force in 1873, when the *Virginius* crisis threatened war with Spain,[38] brought together a collection of "antiquated and rotting ships,"[39] which a single "modern war-vessel" could probably have destroyed "without serious damage to herself."[40] A canvass of professional opinion in 1876 disclosed practically universal dissatisfaction with the Navy's physical deterioration.[41] In 1880, the House Naval Affairs Committee found that there were not more than forty-eight vessels "capable of firing a gun." Not one of these was a first-class modern warship; and five of them were "old obsolete sailing vessels."[42]

Dynamics of Naval Policy in the 'Seventies

How is one to account for this material decline and intellectual stagnation? Doubtless a great many factors were involved, some of which we may briefly note. It is clear in retrospect that the psychological environment was not favorable. A reaction against things military had set in even before the final downfall of the Confederacy. It was widely believed that the American people had probably fought their last war. The United States had no oversea colonies to defend. We had no incentive to interfere in the periodic crises of the Old World. It was then deemed unthinkable that we would ever embark upon a war of conquest. Wide oceans separated us from all

[38] A Spanish cruiser captured the ship *Virginius* running arms to Cuban insurgents. Spanish authorities in Santiago, Cuba, executed several dozen of the passengers and crew as pirates. Many of them, including the captain, were United States citizens. For an excellent account which takes cognizance of the naval situation, see Allan Nevins, *Hamilton Fish* (1936), Chap. XXVIII.

[39] J. D. Long, *The New American Navy* (1903), Vol. I, p. 7.

[40] Captain A. C. Rhind to W. C. Whitthorne, Chairman of the House Naval Affairs Committee. 44 Cong. 1 Sess., *H. Misc. Doc.* No. 170, Pt. VIII, p. 93; and see Captain R. D. Evans, *A Sailor's Log* (1901), p. 171.

[41] 44 Cong. 1 Sess., *H. Misc. Doc.* No. 170, Pt. VIII, pp. 2, 7, 9, 45, 52, 57, 58, 61, 71, 93, 102, 104, 128, 142, and *passim*.

[42] 45 Cong. 2 Sess., *H. Rept.* No. 169, p. 11.

potential enemies. And the unstable balance of power in Europe would effectually deter any of the Great Powers from adopting "an aggressive policy toward the United States." All things considered, there seemed to be slight justification for maintaining a powerful navy patterned after those of the European Powers.[43]

Political and economic developments also militated against a positive naval policy. Decline of our merchant marine during and after the war weakened one of the traditionally strong arguments for increasing the Navy. The abolition of slavery removed one great incentive for southward expansion, which had contributed directly and indirectly to the naval development under Democratic administration in the 'fifties. Even more important, perhaps, was the sectional realignment that marked the rise of the Republican Party. By means of a liberal land policy and a high protective tariff, a political alliance was forged between the industrial East and the agrarian West, uniting under one banner the two sections whose antithetical views on naval policy were traditional and notorious. Rapid settlement of the West, together with unrestricted immigration, created an apparently insatiable home market for the factories growing to maturity in the warm atmosphere of protectionism. While this situation lasted, there was little incentive to look abroad for colonies or foreign markets in which to dispose of the country's "surpluses." Comparatively little was said about the Navy as an agency for promoting foreign trade. Thus it was perhaps not altogether fortuitous that neither major party took a strong stand for naval reconstruction during sixteen years after the Civil War.

The desperate partisan struggle over Southern reconstruction likewise had a depressing effect on the Navy. Gideon Welles, who had stayed on as Secretary of the Navy after the assassination of Lincoln, strove tirelessly, and on the whole

[43] For typical expositions of this point of view, see the annual reports of the Secretary of the Navy for 1876 and 1877. 44 Cong. 2 Sess., *H. Ex. Doc.* No. 1, Pt. IV, pp. 5–7; and 45 Cong. 2 Sess., *H. Ex. Doc.* No. 1, Pt. III, Vol. VII, pp. 7–13.

intelligently, to reorganize the naval establishment on a sound peace footing. Orderly demobilization of the mushroom war-navy would have been difficult in any event. With his department and his policies involved in the Radical Republicans' savage assaults on President Johnson, formulation and administration of an intelligent and consistent naval policy became virtually impossible.[44]

There was greater harmony between Executive and Congress after the inauguration of President Grant in 1869; but improvement in this direction was largely offset by the Administration's surrender of initiative and leadership on naval question to an ultraconservative professional group within the Service.

The line officers had long regarded themselves as the Navy's aristocracy, superior to the so-called staff departments such as the pay corps (supply and accounts), the medical corps, and the engineer corps. The war had emphasized the importance, and enhanced the prestige of the staff departments in general, and the engineers in particular. Indeed, it seemed likely that the complete and final triumph of steam over sails would put the engineers permanently on a par, socially and professionally, with the Line. This prospect, together with the average line officer's prejudice against steam *per se,* led in the postwar years to a series of efforts to humble the engineer corps and to check the trend toward steam.[45]

These efforts began during the Johnson administration. Admiral David D. Porter, an officer of the old school who had risen during the war to a position second only to Admiral Farragut, was charged with various intrigues designed to put the Line in control, with himself at the helm. His favorite scheme, according to Gideon Welles, was to have Congress set up a board of line officers to take over the duties of the civilian Secretary, who would thereafter become largely an

[44] *Diary of Gideon Welles* (edited by J. T. Morse, 1909), Vol. II, pp. 340, 430; Vol. III, pp. 264, 325; and *Cong. Globe,* 40 Cong. 2 Sess., p. 1320.

[45] See Bennett, *Steam Navy,* Chap. XXXI.

ornamental figurehead.[46] The election of General Grant to the Presidency, in 1868, opened the way. Porter had assiduously cultivated Grant whose temperament and military background rendered him receptive to the former's ideas. Grant appointed an elderly Philadelphia merchant, Adolph E. Borie, Secretary of the Navy, with the understanding that Porter was to run the Department.[47] For three months Porter was Secretary of the Navy in everything but name. One of his first acts was to have Borie dismiss Benjamin F. Isherwood who, as Chief of the Bureau of Steam Engineering, had led the revolt against sails and developed the fast steam cruisers begun during the war and completed soon thereafter.[48] Porter next struck at the engineer corps as a whole, reducing the relative rank of each grade as compared to the corresponding grade in the Line.[49] He then turned to the ships, ordering their sail power increased, their steam power reduced, and threatening dire penalties for burning coal save in emergencies.[50]

Borie's resignation in June 1869 cut short Porter's rule, but did not remove his influence from the Department. Borie's successor, George M. Robeson of New Jersey, while a somewhat more energetic executive, was a careless administrator, an active party politician, and a complacent follower on questions of policy.[51] Like many a Secretary before him, Robeson

[46] *Diary of Gideon Welles,* Vol. III, pp. 252–3, 283.

[47] J. R. Soley, *Admiral Porter* (1903), pp. 458–60; M. E. Dahlgren, *Memoir of John A. Dahlgren* (1882), p. 642; *Diary of Gideon Welles,* Vol. III, pp. 549–64; G. S. Boutwell, *Reminiscences of Sixty Years in Public Affairs* (1902), Vol. II, p. 212; and Nevins, *Hamilton Fish,* pp. 109–10.

[48] *Diary of Gideon Welles,* Vol. III, p. 551; and Bennett, *Steam Navy,* p. 608.

[49] Bennett, *Steam Navy,* pp. 610–21.

[50] We described this phase of Porter's policy in the early pages of this chapter. Altogether, Porter promulgated forty-five general orders within three months, whereas Welles had issued only five during the last two years of his administration. C. O. Paullin, "A Half Century of Naval Administration in America, 1861–1911" (Parts III and IV), *Proceedings of the United States Naval Institute,* Vol. XXXIX (1913), pp. 735, 749.

[51] Boutwell described Robeson as "a man of singular ability, lacking only the habit of careful, continuous industry." *Sixty Years,* Vol. II, p. 212. For a less favorable characterization, see Nevins, *Hamilton Fish,* p. 281.

entered the Department without previous experience with naval affairs. But he quickly acquired opinions, remarkable chiefly for their resemblance to those of the more conservative line officers.[52]

Throughout Robeson's long term of nearly eight years (1869–1877), the Administration's naval policy continued to reflect views prevailing among the senior line officers; and conditions within the Department were not such as to encourage criticism from the lower ranks. On the death of Admiral Farragut in 1870, Porter became Admiral of the Navy, the highest post in the Service, a position of great prestige from which he continued to influence the course of policy.[53] In 1871, Admiral Daniel Ammen one of Grant's close friends,[54] was appointed Chief of the Bureau of Navigation. The incumbent of this position controlled the assignments of all officers. He was, therefore, a powerful figure whom junior officers would hesitate to offend by too freely expressing critical or unorthodox opinions.[55] And Ammen, who held this key post until 1877, was as conservative as any member of the Service.[56]

While jealous of their prestige and position, and unyielding in their reactionary views on motive power, naval architecture, and strategy, the senior line officers as a class regarded themselves as reformers. And on some questions, they were genuine reformers. In particular, they were keenly distressed by the rapid deterioration of ships and equipment during the Grant

[52] Porter's influence at the beginning of the Robeson administration is easily seen by comparing certain of the former's earlier general orders with the views expressed in Robeson's first annual report. 41 Cong. 2 Sess., *H. Ex. Doc.* No. 1, p. 6.

[53] Compare, for example, Porter's annual reports as Admiral of the Navy, with Robeson's annual reports for the years 1870–1876.

[54] See Nevins, *Hamilton Fish,* pp. 140, 263.

[55] Paullin, "Half Century of Naval Administration," p. 734.

[56] For Ammen's reactionary views, see his articles in *The United Service,* Vol. I (April 1879), pp. 245–50; and Vol. II (April 1880), pp. 397–403. As late as 1891, several months after the publication of Captain Alfred T. Mahan's *Influence of Sea Power Upon History, 1660–1783,* Ammen was reiterating the same doctrines. See his book, *The Old Navy and the New* (1891), p. 473.

administration.[57] On this issue, they definitely parted company with the easy-going Robeson, whose annual reports conveyed the impression that the Navy was steadily growing stronger.

Another factor contributing to the decline of the Navy was a virulent attack of politics, graft, and corruption which ate at the vitals of the establishment during Grant's administration. With the tacit consent, if not the actual connivance, of Senators and Representatives who annually voted large naval appropriations,[58] the Navy Department spent millions of dollars for materials and labor, with little in the end to show for it, save a collection of worthless antiquated ships, an army of enriched contractors, a host of political retainers, and partisan strength at the polls in the favored constituencies. Yet, after public disclosure of these conditions in 1876,[59] Robeson in his valedictory report pointed with pride to the condition of the Navy, and observed complacently that we should "perhaps congratulate ourselves" for not having followed other maritime nations in building fleets of expensive "armor-plated, gun-bearing vessels. . . ." It was sufficient for us to have the "means of destroying such vessels should they appear in hostile attitude on our coasts. . . ." While our Navy did "not compare, either in number or character of vessels, with the expensive establishments" of certain European nations, it was nevertheless quite sufficient for the "defensive purposes of a peaceful people, without colonies, with a dangerous coast, and shallow

[57] See, for example, Porter's annual reports as Admiral of the Navy; and the answers to Representative Whitthorne's "circular letter" in connection with the navy investigation of 1876. 44 Cong. 1 Sess., *H. Misc. Doc.* No. 170, Pt. VIII.

[58] Congress appropriated altogether approximately $147,500,000 for the Navy for the years 1870–1876 inclusive, as compared with only $87,000,000 for the years 1854–1860, the period of greatest naval expansion before the Civil War. 45 Cong. 1 Sess., *S. Ex. Doc.* No. 3, pp. 156, 157.

[59] For the report of the congressional investigating committee, see 44 Cong. 1 Sess., *H. Rept.* No. 784; for the evidence in the case, see 44 Cong. 1 Sess., *H. Misc. Doc.* No. 170. The voluminous findings of the committee are well summarized in E. P. Oberholtzer, *History of the United States Since the Civil War* (1917–1937), Vol. III, pp. 172–81.

harbors, separated from warlike naval powers" by a wide ocean.[60]

The outlook for naval reform was just as unfavorable during the Hayes administration (1877–1881). Fiscal and social problems stemming from the business depression of the 'seventies crowded less pressing matters into the background. The Republican administration had to deal with Democratic majorities in the House (1877–1881) and in the Senate (1879–1881). And a war within the Republican Party, over the President's conciliatory Southern policy, his appointments to office, and his attack on the spoils system, further darkened the outlook for constructive legislation on any subject.[61]

The Hayes administration, moreover, showed little interest in improving the Navy. The President seemed wholly unaware of the real state of affairs, intimating from year to year that the Navy was in a generally satisfactory condition.[62] His Secretary of the Navy, Richard W. Thompson of Indiana, was so densely ignorant of naval affairs as to have expressed surprise, so it was reported, on learning that ships were hollow.[63] Whether true or not, this story fairly suggests the caliber of the man who presided over the Navy Department in this unique period of American naval history. Ignoring the inadequate condition of the regular Navy, Thompson talked largely about the advantages of a strong merchant marine, from which we could easily "improvise a navy in . . . an unexpected emergency."[64] With astonishing ignorance of readily available facts regarding naval progress abroad, he declared, in 1877, that "heavy armor-plated, gun-bearing vessels" were "not capable of sea-service";

[60] 44 Cong. 2 Sess., *H. Ex. Doc.* No. 1, Pt. IV, Vol. III, p. 6.

[61] See J. F. Rhodes, *History of the United States from Hayes to McKinley* (1920), pp. 104*ff.*; and Oberholtzer, *History*, Vol. IV, Chap. XXV.

[62] *M. & P.* (Richardson), Vol. VII, pp. 473, 500, 573.

[63] H. J. Eckenrode, *Rutherford B. Hayes, Statesman of Reunion* (1930), p. 242. One is reminded in this connection of the famous observation of Mr. Dooley (Finley Peter Dunne), that the first qualification of a Secretary of the Navy was that he should never have seen salt water outside of a pork barrel.

[64] Annual reports for 1877 and 1879. 45 Cong. 2 Sess., *H. Ex. Doc.* No. 1, Pt. III, Vol. VII, p. 10; and 46 Cong. 3 Sess., *H. Ex. Doc.* No. 1, Pt. III, Vol. VIII, p. 35.

that they were "suited for but little else than harbor defense" and might "be likened to movable fortifications."[65] And, in 1879, after two years in office, he still professed to believe that it was an open question whether European navies were really superior to our own.[66]

Lacking intelligent executive leadership, preoccupied with internal problems, and torn by partisan strife, Congress did little but mark time. The Democratic majority in the House, eager to expose Republican derelictions, probed into the administration of the Navy Department.[67] Increasingly aware that something was radically wrong with the Navy, Senators and Representatives showed a strong disposition to curtail appropriations pending a thorough overhauling.[68] But congressional steps in the direction of reform were halting and inconclusive. The House and Senate Naval Affairs Committees deprecated the situation, but had little to offer in the way of a constructive legislative program.[69] And a serious, if inadequate, reform measure, after passing the House of Representatives, was shelved in the Senate on the last day of February 1881.[70]

Nevertheless, the United States was at this very moment on the threshold of a new era in naval development. As we shall see in the next chapter, a fortuitous concurrence of events, following the succession of General James A. Garfield to the presidency, in March 1881, set in motion the long-delayed process of rejuvenation that resulted in the rise of the New Navy.

[65] 45 Cong. 2 Sess., *H. Ex. Doc.* No. 1, Pt. III, Vol. VII, p. 13.

[66] 46 Cong. 2 Sess., *H. Ex. Doc.* No. 1, Pt. III, Vol. VIII, p. 25.

[67] See 45 Cong. 2 Sess., *H. Misc. Doc.* No. 63; and 45 Cong. 3 Sess., *H. Misc. Doc.* No. 21.

[68] Naval expenditures were curtailed from an average of approximately $20,000,000 per annum for the period 1869–1877, to an average of only $15,000,000 for the period 1877–1881.

[69] See 45 Cong. 3 Sess., *H. Rept.* No. 112; 46 Cong. 2 Sess., *H. Rept.* No. 169; and 46 Cong. 2 Sess., *S. Rept.* No. 653.

[70] 46 Cong. 2 Sess., *Congressional Record* (Vol. X), pp. 618, 2410–17, 2441, 3600; and 46 Cong. 3 Sess., *op. cit.* (Vol. XI), pp. 2196–205.

CHAPTER TWELVE

☆ ☆

Beginnings of the New Navy (1881–1889)

THE year 1881 was an historic milestone in the rise of American naval power. The process of naval reconstruction was commenced in that year. This work proceeded haltingly at first, encumbered with strategic and technological prejudices carried over from the previous period. Nearly a decade was to elapse before Captain Alfred Thayer Mahan's great book, *The Influence of Sea Power Upon History, 1660–1783,* cleared the way for a revolutionary advance in American thinking on the subject of naval strategy and defense, comparable to the revolution in naval technology which had been in progress for more than a quarter of a century. And a generation was to elapse before Mahan's capital-ship, or command-of-the-sea, theory finally and conclusively superseded the commerce-raiding and passive-coast-defense theories as the basic doctrine of American naval policy.

Political and Economic Background of Reform

When James A. Garfield entered the White House, March 4, 1881, conditions were at last favorable for naval reconstruction. In the economic sphere, the country had recovered substantially from the depression of the 'seventies. Beginning with 1880, the Federal Treasury showed a large and increasing surplus revenue. This surplus, despite a momentary contraction in the middle 'eighties, averaged more than $100,000,000 a year from 1881 to 1889, giving a strong incentive to increased governmental expenditures.[1] During this decade, American industries in general, and manufacturing in particular, were undergoing a phenomenal development. Along with this went a corresponding growth of foreign trade, especially exports, which was to bring the United States increasingly in conflict with the imperialistic and mercantilistic policies of the European Powers. An excess of merchandise exports over imports, popularly known as a "favorable" balance of trade, had by now become the rule. With the rapid growth of exports went a reviving interest in rebuilding the American merchant marine which, it was believed, would further stimulate the country's foreign trade. And all this gave added impetus to the rising movement for naval reconstruction.[2]

The political situation was also propitious. As the *New York Herald* put it: "The accession of General Garfield to the presidency" closed "the cycle in which our politics turned upon the Civil War and its immediate consequences. . . ."[3] Moreover, for the first time in six years, one political party, and that one the Republican Party, controlled both branches of Congress as well as the presidency. With relative quiet prevailing in domestic politics, the incoming Administration was free to look abroad. It was suddenly realized with alarm that several South American republics had been acquiring warships, any one of which single-handed could probably destroy the entire United States Navy.[4] It was rumored that the Great Powers of Europe were contemplating joint control of the canal which a French company was projecting across the Isth-

[1] See E. M. Earle, "The Navy's Influence on Our Foreign Relations," *Current History,* Vol. XXIII (Feb. 1926), pp. 648, 650. For further details, see D. R. Dewey, *Financial History of the United States* (6th ed., 1918), Chap. XVIII.

[2] For commercial and industrial aspects, see any of the standard economic histories. H. U. Faulkner, *American Economic History* (1924), Chap. XXIII, is especially good in this connection.

[3] Feb. 10, 1881, p. 6.

[4] This point was frequently raised in congressional debates on naval reconstruction. See, for example, 47 Cong. 2 Sess., *Congressional Record* (Vol. XIV), pp. 1404, 1420, 1563; and 48 Cong. 1 Sess., *op. cit.* (Vol. XV), p. 1421.

mus of Panama. In the islands of the Pacific, in the Far East, and elsewhere, Americans were dabbling in a small way in the imperialistic struggle that was steadily gathering momentum. President Garfield's Secretary of State, James G. Blaine of Maine, was a harbinger of that union of militant nationalism and resurgent mercantilism that was soon to sweep the American people into the tide-rip of world politics. Blaine's aggressive utterances, especially his stern denunciation of European control of the proposed isthmian canal, focused public attention on the antithetical interests of the European Powers and the United States, and called forth an imperious demand for a navy to put teeth into the Monroe Doctrine and other policies of the United States.[5]

Another source of pressure was the Navy itself. For years, various groups within the Service had been fighting doggedly for reform. While there was little agreement among these groups as to how large, or what kind of, a navy the United States should have, there was universal dissatisfaction with the negative policy which was destroying this branch of the national defense.[6]

Finally, as noted in the preceding chapter, there were accumulating indications of congressional dissatisfaction. The House Naval Affairs Committee, beginning with the famous Navy Department Investigation of 1876,[7] had collected and

[5] See, for example, the following editorials in the *New York Herald*: "An Imperative Duty" (Dec. 5, 1881); "The Panama Canal and the Navy" (Dec. 9); "Our Foreign Relations and the Need of a Navy" (Dec. 12); "The Isthmian Canal and the Monroe Doctrine" (Dec. 17).

[6] For a cross-section of professional naval opinion on the condition of the Navy at the close of the Grant administration, see 44 Cong. 1 Sess., *H. Misc. Doc.* No. 170, Pt. VIII. In 1877, the Senate published a comprehensive report by Chief Engineer J. W. King, on European ships of war, etc., 44 Cong. 2 Sess., *S. Ex. Doc.* No. 27. This excellent report, revised and enlarged to include all the navies of the world, was published in book form under the title, *The Warships and Navies of the World.* Following the publication of King's book, in the summer of 1880, Lieutenant E. W. Very brought out, later in the same year, a similar book entitled *Navies of the World.* In January 1879, there appeared the first issue of a new periodical entitled *The United Service*, which henceforth became a forum of professional opinion, supplementing the older *Army and Navy Journal* and *Proceedings of the United States Naval Institute.*

[7] 44 Cong. 1 Sess., *H. Misc. Doc.* No. 170.

analyzed a great deal of information on naval policy and administration.[8] And despite the partisan motives which had obviously inspired much of this activity, the effect of such persistent criticism was to foster a demand for reform, which had begun to find expression in the forty-sixth Congress (1879–1881),[9] and which awaited only intelligent and vigorous executive leadership to set in motion the process of naval reconstruction.

Naval Progress in the 'Eighties

With the stage thus set for reform, President Garfield invited William H. Hunt of Louisiana to preside over the Navy Department. Hunt was selected chiefly because of Garfield's desire to give the South some representation in his Cabinet.[10] But it was a fortunate if fortuitous choice, for Hunt possessed not only a long-standing personal interest in the Navy,[11] but also the energy, tact, and managerial skill so essential to tangible progress at this critical juncture.

Hunt's first move was to surround himself with the ablest professional advisers available. His second was to appoint a board of naval officers to formulate plans for rebuilding the Navy. His third was to send this board's report to Congress with a strong plea for immediate action. And his fourth was to bring together selected Senators, Representatives, and naval officers for a general discussion of naval policy, a new de-

[8] See 45 Cong. 2 Sess., *H. Misc. Doc.* No. 63; 45 Cong. 3 Sess., *H. Misc. Doc.* No. 21; 45 Cong. 3 Sess., *H. Rept.* No. 112; and 46 Cong. 2 Sess., *H. Rept.* No. 169.

[9] 46 Cong. 2 Sess., *Cong. Record* (Vol. X), pp. 618, 2410–17, 2441, 3600; and 46 Cong. 3 Sess., *op. cit.* (Vol. XI), pp. 2196–205.

[10] See Thomas Hunt, *Life of William H. Hunt* (1922), p. 216; and *New York Herald*, March 3, 1881, p. 3.

[11] As a Union man in New Orleans during the Civil War, Hunt had thrown open his home to the officers of Admiral Farragut's fleet. See letter signed "a line officer" in *New York Herald*, Dec. 12, 1881, p. 4. In addition, one of Hunt's sons was an officer in the Navy, a fact which unquestionably enhanced his interest in naval reform. See B. A. Fiske, *From Midshipman to Rear Admiral* (1919), p. 80.

parture which materially helped to overcome the mutual prejudice and misunderstanding between Congress and the Service.[12]

The assassination of President Garfield unsettled the Administration before it fairly got under way. But this tragic event, while it interrupted the process of naval reconstruction, did not permanently halt the work which Hunt had so auspiciously inaugurated. President Arthur strongly endorsed Hunt's program.[13] And when the latter presently resigned, the man whom Arthur, for purely political reasons, selected to succeed Hunt, brought to the Navy Department, also quite by accident, an abundance of energy, a marked talent for organization, and a strong personal interest in naval reconstruction.[14] This man, William E. Chandler of New Hampshire, presided over that department for three critical years. He was severely criticized, then and later, both for blunders that held back the work of reconstruction, and for playing favorites, in particular with John Roach, the shipbuilder, to whom were awarded the contracts for the first ships of the New Navy.[15] But such criticism, much of it well founded, should not obscure Chandler's service in pushing forward the rebuilding of the Navy in the face of discouraging technical and political obstacles.[16]

This work of naval reconstruction involved two distinct problems. The first was to get rid of the wooden vessels of the Old Navy, which were potentially useless for war, and a constant source of expense in peace. The second was to replace these obsolete craft with modern warships, embodying the

[12] Hunt, *Hunt*, pp. 218–38; 47 Cong. 1 Sess., *H. Rept.* No. 653, pp. xxi–xxii, 190–213.

[13] *Messages and Papers of the Presidents* (Richardson's 1st ed.), Vol. VIII, pp. 51–2; G. P. Howe, *Chester A. Arthur, A Quarter Century of Machine Politics* (1934), pp. 232–3.

[14] F. L. Paxson, "William Eaton Chandler," *Dict. Am. Biog.*, Vol. III, pp. 616–18; Fiske, *Midshipman to Rear Admiral*, p. 81; Howe, *Arthur*, p. 233.

[15] See E. P. Oberholtzer, *History of the United States Since the Civil War* (1917–1931), Vol. IV, pp. 341–7.

[16] See Chandler's annual reports, 1882–1884; and Howe, *Arthur*, Chap. XXI.

revolutionary advances that had been, and were still, taking place in naval architecture.

Congress met the first problem by limiting repairs on the old men-of-war. It was enacted in 1882, that no wooden warship should receive repairs amounting to more than 30 per cent of the cost of a new vessel of the same size and class.[17] The following year this limitation was changed to 20 per cent, which insured the still earlier retirement of the remaining vessels of the Old Navy.[18]

Congress also attacked the second problem in 1882,[19] but the real legislative origin of the New Navy dates from the authorization in 1883, of four steel vessels—the protected (but unarmored) cruisers[20] *Chicago, Boston,* and *Atlanta,* and the so-called dispatch boat *Dolphin.* These ships emphasized the transition through which the Navy was then passing. They carried the familiar rigging and sails of the earlier period. The *Chicago,* largest of the four, was only 325 feet long and displaced only 4,500 tons. They showed serious defects of design. Only the *Chicago* attained a speed as high as 18 knots.[21] Yet with all their defects, these ships, completed between 1885 and 1887, and popularly known and publicized as the "White Squadron," provided tangible evidence of the physical rebirth of American naval power, and aroused the

[17] *Statutes at Large,* Vol. XXII, p. 291; 47 Cong. 1 Sess., *Cong. Record* (Vol. XIII), p. 5568. The idea apparently originated in Congress rather than in the Navy Department. 46 Cong. 2 Sess., *Cong. Record* (Vol. X), p. 2411.

[18] Act of March 3, 1883, reprinted in 65 Cong. 3 Sess., *S. Doc.* No. 418, p. 14. This document, entitled *Navy Yearbook, 1917 and 1918,* is one of a long series of annual reference books of the same name, published each year down to 1921, as a congressional document. For the sake of uniformity and brevity we have invariably cited the one just designated by the short title, *Navy Yearbook, 1917.*

[19] For a concise review of the proceedings in Congress during 1881–1882, see 47 Cong. 2 Sess., *Cong. Record* (Vol. XIV), pp. 1562*ff.*

[20] The term "protected cruiser," no longer used, designated a warship with a thick steel deck designed to give some protection to the vessel's interior. Armored warships—battleships and armored cruisers (which latter evolved into the battle cruiser)—carried armor plate on their sides as well as on their decks.

[21] *Navy Yearbook, 1917,* p. 738; Allan Nevins, *Grover Cleveland* (1932), pp. 219*ff.*; Ann. Rept., Sec. of the Navy, 1885, 49 Cong. 1 Sess., *H. Ex. Doc.* No. 1, Pt. III, pp. xix*ff.*

popular enthusiasm necessary to sustain further progress in naval reconstruction.

After its first tentative steps in 1883, Congress voted no more ships for two years. And when it did, in March 1885, the authorization was limited to two additional small cruisers and two still smaller so-called gunboats.[22] Change of administration immediately thereafter, gave a fresh impetus to naval reconstruction. While neither President Cleveland nor his Secretary of the Navy, William C. Whitney, a prominent New York financier, were advocates of extravagant naval expansion, both of them were easterners with the prevailing seaboard attitude toward the Navy. In this respect, they were decidedly out of line with the negative naval policy associated with the party of Jefferson and Jackson. And their efforts were constantly impeded by the hostility toward the Navy still prevailing among a large segment of their party supporters in Congress and the country at large. Nevertheless, they accomplished a great deal. Whitney instituted long-overdue administrative reforms. And Congress, under strong Administration leadership, authorized during the next four years (1885–1889) thirty naval vessels of different classes, with an aggregate displacement of nearly 100,000 tons.[23]

These authorizations ranged all the way from fairly large armored ships down to naval tugs. They included two second-class battleships, one armored cruiser, six coast-defense monitors, six protected cruisers, and fifteen smaller vessels of different classes. The battleships were the *Texas* (later renamed the *San Marcos*) and the ill-fated *Maine* whose destruction in Havana Harbor in February 1898, by an explosion of unknown origin, was one of the precipitating causes of the war with Spain. Judged by present-day standards, these ships were scarcely more than gunboats. They displaced less than 7,000 tons, and had a max-

[22] The protected cruisers *Charleston* (3,730 tons) and *Newark* (4,083 tons), and the gunboats *Petrel* (890 tons) and *Yorktown* (1,710 tons). *Navy Yearbook, 1917*, pp. 29, 738.

[23] Nevins, *Cleveland*, pp. 217*ff.*; *Navy Yearbook, 1917*, p. 738.

imum speed of less than eighteen knots. The *Texas* carried only two heavy (twelve-inch) guns, and the *Maine* only four moderately heavy (ten-inch) guns. Another famous member of this group was the armored cruiser *New York*, renamed *Saratoga*, and later *Rochester*. This vessel, which served as the flagship of Admiral Sampson's fleet in the war with Spain, carried a main battery of six eight-inch guns, displaced slightly more than 8,000 tons, and could attain a speed of twenty-one knots. The third famous warship authorized during this period was the protected cruiser *Olympia*, 5,800 tons, four eight-inch guns, and nearly twenty-two knots speed, remembered as Admiral Dewey's flagship in the battle of Manila Bay, May 1, 1898.

Obstacles to Naval Progress in the 'Eighties

It would be a mistake to conclude that naval reconstruction proceeded smoothly, in accord with any prearranged plan. On the contrary, as already intimated, the work went forward spasmodically, with very little planning at all, and in spite of serious difficulties and obstacles.

Party spirit was one of the most serious of these obstacles. By 1881, the congressional leaders of both major parties were committed to rebuilding the Navy. Republican leaders, perhaps because of their party's industrial affiliation, generally stood for larger and more rapid reconstruction than did the Democrats who still showed a tendency to revert to the small-navy tradition of the Jeffersonian and Jacksonian periods. Honest differences of opinion as to pace, method, and procedure, however, tended constantly to give way before such partisan considerations as desire to discredit the opposing party and to claim for one's own party a monopoly of patriotic zeal and purpose. Thus the Democrats, when in the minority, obstructed Republican naval bills on the stated ground that we should experiment cautiously with new types of naval construction. And the Republicans, when in the minority, criticized the Democrats for not going fast enough or far enough, yet voted against the constructive proposals which the Democratic leadership did offer.

With party spirit running high, the party complexion of Congress changing every two years, and opinion on future naval policy decidedly in flux, it was practically impossible to carry out any consistent program of reconstruction. When, as in 1881–1883, the Republicans controlled both branches of Congress as well as the presidency, it was possible to override partisan opposition.[24] When, as between 1885 and 1889, a Democratic administration had to deal with a Republican majority in one branch of Congress, progress was difficult but still possible because of the generally big-navy trend of Republican leadership.[25] But when, as in the last two years of Arthur's administration (1883–1885), a Republican President faced a hostile Democratic majority in the House, the legislative machinery all but came to a standstill.[26]

Patronage, favoritism, and the spoils system in general, constituted other obstacles to naval reconstruction. A certain class of politicians had long regarded the Navy as legitimate party plunder. As previously noted, seaboard Senators and Representatives had traditionally combined to secure large appropriations for unneeded navy yards. They had utilized every opportunity to expand these establishments which provided jobs for a multitude of party workers. One of the greatest scan-

[24] See the debates on the naval appropriation bills of 1882 and 1883, especially the rollcalls in the House on July 6, 1882, and Jan. 25, 1883. 47 Cong. 1 Sess., *Cong. Record* (Vol. XIII), p. 5698; 47 Cong. 2 Sess., *op. cit.* (Vol. XIV), pp. 1581–2.

[25] See the debates and votes on naval bills in the 49th and 50th Congresses, especially the rollcall in the House on July 24, 1886, on the special bill for increase of the Navy. 49 Cong. 1 Sess., *Cong. Record* (Vol. XVII), p. 7503.

[26] In the summer of 1884 the Republican Senate and the Democratic House reached an impasse over the absolute refusal of the latter to authorize the construction of additional warships recommended by the Administration. 48 Cong. 1 Sess., *Cong. Record* (Vol. XV), proceedings on Senate Bills No. 690, 698, and on House Bill No. 4716, especially pp. 1496, 1667, 2317, 2834, 2923, 5858. This deadlock, continuing to the end of that session and on into the next, prevented any further constructive naval legislation until the closing days of the Arthur administration. 48 Cong. 2 Sess., *Cong. Record* (Vol. XVI), further proceedings on House Bill 4716, and proceedings on House Bills No. 7510, 7791, 7874, 8239.

dals had been the periodic rebuilding of obsolete and worn-out naval vessels under the fiction of necessary repairs. These "repairs" provided work for the navy yards and a market for the materials which favored producers and middlemen furnished at inflated prices. Even after full exposure of these conditions in 1876,[27] the politicians had stubbornly resisted any reform that would deprive them of this highly valued patronage. In particular, they had resisted the movement to curtail repairs on old vessels, and had blocked every attempt to close superfluous yards. As Secretary Chandler well said in 1884: ". . . instead of maintaining such yards . . . only as were necessary for the . . . benefit of our ships, the ships have been made to drag out a protracted existence for the benefit of the yards."[28]

Chandler's cure, however, was almost as bad as the disease. Instead of leading a politically unpopular drive to cut down the Navy's costly and topheavy shore establishment, he merely sidestepped the politics-ridden yards, letting out new construction to private contractors—or rather to one contractor. Under conditions which led to well founded charges of favoritism, Chandler awarded to his shipbuilder friend, John Roach, all the contracts for the new cruisers begun during Arthur's administration.[29]

Another inhibiting factor was inexperience. American naval architects had had no practice in designing modern warships, or American manufactures in building them. The advisory board, designated to draw plans and supervise construction of the vessels authorized in 1883, made costly blunders. And the favored contractor proved unable to adapt his shipbuilding practice to the exacting requirements of modern warship construction. The vessels of the White Squadron, while significant as symbols of our reviving naval power, were of decidedly limited value as instruments of war. As previously noted, these

[27] See 44 Cong. 1 Sess., *H. Misc. Doc.* No. 170.

[28] 48 Cong. 2 Sess., *H. Ex. Doc.* No. 1, Pt. III, p. 16. And see Oberholtzer, *History,* Vol. IV, p. 345; Howe, *Arthur,* p. 235; Nevins, *Cleveland,* pp. 219*ff*.

[29] See Oberholtzer, *History,* Vol. IV, pp. 342–3; Nevins, *Cleveland,* pp. 218–19.

ships were unarmored cruisers, useful only as commerce raiders; yet they lacked the speed absolutely necessary to overhaul fast merchant steamers or to escape from hostile battleships. And the so-called dispatch boat *Dolphin* had numerous fatal defects, not the least of which was the location of its machinery so that a single well placed shell could have utterly disabled it.[30]

Another source of difficulty was defective administrative organization. The Navy Department was still functioning under the bureau system instituted back in 1842 to supersede the Board of Navy Commissioners. There was no inter-bureau coordination except through the political Secretary who was thus burdened with a rapidly growing volume of increasingly technical detail. Although congressional inertia and opposition prevented any comprehensive reorganization of the Department, Secretary Whitney effected numerous administrative reforms between 1885 and 1889, which prepared the way for the rapid expansion of the whole naval establishment in the 'nineties.[31]

Lack of manufacturing facilities also delayed naval reconstruction in the 'eighties. There were no steel mills equipped to roll steel for ship-plates. There were no plants capable of producing armor or gun forgings.[32] To free the United States from a precarious dependence upon foreign producers of these and other essential articles, Congress, in 1886, decreed that builders of American naval vessels use only materials of "domestic manufacture."[33] This requirement, designed to foster Amer-

[30] Ann. Repts., Sec. of the Navy, 1885 and 1886, 49 Cong. 1 Sess., *H. Ex. Doc.* No. 1, Pt. III, p. xix; and 49 Cong. 2 Sess., *H. Ex. Doc.* No. 1, Pt. III, p. 5. And see Nevins, *Cleveland,* p. 219; statement of Representative Abram S. Hewitt, Feb. 23, 1885, 48 Cong. 2 Sess., *Cong. Record* (Vol. XVI), p. 2038.

[31] Nevins, *Cleveland,* p. 221.

[32] Report of the Gun Foundry Board, Feb. 20, 1884, 48 Cong. 1 Sess., *H. Ex. Doc.* No. 97; Arthur's special message to Congress, March 26, 1884, 48 Cong. 1 Sess., *Cong. Record* (Vol. XV), p. 2317; *ibid.,* pp. 2759–64; Ann. Rept., Sec. of the Navy, 1888, 50 Cong. 2 Sess., *H. Ex. Doc.* No. 1, Pt. III, p. iii; and Nevins, *Cleveland,* p. 218.

[33] *Navy Yearbook, 1917,* pp. 33–4, and index, title: "domestic materials"; also Ann. Repts., Sec. of the Navy, 1886 and 1887, 49 Cong. 2 Sess., *H. Ex. Doc.*

ican steel and munitions industries, inevitably delayed construction of the New Navy. But it did have the desired effect, and by the end of Cleveland's first term (1889), the day was in sight when the country's industrial plants would be able to cope with any type of naval construction.[34] Incidentally, this requirement also had the exceedingly important, if perhaps not wholly foreseen, result of building up a group of industries with a vested interest in a continuous and progressive development of the Navy. These industries were to become active lobbyists and propagandists for naval expansion. And the desirability of keeping these industries prosperous and abreast of new developments in naval technology, was to provide the Navy's official spokesmen with a telling answer to all proposals to curtail naval construction.[35]

Certain prejudices carried over from the period of neglect and decay still further retarded the work of naval reconstruction. One of the most persistent of these was the prejudice against armored cruising vessels. A prominent officer voiced a sentiment still popular in naval circles, when he declared, in 1881, that the time was approaching "when ships of war will throw off their armor and fight in the lightest rig."[36] And Senator Washington C. Whitthorne of Tennessee expressed an opinion equally popular in congressional circles, when he likened the unarmored cruisers of the New Navy to the cavalry of an army, and argued that these cruisers could so harry an approaching fleet of battleships as to exhaust, if not destroy, them before they ever reached our shores.[37]

Another inhibiting prejudice was the reluctance to give up sails. In the summer of 1882, Congress resolved that the cruising vessels of the New Navy should have "full sail-power" as

---

No. 1, Pt. III, pp. 10–12; and 50 Cong. 1 Sess., *H. Ex. Doc.* No. 1, Pt. III, pp. iii–v.

[34] Ann. Rept., Sec. of the Navy, 1888, 50 Cong. 2 Sess., *H. Ex. Doc.* No. 1, Pt. III, pp. iv, viii; and Nevins, *Cleveland,* p. 222.

[35] See, for example, 53 Cong. 3 Sess., *H. Ex. Doc.* No. 1, Pt. III, p. 49; and 55 Cong. 2 Sess., *H. Ex. Doc.* No. III, p. 41.

[36] Rear Admiral John Rodgers, *New York Herald,* Dec. 6, 1881, p. 7.

[37] Speech in the Senate, Feb. 15, 1887. 49 Cong. 2 Sess., *Cong. Record* (Vol. XVIII), p. 1762.

well as "full steam-power."[38] In 1884, Admiral Porter who, it is recalled, was the highest ranking officer in the Navy, insisted that the new cruisers "have enough sail power . . . to go around the world without touching their coal."[39] In that year also, the Secretary of the Navy noted that there was great opposition to equipping these vessels with only partial sail-power.[40] In 1886, another prominent officer described the new cruisers, *Chicago* and *Atlanta,* as a "frigate" and a "sloop-of-war," obsolescent terms harking back to the era of sails.[41] And in that same year, Admiral Porter was heard again, pleading for the retention of sails, and arguing that the Confederate *Alabama* of Civil War fame was a better cruiser than any of the new steel vessels under construction.[42]

Still another inhibiting influence was the continued vogue of those strategic theories which had so long dominated American naval policy. The plan, formulated in 1881 by Secretary Hunt's advisory board, rested upon the characteristic American assumption that commerce raiding and passive coast defense were the Navy's two wartime functions,[43] a view which overwhelmingly prevailed in naval and congressional circles through the 'eighties. All we needed for offensive purposes, according to the controlling opinion of that day, was a fleet of fast unarmored cruisers to raid hostile merchant shipping, to engage an enemy's light cruisers, and to harry the battleships of an attacking fleet. The day had not yet come when any considerable segment of American opinion would grasp the risk of relying chiefly upon this type of offensive strategy in case of war with a major naval Power.[44]

[38] *Navy Yearbook, 1917,* p. 5.

[39] 48 Cong. 1 Sess., *S. Rept.* No. 161, p. 87.

[40] 48 Cong. 2 Sess., *H. Ex. Doc.* No. 1, Pt. III, pp. 4–5.

[41] Rear Admiral Edward Simpson, "The United States Navy in Transition," *Harper's Monthly Magazine,* Vol. LXXVIII (June 1886), pp. 3–26.

[42] 49 Cong. 2 Sess., *H. Ex. Doc.* No. 1, Pt. III, pp. 54, 65.

[43] 47 Cong. 1 Sess., *H. Ex. Doc.* No. 1, Pt. III, pp. 27–38.

[44] Discussions of commerce-raiding recur frequently in congressional debates on naval bills during the 'eighties, especially after 1885 when the question of building armored cruising vessels came to the fore. For representative samples of this view, see 49 Cong. 2 Sess. *Cong. Record* (Vol. XVIII), pp. 1762, 2346; and 50 Cong. 1 Sess., *op. cit.* (Vol. XIX), pp. 6719, 6720.

The prevailing defensive strategy still rested on the ancient doctrine of stopping an enemy at the coast. This strategy envisaged little more than defending our principal seaports from actual bombardment and hostile occupation, and practically ignored the problem of dealing with commercial blockades such as those which played so decisive a rôle in the War of 1812 and the Civil War. Discussion of rams, mines, torpedo boats, gunboats, and monitors, running to scores of pages in the *Congressional Record*, revealed the extent to which Senators and Representatives were still thinking in terms of passive coast defense. In 1882, George M. Robeson, formerly Secretary of the Navy (1869–1877), and now a member of the House of Representatives, led a movement to complete the still unfinished double-turreted monitors, declaring dogmatically, and also incorrectly, that monitors were "the accepted type which the experience of all maritime nations . . . has adopted as the most efficient vessels for . . . harbor and coast defenses."[45] And as late as 1887, Admiral Porter advised repairing the aged and rotting single-turreted monitors of the Civil War period, and recommended building as many new monitors as cruisers, arguing that vessels of the monitor type, properly equipped and handled, "would be a match for the heaviest European ironclad that could reach our shores."[46] While grave doubts were expressed as to the value of these ancient floating batteries,[47] it was nevertheless decided to complete several of the better ones.[48] The continued vogue of the monitor type of warship, together with an amazing proposal to revive and adapt Jefferson's

[45] 47 Cong. 1 Sess., *op. cit.* (Vol. XIII), p. 5453.

[46] 49 Cong. 2 Sess., *H. Ex. Doc.* No. 1, Pt. III, pp. 54, 55, 60, 61; and 50 Cong. 1 Sess., *H. Ex. Doc.* No. 1, Pt. III, pp. 27, 69.

[47] See, for example, 47 Cong. 1 Sess., *Cong. Record* (Vol. XIII), pp. 5453, 5463; 47 Cong. 2 Sess., *op. cit.*, (Vol. XIV), pp. 1404, 1509; 48 Cong. 1 Sess., *op. cit.* (Vol. XV), p. 5860.

[48] See Report of the second Advisory Board, Dec. 30, 1882. 47 Cong. 2 Sess., *H. Ex. Doc.* No. 28; Ann. Rept., Sec. of the Navy, 1883, 48 Cong. 1 Sess., *H. Ex. Doc.* No. 1, Pt. III, p. 6; President Arthur's special message to Congress, March 26, 1884. 48 Cong. 1 Sess., *Cong. Record* (Vol. XV), p. 2317; and statutory provisions reprinted in *Navy Yearbook, 1917*, pp. 22, 33, 42, 52.

discredited gunboat system.[49] speaks eloquently of the extent to which the strategic fallacy of passive coast and harbor defense still dominated the naval policy of the United States.[50]

Finally, one should not overlook the inhibiting effects of our geographical and political isolation. Senators, Representatives, and Secretaries of the Navy pointed frequently to the rapid progress and vastly superior power of European navies, but practically no one felt any grave anxiety on that score.[51] The possibility of war with a European Power was "not lost sight of," but "our isolated location" and our "traditional" policy of peace rendered it "a remote contingency. . . ." We should maintain an "ascendancy in the affairs of the American hemisphere," but it was not our policy "to maintain a fleet able at any time to cope on equal terms with the foremost European armaments,"[52] and certainly not to carry a war into European waters.[53] It was even frequently suggested that we should leave European admiralties to carry on costly experiments in naval ordnance and architecture, doing little or nothing ourselves until naval technology should have reached a point of static perfection.[54]

[49] See an anonymous article entitled "Naval Reorganization" in *The United Service*, Vol. II (April 1880), pp. 460–7; 48 Cong. 1 Sess., *S. Rept.* No. 161, p. 90; and 48 Cong. 1 Sess., *Cong. Record* (Vol. XV), pp. 1208–9.

[50] Not until 1892 did the Navy Department formally reverse its position with regard to the monitor. See 52 Cong. 2 Sess., *H. Ex. Doc.* No. 1, Pt. III, p. 32.

[51] Representative Hiscock of New York, himself an advocate of naval preparedness, well said, in 1883: ". . . . if there were any deep-seated . . . sentiment among the people that we ought to increase and build up our Navy, the present Congress as well as past Congresses would have received demonstrations upon this subject which would have demanded an affirmative answer." 47 Cong. 2 Sess., *Cong. Record* (Vol. XIV), p. 1556.

[52] Report of the Secretary of the Navy for 1883. 48 Cong. 1 Sess., *H. Ex. Doc.* No. 1, Pt. III, p. 8.

[53] Statement of Rear Admiral Robert W. Shufeldt before the Senate Naval Affairs Committee. 48 Cong. 1 Sess., *S. Rept.* No. 161, p. 21.

[54] For a typical sample of this argument, see the plea of Representative Atkins of Tennessee, July 5, 1882: "Now, I do not see any very great necessity for being in a hurry about building up a navy. Let us wait, sir, until naval invention and naval construction shall have reached that perfection which will present a model that we may safely adopt." 47 Cong. 1 Sess., *Cong. Record* (Vol. XIII), p. 5651. And see the critical comment on this argument in Alfred T. Mahan's *From Sail to Steam*, p. 268, and in a speech by Representative Herbert of Alabama, 49 Cong. 1 Sess., *op. cit.* (Vol. XVII), p. 7475.

One remarkable episode in particular reveals the state of mind then prevailing even within the Service. During the 'eighties, a talented young officer, Lieutenant (later Rear Admiral) Bradley A. Fiske, invented a number of precision instruments for range-finding, gun-pointing, and gun-sighting. Exclusive possession of such instruments would obviously give a decisive advantage over navies relying on more primitive methods of fire control. Yet the Navy Department not only allowed Fiske to manufacture and market these instruments freely, but also to advertise and sell them to the leading European admiralties. Years afterward, Fiske was to marvel that he should have done such a thing, or that the authorities should have allowed it. The explanation, he believed, lay in the "state of public opinion then even in the Navy . . . absolute conviction in the minds of everybody that the United States would never go to war again, and that our Navy was maintained simply as a measure of precaution against the wholly improbable danger of our coast being attacked."[55]

Strategic Ideology in Transition

At this very moment, however, the ideology of American naval policy was undergoing a profound, if belated, transformation. Here and there for years, as we have noted in earlier chapters, there had been isolated and sporadic dissents from the prevailing doctrines of American naval policy. Now, in the 'eighties, there were unmistakable indications of growing unrest and dissatisfaction with these traditional doctrines. "Masts and sails," it was argued, cut down a warship's speed and detracted from its "fighting qualities."[56] And there was a dawning recogni-

[55] *From Midshipman to Rear Admiral,* p. 133. The sequel was no less illuminating. While in France, Fiske was allowed to witness the maneuvers of the French fleet. "As I was only an American naval officer," he noted in retrospect, "I was accorded privileges that would not have been accorded to a European officer, and permitted to see things such as would have been kept close secrets from an officer of a navy that was seriously regarded." *ibid.*, p. 141.

[56] See Ann. Rept., Sec. of the Navy, 1884. 48 Cong. 2 Sess., *H. Ex. Doc.* No. 1, Pt. III, p. 5; and see 48 Cong. 1 Sess., *S. Rept.* No. 161, p. 19; and 49 Cong. 1 Sess., *H. Rept.* No. 993, pp. 8–9.

tion that an unarmored cruiser must have speed. Such a vessel was a "commerce destroyer." "If slower than ironclads," she "could not keep the sea, and if slower than merchantmen she might as well stay in port."[57]

Especially significant was the mounting criticism of the strategic postulates of our traditional naval policy. In 1881, four members of Secretary Hunt's Advisory Board dissented from the majority's decision to recommend only unarmored cruisers. Such vessels, argued the minority which included John Lenthall and Benjamin F. Isherwood, who had advocated sea-going ironclads as far back as 1862, could "not be properly considered as fighting machines, although they carry a respectable armament," for they would have "to fly the presence of all foreign ironclads, even those of the least dimensions and thinnest armor."[58] Subsequently, in conference, Isherwood reiterated that we must eventually have sea-going armored warships "to prevent our ports being blockaded by foreign ironclads." Otherwise, we would encounter "the same difficulty as was experienced in the War of 1812," when our privateers captured many prizes but could not get them into port.[59]

In 1885, the Navy Department moved cautiously and tentatively in this direction, recommending construction of one large "sea-going armored vessel. . . ."[60] The House Naval Affairs Committee, reporting a bill to authorize two such vessels, explained that we needed powerful battleships "capable of keeping the sea for long periods" and of following an enemy's forces to any menaced point along our coast.[61]

In 1886, a board appointed to survey the problem of coastal fortifications, the so-called Endicott Board, based its report on the assumption that if the United States should "hereafter" build a considerable number of "armored sea-going ships,"

[57] Ann. Rept., Sec. of the Navy, 1886. 49 Cong. 2 Sess., *H. Ex. Doc.* No. 1, Pt. III, p. 5; and 50 Cong. 2 Sess., *H. Ex. Doc.* No. 1, Pt. III, p. viii.

[58] 47 Cong. 1 Sess., *H. Ex. Doc.* No. 1, Pt. III, p. 42.

[59] Navy Department Conference, Feb. 15, 1882. 47 Cong. 1 Sess., *H. Rept.* No. 653, p. 198.

[60] Report of the Bureau of Construction and Repair for 1885. 49 Cong. 1 Sess., *H. Ex. Doc.* No. 1, Pt. III, p. 253.

[61] 49 Cong. 1 Sess., *H. Rept.* No. 993, p. 8.

these ships "would act offensively and [would] not be confined to the defense of ports."[62]

Senator Matthew C. Butler of South Carolina carried the argument a step further. In 1887 and again in 1888, he characterized commerce raiding as an "insignificant kind of guerrilla, bushwhacking warfare," and brushed aside the strategy of passive coast and harbor defense. Give us a strong fleet of first-class battleships, he argued, and the coast would take care of itself.[63]

In retrospect, it is clear that these scattered utterances were harbingers of a coming revolution in American naval policy. At the moment, however, they attracted little attention. In 1886, it is true, Congress authorized the two armored warships recommended by the House Naval Affairs Committee,[64] and two years later, voted a still larger "armored cruiser."[65] But a visitor in the congressional galleries, while these and other capital-ship proposals were being debated, would have heard very little intelligent discussion of the strategic implications of this new trend in naval construction.[66] Legislation, in short, was outrunning theory. This had happened before, notably in 1816 when Congress had authorized building a fleet of "seventy-fours," capital ships of the era of sails.[67] On that occasion, an auspicious beginning had degenerated into haphazard development, in part because of confused notions as to the function of capital ships. Now, a somewhat similar beginning was destined to usher in a revolution in American naval strategy, partly because conditions were generally more propitious, but also

[62] The naval members of this board, Commanders W. T. Sampson and C. F. Goodrich, were undoubtedly the authors of this passage. 49 Cong. 1 Sess., *H. Ex. Doc.* No. 49, Pt. I, p. 9.

[63] 49 Cong. 2 Sess., *Cong. Record* (Vol. XVIII), p. 1807; and 50 Cong. 1 Sess., *op. cit.* (Vol. XIX), p. 6720.

[64] *Navy Yearbook, 1917*, p. 33.

[65] *ibid.*, p. 46.

[66] See, for example, 49 Cong. 1 Sess., *Cong. Record* (Vol. XVII), pp. 7474–502; 49 Cong. 2 Sess., *op. cit.* (Vol. XVIII), proceedings on Senate bill 3288; and 50 Cong. 1 Sess., *op. cit.*, (Vol. XIX), proceedings on House bill 10556.

[67] See pp. 88*ff.*, *supra.*

because theory overtook and then kept pace with legislation. As the 'eighties had witnessed the beginnings of the New Navy, so were the 'nineties to be remembered for the beginnings of the new naval policy that stemmed from the teaching and writing of Captain Alfred Thayer Mahan.

CHAPTER THIRTEEN

☆ ☆

Alfred Thayer Mahan: Sea Power and the New Manifest Destiny (1889–1897)

THE intellectual awakening foreshadowed in the 'eighties was fortuitously hastened by the establishment, in 1884, of the Naval War College at Newport, Rhode Island. While this institution was founded for the express purpose of providing post-graduate instruction in history, international law, and the higher branches of naval art and science, there is little evidence that either the forward-looking officers who sponsored this project, or the Secretary of the Navy who put it into execution, envisaged the far-reaching consequences that were to follow within a very short time.

These consequences arose from the early appointment to the War College faculty of a middle-aged officer named Alfred Thayer Mahan who was chosen to lecture on naval history and tactics. While Captain Mahan had published a book on the naval operations of the Civil War,[1] neither that work nor other phases of his previous career would have led one to predict the brilliant future that now lay before him.[2] Released from routine duties, Mahan developed a remarkable talent for scholarship. And out of his studies and lectures, there grew a book entitled *The Influence of Sea Power upon History, 1660–1783,* which not only took the leading admiralties by storm,

[1] This book was entitled *The Gulf and Inland Waters* and was published in 1882.

[2] See C. C. Taylor, *The Life of Admiral Mahan* (1920), Chaps. I–III.

but also profoundly affected civilian thinking and public policy in America, Europe, and even the Far East.

Mahan's Philosophy of Sea Power

In this remarkable book, published in 1890, Mahan presented a philosophy of world politics deducible from his studies of the diplomacy, commerce, and wars of the seventeenth and eighteenth centuries. This philosophy was compounded from two distinct, if related, theories. One was a theory of national prosperity and destiny founded upon a program of mercantilistic imperialism. The other was purely and simply a theory of naval strategy and defense.

According to Mahan's imperialistic hypothesis, an expanding foreign commerce was essential to national power and prosperity. To compete successfully in the world-wide struggle for markets, a nation must have a strong merchant marine. Also, by earning the freights that would otherwise go to foreign shipping, such a marine was in itself a source of national prosperity. It was the "wish of every nation" to confine "this business" to "its own vessels."[3]

These merchant vessels must have secure ports at their destinations, and protection throughout their voyages. For the first, a nation must have oversea colonies; for the second, a powerful navy. Such a navy was likewise essential to defend the colonies; and the colonies, in turn, provided indispensable bases to support oversea naval operations.[4]

While a strong navy was necessary to guarantee security to a nation's merchant shipping, a prosperous merchant marine was, at the same time, the backbone of its naval power. Such a marine fostered seafaring and maritime industries. Merchant shipping, a seafaring class, and strong maritime industries, provided "a shield of defensive power behind which" a people could gain

[3] Captain A. T. Mahan, *The Influence of Sea Power upon History, 1660–1783* (1890), p. 26.

[4] *ibid.*, pp. 26–7, 82–3.

time "to develop its reserve of strength."[5] And in countries with representative institutions, such maritime interests would, in turn, exert the pressure necessary to keep the navy at a high standard of power and efficiency.[6]

When, however, as in the case of the United States, a nation had neither colonies nor a large merchant marine engaged in foreign commerce, the problem was altogether different. For us, the present object of naval policy was not to support a program of politico-commercial expansion overseas, but rather to insure foreign neutral shipping free access to our ports whenever we should be involved in war.[7] It was not sufficient that we be able to stop an enemy at the coast.[8] Hostile fleets, well beyond sight of land, could maintain an effective blockade of our principal ports. The only way "to avoid such blockades" was to have "a military force afloat" able at all times to "so endanger a blockading fleet" that it could "by no means keep its place."[9]

Cruisers would not suffice for this purpose. They could not drive off an enemy's capital ships blockading our seaboard. And commerce raiding, the chief function of cruisers, while an important "secondary operation," would neither relieve our own coast nor in itself cripple a powerful maritime enemy. Moreover, commerce raiders, especially since the advent of steam, must have secure and open ports to which they could frequently return for fuel, supplies, and repairs.[10]

Only a fleet of capital ships could keep open our ports, whether to admit neutral foreign shipping or to receive our own cruisers. And this battleship fleet must have the power to drive from the vicinity of our coast any force that any enemy could send against us. While Mahan clearly hoped that the time would soon come when the United States would embark upon a program of expansion overseas, which in turn would neces-

[5] *ibid.*, p. 49.
[6] *ibid.*, p. 88.
[7] *ibid.*, p. 84.
[8] *ibid.*, p. 87.
[9] *ibid.*, p. 86.
[10] *ibid.*, pp. 31, 132, 136–8, 539.

sitate greatly increasing the Navy,[11] our requirements for the time being were comparatively modest. We needed a fighting fleet strong enough to give us battle supremacy, or command of the sea, not in the English Channel, the Indian Ocean, the Western Pacific, or some other remote quarter, but simply throughout a wide zone contiguous to our continental coastline.[12]

Mahan's Impact on American Naval Policy

The conception of command of the sea, which for convenience one may designate simply the capital-ship theory, was not wholly original with Mahan. His contribution lay rather in organizing into a coherent system, or philosophy, the strategic principles which the British Admiralty had been following more or less blindly for over two hundred years. These principles, moreover, had recurrently entered into discussions of American naval policy at different periods of our national development.[13] But these principles had never received official endorsement, either in the utterances of executive statesmen or in the enactments of Congress. It remained for Mahan to restate the capital-ship theory in a clear and forceful manner at a moment when conditions were unusually propitious for its formal adoption as the basic doctrine of American naval policy.

The moment was propitious for several reasons. Naval reconstruction had been steadily gaining momentum during the 'eighties. Thanks to the legislative stipulation requiring "materials of domestic manufacture," and to the efforts of Secretary of the Navy Whitney (1885–1889), our heavy industries would soon be able to supply machinery, ordnance, and armor plate for battleships of the largest size and power.[14]

[11] *ibid.*, pp. 83–4, 88.

[12] This conclusion, while not expressly stated in Mahan's first book, is a necessary inference from his argument. See especially pp. 83–8.

[13] See pp. 13*ff.*, 41*ff.*, 87*f.*, 159, 198*ff.*, *supra*.

[14] See Annual Report of the Secretary of the Navy, 1888. 50 Cong. 2 Sess., *H. Ex. Doc.* No. 1, Pt. III, pp. iii–viii; and C. O. Paullin, "A Half Century of

The domestic political situation was also favorable. Benjamin Harrison, who became President March 4, 1889, was an outspoken advocate of a big navy.[15] His Secretary of the Navy, Benjamin F. Tracy of New York, was a man of marked ability and initiative.[16] For the first time since 1875, a Republican administration had clear Republican majorities in both branches of Congress.[17] And if the Republican majority in the House was rather slender,[18] it was under the firm hand of the new speaker, Thomas B. Reed of Maine, a consistent, if unostentatious, advocate of naval expansion.[19]

The international outlook was also propitious. James G. Blaine's return to the Secretaryship of State foreshadowed an aggressive foreign policy. And in the winter of 1888–1889, a drama was unfolding in the Southern Pacific that was to give a decided impetus to naval development. As the Cleveland administration drew to a close, the relations of Germany, Great Britain, and the United States were rapidly approaching a crisis over conflicting interests in the Samoan Islands. The American interest, centering chiefly on a prospective coaling station in these islands, immediately brought the Navy into the picture. An unfounded rumor, early in March, of a clash between German and American forces in Samoan waters, caused a flurry of excited talk about war, and called attention to the Navy's unreadiness for any such contest.[20] When, a few days later, a terrible hurricane destroyed or disabled three American warships in the Samoan harbor of Apia, the United States was left with

---

Naval Administration in America, 1861–1911," Parts VIII–IX, *Proceedings of the United States Naval Institute,* Vol. XXXIX (1913), pp. 1469, 1480*ff.*

[15] See *New York Herald,* Feb. 20, 1889, p. 5.

[16] See E. C. Smith, "Benjamin Franklin Tracy," *Dict. Am. Biog.,* Vol. XVIII, p. 622.

[17] Between 1881 and 1883 there was a Republican administration and Republican control of both chambers, but the Republicans lacked a clear majority in the Senate. See J. F. Rhodes, *History of the United States from Hayes to McKinley* (1920), p. 341n.

[18] House composition: 156 Democrats, 173 Republicans, 1 Independent.

[19] This conclusion is based on Reed's speeches and votes on naval bills before he became Speaker.

[20] See *New York Herald,* March 9, 1889, p. 3.

"almost no . . . war vessels worthy of the name in the Pacific Ocean."[21] The failure of these old warships to get to sea where they could ride out the storm, tragically advertised their "old fashioned engines and defective steam power,"[22] providing first-rate arguments for a program of accelerated naval construction.

With this background of conditions, events, and personal predilections, naval policy early occupied the attention of the Harrison administration. And Mahan, whose book was approaching completion in the summer and autumn of 1889,[23] provided an ideological basis which made Secretary Tracy's annual report for that year one of the most forceful documents in the entire history of American naval policy. Whether Mahan drafted certain passages, whether Tracy had access to Mahan's manuscript, or whether he merely consulted him, it is difficult to say, but the ideas were indubitably Mahan's.[24]

Defense, not conquest, Tracy held, was the object of American naval policy. But defense required "a fighting force." Unarmored cruisers did not constitute a fighting force, "even when . . . intended exclusively for defense." Such vessels were primarily commerce destroyers. "Destruction of two or three dozen or two or three score of merchant vessels" would "not . . . prevent a fleet of ironclads from shelling our cities. . . ." We must have "armored battleships" with which "to raise blockades" and to "beat off the enemy's fleet on its approach. . . ." We must have a fleet capable of diverting a hostile fleet from our coast "by threatening his own, for a war, though defensive in principle, may be conducted most effectively by being offensive in its operations."[25]

Specifically, the Secretary advocated building "two fleets of

[21] *ibid.,* March 31, 1889, p. 13.

[22] Ann. Rept., Sec. of the Navy, 1889, 51 Cong. 1 Sess., *H. Ex. Doc.* No. 1, Pt. III, p. 36.

[23] Mahan's preface was dated December 1889. The book was published the following May. See Mahan, *From Sail to Steam,* p. 302.

[24] We do know that Tracy and Mahan quickly became intimate, and that Tracy had the highest regard for Mahan. See *ibid.,* pp. 303, 312.

[25] 51 Cong. 1 Sess., *H. Ex. Doc.* No. 1, Pt. III, pp. 3, 4.

battleships," twelve for the Atlantic, eight for the Pacific. Each one should equal the best in existence with respect to "armament, armor, structural strength, and speed." Superior speed was particularly important, for it enabled a fighting ship to "choose her position and keep the enemy at a disadvantage." And the ships must have "uniformly high" speed, for the speed of a fleet was no greater than that of its slowest vessel.[26]

In addition to twenty battleships, we should have at least sixty fast cruisers. Such vessels were "essential adjuncts of an armored fleet. . . ." And they were indispensable for the important, if secondary, functions of attacking an enemy's merchant shipping, and of defending our own against hostile cruisers.[27]

Finally, we should have "at least twenty vessels for coast and harbor defense"—"floating fortresses" with "a powerful battery and the heaviest armor, combined with moderate draft." Such vessels, "although restricted in their range of effectiveness," were nevertheless recommended as "necessary components of a naval force which has a sea-coast to defend."[28]

This official reendorsement of the unseaworthy monitor presents somewhat of an enigma. It possibly reflected the influence of ultraconservative opinion within the Navy Department. Or it may have been a political maneuver to win congressional support for the battleship program. On the whole, we incline to the latter explanation. While it was contended, apparently in good faith, that warships of the monitor type might render valuable service as adjuncts to land fortifications in case a hostile force should evade or break through our battleship fleet,[29] monitors also had political value. Congressmen, especially those from seaboard constituencies, might hesitate to endorse a system that concentrated our fighting forces into

[26] *ibid.*, pp. 10, 11.
[27] *ibid.*, pp. 11, 12.
[28] *ibid.*, p. 11.
[29] Ann. Rept., Sec. of the Navy, 1890. 51 Cong. 2 Sess., *H. Ex. Doc.* No. 1, Pt. III, p. 40; and A. T Mahan, "The United States Looking Outward," *The Atlantic Monthly,* Vol. LXVI (Dec. 1890), pp. 816, 822.

cruising fleets, and thus left the seaboard without visible symbols of naval power. Monitors, even though practically worthless, looked formidable. Stationed permanently in the harbors of our larger port cities, they would inspire confidence and afford training facilities for a naval militia,[30] and incidentally strengthen the political fences of seaboard Senators and Representatives.[31]

Closely following Tracy's report came a still more revolutionary document. This was the report (January 1890) of the so-called Policy Board, a committee of six naval officers[32] whom Tracy had appointed to study the naval requirements of the United States.[33] This board, taking a broad view of its commission, outlined a naval program in terms, not of present requirements, but of the imperialistic program envisaged in Mahan's larger conception of sea power.

The board's analysis of existing conditions disclosed the following: We had "no colonies, nor any apparent desire to acquire them. . . ." Our oversea commerce was largely "carried in foreign vessels. . . ." And our manufacturers were competing "with those of other nations in but few markets. . . ." We had therefore only our continental seaboard to defend. No transoceanic Power could carry on war against us without naval bases in this hemisphere. Only Great Britain, France, and Spain had such bases. Barring hostile combinations—and it was assumed that we could make more favorable alliances than our enemies—we had only Great Britain seriously to consider. And the "conditions" would "not arise" when

[30] Ann. Rept., Sec. of the Navy, 1890, 51 Cong. 2 Sess., *H. Ex. Doc.* No. 1, Pt. III, p. 41.

[31] While such an interpretation may seem rather sophisticated, it is nevertheless a fact that, in 1892, when the battleship program was fairly under way, and Mahan's writings had begun to receive wide currency and acceptance, the same Administration abruptly reversed its earlier stand, declaring flatly that monitors were utterly worthless even as adjuncts to land fortifications. See 52 Cong. 2 Sess., *H. Ex. Doc.* No. 1, Pt. III, pp. 32–3.

[32] The members of this Board were Commodore W. P. McCann, Chairman; Captain R. L. Phythian; Captain W. T. Sampson; Commander W. M. Folger; Lieutenant Commander W. H. Brownson; and Naval Constructor R. Gatewood.

[33] 51 Cong. 1 Sess., *S. Ex. Doc.* No. 43, p. 55.

Great Britain "or any other nation possessing an important commerce" could "detach all her effective navy from her own coast for distant operations." In consequence of all these facts, the chances of our getting into war seemed "to be at a minimum."[34]

However, despite this remarkable security on all frontiers, the board advised immediately building more than two hundred modern warships of all classes, for there were "indications" that we were entering a period of "commercial competition" when we would be "certain to reach out and obstruct the interests of foreign nations"; when we would "compete in earnest . . . for the vast and increasing ocean-carrying trade"; and when the opening of an isthmian canal would "place this nation under great responsibility which may be a fruitful source of danger."[35]

For the defense of our continental coastline, the board recommended a large number of sea-going battleships, "heavily armed and armored," but with limited fuel capacity. These vessels, "all having the same general characteristics of speed and maneuvering power, in order that they might act together as a unit, or in squadrons . . . would serve the purpose of keeping our ports open and destroying an enemy's bases of supplies within a thousand miles of our coast."[36]

For offensive operations, the board advocated a fleet of battleships with a cruising range of 15,000 miles.[37] Such a fleet, able to "remain at sea during a long period," was for cruising "against the enemy," and for attacking "points on the other side of the Atlantic." Ignoring the international repercussions of such a policy, and disclaiming any thought of aggression on our part, the board recommended such a fleet simply as a means of utilizing the old military maxim, that offense is the best defense.[38]

[34] *ibid.*, pp. 3, 4, 9, 10.
[35] *ibid.*, pp. 4, 12, 13.
[36] *ibid.*, p. 11.
[37] That is, 13,000 knots, the expression used by the board.
[38] 51 Cong. 1 Sess., *S. Ex. Doc.* No. 43, p. 11.

This report raised a storm of protest. Although it differed from his own program merely in the larger navy proposed, Secretary Tracy promptly washed his hands of it.[39] Eugene Hale, Republican Senator from Maine, and second ranking member of the Naval Affairs Committee, stated that it "would be difficult . . . to find a Senator" or any "responsible" government "official" who "in the least degree" endorsed the Policy Board's report.[40] Even the pro-navy *New York Herald* damned it as a piece of "naval fanaticism"; and predicted that it would "meet with slender approval unless the spirit and temper of the American people have suddenly and radically changed."[41] From the scores of petitions that descended upon Congress,[42] and from what was said in the two chambers, it would certainly appear that, in the spring of 1890, no such change in opinion had yet occurred.

The House Naval Affairs Committee, however, endorsed that part of the Policy Board's plan that looked toward establishing battleship fleets to command the Western Atlantic, the Caribbean, and the Eastern Pacific. With such an end in view, this committee, at the instigation of its able chairman, Representative Charles A. Boutelle of Maine, made provision in the naval appropriation bill for what he termed[43] "three sea-going, coastline battleships designed to carry the heaviest armor and most powerful ordnance upon a displacement of about eight thousand five hundred tons, with a coal endurance of about five thousand knots. . . ."[44]

In explanation, Boutelle took the position that we did not want a fleet of long-range battleships, but simply a "squadron of defense that will be able to protect our own country from any assault that may be made by sea." But, he continued, tacitly endorsing the arguments of both Tracy and the Policy Board,

39 See *ibid.*, pp. 1–2.

40 51 Cong. 1 Sess., *Congressional Record* (Vol. XXI), p. 5277.

41 Jan. 31, 1890, p. 6.

42 These petitions came from various types of groups, but the most numerous by far were those from the Society of Friends.

43 See 54 Cong. 1 Sess., *Cong. Record* (Vol. XXVIII), p. 3193.

44 51 Cong. 1 Sess., *H. Rept.* No. 1178, p. 16.

such a squadron must consist of "fighting ships," able to keep the sea, and "stand against any that they may have to encounter."[45]

Boutelle developed this argument in debate. We needed a fighting fleet "powerful enough . . . to break the blockade of any of our great maritime ports . . . to drive off foreign aggression from our shores, and to seize and hold those bases of supply in the immediate vicinity of the American coast," possession of which in war "would be absolutely essential to . . . the safety of our coast line." These objectives did not call for vessels of great cruising range. By cutting down fuel endurance to five thousand nautical miles, our battleships could carry heavier armor and larger guns, and still have sufficient radius of action to command the sea from Nova Scotia to the Isthmus of Panama.[46]

The battleship clause evoked great opposition which ranged over a broad field, including all the traditional objections to increasing the Navy and some new ones besides.[47] But the objectors were overruled, the House voting 131 to 105, and the Senate 33 to 18, to build the proposed battleships.[48] While the sectional and partisan cleavage in the Senate was somewhat blurred, that in the House was sharp and clear-cut. In the latter, only 26 Democrats voted for the battleships, only 23 Republicans against them. Of these 26 Democrats, 24 represented constituencies in seaboard States; and of the 23 opposition Republicans, 22 represented interior districts.

Very few Senators and Representatives, however, seemed to understand the implications of what they were doing. Most of the advocates, and practically all the opponents of the proposed legislation, still spoke in terms of local coast defense and commerce raiding. Even Henry Cabot Lodge, then second ranking member of the House Naval Committee, and already

[45] *loc. cit.*

[46] *Cong. Record,* Vol. XXI, p. 3163.

[47] For the debates on the battleship clause in the House, *Cong. Record,* Vol. XXI, pp. 3161–71, 3221–3, 3256–71, in the Senate, pp. 5173–82, 5236–8. 5276–97.

[48] *ibid.,* pp. 3395, 5297.

posing as an authority on naval affairs, asserted with palpable inaccuracy that the battleship proposal introduced nothing new, but was "merely the continuance" of a policy "settled" by the War of 1812, and followed consistently thereafter.[49]

On the contrary, the battleship section of the Act of 1890 implied congressional endorsement of a revolutionary departure in our system of naval defense. This legislation, as its sponsors openly admitted, was but the first step toward creating a fighting fleet to seize command of the open sea;[50] but not all the open sea. The Act carried highly important qualifying words. The phrase "sea-going, *coast-line* battleships," and the stipulated fuel endurance of only five thousand nautical miles, obviously implied, and were unquestionably intended to imply, that our bid for naval supremacy was not to extend much, if at all, beyond a thousand miles or so from the continental seaboard of the United States.

We may note briefly, in concluding this section, that this Act also resulted in the construction of some famous ships. These were the battleships *Indiana, Massachusetts,* and the famous *Oregon* whose spectacular voyage around Cape Horn to join the Atlantic Fleet in the war with Spain provided excellent publicity for the Navy and undoubtedly hastened the building of the Panama Canal. These ships were designed for a standard displacement of slightly more than 10,000 tons. Their speeds varied from 15.5 to nearly seventeen knots. Each carried four thirteen-inch rifles and eight eight-inch pieces in its main battery, a very formidable armament for that day. And their total cost varied from $5,500,000 to $6,500,000.[51]

Sea Power and the New Manifest Destiny

With the passage of the Naval Act of 1890, Congress was clearly reaching out toward the naval policy implicit in Mahan's

[49] *ibid.*, p. 3170.
[50] *ibid.*, pp. 3161, 5276.
[51] *Navy Yearbook, 1917,* pp. 739, 758, 766.

analysis of the existing requirements of the United States. But Mahan, as previously noted, did not regard the United States as permanently destined to remain an isolated, continental Power. On the contrary, he believed that we were destined to become a world Power, with interests and policies calling for the larger conception of sea power set forth in his interpretation of history.

Already, in 1890, he beheld indications that the American people were at last awakening to the greater opportunities awaiting them overseas.[52] And with a view to hastening this process, he plunged into the congenial task of indoctrinating his countrymen with his vision of national power and destiny. In a series of magazine articles, appearing at intervals between 1890 and 1897, and marvellously synchronized with the march of events and the "broadening horizons" of the 'nineties,[53] he set forth his view of America's imperial destiny.[54]

According to Mahan's imperialistic thesis, a nation must expand or else decline. It was impossible to stand still. The American people, after a period of preoccupation with internal development following the Civil War, were again "looking outward" toward foreign lands and markets in search of a richer life and a larger prosperity. But these things were not to be had without a struggle. A restless spirit was stirring other Western peoples who also cherished "aspirations for commercial extension, for colonies, and for influence in distant regions, which may bring . . . them into collision with ourselves."[55]

The American Isthmus, in Mahan's opinion, was the key position in this coming struggle. A canal across the Isthmus would "enable the Atlantic coast to compete with Europe, on equal terms as to distance, for the markets of eastern

[52] See his essay entitled, "The United States Looking Outward," *The Atlantic Monthly*, Vol. LXVI (Dec. 1890), pp. 816*ff*.

[53] See J. W. Pratt, *Expansionists of 1898* (1936), pp. 152, 222, and Chaps. V–VI, *passim*.

[54] These articles were subsequently collected into a single volume entitled, *The Interest of America in Sea Power, Present and Future* (1898).

[55] "U. S. Looking Outward," p. 818.

Asia. . . ."[56] Such a waterway, shortening by thousands of miles the distance between Europe and our Pacific seaboard, would also weaken incalculably the strategic security of our western continental frontier, necessitating large additions to our Navy.[57] "The canal [would] itself . . . become a strategic centre of . . . vital importance."[58] Its security would necessarily become a paramount object of national policy. Realization of this object would hinge on establishing indisputable naval supremacy over the Caribbean and the Eastern Pacific, which would require a further strengthening of our fighting forces afloat, exclusion, as far as possible, of European power from these areas, and acquisition and development of naval bases at strategic points—especially in Cuba[59] and the Hawaiian Islands.[60] The latter, the crossroads of the Pacific, had a threefold importance. Dominion over these islands was essential not only for control of an isthmian canal, but also for defense of our Pacific seaboard, and for supporting American commercial enterprise pushing westward toward Asia.[61] Mahan, indeed, anticipating the "yellow peril" bogey of the next generation, believed that these islands might one day become a vital strategic "outpost" against a "wave of barbaric invasion" from the Far East. To hold this outpost of Western civilization, whether against aggression from the Orient or from Europe, implied "a great extension of our naval power."[62]

The menace of an aggressive, awakened East was a disturbing factor never to be forgotten. Our Western States as well as the Pacific dominions of Great Britain, "with an instinctive shudder have felt the threat," declared Mahan, "which able Europeans have seen in the teeming multitudes of central and

[56] "The Isthmus and Sea Power," *Atlantic Monthly,* Vol. LXXII (Oct. 1893), p. 471.

[57] "U. S. Looking Outward," p. 819.

[58] *loc. cit.*

[59] "The Strategic Features of the Gulf of Mexico and the Caribbean Sea," *Harper's Magazine,* Vol. XCV (Oct. 1897), pp. 680*ff.*

[60] "Hawaii and Our Future Sea Power," *Forum,* Vol. XV (March, 1893), pp. 1*ff.*

[61] *ibid.,* pp. 6–8.

[62] Letter to the *New York Times,* Jan. 31, 1893.

northern Asia. . . ."[63] The emergence of Japan as a rising military power "has fairly startled the world . . ." he added, in 1895, at the close of the Sino-Japanese War.[64] And, two years later, he saw the world entering a period which would decisively settle the question "whether Eastern or Western civilization is to dominate throughout the earth and to control its future." The "mission" of Christian civilization, "which it must fulfil or perish," was to overspread and to assimilate to its "own ideals those ancient and different civilizations . . . at the head of which stand China, India, and Japan."[65]

This crusade called for armed force and a martial spirit. In the imperialistic "rivalries" and conflicting "ambitions" of the Western peoples, Mahan beheld the means of preserving the "martial spirit," which alone could cope "with the destructive forces which from outside and from within threaten to submerge all that the centuries have gained."[66] In the "immense armaments of Europe," he beheld not a "provocation to war," but rather an insurance of peace among the Western Powers,[67] and the elements of a united armed front against a militant, awakened East.[68] In this struggle, sea power would inevitably play an important rôle. And in respect to sea power, no state, in Mahan's view, was "charged with weightier responsibilities than the United States"[69]—responsibilities calling for a development of American naval power far beyond anything yet envisaged in existing plans and legislation.[70]

Mahan was by no means the only prophet of America's im-

[63] "Possibilities of an Anglo-American Reunion," *North American Review,* Vol. CLIX (Nov. 1894), pp. 558–9.

[64] "The Future in Relation to American Naval Power," *Harper's Magazine,* Vol. XCI (Oct. 1895), p. 773.

[65] "A Twentieth Century Outlook," *Harper's Magazine,* Vol. XCV (Sept. 1897), p. 527.

[66] "Anglo-American Reunion," p. 558.

[67] "Isthmus and Sea Power," p. 472; and "Future in Relation to American Naval Power," p. 775.

[68] Letter to the *New York Times,* Jan. 31, 1893.

[69] "Twentieth Century Outlook," p. 532.

[70] See "Future in Relation to American Naval Power"; and "Preparedness for Naval War," *Harper's Magazine,* Vol. XCIV (March 1897), pp. 579*ff.*

perial destiny. Prominent political scientists, sociologists, and historians were also propagating the gospel of imperialism in the early 'nineties.[71] But it was Mahan, and his politically influential friends and satellites, Henry Cabot Lodge and Theodore Roosevelt,[72] who sounded the call to action, marshalling the ideas of national security, commercial expansion, cosmopolitan philanthropy, national honor, and national prestige, in support of a breath-taking program of imperialism and naval aggrandizement.

The Growing Influence of Mahan

While Mahan was propagating the doctrines of sea power and manifest destiny, Congress and the Navy Department were struggling to grasp and to apply the new strategy of naval defense. In 1889, the Department instituted a so-called "squadron of evolution."[73] This squadron, consisting wholly of new vessels, and kept together as a tactical unit, marked an important step toward creation of a fighting fleet.[74] In 1894, the Department reorganized the cruising stations, and arranged to have all vessels on each station assemble periodically for exercises and maneuvers.[75] And by 1897, the North Atlantic Squadron, which then included three first-class battleships, two second-class battleships, and two armored cruisers, had developed into a force which might realistically be called a fighting fleet.[76]

Meanwhile, the process of naval reconstruction was continuing under Democratic leadership. The Fifty-second Congress (1891–1893), in which the Democrats ruled the Lower House

[71] See J. W. Pratt, "The 'Large Policy' of 1898," in *Mississippi Valley Historical Review*, Vol. XIX (Sept. 1932), pp. 219*ff*.

[72] See J. W. Pratt, *Expansionists of 1898*, index, items: Lodge, Roosevelt.

[73] Annual Report of the Secretary of the Navy, 1889. 51 Cong. 1 Sess., *H. Ex. Doc.* No. 1, Pt. III, pp. 87–8.

[74] Strictly speaking, the squadron of evolution was not at the outset a fighting force, since it contained only unarmored cruisers.

[75] Ann. Rept., Sec. of the Navy, 1894. 53 Cong. 3 Sess., *H. Ex. Doc.* No. 1, Pt. III, p. 23.

[76] Ann. Rept., Sec. of the Navy, 1897. 55 Cong. 2 Sess., *H. Doc.* No. III, p. 8.

with an overwhelming majority, voted a fourth first-class battleship,[77] a large armored cruiser,[78] an experimental submarine boat, and three more gunboats.[79] In March 1893 Grover Cleveland began his second term as President. And the following November, his Secretary of the Navy, Hilary A. Herbert of Alabama,[80] inspired by Mahan's second large work, *The Influence of Sea Power upon the French Revolution and Empire, 1793–1812,*[81] endorsed the capital-ship theory of naval defense in terms even stronger than those used by his Republican predecessor.[82]

Herbert took particular exception to the policy of building so many unarmored cruisers,[83] of which Congress had authorized sixteen between 1883 and 1891. Such craft were "not, properly speaking, fighting vessels." They could "destroy merchant ships" and "fight vessels of their own class"; but they could "not meet armored" ships. Furthermore, it was easy to overrate the "military value" of commerce raiding. Cruiser warfare "directed against an enemy's wealth afloat" could do "great damage." French raiders had caused great injury to British commerce during the Napoleonic wars. Confederate raiders had wrought havoc with Union merchant shipping in our own Civil War. But in neither case had such operations affected the outcome in the slightest. On the other hand, the British fleets of capital ships "hunted and destroyed the French vessels of war

[77] U. S. S. *Iowa,* 11,346 tons, seventeen knots, four twelve-inch and eight eight-inch guns, cost about $5,000,000. This ship played a leading rôle under Captain ("Fighting Bob") Evans in the naval battle off Santiago, Cuba, July 3, 1898. *Navy Yearbook, 1917,* pp. 739, 758, 766.

[78] U. S. S. *Brooklyn,* 9,215 tons, flagship of Commodore Winfield S. Schley's "flying squadron" which formed part of Rear Admiral William S. Sampson's fleet in the battle off Santiago.

[79] *Navy Yearbook, 1917,* p. 739.

[80] Herbert came to the Navy Department from the Chairmanship of the House Naval Committee, in which position he had acquired a wide knowledge of naval affairs.

[81] A sequel to *The Influence of Sea Power upon History.* The second work was published in December 1892. See Mahan, *From Sail to Steam,* p. 312.

[82] For Mahan's influence on Herbert, see Taylor, *Life of Mahan,* pp. 34–5.

[83] Technically sub-classified as "protected" and "unprotected" cruisers. Neither class carried any side-armor, but the protected cruisers did have a thick steel deck which afforded some protection against falling projectiles.

at the battle of the Nile, at Cape St. Vincent, and at Trafalgar," and were able as a result to "cut off Napoleon's communications by water." In our Civil War, command of the sea enabled the Union squadrons to blockade the "ports of the Confederacy . . . penetrate its rivers [and] cut off its interior communications" —services which the "public has never yet fully appreciated." The inference was clear. The crying need of the Navy was not more cruisers, but more battleships.[84]

All this was utterly alien to Democratic traditions, but not more so than Herbert's further justification of naval expansion. The Navy was not merely an agency for the defense of the homeland in war, but also an instrument of power with which to promote national interests abroad and generally to put teeth into civilian diplomacy in time of peace. The Navy was to be the spearhead of commercial expansion, to advance and protect American interests in the Far East, the South Seas, Central and South America, and other distant places. "We must make and keep our Navy in such a condition of efficiency as to give weight and power to whatever policy it may be thought wise on the part of our government to assume."[85] And three years later this same Democratic statesman closed his administration of the Navy Department with the parting admonition, that we must have a navy strong enough not merely "to defend our long line of seacoast," but also to "afford unquestionable protection to our citizens in foreign lands, render efficient aid to our diplomacy, and maintain under all circumstances our national honor."[86] From this emphatic endorsement of power politics, it was obviously but a step to Mahan's thesis that oversea colonies were necessary to sustain the naval power deemed so essential for the support of national diplomacy, prestige, and commerce in distant lands and seas.

The financial panic of 1893 and the subsequent depression, resulting in a serious shrinkage of Federal revenue, temporarily

[84] Ann. Rept., 1893. 53 Cong. 2 Sess., *H. Ex. Doc.* No. 1, Pt. III, pp. 37–8.
[85] *ibid.*, pp. 40–1.
[86] Ann. Rept., 1896. 54 Cong. 2 Sess., *H. Doc.* No. III, p. 7.

retarded the Administration's program of naval expansion.[87] But in 1895, though the Treasury was still "in the red," there developed a strong movement to resume the battleship program. Secretary Herbert expressed anxiety lest cessation of naval construction jeopardize the newly established armor-plate and other industries upon which the Navy so heavily depended.[88] At the same time, evidence was not lacking that these same industries were themselves actively striving to bring about a resumption of battleship construction.[89]

Other forces were also working toward this end. The naval battles of the Sino-Japanese War (1894–1895), widely interpreted as proving the fighting value of capital ships, gave a fresh impetus to battleship building.[90] Several controversies with Great Britain, culminating in the Venezuelan Boundary crisis of 1895–1896, furnished effective propaganda material, as did also the Cuban crisis with Spain which finally led to the War of 1898.[91]

Most important, perhaps, of all the factors pointing toward an early resumption of the battleship program was the steadily increasing vogue of Mahan. The Captain's name was not even mentioned in the naval debate of 1890. There was no indication that Senators and Representatives had heard of either his War College lectures or his forthcoming book. Even the congressional leaders who sponsored the initial battleship authorization, seem to have derived their strategic ideas second-hand, through the reports of Secretary Tracy and the Policy Board. By 1895, however, Mahan's name and ideas were well known, frequently cited, and widely if not universally endorsed in congressional circles.[92]

[87] See President Cleveland's Annual Message, 1893, *Messages and Papers of the Presidents* (Richardson's 1st ed.), Vol. IX, p. 451; 53 Cong. 2 Sess., *H. Rept.* No. 728, p. 8; and *Navy Yearbook, 1917*, p. 739.

[88] Annual Report, 1894. 53 Cong. 3 Sess., *H. Ex. Doc.* No. 1, Pt. III, p. 49.

[89] See, for example, 53 Cong. 3 Sess., *Cong. Record* (Vol. XXVII), p. 3113.

[90] 53 Cong. 3 Sess., *H. Rept.* No. 1675, p. 9.

[91] 54 Cong. 1 Sess., *Cong. Record* (Vol. XXVIII), pp. 3239, 4512, 4713, and *passim*; and J. W. Pratt, *Expansionists of 1898*, pp. 204–8.

[92] See, for example, 53 Cong. 3 Sess., *Cong. Record* (Vol. XXVII), pp. 2247, 2251–6, 2307, 3105–13; and 54 Cong. 1 Sess., *op. cit.* (Vol. XXVIII), p. 3249.

Against this background of conditions, events, ideas, and personalities, a Democratic administration and Democratic majorities in House and Senate, carried on the work of creating a fighting fleet. In December 1894, President Cleveland endorsed Secretary Herbert's "plea for . . . three additional battleships."[93] After a strenuous debate in which more speakers than on any previous occasion showed knowledge of the function of battleships, the House passed the requested authorization, voting down, 202 to 67, a motion to strike out the battleship clause.[94] The Senate, where anti-navy sentiment was stronger[95] and more articulate, reduced the number from three to two;[96] and the House concurred in the reduction to save the bill in the last days of the short session.[97]

A year later the drama was reenacted with variations. This time the Administration asked for two battleships;[98] the House, once more under Republican control, voted four;[99] the Senate reduced the number to two;[100] and the chambers finally compromised on three.[101]

Passage of these bills registered explicit and conclusive congressional endorsement of the capital-ship theory of naval defense. In the naval debates of 1895 and 1896, a really substan-

[93] *M. & P.* (Richardson), Vol. IX, p. 540.

[94] 53 Cong. 3 Sess., *H. Rept.* No. 1675, pp. 8*ff*.; and *Cong. Record*, Vol. XXVII, pp. 2240–62, 2301–10, 2460–9.

[95] The greater strength of the anti-navy sentiment in the Senate, which was to persist into the twentieth century, was partially attributable, it would appear, to the equal representation of the States, which resulted in giving an undue influence to the less densely settled States of the Interior.

[96] *Cong. Record*, Vol. XXVII, pp. 3074–125.

[97] *ibid.*, pp. 3232–7. The 53rd Congress (1893–1895) authorized altogether two first-class battleships (*Kearsarge* and *Kentucky*, 11,520 tons, seventeen knots, four thirteen-inch and four eight-inch guns, cost about $5,000,000 each), six torpedo boats, and eight smaller vessels of different types. *Navy Yearbook, 1917*, pp. 739, 758, 766.

[98] See 54 Cong. 1 Sess., *H. Doc.* No. 3, p. lvii.

[99] 54 Cong. 1 Sess., *H. Rept.* No. 904, p. 2; and *Cong. Record*, Vol. XXVIII, pp. 3192–5, 3257.

[100] *ibid.*, pp. 4512, 4651, 4652.

[101] *Navy Yearbook, 1917*, p. 111. These were the first-class battleships *Alabama, Illinois,* and *Wisconsin* (11,552 tons, seventeen knots, four thirteen-inch guns, cost about $4,600,000 each). In addition the 54th Congress authorized thirteen more torpedo boats. *ibid.*, pp. 740, 758, 766.

tial number of Senators and Representatives, for the first time, displayed a fair understanding of the strategic theory implicit in all naval legislation since 1890. And the general endorsement of this theory, that accompanied the process of congressional reorientation, squarely aligned the national legislature with the political executive and with the Service, both of whom were now thoroughly committed to the policy of seizing indisputable command of the sea throughout a wide zone extending outward from our continental seaboards on the Atlantic, the Gulf, and the Pacific.

When the Cleveland administration drew to a close in the winter of 1896–1897, the United States possessed—built, building, or authorized—a navy which, when completed, would go far toward attaining that objective. It would not equal the major European fleets. Such equality was not necessary. The growing instability of the European political equilibrium seriously tied the hands of the Great Powers of that Continent, and rendered progressively improbable any determined aggression from that quarter against the interests of the United States in the northern part of the Western Hemisphere. European instability, in short, enhanced the *relative* power and security of the United States. And in 1897, the day was not far distant when the American Navy, though numerically inferior to those of several European Powers, would hold indisputable command of all the strategic marine approaches to the continental United States.

At the same time, a succession of events, already in process, was to render this strategic objective obsolete even before it could be conclusively realized, and was to launch the American ship of state upon the much bolder and more comprehensive program of politico-naval imperialism which was envisaged and justified in Mahan's larger philosophy of sea power.

CHAPTER FOURTEEN

☆ ☆

Mahan Vindicated: The War with Spain (1897–1901)

THE war with Spain was another historic milestone in the rise of American naval power. Decisive and duly publicized victories enhanced the Navy's popularity at home and prestige abroad. The war, coming after a decade of rapid and highly experimental development, tested the New Navy under conditions sufficiently arduous and exacting to reveal hitherto concealed or unsuspected weaknesses.[1] The wave of popular hysteria produced by the fantastic rumor that the Spanish fleet was steaming across the ocean to attack our Atlantic seaboard, dramatically reemphasized the need of thoroughly informing the American public as to the fundamental principles of naval strategy. At the same time, the war, in plainly demonstrating these fundamentals recently systematized in Mahan's books and articles, provided splendid material for popular education designed to avoid a similar panic in the future.

The war also advanced the imperialistic process envisaged and propagandized by Mahan. The insular accessions which accompanied and followed the war provided the territorial outposts necessary, according to Mahan, to sustain the naval power which was deemed essential for the support of American diplomacy in the Far East. But these outposts themselves required defense. Their acquisition revolutionized the strategic

[1] See *America of Yesterday, as Reflected in the Journal of John Davis Long* (edited by L. S. Mayo, 1923), p. 167.

and political situation of the United States. Like the partition of Oregon and the conquest of California fifty years before, the projection of American sovereignty across the Pacific added enormously to the Navy's responsibilities. And as we shall see in the ensuing chapters, these responsibilities raised all but insoluble problems for American statesmen and their professional naval advisers in the opening years of the twentieth century.

THE NAVY'S APPROACH TO THE WAR: THE RÔLE OF THEODORE ROOSEVELT

The presidential succession of 1897 seemed at the outset to foreshadow another pause in naval reconstruction. The Republican platform of 1896, consistent with that party's well established policy, had advocated "continued enlargement of the Navy," and the National Convention had applauded the reading of this clause;[2] but the naval issue slipped into the background as Republican campaigners fought desperately to stop the Bryan agrarian crusade. Though William McKinley, the Republican nominee, casually endorsed his party's naval plank,[3] he subsequently showed little interest in, or knowledge of, the needs of the Navy.[4] McKinley's choice of John D. Long to head the Navy Department seemed to confirm the forecast of a passive naval policy. Long, former Governor of Massachusetts, was a man of sterling qualities but he had a cautious temperament, and impressed his chief subordinate as being lukewarm, if not actually hostile, to further rapid expansion of the Navy.[5] The outlook for leadership from within the Service seemed especially unfavorable at this time, with an ultraconservative officer

[2] *Official Proceedings of the Republican National Convention of 1896*, p. 84.

[3] McKinley's letter of acceptance, *ibid.*, p. 158.

[4] There are few references to naval policy in McKinley's public addresses, and in his annual messages to Congress he did little more than formally endorse the recommendations of his Secretary of the Navy.

[5] *Selections from the Correspondence of Theodore Roosevelt and Henry Cabot Lodge* (edited by H. C. Lodge, 1925), Vol. I, pp. 268, 273; Ann. Rept., Sec. of the Navy, 1897, 55 Cong. 2 Sess., *H. Doc.* No. 3, p. 41; J. B. Bishop, *Theodore Roosevelt and His Time* (1920), Vol. I, p. 82.

in charge of the Bureau of Navigation,[6] where he was *ex-officio* the Secretary's chief professional adviser on personnel and technical questions. The outlook for congressional initiative was likewise clouded. The Fifty-fifth Congress, though strongly Republican, and seething with war sentiment, took no important steps, during the special session of 1897, either toward strengthening the Navy in general, or toward preparing it for the approaching struggle with Spain.

At this juncture, however, there strode noisily upon the national stage a man who was to dominate American naval development for nearly a generation, and whose influence on policy was to rank second only to that of Mahan. This man was Theodore Roosevelt, whom McKinley, at the behest of the former's influential friends, had just appointed in March 1897 to the post of Assistant Secretary of the Navy.

A systematic attempt to explain the personality and ideas of this extraordinary man might perhaps terminate amid the mazes of endocrinology and psychoanalysis. While such an excursion obviously lies beyond the scope of this study, one cannot hope to understand either the naval background of the war with Spain or American naval policy in the twentieth century, without taking some account of Roosevelt's temperament, personality, and intellectual equipment.

Roosevelt began life with a puny body and a frail constitution. Proud, vain, egotistical, ambitious, and intellectually brilliant, he struggled desperately to overcome his physical handicap. His remarkable success filled him with an "evangelical vitality," a devotion to the "strenuous life," that colored every phase of his subsequent career. And his struggle for health and bodily strength, along with his other temperamental qualities, gave a cast to his personality which has been described by the phrase "perpetual adolescence," one manifestation of

[6] Rear-Admiral A. S. Crowninshield, *Autobiography of George Dewey* (1913), p. 167. For samples of this bureau chief's failure to profit from wartime experience, see Annual Reports, Bureau of Navigation, 1899, 1900, 56 Cong. 1 Sess., *H. Doc.* No. 3, pp. 401*ff.*; and 56 Cong. 2 Sess., *H. Doc.* No. 3, pp. 447*ff*.

which was an unusual interest in, and admiration for, things military.[7]

This interest began to overshadow all others while Roosevelt was still an undergraduate at Harvard. There he conceived the idea of writing a book on the naval operations of our second war with Great Britain. Research for this book took him to the Navy Department at the historic moment of the great awakening of 1881.[8] Roosevelt's book, *The Naval War of 1812,* published in 1882 when the author was but twenty-four years old, showed both a remarkable grasp of naval principles, and also the distinctly militaristic trend in his thinking. Occasional glimpses of his views during the next fifteen years reveal a steady drift in this direction.[9] In Henry Cabot Lodge, a rising Massachusetts politician, Roosevelt early discovered a congenial friend whose nationalism matched his own.[10] And in Captain Mahan he found a preceptor whose writings clarified and advanced his own ideas, and who led him willingly along the dazzling highway toward world power and imperial grandeur.[11]

When Roosevelt joined the McKinley administration in 1897, he was, it is fair to say, a rabid "jingo," outspoken in advocating a big navy, an aggressive foreign policy, and, in particular, armed intervention in Cuba and territorial expansion overseas. It is readily understandable why McKinley, a man of peace, who in 1897 earnestly desired to avoid war with Spain, should have felt grave misgivings on appointing this firebrand to so influential a post in his Administration.[12]

The President's doubts were soon justified. Roosevelt went at his work hammer-and-tongs, riding roughshod over bureau-

[7] See Henry Pringle, *Theodore Roosevelt* (1931), *passim;* and E. P. Oberholtzer, *History of the United States Since the Civil War* (1917–1937), Vol. V, p. 517n.

[8] Roosevelt, *The Naval War of 1812* (1882), p. vi; and Pringle, *Roosevelt,* pp. 36, 46, 47, 60.

[9] See Pringle, *op. cit.,* pp. 166–7.

[10] *Roosevelt-Lodge Correspondence,* Vol. I, *passim.*

[11] See Roosevelt's review of Mahan's first two books in *The Political Science Quarterly,* Vol. IX (March 1894), p. 171; and J. W. Pratt, *Expansionists of 1898* (1936), pp. 21, 222.

[12] Pringle, *Roosevelt,* pp. 165–6.

cratic routine, laboring night and day to weld ships, men, equipment, and supplies into an efficient fighting machine, and striving meanwhile to indoctrinate his superiors and the public in general with his militant views on national power and policy.[13]

These views, reiterated again and again throughout his long public career, were first set forth in detail in a lecture delivered in June 1897 before the Naval War College. Scattered through this address were the elements of Mahan's philosophy of sea power with which Roosevelt was thoroughly conversant. Interspersed between Mahan's ideas were Roosevelt's own contributions of which the following is a brief summary: We needed a great navy to overawe potential aggressors, and if necessary to resist aggression. Possession of such a navy would not transform us into a militaristic nation as some people feared. The United States was inherently a peace-loving nation, "a nation of merchants and manufacturers, of farmers and mechanics; a nation of workingmen, who labor incessantly with head or hand." There was no danger that "possession of a sufficient navy" would lead "such a nation" into "wanton aggression or needless conflict with military powers. . . ." Indeed, the danger was "precisely the opposite": that insufficient power would invite aggression, and render us "an easy prey for any people which still retains those most valuable of all qualities, the soldierly virtues." Diplomacy and arbitration could not compensate for military weakness. Arbitration was an "excellent thing, but ultimately those who wish to see this country at peace with foreign nations will be wise if they place reliance upon a first-class fleet of first-class battleships, rather than on any arbitration treaty which the wit of man can devise." As for diplomacy, it was "utterly useless" without "force behind it," for the diplomatist was the "servant, not the master, of the soldier." Furthermore, attractive as was the ideal of peace, it was a mistake to regard war as an unmitigated evil. War stimulated man's moral fiber. "All the great masterful races have been

[13] *ibid.*, Chap. XIII, *passim.*

fighting races, and . . . a race [which] loses the hard-fighting virtues . . . no matter how skilled in commerce and finance, in science or art . . . has lost its proud right to stand as the equal of the best." War was always preferable to peace at the price of national honor, or even at the price of suffering humanity in other lands. Against such obligations, considerations of national cost and individual prosperity had "no weight whatever. . . ." For there were "higher things . . . than the soft and easy enjoyment of material comfort." Yet, closing on the same chord with which he had opened, he favored a great navy, not "primarily to fight, but to avert fighting"; a navy which would provide the "means to ensure that honorable peace which alone is worth having."[14]

Along with public speeches and administrative activities, Roosevelt labored to convert Secretary Long and President McKinley to his view of naval needs and policy.[15] But these efforts produced slight results. Despite all Roosevelt's exertions during the summer and autumn of 1897, the Administration in December publicly called a halt to rapid naval expansion. Recommending only one new battleship, Secretary Long reminded Congress and country that "our remoteness from foreign powers, the genius of our institutions, and the devotion of our people to education, commerce, and industry, rather than to any policy that involves military entanglements, make war to be thought of only as a last resort in defense of our rights, and our military and naval establishments as a police force for the preservation of order and never for aggression." Future additions to the Navy might be necessary, but it was a

[14] First published in *Proceedings of the United States Naval Institute*, Vol. XXIII (1897), pp. 447*ff*.; reprinted in collection of Roosevelt's essays entitled *American Ideals* (1907), Vol. II, pp. 66*ff*. See also address delivered to Ohio Naval Reserve, reported in *New York Herald*, July 24, 1897. And see comments on these addresses in Bishop, *Roosevelt*, Vol. I, p. 77; and Pringle, *Roosevelt*, pp. 172–3.

[15] J. D. Long, *The New American Navy* (1903), Vol. II, pp. 173–4; *Roosevelt-Lodge Correspondence*, Vol. I, pp. 276–8, 284; *Letters of Theodore Roosevelt to Anna Roosevelt Cowles* (edited by A. R. Cowles, 1924), p. 209; Bishop, *Roosevelt*, Vol. I, pp. 82–4; Herman Hagedorn, *Leonard Wood* (1931), Vol. I, p. 141; Walter Millis, *The Martial Spirit* (1931), p. 81.

"mistake," on the other hand, "not to recognize that our naval power has more than doubled within the last few years; that the case of an emergency beyond our present resources is the very rare case; that until it comes ships will be gradually taken out of commission and put into reserve in order to reduce running expenses; and that a due regard is necessary to the relation of national expenditures to national resources."[16]

Meanwhile, Roosevelt was doing what he could to get ready for the war which he hoped, and felt sure, would come. He gathered around him a group of ambitious and forward-looking officers, with whom he "went over and over . . . everything necessary . . . to put the navy in trim to strike quick and hard" the moment war was declared.[17] He persuaded Secretary Long to take a few precautionary measures.[18] And on February 25, a few days after a mysterious explosion had destroyed the battleship *Maine* in Havana harbor, Roosevelt seized the opportunity, while Long was away for a few hours, to put the Navy on a full war footing.

Long returned to his office the next day to "find that Roosevelt, in his precipitate way," had "come very near causing more of an explosion than happened to the Maine. . . . The very devil seemed to possess him yesterday afternoon," Long confided to his diary. "Having the authority for that time of Acting Secretary, he immediately began to launch peremptory orders; distributing ships; ordering ammunition, which there is no means to move, to places where there is no means to store it . . . sending messages to Congress for immediate legislation, authorizing the enlistment of an unlimited number of seamen . . ." etc. etc.[19]

Especially important, in view of subsequent events, was Roosevelt's part in planning the naval assault on the Philippine

[16] 55 Cong. 2 Sess., *H. Doc.* No. 3, p. 41; and see *Messages and Papers of the Presidents* (Bur. Nat. Lit. ed.), Vol. XIII, pp. 6268–9.

[17] Theodore Roosevelt, *The Rough Riders* (1921), p. 2.

[18] See Appendix to Ann. Rept., Bureau of Navigation, 1898, 55 Cong. 3 Sess., *H. Doc.* No. 3, pp. 21–6, and *passim.*

[19] *America of Yesterday,* pp. 169–70.

Islands. Whether simply as a means of striking Spain at a weak point, or as part of a grand scheme of imperial expansion, he early conceived the idea of sending the Asiatic Squadron against the decrepit Spanish force stationed in Philippine waters. For this undertaking he selected Commodore George Dewey, an enterprising naval officer who was receptive to his plans. Political influence secured the latter's assignment to command of the Asiatic Station. Dewey departed for the Far East in December 1897, and with Roosevelt's coaching and assistance, collected the ships, put them in condition, procured fuel and ammunition, and was ready to strike as soon as war was declared late in April 1898.[20]

Without Roosevelt's preliminary labors, Dewey's naval victory at Manila Bay would have been impossible, and the subsequent annexation of the Philippines improbable.[21] The latter event, as will become increasingly clear, profoundly altered the situation of the United States, transforming us from a geographically isolated continental Power into a scattered empire with a strategic problem virtually insoluble without recourse to alliances absolutely incompatible with the traditions of American foreign policy. And through one of the fateful accidents of history, this gigantic problem was soon to devolve upon the same aggressive militarist who had contributed so largely to its creation, with results that were to affect American naval policy for decades to come.

Naval Lessons of the War

The War with Spain was launched as a crusade to liberate Spain's Cuban colony. The sole object, set forth in the congressional joint resolution of April 20, 1898, was to end Spanish misrule in the island, to compel the Spanish government "to

[20] Dewey, *Autobiography,* Chaps. XIII–XIV; Appendix to Ann. Rept., Bureau of Navigation, 1898, pp. 65*ff*.; and *Theodore Roosevelt—An Autobiography* (1920 ed.), p. 213.

[21] See Bishop, *Roosevelt,* Vol. I, pp. 92–8; and Dewey, *Autobiography,* pp. 170–2.

relinquish its authority," and "to withdraw its land and naval forces from Cuba and Cuban waters."[22] Yet there was a growing opinion in certain quarters, that we should not neglect this great opportunity to seize the Spanish islands in the Western Pacific.[23] And thanks largely to the preparatory labors of Theodore Roosevelt, the first blow for Cuban freedom was struck, not in the Caribbean, but upon the opposite side of the globe on the waters of Manila Bay.

On April 27, Commodore Dewey left Hong Kong with his Asiatic Squadron consisting of the cruisers *Olympia, Baltimore, Raleigh,* and *Boston;* the gunboats *Concord* and *Petrel;* the revenue cutter *McCulloch*; and two hastily purchased colliers in train. During the night of April 30, the squadron crept into Manila Bay, and the following morning destroyed the feeble Spanish force anchored there. Dewey's decisive victory of May 1 had no material effect on the war, however. The Spanish vessels in Philippine waters were too decrepit and too far removed ever to have become a factor in the Atlantic.[24] And it would have been a physical impossibility for those antiquated, rundown, and ill-manned craft to have steamed across the Pacific Ocean to raid our western seaboard.[25]

The campaign in the Caribbean, the main theater of war, developed less rapidly. There as in the Far East, American naval forces were overwhelmingly superior to those of Spain.[26] There also, thanks again largely to the energy and foresight of Theodore Roosevelt, the Navy was ready to strike as soon as Congress declared war.[27] But the Navy's operations in this theater lacked the singleness of purpose and dispatch in execution that so conspicuously characterized Dewey's descent on Manila.

[22] *Statutes at Large,* Vol. XXX, pp. 738–9.

[23] See *New York Herald,* March 10, 1898, p. 6; and Pratt, *Expansionists of 1898,* pp. 227–9.

[24] Rear Admiral F. E. Chadwick, *The Spanish American War* (1911), Vol. I, Chap. II, and p. 90.

[25] *ibid.,* pp. 90–1.

[26] *ibid.,* Chap. II.

[27] *ibid.,* Chap. I; Rear Admiral R. D. Evans, *A Sailor's Log* (1901), pp. 407–12; Appendix to Ann. Rept., Bureau of Navigation, 1898, pp. 163*ff.*

The strategic situation hinged on naval command of the Caribbean and Western Atlantic. The avowed objective was to drive the Spanish forces from Cuba and Cuban waters. A naval blockade of the island would eventually starve out the Spanish garrisons; and a military invasion might hasten the collapse of Spanish power there. To avoid these disasters, the Madrid government would have to maintain sea communications with Cuba. And to do so, the Spanish Navy would have to destroy, drive off, or at least threaten the naval forces of the United States. At the same time, blockade or invasion of Cuba was just as contingent upon American command of the Caribbean. And such command was to be established only by destroying or immobilizing the naval forces of Spain. Until that was achieved, it would be dangerous to send our military transports to sea at all.[28] Until then also, the widely distributed, and necessarily weak, blockading divisions would theoretically be in constant danger of attack by stronger hostile squadrons.[29] Thus for the United States as for Spain, everything turned on seizing and holding indisputable command of the Caribbean and adjoining waters.[30]

The overwhelming superiority of American naval resources foreshadowed an early realization of this objective. Spain's Navy appeared rather formidable on paper.[31] But the effective and available force in the Atlantic, embraced only four armored cruisers and a few torpedo boats and destroyers. These units, under command of Admiral Cervera, constituted Spain's sole naval threat to the United States in the Caribbean. While Cervera's ships had a paper rating about as high as corresponding units of the American Navy, they were inadequately equipped, out of repair, and wretchedly manned. Cervera, moreover, had no ships at all comparable to our Navy's four

[28] See Chadwick, *Spanish American War,* Vol. I, p. 57; and *America of Yesterday,* p. 183.

[29] See Chadwick, *Spanish American War,* Vol. I, p. 57.

[30] G. S. Clarke, "Naval Aspects of the Spanish American War," *Brassey's Naval Annual, 1899,* p. 125.

[31] Chadwick, *Spanish American War,* Vol. I, pp. 33-9.

new first-class battleships, three of which were in the North Atlantic when war was declared.[32]

The geographical situation further increased the disparity of power in the Caribbean. The Spanish fleet would have to operate several thousand miles from its home ports, in what were virtually the enemy's home waters. Puerto Rico, the most easterly Spanish naval depot in the West Indies, lay more than twice as far from Spain as from the United States. Viewed in retrospect, the disparity of strength and advantage seems so obvious and so overwhelming, that one marvels how presumably well informed neutral experts could have asserted, as they did in 1898, that the contending forces were about equally matched, with Spain possibly holding a slight advantage.[33]

While American naval authorities seem to have felt little doubt as to their superior power, they took the obvious precaution of transferring the new battleship *Oregon* from the Pacific Coast where it was utterly useless, to the Atlantic where it would materially strengthen the fleet assembling at Key West.[34]

The *Oregon's* famous voyage had a significance far beyond what was anticipated. It required sixty-eight days to steam from San Francisco to Key West by way of Magellan Strait, a distance of nearly 13,000 nautical miles. That the *Oregon* could make such a voyage and arrive at her destination in good condition testified both to the excellence of the vessel and to the efficiency of her personnel.[35] The superior performance of the *Oregon* at the Battle of Santiago emphatically demonstrated the value of the training and experience gained on the long voyage.[36] And the voyage itself advertised, as almost nothing

[32] These were the *Iowa, Massachusetts,* and *Indiana.* The *Oregon* was on the Pacific coast. For characteristics of these ships, see pp. 213, 218 n., *supra.*

[33] See Chadwick, *op. cit.,* pp. 39–40; *The Times* (London), April 14, 1898, p. 6; April 23, p. 12; April 27, p. 8; *Living Age,* Vol. CCXVII (1898), p. 436.

[34] Chadwick, *Spanish American War,* Vol. I, pp. 12–16; Long, *New Navy,* Vol. II, pp. 52–3; and Appendix to Ann. Rept., Bureau of Navigation, 1898, p. 475.

[35] Chadwick, *Spanish American War,* Vol. I, p. 16.

[36] Clarke, "Naval Aspects of the War," pp. 155–6.

else could have, the strategic necessity for building an inter-oceanic isthmian canal.

Returning to the main theater of war, it seemed highly probable that Cervera's fleet, then in the Cape Verde Islands, would attempt a "dash" for the Caribbean. Its ultimate destination might be either Havana or San Juan (P.R.) since the latter was so situated as to command the eastern approaches to the Caribbean, and had a coaling and repair station. Several courses lay open to the United States, two of which were proposed by Admiral William T. Sampson, commander of the fleet in the Caribbean. His first plan was to make a quick descent on Havana, calculated to end the war before Spanish reenforcements could arrive; his second, to seize San Juan, and then to locate and destroy the Spanish fleet on its arrival in the West Indies.[37] Both plans were strategically sound. And the second at least would have been feasible had the authorities in Washington given Sampson a free hand and all available forces.

Actually, he was given neither, largely because of the clamor which the newspapers stirred up in the United States. News and rumors of Spanish naval preparations, sensationally spread upon the front page, greatly alarmed the population of the Atlantic seaboard, and even infected the naval authorities in Washington. As a result, the Navy Department vetoed Sampson's plans for striking quick and decisive blows at Havana or San Juan, directing him instead to limit his operations to blockade and cautious bombardments, and warning him expressly against taking risks until the "more formidable Spanish vessels" were immobilized or destroyed.[38] Furthermore, in deference to pressure exerted by Senators, Representatives, State governors, mayors, and other influential persons and groups, the Department temporarily withheld some of the best fighting ships from Sampson's fleet, organizing them into a separate, so-called Flying Squadron, to be held at Hampton Roads against

[37] Chadwick, *Spanish American War,* Vol. I, pp. 63, 88.
[38] *ibid.,* pp. 64, 74.

the wholly improbable contingency of naval raids on our seaboard.[39] The alarm increasing with the approach of war, the Department, on April 20, created a second defense force, called the Northern Patrol Squadron, to which were assigned several cruisers, which were distributed along the coast from Maine to Virginia.[40] News of Cervera's departure from the Cape Verde Islands, on a westward course,[41] threw the Atlantic seaboard into a panic which verged on hysteria as days passed with no further intelligence. Rumor quickly had the Spanish fleet steaming at full speed for New York, Boston, or some other defenseless seaboard city. Although Cervera was eventually located in the Caribbean, Congress, as a further precautionary measure, directed the Navy Department to mobilize the naval militia of the States into an Auxiliary Naval Force, which eventually manned a collection of ancient Civil War monitors, converted yachts, armed tugs, and other makeshift men-of-war, which were stationed along the seaboard from Maine to the Gulf.[42] Only with the greatest difficulty did the Navy Department prevent the unreasoning and preposterous panic from forcing a complete disruption of the fighting fleet, and the scattering of its units, to guard two thousand miles of coastline against wholly improbable, if not utterly impossible, raids by Cervera's decrepit cruisers.[43]

Perhaps no revelation of the war had greater significance than this startling exhibition of public ignorance and mob psychology. Secretary Welles had faced, and to a large extent had successfully resisted, similar pressure in the Civil War.[44]

[39] See *New York Herald,* March 9, 1898, p. 6; Ann. Rept., Sec. of the Navy, 1898, 55 Cong. 3 Sess., *H. Doc.* No. 3, p. 4; and Chadwick, *op. cit.,* Vol. I, pp. 62–3.

[40] Chadwick, *op. cit.,* p. 63; Ann. Rept., Sec. of the Navy, 1898, p. 5; and Appendix to Ann. Rept., Bureau of Navigation, 1898, pp. 53, 60.

[41] *New York Herald,* May 1, 1898, Sec. I, p. 3.

[42] *Statutes at Large,* Vol. XXX, p. 744; and Ann. Rept., Sec. of the Navy, 1898, pp. 19–20.

[43] For some of the comic but portentous details of this panic, see Roosevelt, *Autobiography,* pp. 214–16; *America of Yesterday,* p. 185; Millis, *Martial Spirit,* pp. 202–3; and Pringle, *Roosevelt,* p. 179.

[44] See pp. 162*ff.*, *supra.*

But the phenomenon had not then assumed either the magnitude or the sinister cast which characterized its reappearance in the war with Spain. The panic was all the more amazing, coming as it did on top of Mahan's widely heralded books and articles, which presumably had acquainted a large fraction of the American public with the fundamental principles of naval strategy. Even if Spain's Navy had actually been the menace conjured up in popular imagination, the very best coast defense was a united fighting fleet under a single command. The pressure which forced even a partial scattering of the Navy's fighting units, might well have produced grave and disastrous consequences in a war with a stronger naval Power.

To avoid future repetition of "the preposterous and humiliating terrors of the past months," Mahan proposed to build up the country's coastal fortifications. Such works, he hoped, would inspire confidence, and relieve pressure from the Navy which could then proceed unhampered with the serious business of war.[45] An eminent foreign critic, Colonel George S. Clarke, of the British Army, took issue with Mahan's solution. Clarke agreed that the American seaboard had little or nothing to fear from naval raids in future wars. But he believed it would be easier as well as cheaper to educate the public, than to expend vast sums on coastal fortifications.[46]

Whether any system of fortifications would sufficiently inspire public confidence in a future crisis, or whether any amount of education could fortify the country against panic, were unanswerable questions. But they posed a fundamental problem, which challenged the capacity of the American people to act rationally in time of war, and foreshadowed a possibility of the government seeking a solution along lines incompatible with that freedom of speech which is the cornerstone of political democracy.

Popular clamor for invasion of Cuba raised the same prob-

[45] "The War on the Sea and Its Lessons," Part III, in *The Times* (London), Dec. 26, 1898, p. 11.

[46] "Naval Aspects of the War," pp. 123, 172–3.

lem in another form. No naval officer would consider sending a fleet of transports to sea while enemy squadrons were still at large. But the civilian public in general, and the daily press in particular, while succumbing to panic over improbable rumors of prospective naval assaults on our seaboard, recklessly demanded that the Government dispatch the Army to Cuba without waiting for the Navy first to dispose of the Spanish fleet. Public opinion thus presented the amazing paradox of ignoring the enemy's naval power where it was most formidable, and of dreading it where it was palpably weakest.[47]

The agitation for invasion of Cuba was resisted, however, until the Spanish fleet was finally located and blockaded in the harbor of Santiago on the southern coast of the island. From May 29 to July 3, this blockade was steadily maintained by Admiral Sampson's fleet which now included the battleships *Iowa, Oregon, Massachusetts, Indiana* and *Texas*; the armored cruisers *New York* and *Brooklyn*; and a number of smaller vessels. The sortie and total destruction of Admiral Cervera's ships on July 3, 1898, is a familiar story which does not need retelling. It is sufficient to say that this action conclusively established the American Navy's absolute command of the Caribbean, and virtually ended the war upon the sea.[48]

Viewed as a whole, the war taught little that was new regarding the fundamentals of sea power and naval warfare. While naval power determined the outcome at every stage, the operations themselves presented few great questions of strategy.[49] Aside from confirming Mahan's thesis and revealing the previously unappreciated potentialities of an ignorant and alarmed public opinion, the war's chief contributions to naval art and science lay in the realm of technology. While many of these lessons were so technical as to interest only qualified experts, some of them bore directly on larger aspects of our

[47] *ibid.*, p. 173.

[48] The best narrative is Rear Admiral Chadwick's two-volume work, *The Spanish American War,* frequently cited in these pages.

[49] See Clarke, "Naval Aspects of the War," p. 172.

defense problem, regarding which it was highly desirable to secure enlightened public opinion. Clearly falling in the latter category was war experience which cast new light on the rôle and potentialities of naval power in general, and on the needs and efficiency of the American Navy in particular.

First, in this connection, were the revelations regarding the rigid limitations which technology imposed on a modern navy's radius of operations. According to international law, belligerent men-of-war might secure in neutral countries only such repairs, fuel, and supplies, as to enable them to reach their nearest home port. Yet the insatiable furnaces and complicated machinery of modern warships required ready access to fuel supplies, drydocks, and machine shops. It was difficult enough to procure the coal, ammunition, and supplies necessary for Dewey's descent on the Philippines. It was even more difficult to maintain his squadron in the Philippines. Had the Spaniards driven off the attacking force, or even inflicted serious injury, the American commander might have found himself stranded with partially or totally disabled vessels, and depleted bunkers, magazines, and stores, seven thousand miles from the nearest American dock yard. Even in the Caribbean, where the American forces were much nearer home, and where distances were comparatively small, the Navy Department experienced no little difficulty in solving the problems of fuel, service, and repairs. It was painfully clear that large-scale oversea operations against any first-rate naval Power would encounter appalling, if not insuperable, difficulties, at least until such time as Congress sanctioned development of a network of oversea bases, or an adequate fleet of colliers, transports, floating docks and foundries, and other auxiliaries.[50]

[50] See Rear Admiral G. W. Melville, "Our Actual Naval Strength," *North American Review,* Vol. CLXXVI (1903), pp. 376, 378–9; *idem,* "The Important Elements in Naval Conflicts," *Annals of the American Academy of Political and Social Science,* Vol. XXVI (1905), pp. 123, 126; Clarke, "Naval Aspects of the War," pp. 170–1; *idem,* "The War and Its Lessons," *Proc. U. S. Nav. Inst.,* Vol. XXVI (1900), pp. 127, 134, 139, 140; Captain F. E. Chadwick, "The Navy in the War," *Scribner's Magazine,* Vol. XXIV (1898), pp. 529, 537; Lieutenant-Commander René de Cartout (French Navy), "An Introduction to the

Second, war experience confirmed European expert opinion which held that, under conditions otherwise equal, guns afloat were no match for guns ashore. Because an American squadron of unarmored cruisers steamed into Manila Bay and, without serious damage to themselves, destroyed a Spanish squadron under the guns of supporting shore batteries, it did not follow that we could repeat this exploit against a well prepared enemy. On the contrary, systematic analysis of the hits scored by American warships in the battles of Manila Bay and Santiago, together with the failure of American ships to silence the shore batteries at San Juan, Santiago, and elsewhere, pointed to an altogether different conclusion. With due allowance for the inferior marksmanship then prevailing in the American Navy, war experience emphasized the inherent difficulties arising from the instability of a floating gun platform, as well as from other inescapable conditions of naval gunnery.[51]

Third, the war sounded the long-overdue knell of the monitor type, around which storms of controversy had raged ever since the Civil War. The United States, in 1898, had several recently completed monitors, and Congress, on the eve of the war, authorized four more.[52] These vessels were supposed to provide impregnable, floating fortifications for harbor defense. But there were not enough to go around, and it was realized, at least in naval circles, that one monitor to a port would be no match for a hostile raiding squadron. The alternative was

---

Study of Naval Tactics," translated and reprinted in *Proc. U. S. Nav. Inst.*, Vol. XXVI (1900), pp. 287, 293; C. O. Paullin, "A Half Century of Naval Administration in America, 1861–1911," Part XI, *Proc. U. S. Nav. Inst.*, Vol. XL (1914), pp. 419*ff*.; and Ann. Rept., Sec. of the Navy, 1898, p. 27.

[51] See Clarke, "The War and Its Lessons," pp. 133, 141; Rear Admiral Plüdderman (German Navy), "Main Features of the Spanish-American War," translated and reprinted in *Proc. U. S. Nav. Inst.*, Vol. XXIV (1898), pp. 772, 779; and Commander Jacobsen (German Navy), "Sketches from the Spanish-American War," translated and reprinted in *op. cit.*, Vol. XXV, pp. 11, 23, 33–6; and Captain Rudolf von Labres (Austrian Navy), "Modern Naval Tactics," *op. cit.*, Vol. XXVI, pp. 525, 527.

[52] 55 Cong. 2 Sess., *Congressional Record* (Vol. XXXI), pp. 4148, 4243; and "Battleships and Monitors Now Building for the Navy," in *Proc. U. S. Nav. Inst.*, Vol. XXV (1899), p. 250.

to assemble them into one or more coast-defense squadrons, but this was impracticable, for they were too slow and too unseaworthy to move quickly to any threatened point on the coast. These monitors, in short, were utterly unsuited to the one rôle for which they had been created. Convinced that they were useless for harbor defense, the Navy Department transferred some of them to the fleet in the Caribbean. But they encumbered that fleet more than they strengthened it. Their low freeboard and instability in a seaway made them extremely poor gun platforms; and their slow speed, inadequate fuel capacity, and general lack of seaworthiness, seriously handicapped every squadron to which they were attached.[53]

Finally, the technical difficulties which confronted the United States Navy waging offensive war against Spain, had a larger significance. If the fuel and service requirements of modern warships taxed the naval resources of the United States, and restricted the radius of American operations, these factors would just as certainly limit the operations of future enemies of the United States. According to Admiral G. W. Melville, the highest engineering officer in the Navy, the technical limitations of modern warships created insuperable obstacles to the blockade of our coast by any foreign navy, and rendered it absolutely impossible for such a force to carry a war into our waters at all unless it was at least twice as strong as our Navy.[54] If the war demonstrated the difficulties of naval gunnery, and the inconclusive results to be expected from bombardments, these factors, also, might work as much to the advantage, as to the disadvantage, of the United States in future wars. Furthermore, the revelations as to the comparative efficiency of guns afloat and ashore, provided one more argument for scrapping even the so-called improved monitors,

[53] See Mahan, "The War on the Sea and Its Lessons," Parts II and III, *The Times* (London), Dec. 1 and 26, 1898; and Clarke, "Naval Aspects of the War," pp. 173-4; and *idem,* "The War and Its Lessons," p. 139.

[54] "Our Actual Naval Strength," pp. 378–9; and *idem,* "The Important Elements in Naval Conflicts," pp. 123, 126.

and leaving passive harbor defense to long-range coast artillery. And finally, out of the maze of technical lessons and revelations, analyzed and interpreted in the ensuing years, both naval officers and civilian statesmen were to acquire a clearer understanding of the ramifications of our naval defense problem which, as already intimated and as will further appear, were enormously extended as a result of the political outcome of the war with Spain.

Naval Implications of Territorial Expansion Overseas

The insular accessions of 1898 and 1899 extended the strategic frontier of the United States several hundred miles eastward into the Atlantic, and several thousand westward across the Pacific.

Annexation of Puerto Rico and occupation of Cuba did not materially enlarge or alter our defense problem in the Atlantic. Naval primacy in the Caribbean had become a settled American naval objective long before the war with Spain. The war itself, and the annexations which accompanied and followed it, merely accentuated our strategic need of an isthmian canal, and the necessity of commanding the Atlantic approaches to such a canal. And, as we shall show in due course, the United States, by 1899, had progressed far toward indisputable naval command over the Caribbean.

Turning to the Pacific, we find that the strategic situation of the United States in that ocean was profoundly altered as a result of the insular accessions that accompanied and followed the war. Mahan, Roosevelt, Lodge, and others had long regarded annexation of the Hawaiian Islands as a strategic necessity.[55] These islands, it was claimed, occupied a commanding position which dominated the Eastern Pacific, and hence the west coast of the United States. It was not sufficient merely to have certain naval privileges in the islands, such as those

[55] Pratt, *Expansionists of 1898*, pp. 147–53, 204–5, 218.

acquired by the Hawaiian-American Treaty of 1884.[56] As long as they remained even nominally independent, it was urged that some "foreign Power"—"notably Japan"—might secure a foothold there. The only sure way to avoid such a "grave military danger" was outright annexation.[57] While this argument did not convince everyone, even in professional naval circles,[58] it was generally conceded that annexation of Hawaii clinched our Navy's command of the Eastern Pacific, resulting not only in greater security for our west coast, but also in surer control of the Pacific approaches to the prospective isthmian canal.

Conquest of the Philippine Islands added another argument for annexation of Hawaii, and was perhaps the decisive factor in bringing this about, in the summer of 1898.[59] Few naval vessels of that day could steam from San Francisco to Manila without recoaling on the way. Although the Great Circle route offered the shortest course between these points, and although the United States had, at Kiska, in the Aleutian Islands, a more commodious harbor nearer to Manila,[60] this route to the Philippines passed within a few miles of Japan, and hence might become strategically unavailable in case of war in the Western Pacific.

Of less immediate importance was that part of the Samoan archipelago, which in 1899 passed under the sovereignty of the United States. These islands, located near the steamship route to Australia, about 2300 miles south of Hawaii, 4100 miles southwest of San Francisco, and 5600 miles from Panama, contained the harbor of Pago Pago, long regarded as an excellent site for a naval coaling station in the South Seas. The United States had acquired a franchise for this purpose in

[56] W. M. Malloy (compiler), *Treaties*, Vol. I, p. 219.

[57] Letter from Captain Mahan to Senator James H. Kyle, Feb. 4, 1898, 55 Cong. 2 Sess., *S. Rept.* No. 681, p. 99.

[58] See, for example, Admiral Robley D. Evans, *An Admiral's Log* (1910), pp. 23, 24.

[59] Pratt, *Expansionists of 1898*, pp. 274, 317*ff*.

[60] T. A. Bailey, "The United States and Hawaii during the Spanish-American War," in *Amer. Hist. Rev.*, Vol. XXXVI (1931), pp. 552, 558.

1878.[61] Ten years later, Congress voted a small appropriation for a coaling station, and preliminary steps were taken to establish one.[62] But the project hung fire, and it was not until after the war with Spain that a permanent naval station, with modest facilities for storing and loading coal, was finally established.[63]

Although journalists, politicians, and naval experts dwelt on the value of this strategic and commercial "stepping stone" to the Far East,[64] and President McKinley, in 1899, declared it unthinkable that we should "relinquish our rights" to this "best anchorage in the Pacific,"[65] the strategic importance of these islands was actually not very great at that time. They were far removed from the main stream of traffic to the Far East. They were too far distant to be a vital factor in defense of the prospective canal. And it seemed doubtful if they would figure conspicuously in the defense of the Philippines.

The Spanish island of Guam had far greater strategic potentialities. The distance from Hawaii to the Philippines was about 4800 nautical miles. A naval station on this route, convenient at all times, might become indispensable in case of war in the Western Pacific. Guam, 3300 miles west of Honolulu, was well situated for such a purpose, and the decision to retain the Philippines led logically to inclusion of this island in the peace settlement of 1898.

The extension of American sovereignty over the Philippine Islands added immensely to the already complicated problem of defense in the Pacific; and the naval burden was further

[61] See G. H. Ryden, *The Foreign Policy of the United States in Relation to Samoa* (1933), pp. 196–7.

[62] *Stat. at Large,* Vol. XXV, p. 814; and Ann. Rept., Sec. of the Navy, 1889. 51 Cong. 1 Sess., *H. Ex. Doc.* No. 1, Pt. III, p. 31.

[63] See Ann. Rept., Sec. of the Navy, 1899, 56 Cong. 1 Sess., *H. Doc.* No. 3, p. 27; same for 1900, 56 Cong. 2 Sess., *H. Doc.* No. 3, pp. 24, 292; and Naval Governor 1910–1913 (W. M. Crose), *American Samoa* (1927), p. 44.

[64] Pratt, *Expansionists of 1898,* p. 274; *Literary Digest,* Vol. XIX (1899), pp. 606, 637; H. C. Ide, "Our Interesting Samoa," *North American Review,* Vol. CLXV (1897), pp. 155, 161; J. G. Leigh, "America's First and Latest Colony," *Forum,* Vol. XXIX (1900), pp. 104, 113.

[65] *M. & P.* (Bur. Nat. Lit. ed.), Vol. XIII, p. 6376.

increased by developments in American Far Eastern policy, which followed the war with Spain.[66]

The decision to retain the Philippines turned on expectations of politico-commercial advantage, as well as on considerations of cosmopolitan philanthropy and national prestige.[67] Eastern Asia, by the turn of the century, had become the theater of a ruthless struggle among the European Powers and Japan, each striving to stake out as large a claim as possible in the seemingly moribund Chinese Empire. To realize the commercial hopes and expectations which certain classes of Americans entertained respecting China, the United States government had a choice of two courses. American statesmen might enter the struggle, with a view to securing as much as possible in the partition of the Chinese Empire; or they might simply demand that the other Powers respect that equality of commercial opportunity throughout China, which was guaranteed in our treaties with the latter country.

For various reasons not especially germane to this discussion, American statesmen chose the second course. This decision had far-reaching naval implications. The demand for commercial equality, set forth in the related policies of the open door and integrity of China, placed the United States in opposition to Japan and to the continental European Powers. A territorial foothold in the Western Pacific was highly desirable, if not absolutely necessary, to sustain the naval power deemed essential to command respect for the China policy of the United States. The Philippines were admirably located for such a purpose, and were generally so regarded.[68]

At the same time, the extension of American sovereignty over the Philippines vastly increased the Navy's responsibilities. These remote islands now became national territory, to be defended at whatever cost. Yet provision for their defense raised

[66] See, in general, A. W. Griswold, *The Far Eastern Policy of the United States* (1938).

[67] See Instructions to American Commissioners to Negotiate Peace with Spain, *Foreign Relations, 1898*, pp. 904, 907.

[68] Pratt, *op. cit.*, pp. 329*ff.*; 56 Cong. 2 Sess., *S. Doc.* No. 148, pp. 32*ff.*; and Oberholtzer, *History of the United States*, Vol. V, pp. 571–5.

all but insoluble strategic and technical problems. Thus, while the American flag floating over Manila strengthened the diplomatic arm of the United States in the Far East, that fact in turn enhanced the danger of our eventually becoming involved in war with the rising Japanese Empire. While the Philippines might prove indispensable in prosecuting such a conflict, they might also become a terrific liability, depending upon the balance of naval power in the Western Pacific.

There were even larger naval implications. Security for the Philippines, as well as enforcement of commercial equality in China, might depend in no small degree upon maintaining the multilateral balance of power which was taking form in the Far East. But except for Japan and the United States, the parties to this equilibrium were all European States. A general war in Europe would have incalculable consequences in the Far East. Thus the moment the security of American territory or the enforcement of American policies became even indirectly contingent on the European balance of power, the United States acquired a definite stake in European stability and peace. And the ability of American statesmen to speak with authority in Europe, as in the Far East, would depend in no small degree on the relative power and the prestige of the United States Navy.

No one, at the turn of the century, could have foreseen all these ramifications. But many did perceive, or at least vaguely sense, that the annexation of the Philippines, together with the practically simultaneous strengthening of our Far Eastern policy, had impaired, if not destroyed, both our political and strategic isolation; and that the resulting situation called for thorough reexamination of the naval policy of the United States.

Reaction and Drift, 1899–1901

The inevitable post-war adjustments and reaction delayed reexamination of the postulates of American naval policy. The government discharged the volunteers who had swelled the Navy's ranks and disposed of the makeshift auxiliary cruisers acquired from the merchant marine. Many of the regular men-of-war were laid up for repairs, and those still in active service were once again distributed among the oversea cruising stations.

The dispersion of the armored ships, along with the smaller cruisers, among these oversea stations, revealed a surprising failure to profit by one of the most obvious lessons of the war. That struggle had demonstrated the difficulties of improvising fleet organization in a crisis, and had clearly pointed to the desirability of permanently assigning at least the battleships and armored cruisers to one, or at most two fleets, in order that officers and crews might acquire skill and proficiency in fleet tactics and maneuvers. But the Bureau of Navigation decreed otherwise. This bureau, which largely controlled the movements of vessels, frankly had no fleet policy. Ship assignments were "determined" by the "specific" requirements of the various stations, regardless of the effect on the Navy's efficiency as a war machine. The bureau's nearest approach to a fleet policy was its suggestion that new capital ships be temporarily assigned to either the North Atlantic or the (Eastern) Pacific Squadrons, for a trial period before their departure to one of the oversea stations. This suggestion, inspired by "prudential considerations of defense," would insure the presence of at least three such ships on the Atlantic coast and one on the Pacific.[69]

Actually, the consequences of this reactionary policy were not as bad as they might have been. Circumstances forced the Navy Department to concentrate most of its best vessels on the North Atlantic and Asiatic Stations. Despite frequent interruptions, resulting from detachment of vessels for special service, native insurrections in the Philippines, and civil disturbance in China, the commanding officers on these stations managed somehow to carry on gunnery practice and squadron

[69] Ann. Repts., Bureau of Navigation, 1899 and 1900, 56 Cong. 1 Sess., *H. Doc.* No. 3, pp. 401*ff.*; 56 Cong. 2 Sess., *H. Doc.* No. 3, pp. 447–8.

drills.[70] But these sporadic efforts, highly significant as revelations of the energy and vision of individual officers, merely emphasized the Department's failure to profit from one of the most obvious lessons of the recent war.

Certain other problems, however, were attacked somewhat more constructively. It was immediately recognized within the Navy Department that American battleships and cruisers should hereafter have a larger cruising radius.[71] In response to Service agitation for a professional body to advise the civilian Secretary, and to supervise the departmental bureaus, the Administration in 1900 created the General Board which was in time to assume a large rôle in policy determination.[72] In accord with the advice of this body, the Administration mildly recommended additional construction from year to year.[73] In line with the views of competent officers, the Administration also took steps to improve the Navy's coaling and service facilities overseas, especially in the Pacific.[74] An attempt was even made to secure a secondary naval base on the coast of China opposite the Japanese island of Formosa, but this project was not pushed on account of Japanese opposition.[75] In all these activities, however, there was a conspicuous absence of the vigorous executive leadership which Theodore Roosevelt (at this time Governor of New York) had provided during his brief service as Assistant Secretary of the Navy.

The same trends were perceptible in the sphere of legislation. The war caused an immediate spurt in naval construction. At the beginning of the conflict (May 1898), Congress authorized a long list of new ships, in which three first-class

[70] Ann. Repts., Commanding Officers, 1900 and 1901, 56 Cong. 2 Sess., *H. Doc.* No. 3, pp. 544–9; 57 Cong. 1 Sess., *H. Doc.*, No. 3, pp. 607–23.

[71] Ann. Rept., Sec. of the Navy, 1899, 56 Cong. 1 Sess., *H. Doc.* No. 3, p. 56.

[72] Paullin, "Half Century of Naval Administration," Part X, *Proc. U. S. Nav. Inst.*, Vol. XL (1914), pp. 111, 116; Rear Admiral B. A. Fiske, *From Midshipman to Rear Admiral* (1919), p. 350.

[73] Ann. Repts., Sec. of the Navy, 1900 and 1901, 56 Cong. 2 Sess., *H. Doc.* No. 3, p. 31; 57 Cong. 2 Sess., *H. Doc.* No. 3, pp. 24–5; President's Annual Message, 1900, *M. & P.* (Bur. Nat. Lit. ed.), Vol. XIII, p. 6452.

[74] Ann. Rept., Sec. of the Navy, 1899, pp. 26, 304; same for 1900, pp. 26, 282, 297; same for 1901, pp. 17, 358, 611.

[75] *For. Rels., 1915*, pp. 113–15; A. W. Griswold, *The Far Eastern Policy of the United States* (1938), pp. 83–4.

battleships and sixteen destroyers[76] were balanced against four obsolete monitors, twelve obsolescent torpedo boats, and one gunboat.[77] The decisive and well publicized naval battles of Manila Bay and Santiago, aroused wild enthusiasm which was reflected in the authorization (March 1899) of three more battleships,[78] and three armored cruisers, and several smaller vessels. The session of 1899–1900, to the accompaniment of much patriotic oratory, voted two further battleships, and three more armored cruisers.[79] By this time, however, the momentum was nearly spent. The 1900 bill was passed over rising opposition,[80] and the next session, rejecting the Navy Department's recommendations, voted no ships at all.[81]

Meanwhile, the proceedings which accompanied these enactments were revealing how few Senators and Representatives had any real grasp of the post-war naval problem. Beginning in 1899, it is true, Congress did specify that new ships should have "great radius of action." But the capital ships authorized that year were still officially designated as "coast line" battleships.[82] And no one called attention either to the patent dichotomy involved in these antithetical provisions, or to the equally manifest anachronism implicit in the continued use of the "coast line" formula.[83] The following year, Congress

[76] This type was an outgrowth of the earlier torpedo boat. It was really a larger and faster torpedo boat, designed to destroy the latter craft, hence its original name—torpedo-boat destroyer. The destroyer has survived and today plays an extremely important rôle as the protector of larger naval ships and merchantmen from submarine attack.

[77] The battleships were the *Maine* [2nd], *Missouri, Ohio* (12,500 tons, eighteen knots, main battery of four twelve-inch guns, cost about $5,000,000 each). *Navy Yearbook, 1917,* pp. 133, 740, 759, 766.

[78] The battleships were the *Georgia, Nebraska,* and *Virginia* (14,948 tons, nineteen knots, four twelve-inch and eight eight-inch guns, cost about $6,500,-000). *loc. cit.*

[79] These battleships were the *New Jersey* and *Rhode Island* (14,948 tons, nineteen knots, four twelve-inch and eight eight-inch guns, cost about $6,500,-000).

[80] 56 Cong. 1 Sess., *Cong. Record* (Vol. XXXIII), pp. 4483–92, 5493–7.

[81] 56 Cong. 2 Sess., *H. Doc.* No. 3, p. 31; *Navy Yearbook, 1917,* p. 175.

[82] *Yearbook, 1917,* p. 147.

[83] See 55 Cong. 3 Sess., *H. Rept.,* No. 2168, p. 2; 55 Cong. 3 Sess., *Cong. Record* (Vol. XXXII), pp. 2158–66, 2188–91, 2244–57, 2620, 2639.

dropped this obsolete phraseology; but, with relatively few exceptions, members still displayed either continued ignorance of, or reluctance to accept, the naval implications of their country's territorial and diplomatic commitments in the Pacific.[84] And the same confusion of thought characterized the naval debate in the short session of 1900–1901.[85]

Thus, three years after the war with Spain, one could observe little progress toward a comprehensive restatement of American naval policy, in the light of war experience and of our post-war situation and commitments. And the outlook for an early and vigorous attack on this problem was not propitious. Influential leaders, even within the dominant Republican Party, stood in the way of further immediate expansion of the Navy, notably Joseph G. Cannon of Illinois, Chairman of the powerful House Committee on Appropriations, and Eugene Hale of Maine, Chairman of the Senate Naval Committee.[86] The reelection of McKinley, and the prospect of Secretary Long remaining head of the Navy Department, foreshadowed four more years of executive conservatism in naval policy. And the election of Theodore Roosevelt to the Vice-Presidency, a post of honor without power, seemed to have eliminated the man who had played so radical and dramatic a rôle in preparing the Navy for the war with Spain. Yet through one of the fateful accidents of history, this last event was to alter the whole course of American naval development; for the assassination of McKinley in September 1901 raised Roosevelt to the presidency, thereby giving the United States a Chief Executive equipped with the knowledge, the initiative, and the driving force which were needed to launch imperial America upon an imperial naval policy.

[84] See 56 Cong. 1 Sess., *H. Rept.* No. 930, Pt. I, pp. 18–21; *op. cit.*, Pt. II, p. 6; 56 Cong. 1 Sess., *Cong. Record* (Vol. XXXIII), pp. 4227–72, 4312–47, 4483–92, 4526, 5401–11, 5493–9.

[85] See 56 Cong. 2 Sess., *Cong. Record* (Vol. XXXIV), pp. 1351–8, 1414–28, 1479, for the debate in the House; the sections dealing with increase of the Navy were passed without debate in the Senate.

[86] See *Cong. Record,* Vol. XXXIII, p. 5494; and *Roosevelt-Lodge Correspondence,* Vol. I, p. 511.

CHAPTER FIFTEEN

☆ ☆

Mahan Triumphant: The Naval Policy of Theodore Roosevelt (1901–1909)

MAHAN's philosophy of sea power entered the White House in the person of Theodore Roosevelt, who succeeded to the presidency in the autumn of 1901, following the tragic death of President McKinley. In previous years, as we have repeatedly noted, foreign relations and international crises had frequently influenced naval development. Naval policy now began to influence the spirit and direction of American foreign relations. And so completely did the new President dominate both foreign relations and naval development in these opening years of the twentieth century, that the naval policy of imperial America was, in large degree, the naval policy of Theodore Roosevelt.

Strategic and Political Background

Strategically speaking, the continental United States in 1901, as in 1850, consisted of two long and exposed seaboards, as far apart as if situated on opposite sides of the globe. The shortest distance by water from New York to San Francisco exceeded 13,000 nautical miles, more than twice as far as from San Francisco to Yokohama. It had required the first-class battleship *Oregon* sixty-eight days to steam from San Francisco to Key West. It would require even longer to move a whole fleet from one ocean to the other, and, under conceivable strategic conditions, it might prove impossible to make the transfer at all.

There were two, and only two, solutions to this strategic puzzle. One was to station in each ocean a virtually independent naval force strong enough to cope with any situation likely to arise there. The other was to build an interoceanic isthmian canal which would halve the distance between our Pacific and Atlantic seaboards. The first solution had bristled with difficulties even before the war with Spain. It became utterly impracticable after the annexation of the Spanish islands in the Western Pacific, and the ensuing complication of American political relations in the Far East. Thus the only alternative was to build a canal, and Roosevelt came to the presidency thoroughly committed to this undertaking, the initiation of which was one of the notable achievements of his Administration.

Construction of an isthmian canal would solve one strategic problem but create another. As Roosevelt put it, the canal would "greatly increase the efficiency of our Navy if the Navy is of sufficient size. . . ." Otherwise, the "building of the canal would be merely giving a hostage to any power of superior strength."[1] Or as Mahan had repeatedly pointed out during the 'nineties, an isthmian canal would be a strategic asset only if the United States Navy held indisputable command over the Caribbean and the Eastern Pacific.[2]

The strategic position of the United States in the Caribbean, and indeed throughout the Western Atlantic north of the Equator, was naturally a strong one. After the turn of the century, this position tended to become progressively stronger, as a result of the rapid increase of the United States Navy, the growing complexity of naval technology, and, paradoxically, the rise of German naval power.

[1] *Messages and Papers of the Presidents* (Bur. Nat. Lit. ed.), Vol. XIV, p. 6722.

[2] *Interest of America in Sea Power* (1898), pp. 32*ff*., 59*ff*., 271*ff*.

At the beginning of the twentieth century, Great Britain was the only non-American Power with a considerable naval establishment in the Western Atlantic. Germany's threat to Great Britain's naval supremacy in European waters soon forced the latter to cut down its oversea squadrons, including those in American waters. And the accelerating naval race with Germany, as well as the increasingly unfavorable international outlook in Europe, presently eliminated Great Britain as a possible military aggressor in the Western Hemisphere.[3]

The prospect of German aggression was equally remote. Germany lacked naval bases in the Western Hemisphere, and at home faced potential land enemies on two fronts. And the superior British Navy always stood between Germany and the Americas. Whatever the Kaiser and his fellow imperialists might have liked to do, there was never a time after 1900 when technical and political conditions permitted them seriously to consider the war with the United States which would inevitably have resulted from German military aggression anywhere in the Caribbean, and which probably would have followed in case of such aggression even in the more remote parts of South America.[4] And this conclusion applied with even greater force with respect to the other continental European Powers.

In the light of all these circumstances, it would seem that American statesmen might reasonably have taken a highly optimistic view of the politico-strategic outlook in the Western Atlantic. They might even have concentrated their main fighting fleet in the Pacific where, after 1900, it was more urgently needed than in the Atlantic. Actually, however, Roosevelt and his naval advisers took a somewhat different view. They apparently had little fear of British aggression, and the Presi-

[3] See Auguste Moireau, "La politique nouvelle de l'Amirauté Anglaise," *Revue des Deux Mondes*, Vol. XXVII (1905), pp. 200-8. For the details of this progressive withdrawal, see *Brassey's Naval Annual*. For the European aspects of the progressive concentration of British naval forces in European waters, see E. L. Woodward, *Great Britain and the German Navy* (1935).

[4] See Alfred Vagts, *Deutschland und die Vereinigten Staaten in der Weltpolitik* (1935), Vol. II, Chaps. XIV–XVI.

dent to the end of his life opposed a naval race with that Power. But he regarded Germany in an altogether different light. The specter of German aggression in the Caribbean or elsewhere in Latin America, became a veritable nightmare with him. He was absolutely convinced that the Kaiser would one day start trouble somewhere in this hemisphere.[5] Ignoring or belittling the all but insuperable strategic, technical, and political obstacles in the way of such aggression, Roosevelt harped on this theme until it became almost an obsession. Only a fighting fleet, second to none save Britain's, he firmly believed, could forestall or resist the anticipated aggression, and insure the security of the Panama Canal.[6]

The naval situation in the Eastern Pacific was even more favorable to the United States. European aggression in this sector was too remote to be considered. The only conceivable source of attack was the rising Japanese Empire. And the Pacific Ocean plus the United States Navy constituted an impregnable barrier against aggression from that quarter. Even if the Japanese Navy were stronger than that of the United States, which it decidedly was not, practically insuperable difficulties would have stood in the way of a trans-Pacific assault on the continental United States.

Although we have repeatedly noted the difficulties involved in waging war across the ocean, the recurrent bogey of Japanese aggression renders it highly important to leave no doubts on this point. By the beginning of the twentieth century, thanks largely to the world-wide influence of Mahan, it was recognized practically everywhere that naval operations in war, aside from sporadic raids on coast or commerce, had only one

[5] *Selections from the Correspondence of Theodore Roosevelt and Henry Cabot Lodge* (edited by H. C. Lodge), Vol. I, pp. 485, 494.

[6] Discussion of this problem is scattered through the voluminous literature on Roosevelt's diplomacy relating to the Monroe Doctrine, the Isthmian Canal, etc. See, in particular, H. C. Hill, *Roosevelt and the Caribbean* (1927), Chap. VIII, and *passim*; A. L. P. Dennis, *Adventures in American Diplomacy* (1928), Chap. XI, and *passim*; Henry Pringle, *Theodore Roosevelt* (1931), Pt. II, Chap. IV; Tyler Dennett, *John Hay* (1933), Chap. XXXI; and Vagts, *op. cit.*, Vol. II, Chaps. XIV–XVI.

major objective: destruction or confinement of the enemy's fighting fleet, as a preliminary to commercial blockade or military invasion. A hostile fleet invading the Eastern Pacific in force, would have to bring with it an immense train of auxiliary vessels. These would have to carry the supplies necessary to maintain scores of naval ships of all kinds for weeks or months of continuous sea service thousands of miles from their nearest base. These supplies would necessarily include enormous quantities of fuel and ammunition; materials and equipment for making major structural repairs; spare parts for engines, guns, hoists, and other machinery; medical equipment, food supplies, and the thousand other articles necessary to the maintenance of the complicated fighting machines into which men-of-war had evolved by the opening of this century.

This train of auxiliary vessels would constitute a serious encumbrance, limiting the fleet's speed, and requiring strong escort to guard it against surprise attacks by hostile cruisers. The units of the fleet would have to refuel frequently at sea, a difficult operation at best, and one of extreme hazard in hostile waters. Any ship suffering serious mechanical breakdown or receiving severe injury in battle, would have to limp back to its distant dockyards, across an ocean infested with enemy raiders. To provide escorts for such ships would dangerously weaken the invading fleet. Each successive week at sea would increase the latter's difficulties. Mechanical troubles would accumulate. The ships' bottoms would gradually foul, with progressive loss of speed. Health and morale of officers and men would eventually suffer from the constant strain of continuous service in hostile waters.

The attacking force, as already stated, could accomplish nothing strategically important until it had first destroyed or blockaded the defending fleet. The latter could always choose the time and place of battle, or refuse to fight at all. And the ability of the invaders to blockade the defending forces would depend not only upon a decisive initial superiority but also upon a continued efficiency impossible to maintain over an extended period, thousands of miles from their nearest drydocks and machine shops.

While the foregoing summary by no means exhausts the difficulties which would have beset any trans-Pacific aggressor against the continental United States in the opening years of this century, it is sufficient to indicate the remarkable security which the United States had come to enjoy, as a result of geographical isolation, of its own naval development, and of the increasing complexities of naval technology. No one understood these facts more clearly than did Theodore Roosevelt. Yet when a crisis with Japan arose in 1907 and 1908, he displayed astonishing alarm lest the distinctly inferior Japanese Navy launch an attack in force on our Pacific seaboard.[7]

The strategic problem in the Western Pacific was much more difficult. In Guam and the Philippines, the American people possessed not only exposed dependencies, but also well located sites for the advanced bases necessary to sustain the naval power essential to support the prestige and policies of the United States in the Far East.[8] But these sites had yet to be developed,[9] and the government had yet to build a fighting fleet strong enough to insure their security. Until such developments had taken place ashore and afloat, the strategic value of these insular outposts would remain negligible, and in certain conceivable war situations they might become simply gigantic liabilities.[10]

The peril lay chiefly in the possibility of war with Japan. The European Powers maintained squadrons in Asiatic waters

[7] See T. A. Bailey, *Theodore Roosevelt and the Japanese-American Crises* (1934), pp. 277–8.

[8] Roosevelt frankly viewed the Philippines as valuable chiefly for strategic purposes. See his reply to notification and his letter accepting the Republican nomination in 1904. *Official Proceedings of the Thirteenth Republican National Convention,* pp. 189–215.

[9] When the United States took possession there were no naval works in Guam, and only minor facilities in the Philippines.

[10] See in this connection Rear Admiral G. W. Melville, "The Important Elements in Naval Conflicts," in *Annals of the American Academy of Political and Social Science,* Vol. XXVI (1905), pp. 123, 130–1; J. D. Long, *The New American Navy* (1903), Vol. I, p. 165; and see also review of this work in *The Nation,* Vol. LXXVIII (1904), pp. 52, 54.

which symbolized a continuing threat to Chinese sovereignty, and hence to the Asiatic interests and policy of the United States. But these forces were comparatively weak, and were not generally regarded as a direct menace to the Philippines. With Japan the situation was different. Japanese commitments and ambitions related chiefly to Eastern Asia, and Japanese power was concentrated in Asiatic waters. Japanese ambitions, like those of the continental European Powers, collided with American interests and policies. And in case of war, Japanese strategists would logically strike first at the Philippine Islands.

This situation had far-reaching implications. An American fleet, strong enough to guarantee security to the Philippines, could destroy the Japanese Navy and blockade Japan. On the other hand, a fleet that could defend the Japanese homeland against the United States, would constitute a standing menace to the security of the Philippines. Any aggressive movement on the part of either Power to strengthen its navy would quickly arouse anxiety in the other country. While the United States was potentially the stronger, it was not then certain that the American people would support their government to the bitter end in a naval race with Japan. Yet the recent struggle with Spain had revealed how easily the American public could be stampeded into war. As long as the American flag floated over Manila, it was axiomatic that the Navy must be prepared to defend the Philippines. But no one envisaged more clearly than Roosevelt the desperate struggle that would ensue if the United States, inadequately prepared, should have to fight Japan singlehanded in Asiatic waters.[11]

Thus, briefly, stood the complicated and portentous politico-naval situation that confronted Roosevelt in the Far East. He did not immediately grasp all its elements and implications. At first, he regarded Russia as the greatest menace to American interests in Asia; but he eventually realized that the American people would not fight Russia in Manchuria, and that the Russians, whatever their inclinations, could not attack the

[11] See Pringle, *Roosevelt*, pp. 400–9.

United States in the Philippines or anywhere else.[12] Gradually, as he watched the growing antagonism of Japanese and American interests in the Far East, and the ominous development of anti-Japanese sentiment within the United States, Roosevelt transferred his anxiety to Japan,[13] launched a larger naval program, and finally, as a display of power, sent the battleship fleet into the Pacific, and on around the world.

Meanwhile, the drift of events, his own temperamental preferences, and the course already charted by Secretary of State John Hay, had propelled Roosevelt, via the Far East, into the main stream of world politics, resulting in adventures which further enlarged his conception of naval adequacy. To safeguard American interests in the Far East, he followed a line calculated to foster a balance of power in general and, in particular, to play off Russia and Japan against each other.[14] Since the Great Powers were all involved, any upset in Europe would inevitably produce serious repercussions in the Far East. Hence the United States had a vital if indirect interest in the shaky European equilibrium.[15] And the authority of the United States, whether in Europe or in the Far East, depended, as Roosevelt saw it, on the power and reputation of the American Navy.

Public Opinion and the Navy: Organization of the Navy League

Public opinion, a factor at every stage in the rise of American naval power, underwent an important development early in the administration of Theodore Roosevelt. As pointed out in the foregoing chapters, large sections of the American people

[12] See Tyler Dennett, *Roosevelt and the Russo-Japanese War* (1925), p. 47, and Chap. VI; and *idem, John Hay,* Chap. XXXIII.

[13] See Dennett, *Russo-Japanese War,* pp. 332–3; and Bailey, *Roosevelt and the Japanese-American Crises, passim.*

[14] Dennett, *Russo-Japanese War,* pp. 165*ff.*; and *Roosevelt-Lodge Correspondence,* Vol. II, p. 153.

[15] Dennett, *Russo-Japanese War,* pp. 87, 151, 182.

had traditionally remained apathetic, indifferent, sometimes even hostile toward the Navy. On the other hand, particular groups had shown keen interest. Shipowners, exporters, producers of goods entering largely into foreign commerce, and citizens anxious to enhance the power and prestige of the United States, all had favored increasing the Navy. The same was true of shipbuilders, the metallurgical industries, and others who participated directly or indirectly in the profits of naval construction. Then there were the professional members of the Service who had a perfectly natural desire to see their institution grow and prosper. And finally, there were the politicians, for some of whom, depending largely on the location of their constituencies, liberal naval appropriations served as a means of political advancement at the polls.

The sporadic and largely uncoordinated efforts of these various groups to influence naval legislation have entered repeatedly into this study of the rise of American naval power. And, viewing them in retrospect, it now appears rather surprising that the advocates of naval expansion should have delayed so long pooling their resources in some common organization dedicated to the twofold task of educating the public and of urging their views on Congress and the President.

Europe pointed the way toward such an organization. The British Navy League was founded in 1894, the German Navy League four years later. Similar societies sprang up in Spain, Italy, and France.[16] And in 1903 an American counterpart, the Navy League of the United States, came into existence.

Detailed analysis of this famous association's influence on American naval policy, would constitute a book in itself, but we may note briefly certain features of its composition and activities to which further reference will be made in subsequent connections. The League was from the outset an association of individuals of diverse backgrounds and interests. It included some whose only apparent interest was the national

[16] Lieutenant Commander J. H. Gibbons, "Navy Leagues," *North American Review*, Vol. CLXXVI (1903), pp. 758*ff*.

one of seeing the power and prestige of the United States sustained and increased. It included retired naval officers. And it also embraced prominent financiers, industrialists, and corporation lawyers, at least some of whom had a direct pecuniary interest in progressive naval expansion.[17] It would be as difficult to measure the League's direct influence on legislation as its indirect influence through popular education and propaganda. But in both spheres, it is no exaggeration to say that this influence was great.[18] And the organization and growth of this association in these opening years of the century was unquestionably a factor of no small importance in the remarkable success with which President Roosevelt brought about an increase of naval power, unapproached in any previous comparable period in American history.

Roosevelt's Naval Programs

Executive leadership in naval policy took on new meaning under Roosevelt. Certain Presidents and Secretaries of the Navy had displayed energy and initiative in framing a legislative program. More often the Executive had simply presented more or less specific recommendations, and then left Congress to take whatever action, if any, it saw fit. Now for the first time, Congress, during nearly eight years, faced a Chief Executive who combined an almost fanatical desire for a big navy, expert knowledge of naval affairs, an extraordinary flair for showmanship, and a fighting spirit that would not accept defeat.

The President lost no time getting his naval program under way. In December 1901, he sent Congress a ringing appeal

[17] See 64 Cong. 1 Sess., *Cong. Record* (Vol. LIII), pp. 272–93; C. A. Beard, *The Navy: Defense or Portent?* (1932).

[18] One of the League's more obvious activities was the publication of a monthly magazine. From July 1903 to December 1906, it was *The Navy League Journal*; from January 1907 to December 1916, *The Navy*; overlapping and superseded by *The Seven Seas* from June 1915 to June 1916; in turn superseded by *Sea Power*, June 1916 to July 1921.

obviously intended as much for public as for congressional consumption.[19] He followed this with specific demands,[20] backed by all the influence he could bring to bear on Congress. As on previous occasions, strong executive leadership plus safe partisan majorities produced results. Year after year, a determined minority, recruited from both parties, fought the President, denouncing his naval program as imperialistic, militaristic, grossly excessive, a menace to our peaceful relations, and calculated to impoverish the country.[21] But this opposition, even though it included some of the most distinguished congressional leaders,[22] failed to stop the Administration's drive which did not slacken until 1905.

The results of this drive were impressive. Within four years, Congress had authorized ten first-class battleships,[23] four armored cruisers,[24] and seventeen other vessels of different

[19] *M. & P.* (Bur. Nat. Lit. ed.), Vol. XIII, pp. 6665–9.

[20] 57 Cong. 1 Sess., *H. Doc.* No. 3, pp. 28–9.

[21] For some of the high points in this series of congressional debates, extending from 1902 to 1905, see 57 Cong. 1 Sess., *Cong. Record* (Vol. XXXV), pp. 5372–97, 5438–45, 5517–26, 5598; 57 Cong. 2 Sess., *op. cit.* (Vol. XXXVI), pp. 2316–17; 58 Cong. 2 Sess., *op. cit.* (Vol. XXXVIII), pp. 2064–6, 2075–80, 2148–57, 2223–6, 2228–9, 2231–2, 2332–6, 2373, 2375–9, 2720–36, 2852–67; 58 Cong. 3 Sess., *op. cit.* (Vol. XXXIX), pp. 2666–8, 2672–95, 2791–2, 2937–43, 3484–500.

[22] In particular, Rep. J. G. Cannon (Ill.), Chairman, Committee on Appropriations, and after 1903 Speaker of the House; Sen. Eugene Hale (Me.), Chairman, Senate Naval Committee, Rep. T. E. Burton (Ohio), and Rep. Claude Kitchin (N. C.). For the attitude of Roosevelt and his congressional spokesman, Sen. Henry Cabot Lodge, on the opposition of Cannon and Hale, see *Roosevelt-Lodge Correspondence*, Vol. I, p. 511.

[23] In 1902, *Connecticut, Louisiana* (16,000 tons, 18.5 knots, four twelve-inch and eight eight-inch guns, cost about $7,500,000 each); in 1903, *Idaho, Mississippi* (13,000 tons, 17 knots, four twelve-inch and eight eight-inch guns, cost about $5,800,000 each); also *Kansas, Minnesota, Vermont* (16,000 tons, 18 knots, four twelve-inch and eight eight-inch guns, cost about $7,300,000 each); in 1904, *New Hampshire* (16,000 tons, 18 knots, four twelve-inch and eight eight-inch guns, cost about $7,000,000); and in 1905, *Michigan* and *South Carolina* (16,000 tons, 18.5 knots, eight twelve-inch guns, cost about $6,600,000 each). Statistics from *Navy Yearbook*.

[24] The armored cruisers, disregarding those built before the War with Spain, now numbered ten altogether. These divided into two general classes. The smaller ones, six in number, were ships of 13,680 tons, 22–22.4 knots, four eight-inch guns in main battery, average cost about $5,400,000. The larger ones, four in number, were ships of 14,500 tons, 22–22.8 knots, four ten-inch

classes,[25] the whole aggregating over 250,000 tons displacement. During these four years, naval appropriations had mounted from $85,000,000 to $118,000,000 per year, a record without peacetime precedent.[26] And these results were even more impressive, because achieved in the face of formidable and growing opposition both inside and outside the halls of Congress.[27]

At this point, December 1905, Roosevelt announced a breathing spell. Counting vessels still under construction, he estimated the effective naval strength at forty armored ships—twenty-eight battleships and twelve armored cruisers[28]—which placed the United States second only to France and Great Britain.[29] It did "not seem . . . necessary . . . at least in the immediate future," he declared in December 1905, to increase the fleet "beyond the present number of units." It would suffice merely to replace "worn out" or "inefficient" units, adding "probably . . . a single battleship . . . each year."[30]

Actually, the Administration never put this replacement policy fully into operation. The General Board whose conception

---

guns, average cost about $5,700,000. These ships, whose fighting power was always a matter of controversy, were rendered wholly obsolete by the advent of the battle cruiser, or all-big-gun cruiser, the first group of which were completed by the British Admiralty in 1908–1909. These first battle cruisers mounted eight twelve-inch guns, or the same main battery as was carried by the United States battleships *Michigan* and *South Carolina*, authorized in 1905, but not completed until 1910.

25 These included three so-called scout cruisers, a modified type which was destined to evolve into the fast light cruiser of the present day.

26 *Navy Yearbook, 1917*, pp. 679, 741–2.

27 The growth of this opposition is clearly discernible in congressional debates. It is likewise apparent from the volume and tone of the periodical literature of the period. For representative samples of this trend, see the ex-Secretary of the Navy John D. Long's "Shall the Navy be Increased?" in *The Independent*, Vol. LVIII (March 1905), pp. 639*ff*.; and editorial, "Our Naval Policy," in *The Nation*, Vol. LXXIX (Dec. 8, 1904), p. 454. For Roosevelt's comment on the growth of the opposition, see Bishop, *Roosevelt*, Vol. I, p. 366.

28 This estimate included the five battleships and two armored cruisers completed before the war with Spain. The fighting value of these ships in 1905 was certainly debatable.

29 Bishop, *Roosevelt*, Vol. I, p. 366.

30 *M. & P.* (Bur. Nat. Lit. ed.), Vol. XIV, p. 7000; and letters quoted in Bishop, *Roosevelt*, Vol. I, p. 366; and Allan Nevins, *Henry White* (1930), p. 499.

of an adequate fighting fleet exceeded even Roosevelt's, strongly opposed any slackening in the pace of naval construction.[31] And the President, perhaps because of his rising anxiety over the anti-Japanese movement in California,[32] supported the Navy Department's request for two battleships in the same message in which he announced the one-a-year replacement program.[33] As Senator Lodge had warned, the latter announcement placed the President at a fatal disadvantage in making fresh demands on Congress. The opponents of further naval expansion could, and repeatedly did, cite Roosevelt as authority for the view that the Navy was now large enough. And when the latter launched a second large building program in 1907, they immediately countered it by vociferously endorsing his former one-a-year replacement policy. Meanwhile, in the congressional session of 1905–1906, the lines were forming for the coming struggle, with the advocates of continuous but moderate naval development holding new battleship authorizations down to one instead of two as requested by the Administration.[34]

Before Congress again assembled, in December 1906, events on our Pacific Coast had plunged the United States into a grave political crisis with Japan. This crisis arose from the rising anti-Japanese agitation, especially in California, leading to boycotts and discrimination which culminated, in October 1906, in the segregation of Oriental school children in San Francisco. An alarming situation rapidly developed, with war widely regarded as the possible outcome. Roosevelt strove conscientiously to reach a peaceful settlement, but characteristically determined to prepare for the worst. In public, he spoke

[31] Navy Dept., *Ann. Repts., 1905,* pp. 21–2. It was subsequently revealed that the General Board, from 1903 on, had worked toward a fleet built around forty-eight first-class battleships. Navy Dept., *Ann. Repts., 1913,* pp. 30*ff*.

[32] See Bailey, *Roosevelt and the Japanese-American Crises,* pp. 15*ff*.

[33] *M. & P.* (Bur. Nat. Lit. ed.), Vol. XIV, p. 7002.

[34] *Roosevelt-Lodge Correspondence,* Vol. II, p. 204; 59 Cong. 1 Sess., *H. Rept.* No. 3639, p. 18; 59 Cong. 1 Sess., *Cong. Record* (Vol. XL), pp. 6957–84, 7846–50; *Navy Yearbook, 1917,* p. 247.

calmly of the Navy's readiness for any eventuality. But privately, he sent warning letters to the chairmen of the House and Senate Naval Committees, which foreshadowed early abandonment of his one-a-year replacement policy.[35]

Such action was hastened by a revolutionary advance in naval architecture which fortuitously coincided with the Japanese crisis. This advance was the development of the so-called "all-big-gun" battleship. The first-class battleship of the decade, 1895–1905, carried a main battery of four large (eleven- to thirteen-inch) and a larger number of medium caliber (eight- to nine-inch) guns, mounted usually in pairs in revolving turrets. In December 1906, however, the British Admiralty completed a battleship the main battery of which consisted entirely of twelve-inch guns, ten in number. This battery, together with heavier armor, greater speed, higher freeboard, and hence higher gun-platforms, gave this battleship at least twice the offensive power of any warship in existence. And the advent of this ship, named the *Dreadnought,* rendered immediately obsolete every capital ship afloat.[36]

American naval authorities had anticipated this development. They had already designed two battleships with single-caliber main batteries. These ships, authorized in 1905 but not laid down until the following year, carried eight twelve-inch guns instead of four.[37] And the battleship, authorized in 1906, following completion of the British *Dreadnought,* completed the American Navy's transition to the new standard of capital-ship power. This ship, the *Delaware,* was the first American dreadnought. It displaced 20,000 tons, practically twice as much as the *Oregon,* best American battleship in 1898. The *Delaware* could steam better than 21.5 knots, nearly five knots faster than the *Oregon.* It carried two and one-half times as many big guns, each with longer range, higher power, and

[35] *M. & P.* (Bur. Nat. Lit. ed.), Vol. XIV, p. 7067; Bailey, *op. cit.,* pp. 81*ff.*, 119*ff.*

[36] See *Brassey's Naval Annual, 1907,* pp. 2*ff.*, 391*ff.*

[37] *Michigan* and *South Carolina.* See *ibid.*, pp. 32*ff.*, and note 23 *supra.*

greater accuracy. And its construction marked another stage in rise of American naval power.[38]

The advent of the dreadnought battleship, coming on top of the Japanese crisis, galvanized the President into action. In January 1907, he addressed a warning to the House Naval Committee that we must build dreadnoughts or relinquish our political power and position in both oceans.[39] And when the forces of conservatism in Congress once more authorized only one capital ship,[40] Roosevelt countered, the following December, with a peremptory demand for immediate construction of four all-big-gun ships.[41]

This demand precipitated one of the bitterest legislative struggles in American naval history. The House Naval Committee recommended only two ships.[42] The President's supporters, led by Representative Richmond P. Hobson of Alabama,[43] countered with a motion to restore the number to four.[44] In support of this motion, it was repeated that such an increase was necessary to hold our naval rank among the Powers. It was imperative to maintain that rank, or even to forge ahead, not to support aggressive policies, for we had none; but to compel respect for our commercial rights and interests in the Far East, to maintain the supremacy of the white race in the Pacific, to prevent violations of the Monroe

[38] A detailed, illustrated article entitled, "Ten Years' Development of the Battleship," *Scientific American*, Vol. XCVII (Dec. 7, 1907), pp. 408*ff*., graphically traces the evolution of American capital ship design to the *Delaware*.

[39] He enclosed a remarkable technical report prepared by his friend, Lieutenant Commander (later Admiral) William S. Sims, entitled "The Tactical Qualities of the Dreadnought Type of Battleship." Roosevelt's letter and Sims' report are printed in *Brassey's Annual, 1907*, pp. 387*ff*.

[40] 59 Cong. 2 Sess., *Cong. Record* (Vol. XLI), pp. 2597–605, 2774–8, 3047–69, 3437; *Navy Yearbook, 1917*, p. 261. The ship built under this authorization was the *North Dakota* (20,000 tons, 21 knots, ten twelve-inch guns, cost over $8,500,000).

[41] *M. & P.* (Bur. Nat. Lit. ed.), Vol. XIV, p. 7114.

[42] 60 Cong. 1 Sess., *H. Rept.* No. 1398, pp. 19–20.

[43] Hobson had served in the Navy during the War with Spain, and had achieved fame through his attempt to sink a hulk and thus block the entrance to the harbor of Santiago, Cuba, in which Cervera's fleet was anchored.

[44] *H. Rept.* No. 1398, Pt. II; 60 Cong. 1 Sess., *Cong. Record* (Vol. XLII), p. 4782.

Doctrine, to deter potential aggressors against our continental and oversea territories, and in the final analysis, to repel aggression, if necessary by war.[45]

In reply, advocates of the smaller program scouted the war rumors which, they asserted, were annually cooked up when the naval appropriation bill was under consideration. They flatly rejected the familiar argument that a big navy was cheap insurance against war, contending instead that naval expansion in one country fostered distrust and fear abroad, stimulating armament competition that could end only in national bankruptcy or war, or both. They also made much of our strong geographical position, stressing the all-but-insuperable strategic and technical, as well as political, obstacles which would prevent any Asiatic or European Power from carrying a war across the Pacific or Atlantic. And expressly or by implication, they stood opposed to building up a great navy for waging war overseas.[46]

It was not to be expected that a man of Roosevelt's temper would quietly await the outcome. Already, in December 1907, he had made a bold and dramatic gesture, calculated both to overawe Japan and to popularize the Navy and his latest naval program. This was nothing less than sending a fleet of sixteen battleships to our Pacific Coast, where they arrived in April 1908, when the struggle in Congress was approaching a climax. Meanwhile, he had ordered Congress to authorize his four battleships without further delay.[47] He had also resurrected

[45] See speeches by Favrot (Dem., La.), McKinley (Rep., Cal.), Knowland (R., Cal.), Hobson (D., Ala.), O'Connell (D., Mass.), Cockran (D., N. Y.), Richardson (D., Ala.), Humphrey (R., Wash.), Fassett (R., N. Y.), Robinson (D., Ark.), Hays (R., Cal.), Parker (R., N. J.), Landis (R., Ind.), Longworth (R., Ohio), Talbott (D., Md.), *Cong. Record,* Vol. XLII, pp. 4581, 4596, 4598, 4605, 4647, 4778, 4788, 4789, 4799, 4800, 4801, 4802, 4804, 4805.

[46] See speeches of Foss (R., Ill.), Padgett (D., Tenn.), Bartholdt (R., Mo.), Gregg (D., Tex.), Burton (R., Ohio), Kitchin (D., N. C.), Loud (R., Mich.), Rainey (D., Ill.), Williams (D., Miss.), Tawney (R., Minn.), Lassiter (D., W. Va.), Keifer (R., Ohio), Macon (D., Ark.), Fuller (R., Ill.), Watkins (D., La.), *ibid.,* 4574, 4578, 4584, 4604, 4611, 4620, 4637, 4780, 4781, 4783, 4789, 4797, 4802, 4803, 4804, 4806.

[47] *M. & P.* (Bur. Nat. Lit. ed.), Vol. XIV, p. 7147.

the Japanese crisis, now on the way toward settlement, and exploited it behind the scenes to subdue the opposition.[48] In desperation, he even threatened to veto a special "local public buildings bill," a pork-barrel measure, dear to every Congressman who must soon face his constituents in the rapidly approaching election.[49] These and other maneuvers failed, however, to quell the revolt. The House voted down Hobson's motion, 199 to 83, without the formality of a roll call; then adopted the committee's two-battleship proposal; but appropriated no funds with which to begin work on the vessels thus authorized.[50]

The battleground now shifted to the Senate, where a group of younger members, under the aggressive leadership of Albert J. Beveridge of Indiana, rallied behind the President. But the Senate also was completely out of hand. For seven years, Roosevelt had ridden roughshod over senatorial pride, prestige, and prerogative. He had repeatedly ignored or sidestepped the Senate's rôle in foreign relations. He had pushed sundry social reforms against the wishes of Republican conservatives who dominated the Senate organization. But now his "reign" was swiftly drawing to a close; his "big stick" no longer had its old-time efficacy. As power slipped from his grasp, the Senate conservatives took revenge all along the line.[51] After a savage debate,[52] in which even Roosevelt's ancient friendship with Senator Lodge hung precariously in the balance,[53] the Republican "Old Guard," including a few genuine small-navy men as well as many who would normally have supported a strong

[48] Bailey, *Roosevelt and the Japanese-American Crises,* pp. 207, 247*ff*.; Pringle, *Roosevelt,* p. 409; L. W. Busbey, *Uncle Joe Cannon* (1927), pp. 223–6.

[49] *Cong. Record,* Vol. XLII, p. 4801; *New York Herald,* April 5, 1908, Sec. II, p. 3. The *Herald* reported this revelation under the expressive headline: "No 'Pork' If Big Ships Are Beaten."

[50] *Cong. Record,* Vol. XLII, pp. 4806, 4838; *New York Herald,* April 16, 1908, p. 6.

[51] Pringle, *Roosevelt,* Pt. II, Chaps. XI–XV; E. S. Bates, *The Story of Congress,* pp. 343–53.

[52] *Cong. Record,* Vol. XLII, pp. 5007–20, 5158–75, 5211–36, 5262–93; Claude Bowers, *Beveridge and the Progressive Era* (1932), pp. 277–82.

[53] Bowers, *op. cit.,* p. 280; *Roosevelt-Lodge Correspondence,* Vol. II, p. 293.

naval policy, joined with a majority of the Democrats to vote down the President's four-battleship program.[54] After thus wrecking his favorite project, the Senate relented sufficiently to sustain the two-ship authorization of the House, and to restore, under threat of veto,[55] the appropriation necessary to begin work on the new vessels.[56]

The political implications of this dramatic legislative struggle are by no means clear. Taking the House proceedings as a fair index of public opinion,[57] it would appear: first, that the American people as a whole were overwhelmingly opposed to the President's naval program; and, second, that the Middle West was the stronghold of anti-navy sentiment.[58]

Certain collateral evidence, however, throws some doubt upon these conclusions. Practically all active public opposition to the President's program came not from the Middle West but from the Atlantic seaboard. The active groups consisted chiefly of the Society of Friends, Protestant clergymen, teachers, businessmen, and financiers.[59] A conspicuous leader in the movement was Andrew Carnegie, who appealed personally to the President,[60] and whose name headed an impressive petition,

[54] *Cong. Record,* Vol. XLII, p. 5291.

[55] *The Times* (London), April 23, 1908, p. 3.

[56] *Navy Yearbook, 1917,* p. 282.

[57] The House proceedings were comparatively free from the personal animosities that seriously blurred the Senate scene. Furthermore, unlike Senators elected for long terms by State legislatures, every Representative was coming up for reelection at the polls within eight months.

[58] See *New York Herald,* April 18, 1908, p. 5. The powerful Speaker of the House, Rep. Cannon (Ill.), was notoriously opposed to a big navy; Rep. Foss (Ill.), Chairman of the Naval Committee, was lukewarm even to the two-ship proposal sponsored by his committee; and Rep. Tawney (Minn.), Chairman of the Appropriations Committee, seriously attempted to secure further reduction in the number of battleships authorized. See *Cong. Record,* Vol. XLII, p. 4806. Of the eight representatives from coastal districts who spoke on the question, seven strongly endorsed the four-ship program; of the eight from interior districts of coastal States, five supported that program; but of the fourteen from interior States who spoke, no less than eleven opposed the four-ship program. Since there was no roll call it is impossible to make a closer analysis of the sectional cleavage.

[59] *Cong. Record,* Vol. XLII, pp. 1265, 2361, 2717, 2952, 3421, 3822, 4743.

[60] B. J. Hendrick, *The Life of Andrew Carnegie* (1932), Vol. II, p. 320.

signed by hundreds of prominent New Yorkers.[61] Conspicuous, also, were outspoken criticisms from a committee of the National Association of Manufacturers,[62] and from editors of leading financial journals.[63]

Turning to press opinion in general, one encounters still other puzzling facts. In February 1908, the *Literary Digest* reported a sharp difference of opinion among the newspapers, with respect to the President's battleship program.[64] Two months later, however, a poll of editors[65] and a survey of editorials revealed a press overwhelmingly supporting the President against Congress.[66] Letters and telegrams pouring in upon Congress during the struggle were said also to reflect this later drift of opinion.[67] Yet, as already noted, the House on the eve of a general election voted down the President's program by the decisive majority of 199 to 83.

Whatever inference one may draw from these contradictory indications, certain facts are clear. By demanding four, Roosevelt secured two battleships instead of one, thereby smashing the one-a-year replacement policy, which he had previously endorsed, and which his opponents were now citing against him. And this achievement set a precedent for the next congressional session (1908–1909), in which Roosevelt, using the same strategy, secured two more capital ships in the face of even stiffer opposition.[68]

[61] *Cong. Record,* Vol. XLII, p. 4743.

[62] Nat. Assoc. Manufacturers, *Proc. of 13th Ann. Conv.,* p. 16.

[63] Urging a firm stand against the extravagant demands of Roosevelt, Lodge, and their "sympathizers," *The Commercial and Financial Chronicle* scouted the suggestion that our Navy was inadequate, and observed sourly that "the experience of European governments . . . shows that concessions to demands for a larger navy, instead of leading to expressions of satisfaction, are at once made the foundation for vastly larger demands, and in every country where pressure of taxation and perplexities of the public deficit are recognized, this drift of things in naval construction is frankly admitted to be a peril almost as serious as that of the standing army." Vol. LXXXVI (April 25, 1908), p. 1009. See also *Banker's Magazine,* Vol. LXXVI (May 1908), p. 658.

[64] Vol. XXXVI, p. 253.

[65] *New York Herald,* April 24, 1908, p. 8.

[66] *Literary Digest,* Vol. XXXVI (May 2, 1908), p. 631.

[67] *New York Herald,* April 23, 1908, p. 3.

[68] *M. & P.* (Bur. Nat. Lit. ed.), Vol. XIV, pp. 7236–7; 60 Cong. 2 Sess., *H. Rept.*

With this final compromise, Roosevelt stepped down from the presidency. Since launching his second drive in 1907, he had maneuvered Congress into authorizing four new capital ships, larger, more powerful, and more expensive than their predecessors.[69] In the face of financial panic and industrial depression, he had forced up naval appropriations from $100,-900,000 in 1907 to the unprecedented peacetime figure of $140,-000,000 in 1909. On the other hand, he had secured many less battleships than he had demanded. Except for submarines which Congressmen especially favored because of their presumed utility for coast and harbor defense,[70] the Administration had secured comparatively little besides battleships. After authorizing three scout cruisers in 1904, Congress had ignored all subsequent recommendations for these indispensable "eyes" of a fighting fleet. The Administration had further secured only twenty destroyers, a mere fraction of the number needed for a fleet as large as that of the United States.[71] And in addition to all this, and perhaps even more important, the President's demands had aroused, strengthened, and solidified an opposition, hitherto scattered and largely unorganized,[72] foreshadowing stormy times in case the next Administration should

---

No. 1862, p. 21; 60 Cong. 2 Sess., *Cong. Record* (Vol. XLIII), pp. 1314–22, 2549, 2550; *Navy Yearbook, 1917*, p. 299.

[69] The battleships authorized in 1908 were the *Florida* and *Utah* (21,825 tons, 21 knots, ten twelve-inch guns, cost $10,400,000 and $8,500,000 respectively); in 1909, *Arkansas* and *Wyoming* (26,000 tons, 21-21.6 knots, twelve twelve-inch guns, cost $10,000,000, and $11,000,000 respectively). *Navy Yearbook* statistics.

[70] See, for example, *Cong. Record,* Vol. XLII, pp. 4822, 4823. Between 1902 and 1909 inclusive, Congress authorized twenty-seven submarines, although this type was still in a highly experimental stage.

[71] See 63 Cong. 3 Sess., House Committee on Naval Affairs, *Hearings on Estimates for 1915*, p. 702. While even the professional experts tended sometimes to underestimate the value of cruisers and destroyers as elements of a fighting fleet, it is nevertheless true that both the experts and the Administration had striven year after year to secure more ships of these types. But Roosevelt and his naval advisers consistently sacrificed these latter rather than battleships when it proved impossible to get both.

[72] This was particularly the case in the short session of 1908–1909, in which a motion in the House to strike out the authorization for even two more battleships lost by the narrow margin of 80 to 100. *Cong. Record,* Vol. XLIII, p. 1314; and see Merle Curti, *Peace or War* (1936), pp. 219–20.

undertake to carry on Roosevelt's policy of keeping pace with the still accelerating naval race in Europe.

Building a Fighting Navy

It was one thing to persuade or coerce Congress into authorizing ships. It was another to design and build them. And it was as great a task, if a less spectacular one, to weld the ships, the officers and crews who manned them, and the supporting shore organization into an efficient fighting machine.

When Roosevelt succeeded to the presidency in 1901, the country's warship-building facilities, both public and private, were still far from adequate. The battleship *Illinois*, authorized back in June 1896, was just going into commission in September 1901. It required nearly four and a half years on the average to build each of the ten battleships authorized between 1896 and 1900. And many of them when completed showed defects of design which seriously impaired their fighting qualities. Their protective belt of armor extended insufficiently above the waterline. They had such low freeboard that it was impossible to work some or all of their guns in a heavy sea. A direct vertical shaft from the big-gun turrets to the ammunition-handling rooms opened the way for a powder flash in the turret to explode the magazine. The gun ports were too large to afford adequate protection for gun crews and the elaborate mechanism for handling the guns. And there were other faults too technical to mention here. When Roosevelt left the presidency, most of these defects had either been corrected or were in process of correction. The building time for battleships was less than two years. And a large share of the credit for these achievements belonged to the President.[73]

Roosevelt found the Navy's organization and administration even more defective. Despite the teachings of Mahan and recent

[73] See Henry Reuterdahl, "The Needs of Our Navy," *McClure's Magazine*, Vol. XXX (Jan. 1908), pp. 251*ff*.

experience in the war with Spain, there was still no permanent fleet in being. The capital ships in commission were widely scattered. Ships on oversea stations had to come home frequently for repairs, or else depend upon such facilities as were obtainable in foreign ports. There was an acute personnel shortage, rendering it absolutely impossible to man all the ships built and building. Yet the personnel system in force kept officers in subordinate ranks until late in their careers. Despite recent efforts to adjust the long-standing feud between the Line and engineer corps, ill-will was smoldering between these branches of the Service. Several years of timid and cautious political leadership had tightened the hold of the Navy Department bureaucracy, which now ruled with an iron hand, usually ignoring, sometimes penalizing, those who attempted to introduce reforms and innovations. With Congress, as in earlier years, more interested in naval spoils than in naval efficiency; with the lay public apathetic, as ever, to the details of naval art and science; and with cautious and conservative elderly officers dominating the Service, the need was great and the time was ripe for a thorough housecleaning. Of all men in public life at that time Roosevelt was preeminently the best equipped to wield the broom.[74]

In December 1901, less than three months after taking office, he was ready with a program of reforms. These included: additional officers and seamen; less shore duty; more ships in commission; a new emphasis on efficiency; and constant training under conditions as similar as possible to those of actual warfare. "It is important," he declared, "to have our Navy of adequate size, but it is even more important that ship for ship

[74] For personnel statistics, ships in commission, their disposition, etc., see the *Navy Register, 1901;* for a picture of conditions as they appeared to the Navy Department bureaucracy, see *Annual Reports, 1901,* 57 Cong. 1 Sess., *H. Doc.* No. 3 (2 vols.); for an objective, if not too critical analysis, see C. O. Paullin, "A Half Century of Naval Administration, 1861–1911," Pt. XII, Secs. 1–2, *Proceedings of the United States Naval Institute,* Vol. XL (1914), pp. 673*ff.*, 1059*ff.*; and for graphic personal recollections, see Rear Admiral B. A. Fiske, *From Midshipman to Rear Admiral* (1919), Chap. XXIII; and Rear Admiral R. D. Evans, *An Admiral's Log* (1910), pp. 125*ff.*, 137.

it should equal in efficiency any navy in the world. This is possible only with highly drilled crews and officers, and this in turn imperatively demands continuous and progressive instruction in target practice, ship handling, squadron tactics, and general discipline."[75]

The personnel shortage was so critical as to attract wide attention.[76] It was imperative, in Roosevelt's eyes, to provide officers and crews for all the ships, and then to keep them in commission. Modern warships were complicated mechanisms, formidable when manned by trained personnel, but utterly useless in inexperienced hands.[77] Yet the United States, he declared publicly in 1902, was facing an alarming shortage of enlisted personnel, and had less than half enough officers to man properly the ships already built and under construction.[78] Year after year he pressed these facts on Congress[79] which grumbled but responded after a fashion.[80] The Navy's enlisted strength was stepped up from 25,050 in 1901, to 44,500 in 1909.[81] By increasing admissions to the Naval Academy, and raising the quotas for certain ranks, the "active list" of officers was boosted from 883 to 1,096 in the same interval.[82] But the stringency still continued. The enlisted strength fell short of that authorized by law.[83] And the slight increase in officer personnel failed to keep abreast of the rapidly accelerating pace of naval construction. As a result, by the end of 1908, the United States Navy, ranking second only to Great Britain in first-class capital ships, and third in tonnage built and build-

[75] *M. & P.* (Bur. Nat. Lit. ed.), Vol. XIII, p. 6668.

[76] There is a large contemporary literature on this question which is easily accessible through the periodical indexes. For a terse statement of the problem, see A. S. Hurd, "America's Bid for Naval Supremacy," in *Nineteenth Century*, Vol. LII (1902), pp. 893–904.

[77] *M. & P.* (Bur. Nat. Lit. ed.), Vol. XIII, p. 8867.

[78] *ibid.*, Vol. XIV, pp. 6722–3.

[79] *ibid.*, pp. 6926, 7001, 7068.

[80] Paullin, "A Half-Century of Naval Administration," Pt. XII, p. 681.

[81] *Navy Yearbook, 1917*, p. 901.

[82] *Navy Register, 1901*, pp. 7*ff.*; and same, *1909*, pp. 6*ff.*

[83] Paullin, "Half Century of Naval Administration," Pt. XII, p. 683.

ing, had less than one-third as many line officers as Great Britain, and about half as many as Germany, France, and Japan respectively.[84]

The personnel shortage bore directly on the problem of efficiency. With officers and crews overworked, training and discipline inevitably suffered. Yet the fighting power of the Navy depended no more on the excellence of the ships than on the knowledge, skill, and efficiency of the men who handled them and worked the guns.[85]

The gunnery problem was especially acute when Roosevelt took office. Naval gunnery in the preceding century had occasionally risen to an art, but never to a science. The development of rifle ordnance of great range, power, and potential accuracy, opened the way for a revolution in gunnery. But this revolution hung fire. The Navy Department, it is recalled, had long remained indifferent to precision instruments for range-finding, gun-sighting, and gun-pointing.[86] Though the Spanish War had fully exposed the Navy's low standard of marksmanship, the naval authorities complacently ignored the deficiency. Target practice, traditionally unpopular, was left largely to the discretion of commanding officers on the different stations. And the primitive gunnery and target-practice methods still in vogue effectually blocked any real progress.[87]

Here and there, individual officers, mostly younger men of subordinate rank, were struggling with the gunnery problem. One of them in particular, Lieutenant (later Admiral) William S. Sims, while in Hongkong awaiting his ship, met Sir Percy Scott of the British Navy. To the list of reports which Sims had already written concerning the defects of certain American ships, he now added voluminous accounts of the new system of

[84] Navy Dept., *Ann. Repts.*, 1908, p. 12.

[85] *M. & P.* (Bur. Nat. Lit. ed.), Vol. XIV, pp. 6722, 6806, 6926, 7002, 7067, 7115.

[86] See Fiske, *Midshipman to Rear Admiral, passim.*

[87] Lieutenant Commander Albert Gleaves, "Training Gunners in the United States Navy," *World's Work,* Vol. VIII (June 1904), pp. 4895–903.

continuous-aim firing which Scott was then developing.[88] He even went so far as to write directly to President Roosevelt, at the risk of his future career, pointing out the "very inefficient condition" of the American Navy "as a fighting force." Although Roosevelt did not, as tradition has it, abruptly call Sims home to be Inspector of Target Practice,[89] it is a fact that Sims was made Intelligence Officer and Target Practice Inspector on the China Station. In this capacity he immediately began to work out improved techniques both for aiming and firing guns, and for conducting target practice. These innovations produced marked improvement in gunnery records within a short time.[90]

Some months later, in the fall of 1902, Sims was called back to Washington to take over the post of Inspector of Target Practice for the whole Navy.[91] In the next few years Sims developed an entirely new system of gunnery and fire control, improving existing instruments, devising new ones, and training the men to a high degree of efficiency. Late in 1905 a Board on Fire Control was able to draw up a statement of general principles which constitute the basis of modern gunnery practice.[92]

The new system had to withstand numerous attacks from within the Service. One of the most serious of these resulted from a disastrous explosion which occurred in a main turret of the battleship *Missouri* in April 1904. This accident was ascribed by many officers to the greatly increased rate of gunfire, rather than to faulty design of the ammunition hoists.[93] In this instance, as in many others, Sims received the strong support of the Presi-

[88] Elting E. Morison, *Admiral Sims and the Modern American Navy* (1942), Chap. VII, especially pp. 83*ff*., 96, 99*f*., 101, also pp. 116*ff*., 125. Before this time gunners set their sights and waited for the roll of the ship to bring the sights on the target. The new method kept the sights continuously on the target. The traditional target was a small triangular canvas, and shots which might have hit if the target had been a ship were counted. The new target was a larger rectangular canvas and only actual hits were counted.

[89] *ibid*., pp. 101-5.

[90] *ibid*., pp. 122*ff*., 125*ff*.

[91] *ibid*., pp. 126-130.

[92] *ibid*., Chap. IX.

[93] *ibid*., pp. 138-9, 141, 147. A flareback from the gun ignited a powder charge in the turret and dropping sparks produced a second explosion in the handling room. Five officers and twenty-nine men were killed.

dent. When informed of the move to put target practice back on the basis of percentage of hits, instead of the number of actual hits per minute, Roosevelt, with the forthrightness which characterized so many of his acts, ordered the matter left to him. The new system was retained, and with it the whole system of gunnery which Sims had introduced.[94]

Throughout this period Roosevelt carried on a noisy crusade to enlighten the Navy, Congress, and the public as to the vital importance of efficient gunnery.[95] So remarkable were the results of the new system that in his message to Congress in December 1906, after the conclusion of the first target practice held under simulated battle conditions, Roosevelt conservatively estimated that the Navy's shooting had already improved fully 100 per cent.[96]

Progress in gunnery continued. In the remaining years of the Administration existing fire control equipment was perfected and new instruments, such as range clocks and range deflection transmitters for example, were secured and installed. Training methods underwent further improvement. American gunnery came to rank close to, if not completely on a par with that prevailing in British ships.[97]

Roosevelt was less successful in his attempt to reorganize the Navy Department. Since 1842, the Department had been divided into administrative divisions or bureaus. One bureau had jurisdiction over hulls, another over machinery, another over ordnance, another over navy yards, another over personnel, etc. Each bureau chief was responsible only to the Secretary of the Navy, who was thus the sole coordinator and supervisor of the work of the Department as a whole. Yet the Secretary, invariably a civilian, rarely, if ever, possessed suffi-

94 *ibid.*, pp. 137, 141, 240.

95 Gleaves, "Training Gunners," pp. 4896-7; Fiske, *Midshipman to Rear Admiral*, p. 347; Roosevelt, Autobiography (1913), pp. 232-3; *New York Times*, Sept. 29, 1936, p. 27; and citations in note 85 above.

96 *M. & P.* (Bur. Nat. Lit. ed.), Vol. XIV, p. 7067. In another connection he maintained that the navy's gunnery had improved at least five times. *New York Times*, Sept. 29, 1936, p. 27.

97 Morison, *Admiral Sims*, Chap. XV, especially pp. 236-41.

cient technical knowledge to perform this function well. As a result, there was waste, duplication, and conflict of jurisdiction. Precedent and routine dominated the Department. Complaints multiplied. Yet the Secretary could usually do little more than refer these to the bureau whose work was under fire. And no bureau staff, with personal reputations and even positions at stake, could afford to admit blunders the rectification of which might cost thousands or millions of dollars.[98]

To remedy these conditions, the Line had long advocated a permanent board of line officers, to constitute a general staff. It was urged that such a body should centralize the functions performed by the Naval War College, the Naval Intelligence Office, and the General Board. In addition, it should have broad powers over the bureaus, and advise the Secretary of the Navy on all matters pertaining to policy and administration.[99] While this plan had much to commend it, especially on purely military grounds, and while a similar organization was instituted in the Army during this period, the movement for a Navy general staff made little headway outside the Service. Congress was absolutely opposed from fear that such a body would reduce the Secretary of the Navy to a mere figurehead, and even usurp the policy-determining function of Congress, a function which included the prerogative of the national legislature to exploit the Navy for the mutual benefit of favored districts and electioneering politicians.[100]

Roosevelt, however, with preparedness for war uppermost in his mind, had championed the general staff idea from the beginning of his Administration.[101] He forced the question

[98] For the efforts of Secretary of the Navy Whitney (1885-1889) to grapple with this problem of Navy Department organization, see p. 193, *supra*.

[99] One may easily trace the latter evolution of this movement in the *Proceedings of the United States Naval Institute*, and in the annual reports of the Bureau of Navigation, beginning with 1900. For a more general study, see L. M. Short, *The Development of National Administrative Organization in the United States* (1923), Chap. XIV.

[100] See C. O. Paullin, "A Half Century of Naval Administration in America," Pt. X, *Proc. U. S. Nav. Inst.*, Vol. XL (1914), pp. 111*ff*.

[101] *M. & P.* (Bur. Nat. Lit. ed.), Vol. XIII, p. 6668.

before Congress in 1904, but failed to secure any action.[102] Within the Navy itself a small group of officers known as the "insurgents" were determined to continue the fight for reorganization. Stubborn and solid opposition in the Navy and in Congress blocked every move. By 1907 they were confronted with the realization that they had failed and that the Roosevelt Administration was nearing its end.[103] The only hope was a change of strategy.

In January 1908 an article entitled, "The Needs of Our Navy," appeared in *McClure's Magazine* over the signature of Henry Reuterdahl, American editor of *Jane's Fighting Ships.* The departmental bureaus, Reuterdahl contended, were responsible for grave defects in the design of American ships, such as too low freeboard, badly placed armor belts, and open shaft ammunition hoists. The bureaus had perpetuated these defects, he further charged, to the jeopardy of the sea-going personnel despite repeated complaints from the officers who actually handled the ships. The Navy Department's administrative system he believed quite incapable of keeping the Navy ready for war.[104] It subsequently appeared, if indeed it was not obvious from the subject-matter of the article itself, that Sims, now naval aide to the President, was one of the instigators of this attack.[105]

Reuterdahl's article rocked the Department and produced an explosion in the press. The extent and force of the repercussions led Senator Hale of Maine, chairman of the Senate Naval Committee, to call a congressional investigation on the basis of Reuterdahl's charges.[106]

102 *op. cit.*, Vol. XIV, p. 6806; and Paullin, *op. cit.*, pp. 120-1.

103 Morison, *Admiral Sims*, pp. 177-8, 180-2.

104 *The Navy*, Vol. I (1907), No. 6, p. 13; No. 7, p. 8; Henry Reuterdahl, "The Needs of Our Navy," *McClure's Magazine*, Vol. XXX (1908), pp. 251-63; Morison, *op. cit.*, pp. 182-5.

105 See *New York Times*, Sept. 29, 1936, p. 27; also Morison, *op. cit.*, pp. 183-4.

106 See 60 Cong. 1 Sess., *Cong. Record* (Vol. XLII), pp. 556-60; Senate Naval Committee, *Hearings on S. 3335*; and *S. Doc.* Nos. 297, 298, 427. For press comment, see *Literary Digest*, Dec. 1907 to March 1908, Vol. XXXV, p. 971; and Vol. XXXVI, pp. 1, 79, 176, 290, 355; also Morison, *op. cit.*, pp. 185*ff*.

In his younger days Hale had been a strong supporter of the Navy, but at this time he had already become the center of opposition to progress and expansion in both armed forces.[107] Hale's management of the investigation leaves little doubt that he planned to use it to defeat finally and conclusively the insurgents and all their naval reforms. He secured as witnesses, in defense of the bureau system, Admirals Converse and Capps who proved both able and convincing. He attempted arbitrarily to limit the field of investigation to the technical points raised in the article, thus excluding from discussion the fundamental question of the faulty administrative system which produced the technical defects.[108]

The insurgents succeeded, in spite of heckling and arbitrary procedure, in substantiating many of Reuterdahl's charges. But when the discussions verged "dangerously close" to the real issue of naval administration the committee suddenly went into executive session and adjourned. The records were published, but the committee made no reports or recommendations.[109]

As if the results of the investigation were not sufficiently discouraging to the reformers, Roosevelt himself appeared to be wavering in his support of the cause of reorganization. The President had never entirely approved the Reuterdahl episode, and now he was subjected to strong pressure against making any drastic changes, or in any way antagonizing Senator Hale.[110]

After the abrupt end of the investigation one of the leading insurgents, Commodore A. L. Key, left to get his ship ready for sea. While waiting for the *Salem* he carefully inspected the dreadnought battleship *North Dakota*, sister ship of the *Delaware*, which was in the same yard. He reported to the Secretary of the Navy, as all officers had been invited to do, five respects in which the design of the *North Dakota* seemed to be faulty.[111] Sims sent a copy of this letter to the President and persuaded him to call a

107 Morison, *op. cit.*, pp. 181-2, 185*ff*.
108 *ibid.*, pp. 185-9.
109 *ibid.*, pp. 189-99.
110 *ibid.*, pp. 198-200.
111 *ibid.*, pp. 201-2.

conference composed of members of the General Board and of the War College Staff to consider the matter. Because a large majority of these men had been in some way connected with the design of the *North Dakota* class, Sims prevailed upon Roosevelt to include also a number of younger officers with special knowledge of gunnery.[112]

The conference met at Newport in July 1908 and was pervaded from the first by the bitterness which the congressional investigation had engendered. Sims and his fellow insurgents won the first skirmish when Roosevelt, who had come to Newport to deliver the opening address, checkmated a move to exclude the younger men from the conference, and ruled that voting should be by name. The attackers rejoiced when the conference went on record that the *North Dakota* had a number of defects, including inadequate armor, faulty location of the five-inch battery and of two gun turrets, dangerous position of one magazine, and inferior main battery guns.[113] But when it came to correcting these errors on the *North Dakotas,* or even on the *Utahs* whose keels had not yet been laid, the insurgents went down to defeat. Only minor changes were recommended for the *North Dakotas,* and the basic design was not only continued in the *Utahs* but was endorsed as "excellent." The President accepted the majority report of the conference, though with expressed reluctance; and the General Board promptly drew a "veil of silence" across the whole episode.[114]

The insurgents, anticipating defeat, had already planned a new attack. While still at Newport Sims had secured the support of Admiral Stephen B. Luce. Luce had worked for Navy Department reorganization before his retirement, and afterward had continued to press for this reform. In 1907 he had prepared and sent to the Secretary of the Navy two memoranda on reorganization. He now urged Sims to ask the President for a commission to study the problem.[115] Roosevelt agreed, but months passed

112 *ibid.*, pp. 202-4.
113 *ibid.*, pp. 204-7.
114 *ibid.*, pp. 207-15.
115 *ibid.*, pp. 217-18.

without his taking action. On December 1 Truman Newberry became Secretary of the Navy in place of Victor Metcalf. Newberry had plans of his own for reorganization. He proposed to coordinate the work of the bureaus by including representatives from all of them on the General Board. Roosevelt appears to have temporarily shelved the commission project in favor of Newberry's plan which, although far from satisfactory to the insurgents, had the great advantage of not requiring congressional action.[116]

Late in December Sims wrote to the President reminding him of his earlier stand for a General Staff, and pointing out the defects of the Newberry scheme. The other insurgents followed suit and Roosevelt finally appointed a commission to make recommendations on reorganization. This commission met, with Secretary Newberry as president, and sat just long enough to approve the Newberry proposals.[117] The full report had hardly been published when the President set up a new commission. This body, known as the Moody Commission, deliberated for a month and on February 25 presented to the President a "preliminary report on the principles of naval organization," followed two days later by a list of specific recommendations.[118] These documents were immediately sent to the Senate, but they received little attention. The results could hardly have been otherwise, considering the temper of Congress and the President's unhappy relations with that body during his final years in office.[119]

Roosevelt was almost as unsuccessful in his efforts to develop a system of oversea naval stations. In 1901, and again in 1902,

[116] *ibid.*, pp. 218-21.

[117] *ibid.*, pp. 221-25; see also 60 Cong. 2 Sess., *S. Doc.* No. 693; R. W. Neeser, "The Department of the Navy," *American Political Science Review*, Vol. XI (1917), pp. 59, 66.

[118] Morison, *op. cit.*, pp. 225-30, and sources cited in footnote 117.

[119] The President appointed a commission to report on the organization of the Navy Department; the Senate conducted another investigation, and there the matter rested. See 60 Cong. 2 Sess., *S. Doc.* No. 693; R. W. Neeser, "The Department of the Navy," *American Political Science Review*, Vol. XI (1917), pp. 59, 66.

the Navy Department raised the question,[120] but Congress, while pouring millions into navy yards within the States, ignored the pressing need for well-equipped stations overseas.[121] In 1903, the Administration took a stronger position. The United States, declared the Secretary of the Navy, had a "large fleet" in "Asiatic waters," but "no naval base . . . nearer than Puget Sound or San Francisco Bay." This fleet was having to depend upon "dockyards at Hongkong and in Japan," and to transport its "stores and supplies" across the Pacific. In case of war, under existing conditions, it would be impossible to repair and extremely difficult to supply a fleet in the Western Pacific. "Without a sufficient naval base of our own in Asiatic waters, the position of our fleet would be untenable."[122] The President backed up this plea with a strong appeal for immediate action,[123] but with little effect. Congress authorized slightly larger expenditures on the oversea stations, but failed to go into the matter in a large way, and continued to vote millions for unneeded navy yards in the States.[124]

The explanation was obvious. Political strategy, not naval strategy, dominated the navy-yard policy of Congress. The House and Senate naval committees were invariably loaded with members from seaboard constituencies in which navy yards or stations were located. These seaboard committeemen annually combined to support their respective claims on the public treasury. Partisan differences were forgotten in this conspiracy for political plunder. And through the devious methods of bargaining and trading, which are the essence of the legislative process in the American governmental system, the claims of the seaboard were usually sustained upon the floor of House and Senate.[125]

120 57 Cong. 1 Sess., *H. Doc.* No. 3, pp. 17-18; 57 Cong. 2 Sess., *H. Doc.* No. 3, p. 25.

121 *Navy Yearbook, 1917*, pp. 179-86, 195-200.

122 Navy Dept., *Ann. Repts., 1903*, p. 13.

123 *M. & P.* (Bur. Nat. Lit. ed.), Vol. XIV, p. 6806.

124 Navy Dept., *Ann. Repts., 1907*, pp. 43*ff*.

125 See, for example, R. M. LaFollette, *A Personal Narrative of Political Experiences* (1911), pp. 391*ff*.

Not so fortunate were the oversea stations. They had no Senators and Representatives to press their respective claims, or congressional votes with which to bargain for appropriations.[126] Congressmen were more interested in immediate benefits at home than in prospective national advantages overseas. For years, they were able to justify doing little or nothing, on the ground that experts could not agree as to the best location for permanent naval bases in the West Indies and the Pacific.[127] And in the end Roosevelt left the presidency with this problem still hanging in the air.

His efforts to organize a permanent fighting fleet met with greater success. When Roosevelt took office, the United States had nine armored ships in active service: three in the North Atlantic Squadron, one fitting out for the European Station, three in Asiatic waters, and two in the Eastern Pacific, one of which was soon to leave for the South Atlantic Station.[128] The effect of this dispersion of armored ships was to destroy even a semblance of strategic unity, and to frustrate all efforts to organize a permanent fighting fleet.[129]

Roosevelt promptly took steps to remedy this situation which violated the first canon of sound strategy. Working in cooperation with a group of forward-looking naval officers, he had all battleships withdrawn from the European and South Atlantic Stations. Next, these stations were abolished, and the vessels assigned thereto were merged with the North Atlantic Squadron, which now became the Atlantic Fleet. The Asiatic Squadron was strengthened and renamed the Asiatic Fleet. Next, all battleships were withdrawn from the Pacific, and, in their place, the Asiatic Fleet was supplied with a homogeneous group of heavy armored cruisers. And finally, all forces in the Pacific were placed under one organization which was named

126 *ibid.*, p. 392.

127 See R. D. Evans, *An Admiral's Log* (1910), pp. 300-1, 340-1.

128 See *Navy Register, 1902*, pp. 154*ff.*; and Navy Dept., *Ann. Repts., 1902*, pp. 469, 471.

129 See J. C. O'Laughlin, "The American Fighting Fleet, Its Strategic Disposition," in *Cassier's Magazine*, Vol. XXIV (1903), pp. 375, 385.

the Pacific Fleet. Thus, by the end of 1907, the United States had two great fighting units—the Atlantic Fleet of sixteen battleships, and the Pacific Fleet of eight armored cruisers and an equal number of lighter cruisers.[130]

Roosevelt accompanied this concentration of power with an educational drive, designed to eradicate the ignorance and lingering prejudices, which, despite Mahan's widely publicized writings in the 'nineties, and experience in the war with Spain, still infected American public opinion.[131] As he neared the end of his second term, this matter weighed more and more heavily upon him. Demands from the West Coast that the battleships be divided between the Atlantic and Pacific, drew from him, in December 1907, an eloquent public appeal for a united fighting fleet.

The Navy's true function, he reiterated, was not "to defend harbors and sea-coast cities," but to attack and destroy the enemy's naval forces. In this way, a battle fleet would contribute vitally, if indirectly, to coast defense. In the future as in the past, every crisis was sure to bring forth a "demand, under pressure, of fright," to divide and scatter the Navy's capital ships along the coast, under the mistaken notion that such a dispersion of our forces would best insure security to our coast cities. "Under penalty of terrible disaster, this demand must be refused . . . the ships . . . kept together, and their objective made the enemies' fleet."[132]

No one understood better than Roosevelt the utter impossibility of improvising an efficient fleet in an emergency. Just as it took years to build battleships, and to train officers and crews to handle them, years also were required to weld ships and personnel into a fighting unit. Success in the latter undertaking depended upon keeping the battleships under a single command, and bringing them together frequently for drills,

130 See reports of the Bureau of Navigation, in Navy Dept., *Ann. Repts.*, for the years 1902-1907; and the *Navy Register* for the same period.

131 See, for example, *M. & P.* (Bur. Nat. Lit. ed.), Vol. XIV, pp. 6926, 7001, 7114.

132 *ibid.*, p. 7114.

exercises, and more extended maneuvers. Roosevelt's final "legacy" to his chosen successor, was a solemn warning, never to "divide the battleship fleet between the Atlantic and Pacific oceans prior to the finishing of the Panama Canal."[133]

Roosevelt's crowning achievement was the World Cruise of the Atlantic Fleet. We have previously alluded to the political motives behind this undertaking. Its execution had a significance exceeding even the President's expectations. The Fleet's visit to Japan helped liquidate the crisis that had brought the two countries to the verge of war. The cruise revealed an unsuspected community of feeling among the English-speaking peoples, and greatly enhanced American naval prestige throughout the world. This globe-encircling parade splendidly publicized the Navy, and tremendously increased its popularity at home. But that was not all. This undertaking dramatized, as could nothing else, the inadequacy of the Navy's auxiliary forces, as well as of the privately owned American merchant marine, for transporting fuel and supplies for a large fleet operating overseas. Furthermore, this cruise of an organized fleet, steaming thousands of miles in formation, with constant attention to mechanical and tactical efficiency, provided invaluable training and experience for the officers and crews of the sixteen battleships. The Fleet left Hampton Roads in December 1907, an aggregation of tolerably efficient individual ships; it returned to the same anchorage late in February 1909, a veteran unit of power, a monument to the leadership of a President who had momentarily lifted the American people out of their traditional isolationism and, in the face of stubborn and growing opposition, had led them with pomp and circumstance into the main stream of world politics.[134] But the

[133] Roosevelt to Taft, March 3, 1909, quoted in Bishop, *Roosevelt*, Vol. II, p. 119. Roosevelt had already issued a similar warning to Philander C. Knox who was to become Secretary of State in the Taft Administration. See Bailev, *Roosevelt and the Japanese-American Crises*, pp. 320-1.

[134] The best discussion of the World Cruise and its results is Chap. XII of Bailey's *Roosevelt and the Japanese-American Crises*; and see E. M. Earle, "The Navy's Influence on Our Foreign Relations," *Current History*, Vol. XXIII (Feb. 1926), pp. 648, 653.

President's term was almost over. Within a fortnight, he would have to relinquish the reins once and for all. And the question might well have occurred to him, as he watched the homecoming ships pass in review, whether his chosen successor would, or even could, sustain the rôle that he had created.

CHAPTER SIXTEEN

☆ ☆

Rooseveltian Policy Without Roosevelt (1909–1913)

Naval Implications of Taft's Foreign Policy

THE Presidency of William Howard Taft (1909–1913) spanned a critical period in the world's history. In that period, the international struggle in the Far East revealed more fully its sinister potentialities. In that period also, feverish preparation for war, as well as successive diplomatic crises, both reflected and further aggravated the growing tension and chronic sense of insecurity that pervaded the Old World. And in that period, the United States government, although taking a more aggressive part in the Far Eastern struggle, once more sought security for America and Americans, in the ancient tradition of political isolation which had been partially abandoned under McKinley and Roosevelt.

There was no mistaking the isolationist drift of Taft's foreign policy. An indiscreet utterance by Captain (later Admiral) William S. Sims, before a London audience in 1910, to the effect that Englishmen could always count on their "kindred across the sea," drew from the President a sharp public reprimand.[1] When, in 1911, a second Moroccan crisis shook the European continent, Taft showed no inclination to follow in the steps of his predecessor who had played so prominent a

[1] *New York Times,* Sept. 29, 1936, p. 27; M. A. deW. Howe, *George von Lengerke Meyer* (1919), p. 458.

rôle in the earlier one.[2] The Italo-Turkish War, that same year, evoked a presidential declaration that this struggle, as well as other rumblings in the Near East, while a "cause of uneasiness in European diplomacy" was "without direct political concern" or "interest" to the United States.[3] And the following year, the President took the same stand with respect to the Balkan War, declaring that the United States "was involved neither directly nor indirectly with the causes or questions incident to . . . these hostilities," and had, therefore, "maintained in regard to them an attitude of absolute neutrality and complete political disinterestedness."[4]

While studiedly avoiding political commitments to, or even active collaboration with, the Powers in relation to European questions, the President stood ready to contribute in his own way to peace and stability in the Old World. He repeatedly affirmed his faith in arbitration as a substitute for war, and he was active in the movement to create an efficient international tribunal for the pacific settlement of justiciable disputes. He deplored the struggle for military and naval supremacy, and pursuant to a congressional resolution passed at the instigation of the "peace lobby,"[5] he made cautious advances to ascertain the possibility of securing an international agreement limiting armaments.[6]

Pending tangible progress toward universal arbitration and international limitation of armaments, however, Taft refused

[2] See "America's Interest in the Moroccan Question," *The Independent*, Vol. LXXI (July 27, 1911), pp. 214–16.

[3] *Messages and Papers of the Presidents* (Bur. Nat. Lit. ed.), Vol. XV, p. 7667.

[4] *ibid.*, p. 7782.

[5] This innocuous measure, passed in June 1910, authorized the President to appoint a commission "to consider the expediency of utilizing existing international agencies for the purpose of limiting the armaments of the nations of the world by international agreement, and of constituting the combined navies of the world an international force for the preservation of universal peace. . . ." *Statutes at Large*, Vol. XXXVI, p. 885. For a guide to congressional proceedings on this measure, see 61 Cong. 2 Sess., *Cong. Record* (Vol. XLV), index, H. J. Res. Nos. 187, 223.

[6] Gooch & Temperly, *British Documents on the Origins of the War*, Vol. VI, p. 278; and Vol. IX, p. 252; Merle Curti, *Peace or War* (1936), p. 220; *M. & P.* (Bur. Nat. Lit. ed.), Vol. XV, p. 7494.

even to consider any slackening of his own armament program, designed to keep the United States abreast of the Anglo-German naval race. The Administration's logical steps to this position were not altogether clear. Judging from their public utterances, it would appear that both the President and his Secretary of the Navy believed that failure to keep pace with the European naval race would expose the United States to attack from overseas.[7] Such logic was difficult to sustain. The United States Navy at its then existing strength would probably have been more than a match for any fleet, save possibly Britain's, that could cross the ocean to assail it.[8] And there was little likelihood of any European Power undertaking armed aggression in this hemisphere as long as the Old World continued to seethe from the pressure of imprisoned forces, and the two greatest navies glared at each other across the North Sea.

While the Taft administration publicly advanced no cogent reasons for keeping pace with European naval programs, it did not follow that such reasons did not exist. It was arguable that a great navy was desirable as a means of compelling respect for American neutral interests, in case of a general European war involving Germany and Great Britain. It was also arguable that the United States had a vital interest in helping to maintain the European balance of power and, above all, the Anglo-German naval equipoise, which kept the two greatest European fleets, especially Germany's, confined to European waters. With a navy second only to that of Great

[7] See, for example, *M. & P.* (Bur. Nat. Lit. ed.). Vol. XV, pp. 7371-2; *Addresses of President Taft on Arbitration* (1911), *passim,* especially pp. 4, 10, 11, 15; Navy Dept., *Ann. Repts., 1909,* p. 23; *1910,* p. 41; *1911,* p. 38; and *1912,* pp. 24–6.

[8] This conclusion is of course a speculative inference, but, it would appear, a conservative one, in view of the width of the Atlantic Ocean, the limited sphere of a fleet's operations arising from the fuel and service requirements of modern warships, from the Continental Powers' lack of adequate naval bases in this hemisphere, and the American fleet's immense advantage of operating near its home ports. And it is significant that Great Britain, the only Power potentially capable of operating in the Western Atlantic, was frankly and openly excluded from the list of possible enemies.

Britain, the goal toward which Roosevelt had worked, the United States could play a strong if not a decisive rôle in preventing either of those Powers from destroying the sea power of the other. While such considerations received some public attention during these pre-war years,[9] they were not cited, so far as we are aware, in any public utterance of the Administration, which chiefly supported its policy of keeping pace with European naval development on the ground that European navies constituted a potential standing menace to the territorial security of the United States and the Panama Canal.

In relation to the Far East, President Taft and his financially minded Secretary of State, Philander C. Knox of Pennsylvania, projected an aggressive as well as isolationistic policy. Secretary of State John Hay and President Roosevelt had repeatedly endorsed the open-door principle with regard to China, and had striven discreetly to secure as favorable commercial opportunities as possible for Americans in that country. But Hay and Roosevelt had carefully avoided head-on collisions with the Great Powers, whose claims and activities, despite ostensible acceptance of the open door in principle, still denied to Americans equality of opportunity in practice. Taft and Knox determined to secure the full substance as well as the theory of the open door. To this end they sponsored a scheme for neutralizing the railways in the Russian and Japanese "spheres of interest" in Manchuria; they backed claims on behalf of American capital to share equally in loans to China, and otherwise asserted the right of Americans to participate on an equality with other foreigners in that country.[10]

Such demands naturally irritated all the Powers maintaining special spheres and concessions in China. In particular, it

[9] See, for example, Washington (pseudonym), "The United States and Anglo-German Rivalry," *Littell's Living Age,* Vol. CCLXXVI (Feb. 8, 1913), pp. 323–32.

[10] There is an extensive literature on this subject. For an excellent brief survey, see F. R. Dulles, *Forty Years of American-Japanese Relations* (1937), Chap. VI; for an excellent documented study, see A. W. Griswold, *The Far Eastern Policy of the United States* (1938), Chap. IV.

placed the United States squarely in the way of the imperial progress of Japan. Yet Taft and Knox, pressing their claims as settled rights to which Americans were unquestionably entitled, showed no inclination to approach the Far East in a spirit of compromise, or to offer anything in return for concessions to the United States. Nor did they manifest any disposition to approach the East through Europe as Roosevelt and Hay had done, or even to view American claims in relation to the world situation. On the contrary, they not only pressed their aggressive Asiatic policy without European support or endorsement, but sometimes even with a fine disregard for possible European repercussions.[11]

A strong navy would appear to be an obvious corollary of such a policy of intervention. The Administration's aggressive, singlehanded assault on the entrenched interests of the Powers clearly called for a fleet able if necessary to carry on offensive war in the Western Pacific. And such, it appeared, was the view of the President, who began his Administration with an unqualified endorsement of his predecessor's naval policy, and with the declared intention of "backing up" American "interests" "in the Orient" with something more potent than "mere verbal protest. . . ."[12]

The Revolt of Congress

Events, conditions, and personalities, rather than large conceptions of national interest and policy, set rigid practical limits both to the Administration's naval program and to the response of Congress. In the first place, neither the President nor his otherwise capable Secretary of the Navy, George von Lengerke Meyer, possessed the necessary capacity for political leadership. Second, the Administration inherited a depression, a Treasury deficit, and the incipient political insurgency that traditionally

[11] Tyler Dennett, *Roosevelt and the Russo-Japanese War* (1924), Chap. XII.
[12] *M. & P.* (Bur. Nat. Lit. ed.), Vol. XV, pp. 7371, 7372.

goes with hard times. Finally, a bitter intersectional tariff struggle early in the new régime smashed the discipline and solidarity of the Republican organization in Congress, and all but destroyed the political influence of the President.

Hard times, intersectional warfare, and intraparty strife hardly produced a favorable atmosphere in which to launch a great naval program. Indeed, so unfavorable was the fiscal and political outlook in the autumn of 1909 that the President felt constrained to ask Congress for only two battleships, instead of the four recommended by the General Board and annually demanded by Roosevelt since 1907.[13] And so unfavorable did the outlook continue that the next year's program also was kept down to two capital ships.[14] At this rate, the United States would rapidly lose place in the struggle for naval supremacy. Yet only with great difficulty did the Administration secure congressional sanction to lay down even two battleships in 1910,[15] and, with greater difficulty, to do the same in 1911.[16] And worse was in store!

The congressional elections of 1910 put the Democrats in control of the House, cut down Republican strength in the Senate, and enlarged the so-called Progressive bloc, recruited chiefly from the Middle West. Anticipating trouble, the Administration tried Rooseveltian tactics. A great review of the Atlantic Fleet was staged at New York, and a similar review of the Pacific Fleet at San Diego, in November 1911, shortly before the opening of Congress.[17] These splendid and carefully

[13] *ibid.*, pp. 7429–30; Navy Dept., *Ann. Repts., 1909*, pp. 20–2; Howe, *Meyer*, p. 439.

[14] Navy Dept., *Ann. Repts., 1910*, pp. 39–40.

[15] 61 Cong. 2 Sess., *H. Rept.* No. 796, pp. 41*ff.*; Cong. Record (Vol. XLV), pp. 3778–82, 3806–23, 4061–70, 4162–71, 4422–44, 6592–607, 6722–35. The battleships authorized in 1910 were the *New York* and *Texas* (27,000 tons, 21 knots, ten fourteen-inch guns, cost about $11,000,000). *Navy Yearbook* statistics.

[16] 61 Cong. 3 Sess., *H. Rept.* No. 2006, p. 12; *Cong. Record* (Vol. XLVI), pp. 2989–3001, 3072–3102, 3906–11, 4035–41. The 1911 ships were the *Nevada* and *Oklahoma* (27,500 tons, 20.5 knots, ten fourteen-inch guns, cost about $11,-500,000).

[17] Navy Dept., *Ann. Repts., 1911*, pp. 28–31.

publicized pageants set the stage for public appeals by Secretary Meyer[18] and the President, and for pointed editorials in the pro-navy press.[19]

But Congress ignored Administration appeals, editorial criticism, and pressure by various interested groups. The House Naval Committee, acting under orders from the Democratic congressional caucus, reported a naval appropriation bill without provision for any battleships at all.[20] There was a stormy debate, and numerous attempts to add battleship amendments, but the Democratic lines held, and the bill went to the Senate still lacking any provision for battleships. While it was pending there the Democratic National Convention met at Baltimore, nominated Woodrow Wilson, and adopted a platform calling for a strong navy. Two days later the Senate voted two battleships into the bill.[21] Then, after a deadlock lasting until mid-August, the House Democrats, whose position had been undermined by the turn of events at Baltimore, compromised on one battleship.[22]

Once more the Administration prepared for the struggle. There was another splendid review of the Fleet lasting three days in mid-October, at the height of the presidential cam-

[18] *New York Herald,* Nov. 2, 1911, pp. 3, 4.

[19] *New York Herald,* Nov. 3, p. 3. The *New York Sun,* for example, hoped "that the visiting members of Congress would be duly impressed by today's spectacle." Quoted in *Literary Digest,* Nov. 11, 1911, Vol. XLIII, p. 840. And the *Herald* prophesied that after this popular demonstration it would "be a very rash member of Congress who stands in the way of the proper development of the United States Navy." Nov. 3, p. 10.

[20] *Literary Digest,* Vol. XLIV (March 2, 1912), p. 409; *New York Herald,* May 16, 1912, p. 6; 62 Cong. 2 Sess., *H. Rept.* No. 710, p. 14. This action of the Democratic caucus drew a sharp protest from Sec. Meyer, in which he arraigned the Democratic leaders for rejecting the battleship program, and at the same time failing to abolish "needless navy yards which are costing the government several million dollars a year for maintenance alone." *New York Herald,* Jan. 31, 1912, p. 3; and see *Army and Navy Journal,* Vol. XLIX (Feb. 3, 1912), p. 700.

[21] 62 Cong. 2 Sess., *Cong. Record* (Vol. XLVIII), pp. 7023–62, 7326, 7333–55, 7356, 8664.

[22] *New York Herald,* Aug. 17, 1912, p. 4; Aug. 20, p. 5; Aug. 21, p. 6. The 1912 ship was the *Pennsylvania* (31,400 tons, 21 knots, twelve fourteen-inch guns, cost over $13,000,000).

paign.[23] Speaking before a great banquet in New York City, the President, now campaigning for reelection, made a strong plea for the Navy. And Secretary Meyer, before the same assemblage, took Congress severely to task for obstructing the Administration's program.[24] Even after his crushing defeat at the polls, the President made one more stand, this time for three battleships to make up for the preceding year's deficiency.[25]

The House Naval Committee pared the program down to two.[26] A bipartisan bloc consisting chiefly of Southerners and Middle Westerners[27] forced it down to one, by threatening a filibuster.[28] The upper chamber restored the number to two;[29] the House stood pat; and the Senate finally capitulated as the clock ticked off the final hours of the session, and the crowds gathered for the inauguration of a new President.[30]

One result of Taft's four-year struggle with Congress was the development of a still more "top-heavy" navy. A balanced fighting fleet should have included not only first-class battleships, but also fast scout cruisers, destroyer flotillas to protect the capital ships, and various other classes of vessels in certain recognized proportions. Forced to make compromises at every turn, the Administration had sacrificed cruisers, destroyers, and the other essential components of a fighting fleet, in its desperate, but futile, attempt to keep pace with capital-ship construction abroad. This course was justified on a theory and two hopes.

[23] *Herald,* Oct. 11, 1912, p. 22; Oct. 12, p. 22; Oct. 13, p. 18; Oct. 14, p. 20; Oct. 15, pp. 5–7; Oct. 16, pp. 5–6.

[24] *Herald,* Oct. 15, p. 6.

[25] *M. & P.* (Bur. Nat. Lit. ed.), Vol. XV, p. 7808; Navy Dept., *Ann. Repts.,* 1912, p. 26.

[26] 62 Cong. 3 Sess., *H. Rept.* No. 1557, Pt. I, pp. 1, 13*ff.*

[27] The members of this group who favored economizing on the navy, but did not hesitate to vote millions for pensions, post offices, and other local benefits, were promptly dubbed the "pork-barrel fleet" by the supporters of the Administration's program. See *New York Herald,* Feb. 22, 1913, p. 6; Feb. 25, p. 6; Feb. 26, p. 6; March 5, p. 8.

[28] 62 Cong. 3 Sess., *Cong. Record* (Vol. XLIX), pp. 3813*ff.*; *New York Herald,* Feb. 25, 1913, p. 6.

[29] *Cong. Record,* Vol. XLIX, p. 4321.

[30] *New York Herald,* March 3, 1913, p. 6; March 4, p. 6; and March 5, p. 8. The 1913 ship was the *Arizona* (31,400 tons, 21 knots, twelve fourteen-inch guns, cost over $12,500,000).

The theory was that first-class battleships were the ultimate index of naval power. The hopes were, that the European naval race would slow down, and that the situation in Congress would improve sufficiently to allow the United States to catch up in the so-called auxiliary categories.[31] This policy of sacrificing everything for capital ships, while possibly the best practicable compromise in the circumstances, resulted in a fleet with deficiencies as a fighting organization, which might have proved fatal in a contest with a well balanced hostile fleet.[32]

Another result of Taft's losing struggle with Congress was to emphasize the supreme importance of vigorous executive leadership, party discipline, and one-party control. Lack of astute political leadership handicapped the Taft administration from first to last. Insurgency within the Republican Party aggravated the situation. And Democratic control of the House during the last two years of the Administration insured disaster. Under these conditions, as on previous occasions, the Navy became a football of partisan politics, a victim of patronage, and a subject of pork-barrel legislation. It is significant that Congress, while drastically curtailing the Administration's building program, did not reduce naval appropriations, but, on the contrary, increased them by some sixty million dollars over the last four years of the Roosevelt régime; and that the Democratic House, in the winter of 1912–1913, while ruthlessly paring down the President's battleship program, voted the largest naval appropriation in American history to that date.[33]

Third, the traditional partisan and sectional cleavages were still in evidence. With very few exceptions, seaboard Republicans backed the Administration's program, while many from the interior voted with the opposition. Interior Democrats were preponderantly opposed to increasing the Navy, while

[31] Navy Dept., *Ann. Repts., 1911*, pp. 38–42; same, *1912*, pp. 25–8.

[32] See the attack on this policy in an unsigned article attributed to Rep. Lemuel P. Padgett, Democratic Chairman of the House Naval Committee, in the *National Monthly*, and reprinted in the *Army & Navy Journal*, Vol. XLIX (Jan. 20, 1912), p. 638.

[33] *Navy Yearbook, 1917*, p. 679.

their seaboard colleagues were markedly divided. It was a fatal coincidence that Republican insurgency was strongest in those sections which had traditionally opposed a big navy. And while desire to discredit the Republican President unquestionably determined many Democratic votes, it also happened that some of the strongholds of Democratic power were also regions where small-navy sentiment had traditionally prevailed.[34]

Finally, the progressive revolt of Congress against the naval program of the Taft administration is not without significance as an index of opinion within the national legislature, and possibly also in the country at large, during those final years of peace. Many advocates of a stronger navy were unquestionably sincere. But the number who showed any real anxiety regarding the present or future security of the United States, was virtually negligible. And one rises from reading these debates with a decided impression that the minority report of the House Naval Committee, in February 1913, well summed up the prevailing state of opinion. ". . . For the purpose of defending our country against attacks from any nation on earth we confidently believe that our Navy is amply sufficient and fully adequate, and for any other purpose we need no navy at all."[35]

Politics, Administration, and Naval Strategy

While waging a losing struggle to keep pace with foreign building programs, the Taft administration was simultaneously battling with politics, inertia, and prejudice, in a strenuous effort to carry forward Roosevelt's unfinished work of welding ships, men, and equipment into an efficient fighting machine.

Further progress was made in fleet organization and training. With the completion of additional units, the Atlantic Fleet was increased to twenty-one battleships—four divisions of five ships

[34] These conclusions are derived from a comparative analysis of critical roll calls on naval appropriation bills in the House during the years 1909–1913.

[35] 62 Cong. 3 Sess., *H. Rept.* No. 1557, Pt. II, p. 4.

each, and a flagship. By reducing the necessary periodic overhauls to a system, work at the navy yards was maintained at a fairly uniform level, and four ships in each division were always available for active service. There was no slackening in gunnery training, tactical drills, and fleet maneuvers. And Secretary Meyer was also instrumental in recommissioning and organizing the older vessels into the Atlantic and Pacific Reserve Fleets.[36]

Meyer likewise made some progress with the thorny problem of Navy Department reorganization. Opposition from within the Department, as well as from Congress, it will be recalled, had blocked Roosevelt's efforts to create a general staff of line officers to advise the Secretary on policy, and to direct and coordinate naval administration in the interest of military efficiency. Roosevelt's frontal attacks having failed, Meyer tried a flank movement. Instead of confronting Congress with another general staff proposal, he secured expert advice, and then went ahead on his own responsibility.[37] The Department was divided into four sections: fleet operations, personnel, material, and inspections. The existing bureaus were grouped under these sections, according to the kind of service performed. Over each section was placed a high-ranking line officer with the title of "aid." Individually, each aid was to advise the Secretary on all technical questions within his jurisdiction. Collectively, the four aids were to constitute an advisory council on departmental policy and administration as a whole. This plan was a step toward a general staff, and, in conjunction with other administrative reforms introduced by Meyer, greatly increased the military efficiency of the Navy Department.[38]

The next step was to secure congressional endorsement of these reforms. Successive efforts to this end,[39] however, produced

[36] Navy Dept., *Ann. Repts., 1911,* pp. 29–36; and *1912,* pp. 11–24.

[37] Howe, *Meyer,* pp. 466–8; Navy Dept., *Ann. Repts., 1909,* pp. 5–10.

[38] Navy Dept., *Ann. Repts., 1910,* pp. 5–19; *1911,* pp. 5, 10–18; and *1912,* pp. 5–10; Howe, *Meyer,* pp. 446–70; R. W. Neeser, "The Department of the Navy," in *American Political Science Review,* Vol. XI (Feb. 1917), pp. 59, 67–8.

[39] *M. & P.* (Bur. Nat. Lit. ed.), Vol. XV, pp. 7529, 7695, 7807.

little result. Congress sanctioned a few administrative changes,[40] but ignored requests to put the aid system upon a permanent statutory basis. While there is little direct evidence on this point, one may infer from the general drift of congressional opinion, that many Senators and Representatives preferred to keep the status quo, even at the expense of military efficiency, rather than sanction any concentration of executive power in the hands of the Line, which, as previously stated, might jeopardize the ability of Congress to exploit the Navy for the mutual benefit of favored constituencies and electioneering politicians.[41]

This conflict between politics and military efficiency came to a head in Meyer's attack on the navy-yard problem. Germany at this time was maintaining only three home navy yards, and Great Britain only six. The United States, in contrast, had eleven such establishments, nine on the Atlantic, and two on the Pacific, as well as a variety of smaller naval stations. Yet these eleven yards altogether contained fewer drydocks than the single largest British yard, and they were otherwise inadequately equipped, despite the millions of dollars annually poured into them.[42]

Now as previously, politics barred the way to reform. Secretary Meyer might and did reiterate that the navy yards existed for the fleet; but Congress had long acted on the contrary theory, that the fleet existed for the navy yards. The House and Senate naval committees were invariably loaded with members from constituencies possessing navy yards or stations. These members habitually supported each other's claims on the Treasury. Any move against particular establishments drew protests and even threats of reprisal from the constituencies

40 See L. M. Short, *Development of National Administrative Reorganization in the United States* (1923), p. 319.

41 See, in this connection, the excellent though anonymous article entitled, "Will Congress Put Our Navy on the Sea?", *McClure's Magazine*, Vol. XXXVI (March 1911), pp. 523–35.

42 Navy Dept., *Ann. Repts., 1910*, pp. 30, 35; same, *1911*, pp. 24–7; same, *1912*, p. 43.

and members affected.[43] And if the Administration persisted in its course, these congressional guardians of special privilege could always carry the fight to the floor of House or Senate, where they could usually muster support enough to defeat the proposed reform.[44]

Against this unfortunate situation, Meyer waged unremitting if cautious warfare.[45] In one way or another, he introduced needed reforms in navy-yard management. He closed the yards at Pensacola and New Orleans, as well as smaller coaling stations in Maryland and Connecticut. And he sponsored systematic development of docking and other facilities, with a view to the efficiency and well-being of the Navy as a whole.[46]

Meyer also attacked the closely related problem of developing an adequate naval base in the West Indies. Naval officers had long desired such a base, but had unfortunately disagreed as to the best location.[47] The prospective opening of the Panama Canal forced this question to the front. While the danger of European aggression in the Western Hemisphere was remote, it was nevertheless considered necessary, as a precautionary measure, to equip and fortify an insular station where an American fleet in the Caribbean could readily secure fuel, supplies, and emergency repairs. By 1909, it was decided that the best site was Guantanamo Bay on the southeast coast of Cuba. With a well equipped station at Guantanamo, the American fleet could command all the passages into the Caribbean and the Gulf of Mexico.[48] Development of this site would, there-

[43] See, for example, the revelations published in the *Army and Navy Journal*, Vol. XLIX (Dec. 2, 1911), p. 412; (Dec. 9), p. 431; Vol. L (Jan. 25, 1913), p. 644. On the last cited date, the *Journal* quoted the New Orleans *Picayune* to the effect that "a determined stand" on the part of the Southern members "against any battleship increase . . . would do more to bring the Navy Department to terms [for closing the New Orleans navy yard] than any other course of procedure."

[44] A. W. Dunn, "The Fundamental Cause of Waste in the Army and Navy," *World's Work*, Vol. XXII (May, 1911), pp. 14364–7.

[45] Howe, *Meyer*, p. 463.

[46] Navy Dept., *Ann. Repts., 1909*, pp. 15–19; same, *1910*, pp. 38–9; same, *1911*, pp. 24–8; same, *1912*, pp. 42–51.

[47] R. D. Evans, *An Admiral's Log* (1910), p. 340.

[48] Navy Dept., *Ann. Repts., 1909*, p. 30; same, *1910*, p. 33; same, *1911*, p. 24.

fore, increase the security not only of the Canal, but also of the Gulf seaboard as well, thereby removing the only strategic justification for maintaining any navy yards in the Gulf States.

The United States already had a partially developed station at Guantanamo, but Congress had voted no funds for it since 1904. Finally in 1911, after urgent appeals from the Administration, Congress voted another small appropriation, and work was resumed without delay. But the decision of the Administration to close the Pensacola and New Orleans navy yards, and its request in the interest of economy to transfer some of their equipment to Guantanamo, produced an uproar in the Gulf States, with congressional repercussions that all but wrecked the enterprise and effectually prevented early completion of the station at Guantanamo.[49]

Domestic politics also largely conditioned the disposition of American forces afloat. The North Atlantic Squadron, it will be recalled, had evolved by stages into the great fleet of battleships which Roosevelt sent around the world. On the return of this fleet, it was generally assumed that it would remain in the Atlantic. Yet there was no compelling international reason for keeping it there. The Anglo-German naval race, as well as the growing political tension that was hurrying the Old World on to disaster, at that time precluded any European military aggression in the Western Hemisphere. The declared policy of the Taft administration was rigid abstention from commitments to the European Powers, as well as from entanglement in Old World crises and wars. The presence of the main fleet in the Atlantic, at least in time of peace, had little bearing or effect, therefore, on the political relations of the United States with Europe.[50]

[49] Navy Dept., *Ann. Repts., 1911,* p. 181; same, *1912,* p. 46; *Army & Navy Journal,* Vol. XLIX (Dec. 9, 1911), p. 431; (Dec. 16), p. 477; Vol. L (Jan. 25, 1913), p. 644.

[50] As previously noted there was a tendency within the United States to regard the German Navy as a potential menace. Such sentiments were frequently voiced in Congress and in naval circles. But such anxiety overlooked the political situation in Europe, and minimized the gigantic technical obstacles which the German or any other European navy would have to overcome in order to carry

The presence of the battleship fleet in the Pacific, on the other hand, would have greatly strengthened the Administration's hand in the Far East. Taft's aggressive policy of intervention in China, if not pure bluff, implied ability, even if reluctance, to use force against Japan. In case of a rupture with that country, the theater of war would inevitably embrace a large area in the Western Pacific, with the Philippines as one of the pawns in the game. It is arguable that the presence of the battleship fleet in the Pacific after 1909 might have exerted a strong deterrent influence, as it clearly had in 1908; and that it might possibly have saved the Administration from its diplomatic failures in the Far East.

All proposals to transfer the fleet to the Pacific, however, were flatly rejected. This stand was publicly justified on grounds of expense and inadequacy of existing shore facilities in the Pacific.[51] A far more compelling motive, one strongly suspects, was fear of the political repercussions that such a move would produce on the Atlantic seaboard. The East Coast had long claimed a vested interest in the fleet.[52] And the Administration had to depend on the Eastern seaboard for the congressional votes necessary to save its naval building program from total disaster.

If the Asiatic policy of the Taft administration, as well as the general political situation in the Far East, called for sta-

---

on war four thousand miles from home. The British government, which possessed the best facilities for waging war in the Western Hemisphere, had not the slightest inclination to do so, and was no longer regarded in the United States as a potential menace. And finally, it should be noted that neither in Europe nor in the United States was the American Navy seriously regarded as a factor in the European balance of power. For a representative sample of American naval opinion, see B. A. Fiske, *From Midshipman to Rear Admiral* (1919), pp. 529–30; for the policy of Great Britain, see Gooch & Temperley, *British Documents,* Vol. VI, p. 786; *Brassey's Naval Annual, 1912,* p. 75; and same, *1913,* p. 83; for a thorough analysis of the Anglo-German naval equipoise, with comments on the relation of the United States thereto, see E. L. Woodward, *Great Britain and the German Navy* (1935), especially pp. 289, 368.

[51] Navy Dept., *Ann. Repts., 1910,* p. 24.

[52] As Sec. Meyer frankly admitted, stationing the battleship fleet in the Pacific would "automatically" put "most of the navy yards on the east coast" out of business. Navy Dept., *Ann. Repts., 1911,* p. 28; same, *1912,* p. 43.

tioning a fleet of battleships in the Pacific, these conditions also called for maintaining a first-class naval base either in Guam or in the Philippine Islands. To fight the Japanese Navy without such a base would involve formidable if not insuperable difficulties. Naval officers were generally agreed on this point, and practically unanimous in the opinion that Olongapo, on Subig Bay, about sixty miles north of Manila, was the best site, and the only one defensible against attack by sea. But the Army had demurred on the ground that Olongapo was vulnerable to attack by land. And Admiral Robley D. Evans declared bluntly in 1910 that many had opposed Olongapo because of its isolation from the metropolitan delights of Manila.[53] Be that as it may, the question had dragged along from year to year, with the Navy Department making shift with the old Cavite station in Manila Bay, and gradually developing Olongapo as funds were available.[54] Finally, in 1909, a joint army and navy board ended the impasse by recommending that the government abandon the idea of developing a first-class base in the Philippines, locate its principal insular base at Pearl Harbor in the Hawaiian Islands, and maintain only a small, unfortified station at Olongapo. The Taft administration ratified this decision, and Congress voted the funds necessary to begin work on a large scale at Pearl Harbor.[55]

The decision to establish a strong naval base in Hawaii was unquestionably a sound one. While the possibility of the Japanese Navy ever penetrating into American waters was remote, the strategic importance of the Panama Canal was so great as to justify this development which clinched the American Navy's hold on the Central and Eastern Pacific.

The decision with reference to the Philippines was more questionable. It was publicly explained that "changed conditions in the Pacific" rendered it unnecessary to have a strong

[53] *An Admiral's Log*, pp. 300–2.

[54] One can follow this development through the annual reports of the Navy Department for the years 1903–1908.

[55] Navy Dept., *Ann. Repts., 1909*, p. 30; *Navy Yearbook, 1917*, p. 309.

naval base in the Philippines.[56] Yet it is difficult to escape the conclusion that conditions in the Pacific had changed for the worse, rather than for the better. The immigration question, if momentarily quiescent, was not settled. And the Taft administration had deliberately set out to thwart Japanese ambitions in Asia. As long as the United States followed these policies, there would be tension between the two countries. And as long as the American flag floated over Manila, naval strategists had to envisage a war with Japan, fought in the Western Pacific, to defend the Philippines in the name of national honor and prestige.

Defense of these distant islands hinged on command of what were virtually the home waters of Japan. Command of these waters, which was absolutely prerequisite to sending troops and military supplies to the Philippines, was to be established only by destroying or blockading the Japanese Navy. To expect the United States Navy to accomplish such a gigantic feat without a first-class base in the Western Pacific was to expect something never before achieved in naval warfare.[57]

The retirement of President Taft, in March 1913, closed a strange chapter in the rise of American naval power. Without any comprehensive discussion of national aims, or of the relation of naval power thereto, the Administration had vainly labored to hold the naval rank attained under Roosevelt. Under the capable direction of Secretary Meyer and his well chosen professional advisers, the Navy had attained a new standard of military efficiency. But the exigencies of domestic politics had severely restricted the scope of administrative reform and forced opportunistic compromises in the disposition of the fleet. And there had been an inexplicable failure to face the implications of the Administration's Asiatic policy, and to prepare sys-

[56] Navy Dept., *Ann. Repts., 1909,* p. 30.

[57] See, for example, A. G. McLellan, "British View of American Naval Expenditures," *Atlantic Monthly,* Vol. CVII (Jan. 1911), pp. 34*ff.*; Victor Rousseau, "Japan and the Philippines," *Harper's Weekly,* June 7, 1913, p. 12; comment thereon in *Army & Navy Journal,* Vol. L (June 14, 1913), p. 1263; and letter thereon from J. H. Blount in same (June 28), p. 1332.

tematically for the war that must always lurk just over the horizon as long as the United States tried to block Japanese projects in Asia, while persisting in retaining in the Western Pacific an insular possession which was virtually a hostage to Japan. Thus viewed as a whole, the naval policy of the Taft administration appears as a strange blend of intelligent planning, sound achievement, political opportunism, strategic myopia, inconsistency, and frustration. And in the background, affecting policy at every turn, stood that placid indifference to world affairs, and that pervading sense of security which characterized American public opinion in those final years of peace.

CHAPTER SEVENTEEN

☆ ☆

Politics and Policy on the Eve of the Great War (1913–1914)

THE political campaign of 1912 resulted in the election of a Democratic President, and the return of Democratic majorities to both branches of Congress. President Wilson took office March 4, 1913. The new Administration's policies took form during the ensuing months. In December, its naval program was laid before Congress. In due course, this program was substantially embodied in the regular naval appropriation bill. After a spirited debate in April and May 1914, the bill was passed and sent to the President, who signed it on June 30—two days after the assassination of an Austrian prince had ignited the train leading to the long-feared, long-discussed war which the staggering burden of armaments was supposed to prevent.

That this conflict, the most destructive and widespread of modern times, would profoundly affect the United States, was realized from the very beginning. But few men dreamed of the revolutionary political and naval consequences that were in store for the United States. Even today, it is difficult to appreciate the politico-naval implications of what took place between 1914 and 1918. One can do it, if at all, only by viewing the post-war landscape against the pre-war situation of the United States, against the foreign policy and naval program of the Wilson administration, and against the drift of American naval policy and opinion in that final year of peace.

Politico-Strategic Background

The politico-strategic situation of the United States on the eve of the Great War presented elements both of great strength and of alarming weakness.

Within the Western Hemisphere, the United States had achieved a position of strategic invulnerability. Technical obstacles to military aggression from overseas, as discussed in preceding chapters, gave the United States Navy, at its then existing strength, a wide margin of supremacy throughout the Eastern Pacific, and in the Western Atlantic (including, of course, the Caribbean) at least as far south as the Equator. And the Anglo-German naval equipoise, the complicated balance of power in Europe, and the secondary balance in the Far East, effectually tied the hands of every Great Power whose financial, political, or military leaders might otherwise have seriously contemplated armed aggression against the republics of the Western Hemisphere.[1]

In the Far East the position of the United States was more vulnerable. Though repudiating the methods of the Taft administration, President Wilson showed no disposition to renounce the traditional aims of American diplomacy in Eastern Asia. On the contrary, he expressly affirmed the open-door and integrity-of-China doctrines, in terms which left no doubt of his intention to give at least moral support to the newborn Chinese Republic against all imperialistic aggressors.[2] Simul-

[1] The European Powers, it is true, recognized and otherwise rendered moral aid and comfort, for a time, to the Huerta régime in Mexico, thereby temporarily obstructing President Wilson's efforts to unseat this dictator whom Wilson regarded as an obstacle to orderly constitutional government in that country. It is also true that British, French and German warships, early in 1914, landed forces to protect their respective nationals in Haiti which was rapidly disintegrating into a state of chaotic disorder. But as events soon demonstrated, none of these Powers was prepared to proceed in the face of resistance on the part of the United States. See Harley Notter, *Origins of the Foreign Policy of Woodrow Wilson* (1937), Chap. V, *passim,* especially pp. 250, 255, 264, 274, 281, 283, 284, 296, 361.

[2] *ibid.,* Chap. V, *passim,* especially pp. 196, 202, 207, 210, 216, 231–5, 241–3, 276, 283–4.

taneously, the Japanese question had again flared up in California, this time over discriminatory state legislation pertaining to land ownership. While Wilson and his Secretary of State, William Jennings Bryan, resolutely refrained from warlike gestures,[3] and strove earnestly to save Japanese "face" and prestige, they could make no real concessions, and the basic issue remained unsettled, a potential source of future trouble.[4] The Philippine problem was another disturbing factor in the Pacific. While the Democratic platform of 1912 had promised independence to the Filipinos, the date and extent of American withdrawal was still undetermined.[5] As long as the United States continued to exclude Japanese immigrants, to discriminate against those already in America, and to oppose Japanese expansion in Asia, there would be smoldering ill-will that might at any moment blaze up into another crisis, and even eventuate in war. And as long as the United States, under these conditions, retained any vestige of sovereignty over the Philippines, without a far greater development of American naval power in the Western Pacific, these islands, as already stated, would remain a vulnerable outpost which might become a grave strategic liability.

With respect to Europe, the Wilson administration, like its predecessor, moved cautiously in the traditional path of nonintervention and isolation. The President supported Secretary Bryan's project of negotiating treaties of conciliation and arbitration with European, as well as non-European, states; but these treaties were not regarded as having any entangling political implications.[6] Wilson also permitted Colonal Edward M. House, his intimate friend and counsellor, to visit Europe early in 1914, to explore in a quasi-official capacity the possibility of relieving the political tension of the Old World. But it is not clear that the President fully understood the scope of House's grand project of uniting the German, British, and American

[3] D. F. Houston, *Eight Years in Wilson's Cabinet* (1926), Vol. I, pp. 65–7.

[4] R. S. Baker, *Woodrow Wilson* (1931), Vol. IV, pp. 77*ff*.

[5] *ibid.*, pp. 451*ff*.

[6] *ibid.*, pp. 86*ff*.; Notter, *Origins of Wilson's Foreign Policy*, pp. 205–6, 238–40, 252–3, 298, 300.

Navies to enforce peace. And it may be doubted if Wilson, at that date, would have sanctioned an enterprise so intimately associating the United States in the politics of Europe.[7]

At first glance, the attitude of the Wilson administration toward European affairs might seem to have no naval implications at all. Yet this certainly was not the case. As already noted in several previous connections, the United States derived great strategic advantage from the European balance of power, and especially from the Anglo-German naval equipoise which effectually confined the two greatest fleets within European waters. Destruction of either fleet—especially Britain's—would potentially diminish the security of the United States in the Atlantic. A general war in Europe, moreover, would inevitably cause violent repercussions in the Far East. It would certainly compel at least a temporary withdrawal of European forces, and might possibly eliminate the European Powers from the Far East altogether. Even a temporary withdrawal would jeopardize the position of the United States in that region, and might even force American statesmen to choose between abandoning their time-honored Asiatic policies and attempting singlehandedly to block the imperialistic expansion of a Japan freed from the multiple pressures inherent in the traditional balance of power in the Far East. Thus, taking a long view and considering all possible eventualities, it was arguable that the isolationist trend of American policy on the eve of the Great War called for a greater navy than at any previous period in the history of the United States.[8]

Naval Program of the Wilson Administration

The Democratic Party, it is recalled, had historically stood for a moderate naval policy. A majority of the congressional

[7] Notter, *op. cit.*, pp. 300–1; Charles Seymour, *Intimate Papers of Colonel House* (1935), Vol. V, pp. 37*ff*.

[8] See, for example, Washington (pseudonym), "The United States and Anglo-German Rivalry," *Living Age*, Vol. CCLXXVI (Feb. 8, 1913), pp. 323–32.

opponents of Roosevelt's and Taft's naval programs had been Democrats. And the Democratic caucus in the House had managed the parliamentary strategy which, in 1912, had brought Taft's building program almost to a standstill. On the other hand, the Democratic National Convention of that year had endorsed a platform containing a strong-navy plank. The President-elect was widely regarded as rather a big-navy man.[9] And for Secretary of the Navy, he selected Josephus Daniels, a North Carolina editor who had actively supported the naval policy of the Taft administration.[10] The naval outlook continued a topic of speculation throughout the spring, summer, and autumn of 1913, with frequent predictions that the Administration would present a legislative program as ambitious as that sponsored by the Taft régime.[11]

These predictions were only partially fulfilled. In his first annual message to Congress, President Wilson made no specific reference to naval policy, but merely gave blanket endorsement to the annual reports of the various executive departments.[12] The report of Secretary Daniels embodied a building program not radically different from that of the Taft administration, but his accompanying exposition bore little resemblance to the reports of Secretary Meyer.

Daniels prefaced his concrete demands with a discussion of the armament problem, paying special attention to a recent suggestion, put forward by Winston Churchill, First Lord of the Admiralty in Great Britain, that the Great Powers cease laying down warships for a year.[13] This idea appealed to Daniels, who deplored the feverish competition in armaments. He took the view that no "single nation, with large interests," could by itself, "safely take a vacation in the building of battleships."

[9] See, for example, *Army & Navy Journal*, Vol. L (Nov. 9, 1912), p. 297; *New York Times*, May 25, 1913, Sec. II, p. 13.

[10] See, for example, *New York Times*, March 6, 1913, p. 2; March 9, Sec. II, p. 3; *Army & Navy Journal*, Vol. L (March 8, 1913), p. 833.

[11] See, for example, *New York Times*, April 12, 1913, p. 10; April 21, p. 10; July 14, p. 2; Oct. 9, p. 12; Oct. 12, Sec. IV, p. 4; Oct. 27, p. 1.

[12] *Messages and Papers of the Presidents* (Bur. Nat. Lit. ed.), Vol. XVI, p. 7906.

[13] E. L. Woodward, *Great Britain and the German Navy* (1935), pp. 409*ff*.

Moreover, it was "not [merely] a vacation" that was needed, "but a permanent policy to guard against extravagant and needless expansion." To this end, he proposed that the United States call an international conference to discuss plans for limiting armaments. With refreshing optimism and a fine disregard for political realities, he thought that "it ought not to be difficult to secure an agreement by which navies will be adequate without being overgrown and without imposing overheavy taxation upon the industry of a nation."

Pending such an achievement, Daniels held that the "wise naval policy for the United States" was "to find the golden mean." On the one hand, he rejected all proposals to stop building up the Navy; on the other, he did not fully endorse the program put forward by the General Board, which called for immediate construction of four more battleships and a large number of smaller warships and naval auxiliaries. With a view to keeping naval expenditures "within the limits of the country's probable income," he asked Congress for only two battleships, eight destroyers, and three submarines.[14]

Daniels next turned to matters patently more to his taste. He had ambitious plans for reopening and expanding *all* the government navy yards,[15] and for establishing publicly owned armor-plate, ordnance, and powder factories, oil refineries, and coal mines, as a means of breaking the grip of powerful industrial corporations which, he maintained, were exploiting the government by means of collusive bidding for contracts, and by "exorbitant" prices charged for equipment, supplies, and services. Daniels had equally ambitious plans for developing the Navy into a "great university," for providing religious instruction and leadership, and for otherwise promoting the welfare of the Navy's enlisted personnel.[16]

Nowhere in this document can one detect the slightest trace

[14] Navy Dept., *Ann. Repts., 1913*, pp. 9, 10, 11.

[15] He had repeatedly voiced this intention during the preceding months. See, for example, *New York Times*, June 15, 1913, Sec. II, p. 1; June 17, p. 7; July 14, p. 2.

[16] Navy Dept., *Ann. Repts., 1913*, pp. 5–9, 11–16, 19–23.

of anxiety regarding the country's security. Daniels spoke complacently of the Navy's existing power and efficiency. He had not one word to say with respect to the naval implications of the Administration's foreign policies. And there is little to indicate that he had given any serious consideration at all to this fundamental problem.[17]

The General Board's Program

In 1913, for the first time, the views of the General Board of the Navy were formally spread upon the public record. This body of officers, charged with advising the Secretary on war plans and other phases of policy, had been in existence since 1900. Its recommendations embodied the best professional opinion obtainable. Previous Administrations had frequently acted upon these recommendations, but had generally kept the Board from coming into direct contact with the public or even with Congress. The Wilson administration, for reasons not altogether clear, reversed this precedent, publishing, as an appendix to the Secretary's report, a comprehensive memorandum by the General Board on naval policy and permitting a representative of that body to testify before the naval committees of Congress.[18]

The General Board's memorandum opened with a statement deploring the Navy's haphazard development. The United States had not now, and had never had, a long-term policy. The Board, as far back as 1903, had formulated such a policy, but this had never received executive sanction, and was not "understood by the people or Congress." It was high time that Congress adopt a long-term policy, "founded on our national needs and aims." And to this end, the Board favored "giving the widest publicity" to its own views on policy, "taking the

[17] On this point, see *New York Times*, Jan. 30, 1914, p. 2; Jan. 31, p. 8; Feb. 6, p. 10; and 63 Cong. 2 Sess., *H. Rept.* No. 314, pp. 54–5, 68.

[18] Navy Dept., *Ann. Repts., 1913*, pp. 11, 30–4; *New York Times*, Jan. 29, 1914, p. 21.

people and the Congress into . . . full confidence . . . inviting intelligent criticism as well as support."

The Board's program rested upon the premise that the United States should have a navy "powerful enough to prevent or answer any challenge" to its "well established national policies. . . . The absolute strength necessary to accomplish this" depended "upon the national policies of prospective challengers and the force [which] they can bring [to bear] against us, and, hence, is relative and varies with their naval policies and building program[s]."

The power of a navy depended upon two elements: the excellence of its equipment, and of its personnel. ". . . The two must expand and grow together until the needed power is attained." The unit of power was the first-line battleship. But the life of such ships, and their "continued power to act" in war, depended upon the "assistance of smaller fighting units . . . [and] auxiliaries in recognized proportion. . . ." The Board's program called for 48 battleships, 192 destroyers, 96 submarines, 24 colliers and tankers, 12 destroyer tenders, 12 submarine tenders, 6 ammunition ships, 6 supply ships, 6 transports, and (tentatively) 96 airplanes. This force, "ready for action by 1920," the Board believed to be the smallest that would give us a fleet "equal or superior to that of any probable enemy. . . ."[19]

The specific connotations of this program were more fully developed at a hearing of the House Naval Committee. Asked what well established American policies required a force of this size, Admiral Charles Vreeland, representing the General Board, mentioned the Monroe Doctrine, the open door in China, and exclusion of Asiatics from the United States. Questioned as to probable aggressors, he gave guarded answers which, however, disclosed that Germany and Japan were considered the Powers most likely to challenge one or more of these policies. He frankly admitted that the United States derived great advantage from its geographical isolation. He also

[19] Navy Dept., *Ann. Repts., 1913,* pp. 30–4.

admitted that conditions in the Old World, at least for the time being, effectually tied the French, German, and British Navies to European waters. But he placed little reliance upon political factors, for "no one," he insisted, with complete disregard for the continuity of European politics, could "predict what alliances and ententes may exist a year hence." He felt still greater anxiety regarding conditions in the Pacific. The danger there was not so much that the Japanese Navy would launch an attack against our continental seaboard, as that our anti-Japanese policies might inspire reprisals against American possessions in the Western Pacific. And Japan, unlike the European Powers, could wage war on the United States with the entire naval resources at its command.[20]

Cross Currents in Congress

The Administration's policy of continuing capital-ship construction, with the General Board's larger plans looming in the background, precipitated a parliamentary struggle which brought into sharp relief the antithetical currents of congressional opinion in the spring of 1914. The Administration's program generally pleased the Republican minority, but revealed a deep cleavage within the dominant party. A combination of Republicans and big-navy Democrats reported a bill from the House Naval Committee, substantially in accord with the recommendations of the Secretary of the Navy.[21] A group of four Democratic committeemen carried the fight to the floor with a minority report, vigorously attacking the Committee's Administration bill.[22] This report, as well as the terms of the bill, evoked a debate which continued for weeks during April and May.

At one extreme stood Representative Richmond P. Hobson,

[20] 62 Cong. 2 Sess., *H. Rept.* No. 314, pp. 67–9; *New York Times,* Feb. 9, 1914, p. 1.

[21] 63 Cong. 2 Sess., *H. Rept.* No. 314.

[22] *ibid.,* pp. 48*ff.*

Democrat from Alabama, a former naval officer, and the lower chamber's most vigorous champion of a big navy. The American people, Hobson assumed, had no aggressive designs on any country. But other nations, he maintained, had policies that menaced our national security, and our system of national defense should be framed with a view to the actual situation confronting us. The British Navy gave him no concern, because Britain had no army to follow up a naval victory by invading the United States, and besides, Canada was a hostage that would always restrain Britain's hand. Germany, on the contrary, was a real menace. That Power had a great army and a merchant marine adequate to transport that army across the Atlantic, as soon as the German Fleet should have destroyed our Navy. And Hobson placed no reliance upon the supposedly inhibiting effects of the European balance of power. He also regarded the combined Army and Navy of Japan as a menace, not only to our insular possessions in the Pacific, but even to our western continental seaboard. In his eyes, "America's true naval policy, . . . simple, inevitable, with no idea of aggression upon anyone," was "to have always in the Atlantic a fleet equal to the German Navy and to have always in the Pacific a fleet equal to the Japanese Navy."[23]

At the other extreme stood a group violently opposed to building any more battleships at all, at least for the time being. The leaders of this group, chiefly Middle Western and Southern Democrats,[24] tacitly accepted Hobson's standard, but maintained that our Navy already had indisputable command throughout the Western Atlantic and Eastern Pacific. They cited statistics to show that the fleet was relatively much stronger than the big-navy men admitted.[25] And they stressed the unstable condi-

[23] 63 Cong. 2 Sess., *Cong. Record,* Vol. LI, pp. 7147, 7380.

[24] In particular, Witherspoon (Miss.), Hensley (Mo.), Buchanan (Ill.), and Gray (Ind.), the four members who had signed the Naval Committee's minority report.

[25] This argument turned on the reliability of statistics published in the annual *Navy Yearbook,* compiled by the Senate Naval Committee with the assistance of the Navy Department. In this document, certain obsolescent battleships were dropped from the list of American fighting ships, while similar

tions in Europe and the Far East, which, they sincerely believed, absolutely precluded any aggression against the United States.[26] Disclaiming any hostility to the Navy *per se*, they declared that Congress and the country were simply victims of unfounded rumors and alarms, traceable to various groups interested in building up the Navy for economic, political, professional, or other selfish purposes.[27]

Between these extremes ranged all shades of opinion. Representative William E. Williams, Democrat from Illinois, a member of the Naval Committee, was perhaps the best-informed and most moderate in tone. Williams felt no anxiety regarding an attack on the United States proper. Conditions in Europe and the Far East rendered such an aggression improbable, and our geographical isolation was an all but insurmountable strategic barrier. Our Navy was already more than sufficient to meet any force that could cross the oceans to attack us. But that was only half of the picture. The United States was committed to certain policies—notably the Monroe Doctrine and the open door in China—and we had assumed "gratuitous responsibilities in the Philippines. . . ." With all due respect to the naval experts, he doubted whether anyone could say exactly what measure of naval power might be necessary to halt all possible aggressors in South America or the Far East. Personally, he believed that our existing power was sufficient. But other navies were forging ahead rapidly, and ours must likewise, in order to sustain our relatively strong position. For this reason, there-

---

vessels were retained in the list of German fighting ships. These and other discrepancies drew charges that the big-navy men had deliberately doctored the statistics, to justify their demands for further capital ship construction. *H. Repts.* No. 314, pp. 55–69; *Cong. Rec.*, Vol. LI, pp. 7228*ff*. While the criticism of the *Navy Yearbook* was, at least partially, justified, the little-navy men certainly drew unfounded conclusions from their charges, regarding the actual relative strength of the American and German Navies. For a less biased comparison, see *Brassey's Naval Annual, 1914*.

[26] *Cong. Rec.*, Vol. LI, pp. 7042, 8107.

[27] Among the groups specifically denounced by the little-navy men were the Navy League, the armor plate manufacturers, the shipbuilders, the munitions makers, and the financial interests, as well as the Service itself. See *Cong. Rec.*, Vol. LI, pp. 7020, 7042, 7052, 7218, 7219, 7282.

fore, he intended to support the Administration's comparatively moderate building program.[28]

In the end, such arguments prevailed, and the bill as it finally passed both chambers provided for two more battleships, and also a third, contingent on sale of the relatively new but hopelessly obsolete *Idaho* and *Mississippi*.[29]

Another provision of the Act of June 30, 1914, is likewise significant as indicating the state of congressional opinion in those final weeks before the outbreak of war in Europe. The Administration's program included three submarines, without specification as to type.[30] The bill reported from the House Naval Committee, provided for "one seagoing submarine torpedo boat, three *coast defense* submarine torpedo boats, and four *small* torpedo boats intended for *harbor defense*."[31] And the bill as finally passed authorized one "seagoing" submarine, and *"seven or more"* submarines of *"coast and harbor defense type*."[32] Here, within a few weeks of the Great War, was a surprising congressional revival of the theory of passive defense.

There had been forewarnings, however, of such a revival, in the congressional debates touching on the strategic functions and value of torpedo boats and, later, of submarines; and in the willingness of many members of Congress, in the first decade of the twentieth century, to vote for large numbers of submarines, while opposing additional battleships.[33] But Congress had never gone so far as to authorize submarines specially designed for "coast and harbor defense." And the resort to such

[28] *ibid.*, pp. 7048–52.

[29] The first *Idaho* and the first *Mississippi* were two of the government's costly blunders. Though not completed until 1907, several months after the advent of the *Dreadnought,* these ships were too slow to keep up with the fleet, and were clearly obsolete even before they were launched. The ships built under the 1914 Act were the *New Mexico,* second *Idaho,* and second *Mississippi* (32,000 tons, 21 knots, twelve fourteen-inch guns, $14,000,000 to $16,000,000).

[30] Navy Dept., *Ann. Repts., 1913,* p. 10.

[31] *H. Rept.* No. 314, p. 3 (our italics).

[32] *Navy Yearbook, 1917,* p. 379 (our italics).

[33] See 64 Cong. 1 Sess. House Naval Affairs committee, *Hearings on Estimates for 1915,* pp. 701-3. Between 1900 and 1914, Congress authorized fifty-one submarines.

phraseology in 1914 remains something of an enigma. About all one can say is that this phraseology unquestionably reflected strategic views long associated with the Democratic Party, and still popular in the South and Middle West; and that it may well have been used merely to procure votes needed for the Administration's naval program as a whole.

This revival, in a modern form, of the doctrine of passive coast defense, was symptomatic of the confusion and unreality that still pervaded American civilian discussion of naval policy on the eve of the Great War. The amazing vitality of this doctrine was possibly attributable to our geographical isolation and the consequent sense of security which had traditionally conditioned American thinking on naval matters. Against this pervading conviction of security, advocates of a big navy flung themselves, often without the slightest visible result. In their efforts to break through the wall of public ignorance and apathy, they sometimes indulged in wild flights of imagination as, for example, when they pictured the German Fleet, with the blessing of Great Britain and the Continental Powers, steaming thousands of miles from its nearest bases, to destroy the American Navy, seize the Panama Canal, and open the way for the German Army, following in a great fleet of transports, to invade and lay waste the United States. Such alarms partially served their purpose of frightening people into supporting larger naval appropriations. But such flights transferred the discussion of naval policy from the world of cold reality to the realm of emotion, and may well have contributed, as much as did the ignorance and apathy against which they were directed, to the failure of the American people and their official spokesmen, right down to the war, to develop a sound, realistic opinion on the great question of naval defense.

CHAPTER EIGHTEEN

☆ ☆

Europe at War: Neutrality and Preparedness (1914–1917)

THE outbreak of the Great War in August 1914, foreshadowed an upward surge of navalism within the United States. President Wilson's policy of neutrality which, from the winter of 1914–1915, necessarily envisaged the possibility of American entry into the war, called into question the Navy's readiness and adequacy, whether to support the President's demands on the belligerents, or to play an effective rôle in case the United States joined one of the warring coalitions. Sober consideration of these eventualities, the pressure of special interests, and the exhilarating effects of war viewed from a safe distance, gave rise to an organized agitation for "preparedness," which steadily gathered momentum during the year 1915. The propaganda of individuals and organized groups, the exigencies of domestic politics, the course of events in Europe, the temperament of the President, and above all, the logic of his neutrality policy, impelled the Administration toward a program of warlike preparation which found partial expression in the great Naval Bill of 1916; passage of which marked another milestone in the rise of American naval power.

Initial Impact of the War

The outbreak of war in Europe had surprisingly little immediate effect on naval policy in America. From August until mid-October there was practically no public discussion either of the possibility that the American Navy might eventually play a rôle in this conflict, or of the possible bearing of the war on the future security of the United States.[1] Then, almost overnight, silence gave way to heated debate, following the publication by Representative Augustus F. Gardner, Republican from Massachusetts, of sensational charges regarding the condition of our national defenses, and his introduction in Congress of a resolution calling for public investigation of the military and naval establishments.[2]

The response of the Administration was vigorous and unmistakable. President Wilson at first ridiculed, and then denounced Gardner's proposal.[3] Secretary of the Navy Daniels declared that the Fleet's recent operations in Mexican waters[4] "showed that country that the Navy is always ready; that it lives in a state of preparedness. . . ."[5] And the President went before Congress, early in December, with an annual message designed to silence all the Gardners in the land. The United States, he reminded his countrymen, was "at peace with all the world." And no one, speaking "from a just and candid interpretation of realities" could show "reason to fear" aggression from any quarter. Asserting that "we have always regarded [a powerful navy] as our proper and natural means of defense," he implied that we already had such a navy, deplored current attempts to alarm the public, denied the existence of any emergency, and calmly stated his intention to continue the orderly, unhurried development of our power upon the sea.[6]

[1] For a comment on early discussion in American naval circles of the implications of the war for the United States, see B. A. Fiske, *From Midshipman to Rear Admiral* (1919), p. 544, and Chap. XXXV.

[2] 63 Cong. 2 Sess., *Cong. Record* (Vol. LI), pp. 16694, 16745, 16747. For periodic cross-sections of the ensuing newspaper discussion, albeit somewhat loaded in favor of "preparedness," see *Literary Digest*, Vol. XLIX (Oct. 31, 1914), p. 835; (Dec. 5), p. 1107; (Dec. 12), p. 1159; (Dec. 19), p. 1205.

[3] *New York Times*, Oct. 20, 1914, p. 1; Dec. 8, p. 1.

[4] A reference to the Tampico incident, the dispatch of a naval expedition, and the occupation of Vera Cruz. Navy Dept., *Ann. Repts., 1914*, pp. 141–2.

[5] *ibid.*, pp. 52–3.

[6] *Messages and Papers of the Presidents* (Bur. Nat. Lit. ed.), Vol. XVI, pp. 8021–2. There was some attempt to twist the President's words into a big-navy

This attitude found concrete expression in the Administration's legislative program. The General Board's recommendations for increasing the Navy only slightly exceeded those of the preceding year.[7] Yet Secretary Daniels, as on the previous occasion, drastically pared them down in the interest of economy.[8] He took the same stand with regard to the personnel shortage which, according to expert opinion, was handicapping the Navy in peace, and would seriously curtail its operations in war. Daniels consented to establishing a reserve corps of men who had formerly served in the Navy,[9] but he was immovably opposed to increasing the active enlisted force. When the General Board, in its annual report for 1914, placed the personnel deficiency at 19,600, Daniels refused to publish the report until all specific reference to the shortage was stricken from it. And he took the position, in his own annual report, that the enlisted strength of the Navy was adequate for all existing requirements.[10]

Proceedings in Congress revealed the same pervading sense of security. The House Naval Committee, after listening to a great deal of conflicting testimony on the existing condition of the Navy,[11] reported a bill providing for an increase of only two battleships, six destroyers, three auxiliary vessels, and seventeen submarines[12]—a program, except for the larger number of

---

declaration, as one can see from the following headline selected from the *New York Herald*: "STRONG NAVY NATION'S HOPE OF DEFENSE, PRESIDENT ASSERTS IN HIS MESSAGE," Dec. 9, 1914, p. 3.

[7] The General Board's 1914 program called for 4 battleships, 16 destroyers, 3 fleet submarines, 16 coast submarines, 4 scout cruisers, 4 gunboats, and 6 auxiliary vessels of different types. Navy Dept., *Ann. Repts., 1914,* p. 67.

[8] The Administration's program called for 2 battleships, 6 destroyers, 1 fleet submarine, 7 or more coast submarines, 1 gunboat, and 1 tanker. *ibid.,* p. 8; and Daniels' statement quoted in *Literary Digest,* Vol. XLIX (Dec. 19, 1914), p. 1207.

[9] Navy Dept., *Ann. Repts., 1914,* p. 34.

[10] *ibid.,* p. 31; 66 Cong. 2 Sess., *Naval Investigation, 1920,* Vol. I, pp. 476–7, 508, 1138–40; Fiske, *Midshipman to Rear Admiral,* p. 562.

[11] See 63 Cong. 3 Sess., House Committee on Naval Affairs, *Hearings on Estimates for 1915, passim,* and especially pp. 463–838, 921–1096.

[12] 63 Cong. 3 Sess., *H. Rept.* No. 1287, p. 2; *Cong. Record,* Vol. LII, pp. 2663–6.

submarines, practically identical with the one reported the preceding year, before the outbreak of war in Europe.[13]

The ensuing debate showed a marked disposition to regard the Navy as already adequate, and to discount allegations respecting its unreadiness for war. There was objection to voting more battleships, on the ground that submarines were about to drive heavy armored ships from the sea. While congressional leaders managed to carry the provision for two battleships, it taxed their resources to do so.[14] On the other hand there was little opposition to authorizing as many as sixteen small submarines whose radius of operations in war could not possibly extend very far from the coast.[15]

The prevailing attitude was further revealed in connection with a project for creating an Office of Naval Operations to perform the functions of a general staff. This project was sponsored by Representative Richmond P. Hobson, Democrat from Alabama, who, it will be recalled, was the lower chamber's most outspoken champion of naval expansion. Hobson's plan, drafted in collaboration with Admiral Bradley A. Fiske, called for a Chief of Naval Operations who, with the aid of fifteen assistants, would be "*responsible* for the readiness of the Navy for war and be *charged* with its general direction." As finally enacted, however, the clause provided for a Chief, without any assistants, "who shall, *under the direction of the Secretary of the Navy,* be charged with the operations of the fleet, and with preparation and readiness of plans for its use in war." The change of phraseology, emphasized by our italics, struck at the heart of the plan. And this vital change was said to be the work of certain Administration leaders who were absolutely opposed to strengthening professional influence in the Navy Department.[15a]

[13] 63 Cong. 2 Sess., *H. Rept.* No. 314.

[14] The ships built under this authorization were the *Tennessee* and *California* (32,300 tons, 20.5 knots, twelve fourteen-inch guns, cost over $18,000,000 each).

[15] See *Cong. Record,* Vol. LII, pp. 2666–77, 2679–717, 2721–38, 2741–3, 3106–53, 4609–10, 4694–713; and *Navy Yearbook, 1917,* p. 396.

[15a] See 63 Cong. 3 Sess., *H. Rept.* No. 1287, p. 8; *Cong. Record,* Vol. LII, pp.

The indifference, if not actual hostility, of Wilson, Daniels, and a majority of the Democratic Senators and Representatives, during the winter of 1914-1915, to all projects for military and naval preparedness, apparently reflected the drift of opinion in most of the sections and social groups whose votes had put the Democratic administration and congressional majorities in office and which alone could keep them there.[16] A nation-wide newspaper poll, following Wilson's declaration of policy, early in December, clearly suggested such a conclusion. While 285 out of 400 editors to whom the *Literary Digest* sent questionnaires favored strengthening the Navy, there was no agreement as to how much. This poll also showed big-navy sentiment stronger among metropolitan editors than among those in small towns and cities. Such sentiment was strongest along the Middle and North Atlantic, and Pacific seaboards, weaker in the South Atlantic States, and weakest in the Gulf States and throughout most parts of the Mississippi Valley. The drift of inland opinion was further disclosed by another poll, taken by the *Columbus* (Ohio) *Citizen*. This poll, based upon nearly 150,000 returns from persons in twenty Middle Western cities, showed sentiment running, three to two against increasing the Army and Navy.[17] And these findings coincided with the impressions of competent political observers during the ensuing months.[18]

Thus, while the country as a whole was sharply divided on the issue of national defense, there were indications that those sections which had shown the greatest Democratic voting strength in the presidential election of 1912[19] were generally supporting the Administration and the Democratic majorities

---

2747–8, 4600; *Navy Yearbook, 1917,* p. 383; and Fiske, *Midshipman to Rear Admiral,* pp. 566–71.

[16] Charles Seymour, *Intimate Papers of Colonel House* (1926), Vol. I, p. 298; R. S. Baker, *Woodrow Wilson* (1937), Vol. VI, pp. 5–6; *New York Times,* Dec. 9, 1914, pp. 1, 6; *Literary Digest,* Vol. XLIX (Dec. 19, 1914), pp. 1107, 1207.

[17] *Literary Digest,* Vol. L (Jan. 23, 1915), pp. 137–8, 162–9.

[18] See, for example, Baker, *Wilson,* Vol. VI, p. 13 n.2; Frederick Palmer, *Newton D. Baker* (1931), Vol. I, p. 43; David Lawrence, *True Story of Woodrow Wilson* (1924), p. 158.

[19] E. E. Robinson, "Distribution of the Presidential Vote of 1912," in *American Journal of Sociology,* Vol. XX (July 1914), pp. 18–20, especially map plate II.

in Congress in resistance to the "preparedness" drive that was rapidly getting under way in the winter of 1914–1915.

The Great Preparedness Movement

A detailed study of the great "preparedness" campaign of 1915 would itself fill a volume. But we cannot neglect this movement altogether, for no one can possibly understand either the dynamics of naval legislation during the war, or the drift of American thinking as to naval policy after the war, without some knowledge of the propaganda campaign that preceded the great Army and Navy Acts of 1916. And one cannot fairly analyze or even understand the preparedness campaign and its results without taking cognizance of the intellectual fog that rolled in across the Atlantic after the outbreak of war in Europe and eventually surged westward, blanketing the country with rumors, half-truths, and even falsehoods, all of which stimulated the demand for military preparedness within the United States and, at the same time rendered millions of Americans emotionally receptive to propaganda calculated to produce an unreasoning clamor of fear and hysteria.

The preparedness campaign got under way in the winter of 1914–1915. The leading spirits, chiefly Easterners, included some of the most prominent men in America.[20] Preparedness societies sprang up and grew like mushrooms. The most famous of these was the National Security League, organized late in the fall of 1914, with a notable membership drawn from political, industrial, financial, and professional circles.[21] The already existing Navy League acquired new strength and popularity.[22] Almost without exception, the great metropolitan dailies threw their

[20] Especially conspicuous in the early stages was General Leonard Wood, who had just completed a term as Chief of Staff, the highest position in the United States Army. Herman Hagedorn, *Leonard Wood* (1931), Vol. II, Chap. VII.

[21] See "NOTED MEN DEMAND WE ARM FOR WAR," *New York Times*, Dec. 2, 1914, p. 1, a report of the National Security League's organization meeting in New York City.

[22] See Walter Millis, *The Road to War*, p. 182.

weight into the campaign.[23] The Army and Navy took a strong stand for preparedness.[24] And presently the Administration, reversing its earlier policy, came forward with a great armament program of its own and a supporting propaganda that equalled that of any pressure group in the field.

Many other groups, though less active, were none the less in full sympathy with the preparedness movement. In June 1916, for example, a nation-wide poll of local chambers of commerce and other business groups enrolled in the United States Chamber of Commerce, revealed, among other things, a division of 952 to 10, in favor of immediate measures "to restore the United States at least to its former position of second naval power in the Atlantic, with surplus in the Pacific sufficient to protect its coasts, its possessions, its trade routes, the Canal Zone, and adjacent territory."[25] Other business groups went on record to similar effect.[26] Organized labor swung into line.[27] And what was especially significant, a large segment of the American peace movement cut loose from its ancient moorings of disarmament and arbitration; organized a new society called the League to Enforce Peace; adopted a platform foreshadowing the system of collective security later envisaged in the Covenant of the League of Nations; and endorsed military and naval preparedness as a logical corollary of their program of concerted international action to prevent or if necessary to stop future wars.[28]

[23] See the summaries of editorial opinion collected in two newspaper polls by the *Literary Digest*, published Jan. 23, 1915, Vol. L, pp. 137–8, 162–9, and March 11, 1916, Vol. LII, pp. 617–24, 647–87.

[24] This stand was faithfully mirrored in the editorial columns of the *Army and Navy Journal.*

[25] Chamber of Commerce of the United States, *Special Bulletin,* June 5, 1916.

[26] See, for example, *Proceedings of the Forty-first Annual Convention of the American Bankers' Association, September 1915,* pp. 193–4; *Twenty-first Annual Convention of National Association of Manufacturers, May 1916,* p. 119; and for a large number of other business groups, see *New York Times* Index for 1915 and 1916, title "United States–Armaments."

[27] Samuel Gompers, *Seventy Years of Life and Labor* (1925), Chaps. XXXVIII–XXXIX.

[28] *New York Times,* Sept. 20, 1915, p. 3; *Proceedings of the First Annual As-*

A great variety of motives impelled men into the preparedness movement. There was, for example, a widespread desire, among both Republicans and Democrats, to capture and to capitalize so stirring an emotional issue for the approaching presidential campaign.[29] The personnel of some of the most active groups led to public charges that profit, as well as patriotism, was supporting the preparedness campaign.[30] Some foresaw that events were driving the United States toward war.[31] And countless others flocked to the preparedness standard in a sincere if mistaken belief that the country's security was immediately at stake.

This belief was in large measure a product of the propaganda broadcast over the land during 1915 and 1916. The directors of this propaganda utilized many vehicles and a variety of appeals. From coast to coast, there were preparedness parades, with bands playing and flags fluttering. Citizens' training camps were organized, for publicity as well as military training.[32] The clergy were solicited to preach sermons on the "duty of preparedness."[33] Statesmen like Majority Leader Claude Kitchin of the House of Representatives, who opposed a great armament program, were subjected to scurrilous attacks in the press.[34] But the most effective of all was the appeal to fear. In

---

semblage of the League to Enforce Peace (1916), pp. 29, 84, 50*ff*.; Merle Curti, *Peace or War* (1936), pp. 237–8.

[29] *Selections from the Correspondence of Theodore Roosevelt and Henry Cabot Lodge* (edited by H. C. Lodge, 1925), Vol. II, pp. 461, 463, 471, 474, 476, 480, 489; Hagedorn, *Wood*, Vol. II, Chap. VII; J. R. Tumulty, *Woodrow Wilson as I Know Him* (1921), pp. 240*ff*.

[30] See, for example, Rep. C. H. Tavenner's indictment of the Navy League, in 64 Cong. 1 Sess., *Cong. Record* (Vol. LIII), pp. 272–93; and *ibid., Appendix*, pp. 860–7; and see also the accusations and revelations of Reps. Hensley, Callaway, Kitchin, and Sen. LaFollette, in *Cong. Record*, Vol. LIII, pp. 8812, 8868, 11330, and *Appendix*, p. 1313.

[31] Faced with increasing likelihood of the eventual entry of the United States into the war, high-ranking army and navy officers not unnaturally took a strong stand for preparedness.

[32] Hagedorn, *Wood*, Chap. VIII.

[33] *New York Times*, June 29, 1915, p. 8.

[34] A. M. Arnett, *Claude Kitchin and the Wilson War Policies* (1937), pp. 59-86.

thousands of public speeches,[35] press releases,[36] books and pamphlets,[37] cinema features,[38] and other vehicles of publicity, the point was hammered home that the American people would sooner or later have to face a merciless foreign enemy at their very threshold.[39]

This theme recurred again and again. And in the end, the American public rather generally came to believe: that the European Allies, with their backs to the wall, were fighting desperately to save democracy and liberty from the withering blight of Prussian autocracy and militarism; that the German "war lords," after overrunning France and England, and destroying the British Navy, would then loose their savage, victorious hordes on the republics of the Western Hemisphere; that a "defenseless America" would suffer the fate of the European democracies; that the German fleets could quickly and easily destroy our existing Navy, shell our great port cities, and prepare the way for military invasion; that the German armies, millions strong, would then pour across the Atlantic, land anywhere upon our defenseless coast, brush aside our puny army, and advance at will, destroying our cities, committing unmentionable atrocities, and generally laying waste our fair countryside.[40]

[35] For a fair sample, see the addresses delivered before the National Security Congress at Washington in January 1916, *Proceedings etc., passim.*

[36] See, for example, National Security League release, declaring that the United States lay at the mercy of a foreign enemy, *New York Times,* July 26, 1915, p. 5.

[37] See, for example, Cleveland Moffett, *The Conquest of America* (1916); J. B. Walker, *America Fallen* (1915); H. P. Okie, *America and the German Peril* (1915); Hudson Maxim, *Defenseless America* (1915); and many, many others.

[38] In particular, "The Battle Cry of Peace," a screen version of Maxim's *Defenseless America,* described in the *New York Times* under the caption, "NEW YORK SHELLED ON 'MOVIE' SCREEN," Aug. 7, 1915, p. 8.

[39] Sen. Robert M. LaFollette graphically and accurately summarized conditions as follows: ". . . Everything that could possibly play upon the emotions of the American people has been set to work and paid for in order that this result might be produced: Picture shows; works of fiction, running serially in the magazines; advertisements; editorials, alleging that our country is in danger from a foreign foe: the columns of the newspapers given over to a spurious propaganda, and all with the definite object of terrorizing the public and forcing the enactment of legislation for the great military and naval program now before Congress." 64 Cong. 1 Sess., *Cong. Record* (Vol. LIII), p. 11330.

[40] See, for example, the statement of George H. Putnam, New York publisher,

Now as a matter of actual fact, it was manifest, both from indisputable data publicly available at that time and from inferences easily and fairly deducible therefrom, that such a sequence of events simply could not occur. It was obvious after the first few weeks of the war, and was repeatedly made clear, that the European conflict would so exhaust all the engaged Powers, as to incapacitate them from menacing the United States for years to come.[41] It was well known that any fleet's radius of operations was rigidly and narrowly limited by the fuel and service requirements of modern warships. And if there were any lingering doubts on this point, they were, or should have been, laid to final rest by the emphatic testimony of Admiral Austin M. Knight, President of the Naval War College.

This testimony, given before the House Naval Committee in 1916, dealt specifically with the difficulties of waging naval war across the Pacific; but, as members of Congress expressly pointed out, it applied with only slightly less force to naval war in the Atlantic. "It would take me a very long time," Knight declared, "to go into . . . [all] the difficulties under which a fleet 7,000 miles from its home ports would labor. Ships break down. Out of a large number of ships a certain number are bound to be crippled in one way or another. The supplies needed to maintain the fleet would be very extensive. Five or six hundred thousand tons of coal would be needed as a minimum for a very short campaign there. That coal must be delivered and transferred from colliers to ships. It can not be done at sea except under the most favorable possible conditions. It must be done in sheltered waters. The bottoms of the ships would gradually get foul. They ought to have docks where the bottoms can be cleaned. They are subject in their progress over that

---

at the organization meeting of the National Security League, to the effect that the United States was likely to suffer the fate of Belgium, with a triumphant German Army overrunning the Valley of the Hudson River, on its way to invade Canada. *New York Times,* Dec. 2, 1914, p. 1. And see, in general, the items cited in notes 36–8, *supra.*

[41] See, for example, *New York Times,* Dec. 11, 1914, p. 8; Seymour, *House Papers,* Vol. I, p. 298; Arnett, *Kitchin,* p. 57; *Cong. Record,* Vol. LIII, p. 8868.

7,000 miles, throughout a large part of the time, to the possibilities of attack from the enemy's torpedocraft. . . . Their lines of communication, after they get to the point 7,000 miles away, are constantly liable to interruption and would inevitably be interrupted; and yet they depend on those lines, stretching away back to the home ports, for the very vital things necessary to their life—coal and supplies and reenforcements, if reenforcements are necessary, and all sorts of things. A fleet going out there would be accompanied, necessarily, by a tremendous attendant fleet, a train, as we call it, of auxiliary ammunition ships, hospital ships, and so forth. The problem of conducting such a train as that in going thousands of miles through hostile waters is probably the most serious problem that could possibly be put up to a commander in chief."[42]

In addition, it was likewise well known that guns afloat were no match for guns ashore. Admiral Frank P. Fletcher, Commander in Chief of the Atlantic Fleet, publicly voiced the prevailing expert opinion when he declared that "this war has conclusively demonstrated what every military strategist knew before—that it is impossible for sea craft to successfully attack land fortifications."[43] Qualified experts were equally positive that our coastal fortifications were as good as any in existence.[44] And there was competent military, naval, and lay opinion to the effect that the geographical isolation of the United States, in conjunction with our existing coastal fortifications and Navy, raised insuperable obstacles to any successful attack from overseas.[45]

[42] Quoted in *Cong. Record,* Vol. LIII, p. 8867, and again on p. 11331.

[43] Quoted in *ibid.*, p. 8868.

[44] General E. M. Weaver, Chief of Coast Artillery, publicly testified in 1916 that "I have been a close student of the whole subject, naturally, for a number of years, and I know of no fortifications in the world . . . that compare favorably in efficiency with ours." Quoted in *ibid.*, p. 8812; and to the same effect, see the opinion of General N. A. Miles, former Commander in Chief of the Army, quoted in *ibid.*, pp. 8812–13.

[45] Such, in general, was the purport of the testimony of Admirals C. J. Badger and F. F. Fletcher, before the House Naval Affairs Committee in December 1914; see 63 Cong. 2 Sess., House Naval Affairs Committee, *Hearings on Estimates for 1915,* pp. 463–570, especially pp. 504*ff.*, 536*ff.*, 546*ff.* To the same effect,

Meanwhile, the war was providing graphic demonstration of the limitations of oversea military operations. It was a known fact, and a subject of public comment, for example, that over thirty transports were required to move *one* Canadian contingent of slightly over 30,000 men across the Atlantic, not to mention the warships necessary to protect the transports from enemy submarines through waters in which the Allied Navies had an overwhelming surface command of the sea.[46] It was likewise notorious that the Allies, despite their command of the North Sea, never seriously contemplated a large-scale assault on the German seaboard in the early years of the war. And the utter failure of the Allied attempt to open the Dardanelles publicly revealed and dramatically emphasized the appalling difficulties involved in landing and maintaining an expeditionary force upon a hostile shore, and in protecting the necessary supporting squadrons from torpedoes and mines, even when the assailants had vastly superior resources at their command.[47]

Although it was demonstrable that the continental United States was at that time in no serious danger of attack from overseas, and in no danger whatever of invasion, it did not necessarily follow, therefore, that the Navy was adequate in all

see opinions of Generals E. M. Weaver and N. A. Miles, already cited, and quoted in *Cong. Record,* Vol. LIII, pp. 8812–3, 8867, 8868, 11330–1; and the competent civilian opinion of the veteran war correspondent, Frederick Palmer, in *Newton D. Baker, America at War* (1931), Vol. I, pp. 43–4. While Hudson Maxim, inventor of munitions was broadcasting his "Defenseless America" propaganda, his older brother, Sir Hiram Maxim, British manufacturer of munitions, was going publicly on record to the effect that geographical isolation and other factors rendered it "absolutely impossible for any European nation to invade" the United States. *Everybody's Magazine,* Vol. XXXIV (Jan. 1916), p. 9.

[46] *The Empire at War* (edited by Sir Charles Lucas, 1923), Vol. II, p. 83; and see *Literary Digest,* Vol. XLIX (Dec. 12, 1914), p. 1160, quoting the *Springfield* (Mass.) *Republican* which inferred from this episode that "the invasion of the United States on either ocean by a hostile army strong enough to be an appreciable factor in campaigning . . . must hereafter become a task more formidable than military science has ever contemplated."

[47] See comments on the lessons of the Dardanelles campaign in the congressional naval debate of 1916, in *Cong. Record,* Vol. LIII, pp. 8806, 11331; and see, in general, the editorial comments assembled in the *Literary Digest,* Vol. LI (Oct. 30, 1915), pp. 941–2; Vol. LII (Jan. 22, 1916), pp. 165–6, and (March 11), pp. 633-4.

respects. Partly as a result of the war in Europe, the United States was approaching another crisis with Japan, which compelled naval strategists to reopen the still unsolved problem of conducting a war in the Western Pacific. And, what was even more arresting at the moment, events were driving the United States toward an impasse with Germany. From such an impasse, war might eventually seem to the President and his advisers the only politically feasible escape. But it would not be a war to preserve the integrity of the States, our insular dependencies, or the Panama Canal, but a war carried on in Europe and in European waters, in partnership with the European Allies.

These contingencies which, of course, received due consideration in the thoughts and plans of competent naval experts, were scarcely mentioned by the preparedness propagandists who appealed to the public in terms calculated to arouse hysterical fear of invasion from overseas. And while facts, publicly known or knowable in 1915 and 1916, provided the basis for calm judgment and appraisal of this propaganda, such facts, as well as their logically deducible inferences, were generally brushed aside or ignored altogether, as the preparedness campaign gathered strength and momentum, to culminate finally in the great Army and Navy Acts of 1916.[47a]

Naval Implications of Wilsonian Neutrality

While the events sketched in the preceding section, were taking place upon the propaganda front, President Wilson was

[47a] A by-product of the war in Europe and of the preparedness drive in America was the purchase of the Danish West Indies, renamed the Virgin Islands. Acquisition of these islands, lying east of Puerto Rico, had been repeatedly urged on strategic grounds. Several previous attempts at purchase had failed for one reason or another. The war again raised the issue. It was argued that Germany might overrun Denmark and thereby acquire the Danish oversea possessions. And to forestall such an event the Wilson administration concluded a treaty of purchase (August 4, 1916) which passed the Senate with comparatively little opposition and was ratified in January 1917. See C. C. Tansill, *The Purchase of the Danish West Indies* (1932) Chap. VIII.

advancing step by step upon the diplomatic front, burning his bridges behind him.

The naval phase of the war in Europe had quickly settled down to a problem of commerce destruction, with each belligerent coalition (represented chiefly by Great Britain on one side, and by Germany on the other) striving desperately with all available weapons to stop the flow of munitions, raw materials, and foodstuffs into the territories of its enemies. In this struggle, as in the French Revolutionary and Napoleonic Wars, the measure of neutral "rights" depended from the outset less upon legal principles and arguments than upon the ability and determination of neutral Powers to resist belligerent depredations upon neutral persons, merchandise, and shipping.

The Allies, because of the overwhelming superiority of Great Britain's fighting fleet, immediately established command of the open sea. German merchant shipping was swept from the oceans. And the German battleship fleet was confined within the North Sea and the Baltic. The next step was for the Allies to prevent neutral vessels from carrying neutral goods either to German ports, or to the ports of contiguous neutral countries for transhipment into the territories of the Central Powers. And this the Allies proceeded to accomplish, chiefly by progressively and "illegally" extending the technique of blockade, the list of contraband goods, and the doctrine of ultimate enemy destination.

The Central Powers struck back with the only effective weapon at their command—the submarine. Despite the British Navy's overwhelming supremacy upon the surface of the ocean, the rapid development and high efficacy of the submarine as a commerce destroyer threatened for a time to reduce England to starvation and surrender. The German submarine blockade, like the Allied surface blockade, developed in defiance of generally accepted principles of international law. Technical facts, not legal theories, conditioned the methods of submarine operations. With the Allied Navies in command of the surface, it was impossible for German submarines to take their prizes into port for trial and condemnation. This left them no recourse but to destroy these prizes at sea. Since submarines were small vessels, full of machinery, with scarcely room for operating personnel, and none at all for the crews and passengers of torpedoed merchantmen, the submarine commander could do no more, under the best of conditions, than to set such persons adrift in small boats to save themselves as best they could. And since submarines were highly vulnerable to ramming, and could be easily destroyed by gunfire when upon the surface, the Allied practices of arming merchant vessels, of flying neutral flags, and of disguising warships as innocent merchantmen, left the German submarines no effective recourse but to torpedo merchant vessels without warning.

President Wilson tolerated the illegal depredations of the Allies, but not those of Germany. For reasons immaterial to this discussion, he drew an important distinction between belligerent aggressions which caused neutral property losses, and those which endangered or sacrificed neutral lives. Thus when the German government in February 1915, proclaimed a "war zone" around the British Isles, Wilson countered with a warning that he would hold Germany to "a strict accountability" for the acts of its submarine commanders. The following May, when a German submarine, torpedoed the British passenger steamer *Lusitania*, with a loss of over one hundred American lives, the President lodged a series of protests, culminating with the warning that he would regard further aggressions of such character as "deliberately unfriendly." And in March 1916, when a German submarine sank the French steamer *Sussex*, with Americans on board, Wilson announced that, unless the German government would abandon its unrestricted submarine warfare, the United States could "have no choice but to sever diplomatic relations . . . altogether."

From the day that Wilson delivered his first peremptory warning to Germany, he was advancing along a path from which he could scarcely retreat without a loss of prestige, intolerable to contemplate from the standpoint either of diplomacy or of domestic politics. From that day, if the conflict continued and the German government persisted in using its only effective weapon upon the sea, he had to envisage the entry of the United States into the war. And from that day, a prudent and realistic consideration of eventualities indicated the expediency of making diligent preparation for war. Thus, in the spring and summer of 1915, not only the great preparedness campaign, but also the inexorable logic of his diplomacy was driving Wilson toward military and naval expansion.

President Wilson's Conversion to Preparedness

President Wilson held the balance of power in the great struggle over preparedness. While the preparedness movement showed much strength upon the Atlantic and Pacific seaboards, it made slow headway in many sections of the South and Middle West. The Republican minorities in House and Senate were rather generally in favor of large increases in the Army and Navy; the Democratic majorities, on the other hand, were sharply divided, with a large and influential group, especially in the lower chamber, strongly opposed to the preparedness movement and all its works. Vigorous executive leadership might drive a preparedness program through Congress. Without such leadership, it was doubtful if the advocates of preparedness could carry their legislative program. And it was practically certain that little or nothing could be done in the face of executive opposition. The attitude of the Administration thus became a matter of capital importance. And President Wilson's conversion to preparedness became an episode of lasting significance in the rise of American naval power.

The spectacle of Wilson deserting the congressional representatives of large sections of the country, which had strongly supported his candidacy in 1912, to embrace a policy most popular in the strongholds of Republicanism, is not altogether easy to explain. But the principal stages in Wilson's progress from declared hostility toward, to full endorsement of, the preparedness movement are now fairly clear.

As the first rush carried the German armies into France, the President repeatedly voiced anxiety at the prospect of a German victory. Such a victory, he felt, would "ultimately mean trouble for us"; it would compel us to "build up a military machine of vast proportions"; it might even be "fatal" to American institutions and ideals.[48] Apparently satisfied after the first few weeks that a German victory was not imminent, Wilson strongly resisted for several months the movement to increase the Army and Navy.[49] But in February 1915, he began to show signs of weakening. On the 8th, Wilson received formal notification that, beginning ten days later, German submarines would attempt to destroy all Allied merchantmen within a specified war zone surrounding the British Isles, and that neutral vessels, to avoid danger, should stay clear of this area.[50] *On this same day,* according to Mr. Ray Stannard Baker, Wilson's authorized biographer, the President for the first time seriously turned his mind to the subject of preparedness.[51] And two days later, speaking through the State Department, he sent the German government the "strict accountability" warning.[52]

The *Lusitania* crisis further undermined Wilson's resistance to preparedness. Following the destruction of this ship, on May 6, 1915, Colonel House strove repeatedly to convert Wilson to preparedness, stressing the renewed prospect of a German victory, which House knew to be a weak point in the President's defenses.[53] On July 21, Wilson dispatched his third *Lusitania*

[48] Seymour, *House Papers,* Vol. I, pp. 285, 293; G. M. Trevelyan, *Grey of Fallodon* (1937), p. 355.

[49] *New York Times,* Oct. 20, 1914, p. 1; Dec. 8, p. 1; Seymour, *House Papers,* Vol. I, pp. 298, 299; R. S. Baker and W. E. Dodd, *Public Papers of Woodrow Wilson,* Vol. III, pp. 215, 224; R. S. Baker, *Woodrow Wilson* (1937), Vol. VI, p. 7.

[50] *Foreign Relations, 1915, Supplement,* pp. 95–7. The United States Ambassador in Berlin had previously informed the State Department of this war zone proclamation which was dated Feb. 4. *ibid.,* p. 94.

[51] *Woodrow Wilson,* Vol. VI, p. 8.

[52] *For. Rels., 1915, Supplement,* pp. 98–100.

[53] Harley Notter, *Origins of the Foreign Policy of Woodrow Wilson* (1937), p. 431n.; Seymour, *House Papers,* Vol. II, p. 19; and see Vol. I, pp. 285, 293.

note, warning Germany that further aggressions comparable to the sinking of that ship would be regarded as "deliberately unfriendly" acts.[54] *And on this same day,* by a second coincidence too remarkable to be fortuitous, Wilson directed his Secretaries of War and the Navy to have the experts in their respective departments draw up plans for strengthening the army and navy.[55]

From this time on, Wilson's reiterated fear of the militaristic consequences of a German victory, as well as a growing foreboding of the ultimate failure of his neutrality, forced him step by step toward the program of military and naval expansion demanded by the preparedness leaders.[56] When to the logic of his foreign policy and to his fear of a triumphant Germany, one adds his well known sympathy for the Allies; his own essentially fighting temperament; and above all, the pressure of his political managers who foresaw the electioneering potentialities of the preparedness issue, as well as the necessity of preventing the Republicans from capturing and monopolizing this issue in the approaching presidential campaign,[57] we have the principal factors which seem to have figured in Wilson's progress from declared hostility to any considerable expansion of the army and navy, toward public endorsement of a great legislative program directed to this end.

A Navy Second to None

President Wilson's conversion to the preparedness movement opened the way for an armament program without precedent in American history. And what was even more important in the long run, this program established a new standard of American naval power which hastened the mergence of

[54] *For. Rels., 1915, Supplement,* pp. 480–2.

[55] Baker, *Wilson,* Vol. VI, pp. 8–9.

[56] For further stages in Wilson's conversion to preparedness, see *ibid.*, pp. 9–10, 16; Notter, *Wilson's Foreign Policy,* p. 432; Baker & Dodd, *Wilson Papers,* Vol. III, pp. 373, 388, 406*ff*.

[57] See Tumulty, *Wilson as I Know Him,* Chap. XXVIII.

naval policy with foreign policy, in process since the accession of Theodore Roosevelt to the presidency in 1901.

The standard of naval power generally accepted since that date had been a navy second only to Great Britain's. As late as December 1914, four months after the outbreak of war in Europe, this was still the guiding principle.[58] But it was abruptly repudiated the following summer, after the President's conversion to preparedness.

In response to Wilson's request for expert advice, the General Board prepared a statement, expressly renouncing its earlier views and advocating a navy "ultimately . . . equal to the most powerful maintained by any nation of the world."[59] To attain such rank "not later than 1925," the Board proposed a gigantic five-year building program and a large increase of personnel.[60] This plan, in somewhat modified form,[61] was submitted to Congress in December 1915, with a presidential request for immediate legislation authorizing the Executive to carry it into execution.[62]

This request precipitated a bitter legislative struggle, reminiscent of Theodore Roosevelt's memorable battle with Congress

[58] Testifying before the House Naval Committee, Admiral F. F. Fletcher, Commander in Chief of the Atlantic Fleet, saw "no immediate necessity" for building up our Navy to "equal" that of Great Britain; and, so far as he was aware, no naval expert was "advocating" equality with Britain. Secretary Daniels expressly endorsed the second-best standard. And even the militant Captain Hobson publicly took the same position at this time. See 63 Cong. 2 Sess., House Naval Committee, *Hearings on Estimates for 1915*, pp. 554, 555, 557, 582.

[59] Navy Dept., *Ann. Repts., 1915*, p. 73.

[60] *ibid.*, pp. 77, 80. The Board's program called for 10 additional battleships, 6 battle cruisers, 10 scout cruisers, 50 destroyers, and over 80 smaller warships and auxiliary vessels of different types.

[61] *ibid.*, pp. 1–9, 18.

[62] See Baker & Dodd, *Wilson Papers*, Vol. III, pp. 406, 413*ff*. The Administration's plan envisaged a navy built and building by 1921 to consist of 27 first-line battleships, 6 battle cruisers, 25 second-line battleships, 10 armored cruisers, 13 scout cruisers, 5 first-class (unarmored) cruisers, 3 second-class (unarmored) cruisers, 10 third-class (unarmored) cruisers, 108 destroyers, 18 fleet submarines, 157 coast submarines, 6 monitors, 20 gunboats, 4 supply ships, 15 fuel ships, 4 transports, 3 tenders to torpedo vessels, 2 ammunition ships, and 8 miscellaneous auxiliary vessels, *ibid.*, p. 415.

back in 1908.[63] As already noted, large sections of the South and Middle West, in the winter of 1914–1915, had shown indifference or even hostility to increasing the army and navy. The preparedness campaign not only was making slow headway in some of these regions, but had also stimulated an active anti-preparedness movement which, while winning adherents all over the country, had developed its greatest strength in the interior.[64] Sectional indifference and hostility to preparedness were quickly reflected in congressional circles, where many spokesmen of the interior, including some of the most influential Democratic leaders, received Wilson's armament plea in silence and made preparations to block the Administration's military and naval program.[65]

So formidable did this opposition appear that the President decided, early in January 1916, to carry the issue to the country.[66] Starting with addresses in New York City on January 27, he made a swing through the Middle West, speaking at Pittsburgh, Cleveland, Milwaukee, Chicago, Des Moines, Topeka, Kansas City, and St. Louis. In the last-mentioned city, on February 3, Wilson delivered a stirring extemporaneous plea for "incomparably the greatest navy in the world." In the authorized version of this address, the phrase "most adequate" was substituted for "greatest," but it is now indisputably established that Wilson actually said "greatest."[67]

This speaking tour with its dramatic climax, unquestionably gave fresh impetus to the preparedness movement, especially in the East but also in the anti-preparedness strongholds of the

[63] See pp. 264*ff.*, *supra.*

[64] Mr. Ray Stannard Baker, who alone has access to the Wilson Papers, states that the President had reliable reports in the autumn of 1915 that the preparedness campaign was making little or no headway in Iowa, Maryland, Missouri, Nebraska, Oklahoma, Oregon, Minnesota, Wisconsin, and parts of Pennsylvania and Texas. See Baker, *Wilson,* Vol. VI, p. 13n.

[65] Arnett, *Kitchin,* pp. 47–86.

[66] Tumulty, *Wilson as I Know Him,* p. 242; David Lawrence, *The True Story of Woodrow Wilson* (1924), p. 158; and Baker, *Wilson,* Vol. VI, p. 24*ff.*

[67] Baker, *Wilson,* Vol. VI, p. 29n. And see *New York Times,* Feb. 4, 1916, p. 2; *New York Herald,* Feb. 4, 1916, p. 4; and *Literary Digest,* Vol. LII (Feb. 12), p. 361, in all of which the speech was so reported.

interior.[68] But was the impetus sufficient to carry the Administration's armament program through Congress? The President returned to the Capital to discover the opposition weakened, but still formidable.[69] Hearings before the House Naval Committee, already under way, dragged on for months,[70] with the Republican minority holding out for a program exceeding that of the Administration, the Democratic majority sharply divided, and five "little navy" Democrats holding the balance of power.[71] This deadlock continued past the middle of May, with no group willing to yield, but with Democratic leaders, in and out of Congress, anxious to restore at least a semblance of harmony on the eve of the national convention.[72]

A compromise to this end was finally arranged. The Administration abandoned its five-year building program, consented to accept five battle cruisers in lieu of additional battleships, and made certain other concessions, in return for which the little-navy men acquiesced in a one-year program far exceeding any hitherto enacted.[73] On the understanding that the Administration would faithfully support this compromise through House and Senate,[74] a tolerably united front was restored within the Democratic ranks. After a long and heated debate, characterized by sharp cleavage along party lines,[75] the House voted

[68] See Lawrence, *True Story of Wilson*, pp. 171–4; and Baker, *Wilson*, Vol. VI, pp. 26–31. Another press poll taken by the *Literary Digest* showed a strong trend among editors all over the country toward a "navy second to none," or at the very least, "second only to Great Britain." See issue of March 11, 1916, Vol. LII, pp. 617–24, 647–87.

[69] See Arnett, *Kitchin*, pp. 94*ff*.; and James Kearny, *The Political Education of Woodrow Wilson* (1926), p. 362. The significance of this continuing opposition is all the greater in view of the approaching presidential and congressional campaign, with every member of the House coming up for reelection.

[70] See 64 Cong. 1 Sess., House Naval Committee, *Hearings on Estimates for 1916*, 3 volumes.

[71] Arnett, *Kitchin*, p. 94; *New York Times*, May 18, 1916, p. 1. The five "little-navy" Democrats were Buchanan (Ill.), Callaway (Tex.), Connelly (Kan.), Gray (Ind.), and Hensley (Mo.).

[72] 64 Cong. 1 Sess., *Cong. Record* (Vol. LIII), pp. 12668–9.

[73] *ibid.*, p. 12669; *New York Times*, May 19, 1916, p. 1; 64 Cong. 1 Sess., *H. Rept.* No. 743; Arnett, *Kitchin*, p. 95.

[74] *Cong. Record*, Vol. LIII, pp. 12669, 12697; Arnett, *Kitchin*, p. 95.

[75] *Cong. Record*, Vol. LIII, pp. 8784–828, 8863–99, 8902–9, 8911–22, 9140–6, 9181–90.

down a much larger program sponsored by the Republican minority,[76] and on June 2, 1916, passed the compromise bill.[77]

On this same day, after the bill's passage in the House, by another of those amazing coincidences that have figured so conspicuously in the rise of American naval power, the first reports of the Battle of Jutland reached the United States.[78] This first and only great naval action between the main fleets of Great Britain and Germany, gave fresh impetus to American naval development in general, and to battleship construction in particular.

A brief digression will help explain this result. In 1916, the largest battleships, or super-dreadnoughts as they were popularly called, were vessels generally exceeding 25,000 tons displacement. They varied from 500 to 600 or more feet in length. In speed, they ranged from 21 to 25 knots. They carried eight to twelve heavy guns, the largest of which could throw an armor-piercing, high-explosive shell, weighing nearly a ton, more than thirteen miles. And for protection against the fire of the enemy's heavy guns, the battleships of this period were equipped, at their waterline, gun turrets, and other vital spots, with tough steel armor, ten to fourteen inches thick. Such ships, grouped in divisions of three or four each, formed the nucleus of a fighting fleet, and the principal index of its power.

However, as previously noted, a balanced fleet also required various other classes of warships and auxiliaries. There were destroyers—small, very swift vessels, used to protect the larger ships from torpedo attacks, equipped to lay down concealing smoke-screens in emergencies, and armed with torpedoes of their own for use against a hostile fleet. A fighting fleet also included swift scout cruisers—vessels somewhat larger than destroyers, whose function was to spy out the enemy's fleet, and to keep contact with it until the battleships could arrive.

[76] By a vote of 189 to 183. *ibid.*, p. 9189. For the Republican program, see *H. Rept.* No. 743, Pt. 2.

[77] *Cong. Record,* Vol. LIII, p. 9190.

[78] *New York Times,* June 3, 1916, p. 1.

To support one's own scouting screen, and to break through the enemy's screen of cruisers and destroyers, a still more powerful type of swift warship had been developed in the years immediately preceding the war. This was the battle cruiser. The latest vessels of this type were larger than first-line battleships. Some of them carried guns as powerful as those of the greatest super-dreadnoughts. But to attain the high speed essential for scouting, a great increase in horse-power was necessary. And to allow for the enormous increase in weight which larger engines and additional fuel involved, it was necessary to sacrifice either gun-power or armor protection. The result was a compromise, in which both the number of guns and the thickness of the battle cruiser's armor were somewhat reduced, the proportions varying from ship to ship, and from navy to navy.

The policy which American naval authorities had followed, of keeping pace with foreign battleship programs, if necessary at a sacrifice of other types, had kept the United States from taking an active part in the early stages of battle-cruiser development.[79] After the outbreak of the war, however, German naval raids on the English coast and other operations in the North Sea and elsewhere, considerably enhanced the vogue of the battle cruiser among American experts. In the fall of 1915, after President Wilson's conversion to a strong preparedness program had greatly enlarged the potential scope of American naval development, the General Board took a more decided stand for battle cruisers, including six in its five-year building program.[80] This number was retained in the Administration's program, submitted to Congress in December of that year.[81] For reasons not altogether clear, the little-navy men in Congress, while immovably opposed to more battleships, agreed in the compromise bill to five battle cruisers, to be larger and to cost more than any battleship hitherto author-

[79] Navy Dept., *Ann. Repts., 1911,* p. 39; same, *1912,* p. 26; same, *1913,* p. 29; same, *1914,* p. 60*ff.*

[80] Navy Dept., *Ann. Repts., 1915,* pp. 76, 80.

[81] *ibid.,* pp. 5, 7.

ized, and to have a speed exceeding that of any capital ship afloat.[82] And it was this bill that had just passed the House of Representatives when the first reports of the Battle of Jutland reached the United States.

Garbled and doctored as were those reports, it was soon perceived that the battle cruisers of both fleets had severely suffered. Of the five German battle cruisers engaged, one had been sunk, two others dreadfully battered, and the remaining two considerably damaged. Of the nine warships of this type in the British fleet, German gunfire had blown up and utterly destroyed three, and three others had limped home in crippled condition. The battleships of both fleets, on the contrary, had shown far greater endurance under fire. While it was admittedly true that relatively few of the battleships in either fleet had been subjected to such devastating fire as had the battle cruisers, those that had been had fully demonstrated the protective value of heavy armor.[83]

These events had immediate repercussions within the United States. The Democratic Chairman of the Senate Naval Committee,[84] Benjamin R. Tillman of South Carolina, announced on June 3 that the Battle of Jutland had demonstrated the necessity of building battleships as well as battle cruisers. Within a few days, first the Republican, and then the Democratic National Convention endorsed a strong navy. On June 21, it was announced that a subcommittee of the Senate Naval Committee—consisting exclusively of big-navy men—was reframing the House program so as to provide for several battleships. It was reported the next day that the subcommittee

[82] 64 Cong. 1 Sess., *H. Rept.* No. 743, pp. 4–5.

[83] *New York Herald,* June 5, 1916, p. 10. Admiral George Dewey elaborated this news theme in an article entitled, "Lessons of Skagerrack," *Sea Power,* July 1916, p. 7.

[84] This committee, as usual, was heavily loaded in favor of coastal and industrial States. Its Democratic members were: Chairman B. R. Tillman (S. C.), Swanson (Va.), Bryan (Fla.), Johnson (Me.), Chilton (W. Va.), O'Gorman (N. Y.), J. W. Smith (Md.), Lewis (Ill.), Phelan (Cal.), Pittman (Nev.). Its Republican members were: Penrose (Pa.), Clapp (Minn.), Lodge (Mass.), W. A. Smith (Mich.), Page (Vt.), Poindexter (Wash.), and Fall (N. M.).

would go still further and restore the whole original five-year program. The following day it was intimated that this subcommittee had a still larger project on foot. Three days later, the little-navy Democrats learned to their amazement and consternation that the President, contrary to their understanding of his pledge to support the compromise bill, not only favored restoring the Administration's five-year program, but was even pressing to have it telescoped from five to three years. And on June 30, the Senate Naval Committee brought in a report recommending virtually a new bill in accord with the wishes of the Administration.[85]

This report provoked a second heated debate which lasted intermittently for a week in mid-July.[86] The stubborn opposition of the little-navy men retarded but could not halt the steam roller advancing under the combined power of both the Democratic and the Republican organizations. And on July 21, the amended bill passed the Senate by the decisive vote of 71 to 8.[87]

This action transferred the struggle back to the House where, on August 15, Representative Lemuel P. Padgett, Democrat from Tennessee and Chairman of the Naval Committee, presented a report from a Senate-House conference committee which recommended acceptance of all the salient features of the Senate bill.[88] This report precipitated a third and final debate. The minority floor leader urged all his Republican colleagues to vote for the Senate's program.[89] A few other members reiterated the arguments which the preparedness campaign had carried into almost every household in the

[85] *New York Times*, June 4, 1916, Sec. I, p. 3. The subcommittee was composed of Senators Tillman, Swanson, and Lodge. *ibid.*, June 22, p. 3; June 23, p. 6; June 24, p. 17; June 27, p. 11; 64 Cong. 1 Sess., *S. Rept.* No. 575.

[86] *Cong. Record*, Vol. LIII, pp. 10922–34, 11039–45, 11161–92, 11195–210, 11319–84.

[87] *ibid.*, p. 11384. The eight negative votes came from the following Senators: Democrats: Thomas (Col.), and Vardmann (Miss.); Republicans: Clapp (Minn.), Curtis (Kan.), Gronna (N. D.), LaFollette (Wis.), and Works (Cal.).

[88] *ibid.*, pp. 12652–61.

[89] *ibid.*, pp. 12667–8.

country.[90] But the little-navy bitter-enders held the center of the stage.

Representative Robert N. Page, Democrat from North Carolina, told how he had accompanied Representative Walter L. Hensley of Missouri to the office of Secretary Daniels on May 18; how they had there arranged the famous compromise which had broken the deadlock and reestablished harmony among the House Democrats, and between them and the Administration; and how the little-navy men had loyally supported the compromise bill even though it greatly exceeded what they regarded as an adequate naval program.[91]

Representative Rufus Hardy, Democrat from Texas, dwelt on the growing exhaustion of the warring countries, which was steadily increasing the relative security of the United States; and he deplored the popular "hysteria whipped into fury" that was "driving Republicans and Democrats in the mad race for shelter in the biggest naval program ever adopted by any nation on earth. . . ."[92]

Representative Philip P. Campbell, Republican from Kansas, asked why we should plunge "headlong into immediate preparation for war" at a time when every belligerent nation was "exhausting its resources in men, in money, in everything that makes a nation powerful in war. . . ."[93]

Reiterating the views of the preceding speakers, Representative Frank W. Mondell, Republican from Wyoming, doubted if "a third of the membership of the House here present" believed "this increased program" either "justified or justifiable."[94]

Representative Finly H. Gray, Democrat from Indiana, denounced a policy of building a navy second to none, as utterly

[90] *ibid.*, pp. 12669–72, 12675–9, 12689–95, 12697.

[91] *ibid.*, pp. 12668–9.

[92] *ibid.*, pp. 12672–3. Hardy, along with other bitter-enders, placed the responsibility for the panic squarely upon the "militarists, the jingoes, and the self-interested munitions makers of this country." *ibid.*, p. 12672; and see also, pp. 12679–80, 12696, 12697.

[93] *ibid.*, pp. 12673–4.

[94] *ibid.*, pp. 12679–80.

unnecessary and calculated to involve us in an endless cycle of naval rivalry with other Powers.[95]

Representative Warren W. Bailey, Democrat from Pennsylvania, condemned this "smashing raid on the Public Treasury" to support a naval program "prepared exclusively with reference to remote contingencies . . . about as likely to materialize as a volcanic eruption in the Mississippi Valley. . . ."[96]

Thus, one after another, the little-navy men recorded for posterity their reasons for refusing to join the stampede.[97] Finally, there remained only Claude Kitchin, Democrat from North Carolina, and Majority Leader of the House, whose great personal influence had alone kept the opposition from collapsing altogether.

Kitchin opened by recalling how the House Democrats and the Administration had agreed on the compromise program; how he had been "expressly told" that, in return for united Democratic support, "the Secretary of the Navy and the Administration would get behind it and make it the Administration's program"; how he had urged and persuaded his colleagues to support that program even though it seemed excessive to some of them; how they had united to secure its passage; and how they had defeated "what was then considered an extravagant, wild, and reckless program presented by the Republicans." Now, they were confronted with a bill which exceeded that Republican program and were urged to endorse it by Democratic leaders "from the President down." The utter inconsistency of his party's position seemed the more amazing to Kitchin, when he recalled that, in the interim, a great naval battle had reduced the Navies of Germany and Great Britain by some hundred thousand tons each.[98]

Taking a larger view, Kitchin dwelt on the steadily mounting naval expenditures of the United States during recent

[95] *ibid.*, pp. 12683–5.

[96] *ibid.*, pp. 12685–6.

[97] In addition to those already cited, see the speeches of Lenroot (Rep., Wis.), London (Soc., N. Y.), Burnett (Dem., Ala.), *ibid.*, pp. 12686–7, 12696–7.

[98] *ibid.*, p. 12697.

years. In the last decade before the war, the American Navy had cost more than any other save Britain's—more even than the widely-publicized German Navy. And now, at a single stroke, Congress was about to vote a naval program that would require an *"increase of appropriations over seven times more than the total increase by Great Britain in the ten years prior to the European war . . . sixty times more than the total increase by Germany in the five years preceding the war, and one hundred times more than the total increase by Germany in the three years preceding the war."*[99]

With enactment of this legislation, Kitchin declared, the United States would become "in dollars and cents the greatest military-naval nation the world has ever seen." And he concluded with the prophecy that this would prove only a beginning; that naval appropriations would "never be reduced," but would go on increasing from year to year.[100]

As Kitchin resumed his seat, Padgett arose, to call upon his colleagues, in the name of "patriotic duty" and loyalty to the Administration, to accept the Senate's program.[101] The roll was called, and the result was announced—ayes, 283; noes, 51; not voting, 99.[102] The long struggle was finished, and the United States was launched upon a voyage into uncharted seas whose rocks and shoals and storms only time could reveal.

Naval Act of 1916

The famous Act of August 29, 1916, projected a naval building program at that time without precedent. The origin and evolution of this program is summarized in the following table:

[99] *ibid.*, p. 12698. (Kitchin's italics.)

[100] *ibid.*, pp. 12698, 12699.

[101] *ibid.*, pp. 12699-700.

[102] *ibid.*, p. 12700. Judging from the recorded applause accorded to the opposition speakers, as well as from the number and identity of those who abstained from voting, it is fairly clear that the strength of the opposition greatly exceeded the 51 recorded negative votes. Compare this roll call with the one for recommittal, on June 2, *ibid.*, p. 9189.

Categories of Ships	*Gen. B'd's Program 5-years*	*Admin.'s Program 5-years*	*Compromise Bill 1-year*	*Senate Program 3-years*	*Final Act 3-years*
Battleships	10	10		10	10
Battle cruisers	6	6	5	6	6
Scout cruisers	10	10	4	10	10
Destroyers	50	50	10	50	50
Fleet submarines	9	15		9	9
Coast submarines	58	85	50	58	58
Miscellaneous	13	10	3	14	14

While the building program received the greatest publicity, other provisions of the Act were also highly significant. The Office of Operations, which, it is recalled, had originally been conceived as a step toward a general staff, was enlarged and strengthened, and its chief raised to the rank of Admiral.[103] The Act created a naval flying corps, and appropriated a substantial sum for the development of aviation.[104] There were many provisions relating to personnel, including a considerable increase in both commissioned officers and enlisted strength, and an elaborate reserve organization.[105] Altogether, this enactment was the most comprehensive piece of naval legislation thus far passed, and it was likewise the most expensive. It carried appropriations totaling well over $300,000,000, more than twice the figure for the preceding year, and nearly six times the amount appropriated to carry the Navy through the war with Spain.[106]

Finally, the law concluded with a section renouncing armed aggression and endorsing disarmament—in principle. This section, forced upon Congress and the Administration by Representative Hensley, Democrat, stated that it was "the policy of the United States to adjust and settle its international disputes through mediation or arbitration, to the end that war may be honorably avoided." It stated further that the United States government looked "with apprehension and disfavor upon a general increase of armament throughout the world," but took

[103] See p. 315, *supra;* and *Navy Yearbook, 1917,* p. 400.
[104] *ibid.,* pp. 401, 426*ff.*
[105] *ibid.,* pp. 418*ff.*
[106] *ibid.,* p. 673.

the view "that no single nation" could alone "disarm," and "that without a common agreement upon the subject every considerable Power must maintain a relative standing in military strength." The President was accordingly "authorized and requested to invite, at an appropriate time, not later than the close of the war in Europe, all the great governments of the world to send representatives to a conference" to formulate "a plan for a court of arbitration" and "to consider the question of disarmament. . . ."[107]

For the time being, this section went largely unnoticed. Men were too absorbed in preparing for war, to reflect seriously on the implications and possible future repercussions that might result from their bid for naval supremacy. Only after the restoration of peace would Americans begin to feel the consequences of a naval policy that challenged Britain's traditional supremacy in the Atlantic and the security of Japan in the Western Pacific. Before that day should dawn, the United States was to enter the Great War and play a decisive rôle in the defeat of Germany and the surrender of the German Fleet. And by one of the ironical turns of history, the smashing victory of the Allies (made possible by American financial, military, and naval assistance) was destined, in conjunction with the enlarged naval development projected in the Act of 1916, to complete the mergence of the naval policy and foreign policy of the United States.

[107] *ibid.*, p. 466.

CHAPTER NINETEEN

☆ ☆

America at War: Strategic Lessons and Political Consequences (1917–1918)

THE great preparedness movement and its legislative product, the Naval Act of 1916, framed expressly with a view to post-war requirements, largely ignored the immediate practical problem of getting the Navy ready for the belligerent partnership with the Allies to which, by the spring of 1916, President Wilson was virtually committed if and when the Central Powers resumed unrestricted submarine warfare on merchant shipping.

This omission was symptomatic of a trend in American policy right down to our entry into the war. Certain Administration leaders showed the greatest unwillingness to face the impending contingency of war toward which the logic of events was driving the country during 1916. There was also a rather general failure, even among experts, to anticipate the rôle which the Navy might play if and when the United States cast its lot with the Allies. And it was deemed inexpedient, for reasons to be considered in due course, for the Navy Department even to begin large-scale specific preparations for war with Germany as long as the Administration was attempting to maintain a semblance of neutrality.

Meanwhile, the war upon the sea was moving swiftly toward a crisis which carried the Allies to the verge of irretrievable disaster in the spring of 1917. This crisis resulted largely from the development of new instruments and techniques of naval warfare. It was precipitated by the German submarine offensive against merchant shipping, which challenged some of the most firmly settled doctrines of naval strategy, and threatened for a time to more than offset the Allies' overwhelming surface command of the sea.

The entry of the United States into the war at this juncture put American naval resources and organizing ability to a critical test. The Navy rose to the emergency, and played an important and highly creditable part in saving the Allies. But the stresses and strains of American war experience emphasized certain weaknesses, and gave rise to criticisms which went to the heart of the related problems of securing efficient naval administration and of formulating a coherent naval policy under the American form of government.

Strategy of the Naval War

In order to appreciate the rôle which the American Navy was called upon to play in the later stages of the war, one should have clearly in mind the relative positions of the belligerents and the general course of the war upon the sea from August 1914 to the entry of the United States in April 1917.

Theoretically and mathematically, the Allies possessed in 1914 an overwhelming preponderance of naval power. The British Navy alone exceeded the combined forces of the Central Powers. Although Germany held a slight advantage in submarines, whose potentialities were relatively unknown, and although Britain's margin of superiority in cruisers and destroyers was comparatively small, the latter's main fleet outranked Germany's in first-line capital ships, the traditional index of naval power, by a ratio of three to two.[1]

The fate of the Entente depended in no small degree upon the ability of the British Admiralty to translate its theoretical

[1] For detailed comparison, see Captain T. G. Frothingham, *Naval History of the World War* (1924), Vol. I, Chap. III, and App. A.

primacy into an effective command of the sea. Great Britain was the industrial and financial heart of the Allied war machine. But the peoples and factories of the British Isles were vitally dependent upon food and raw materials drawn from outlying parts of the Empire and from the neutral countries of North and South America. Stoppage of this traffic would soon paralyze British life and halt the flow of men and munitions to France. The integrity of this world-wide network of water communications was, therefore, the paramount objective of British naval strategy. Realization of this objective hinged upon the ability of the British Navy to destroy, or at least to drive from the sea and immobilize, Germany's fighting fleet, commerce-raiding surface cruisers, and, at a later stage, its submarine commerce destroyers. The Allies could, and repeatedly did, suffer reverses on land, and still carry on. But one decisive naval defeat, shattering the sea power of Great Britain, would almost certainly have lost the war.[2]

Sea power figured much less importantly in the war plans of the Central Powers. These countries were not so vitally dependent upon oversea foodstuffs and raw materials. They could easily withstand a commercial blockade for a few weeks or even months. Such a blockade might prove more serious in a long-drawn-out struggle. But German military strategists discounted such a possibility. Counting on a swift land campaign to win the war in a few days or weeks, they largely ignored the superior naval power of the Allies, and neglected the offensive and defensive potentialities of their own splendid Navy, second only to Britain's in size, and second to none in mechanical excellence and technical efficiency.[3]

Events quickly revealed the error in their calculations when war finally broke in August 1914. The initial German drive into France slowed down and shortly came to a full stop. Within a few days the Allies had driven the German mer-

[2] C. R. M. F. Cruttwell, *History of the Great War* (1934), Chap. IV.

[3] Frothingham, *op. cit.*, Vol. I, Chap. I; Captain B. H. Liddell Hart, *The Real War* (1930), Chap. II.

chant flag from the open sea. Within a few weeks the German oversea squadrons were run down and destroyed or driven to cover. Meanwhile, the German High Sea (battleship) Fleet lay at its home bases or made short sallies into the North Sea. And while intact and undefeated, it was at least temporarily confined within a narrow zone by Britain's more powerful Grand Fleet, and powerless to prevent or break up the commercial blockade which the Allies were drawing steadily tighter in the winter of 1914–1915.[4]

In February 1915, the German government countered the Allied blockade, with a submarine offensive against merchant shipping in a "war zone" surrounding the British Isles. Shortage of submarines, threats of American intervention, and other factors led presently to a partial relaxation of this assault on Allied communications, but not until it had revealed the commerce-destroying potentialities of the submarine. Meanwhile, an Allied attempt to open the Dardanelles, and thereby reestablish military communications with Russia, had ended in disaster. And both main fleets had remained comparatively inactive, lying at anchor or cruising in their respective spheres in the North Sea.[5]

Early in 1916, however, these fleets commenced more active operations which culminated the following May in the Battle of Jutland. In this, the only major naval action of the war, the weaker German Fleet, through luck and superior technique, inflicted serious injury[6] and then escaped, though not without casualties,[7] from the annihilation that would almost certainly

[4] Frothingham, *op. cit.*, Vol. I, Chaps. IV–XIV; Cruttwell, *op. cit.*, Chaps. VII, XII; Commander H. H. Frost, *The Battle of Jutland* (1936), Chap. I; Sir Julian S. Corbett, *Naval Operations* (1920), Vol. I, and Vol. II, Chaps. I–V.

[5] Frost, *op. cit.*, Chap. II; Frothingham, *op. cit.*, Vol. I, Chaps. XV–XVII; Vol. II, Chaps. I–XI; Cruttwell, *op. cit.*, Chaps. XII, XVIII; Corbett, *op. cit.*, Vol. II, Chaps. VI–XX; Vol. III, Chaps. I–XII.

[6] British ship losses: three battle cruisers, three armored cruisers, eight destroyers, total displacement 111,980 tons; casualties: 6,097 killed, 510 wounded, 177 prisoners. Frost, *op. cit.*, pp. 506, 541.

[7] German ship losses: one second-line battleship, one battle cruiser, four light cruisers, five destroyers, total displacement 62,233 tons; casualties: 2,545 killed, 494 wounded. *ibid.*, pp. 506, 542.

have resulted from a finish fight with the greatly superior British Fleet.[8]

The Battle of Jutland marked another turning point in the naval war. Though hailed in Germany as a great victory, it had conclusively demonstrated the inability of the Central Powers to smash the Allies' surface command of the sea, and shattered their hope of raising the commercial blockade which was slowly but inexorably reducing them to starvation. This demonstration strengthened the demand for more aggressive use of submarines, which alone, it was contended, could save the Central Powers from ruin. In accordance with this view, U-boat[9] construction was speeded up. The scope and sphere of submarine operations were steadily enlarged. And in February 1917, the German High Command threw off all restraint, and resumed unrestricted warfare on merchant shipping in a desperate effort to starve Great Britain into surrender before an effective anti-submarine defense could be put into operation, and before the now virtually certain entry of the United States into the war could turn the tide for the Allies.[10]

The Crisis of the Naval War

The war now moved swiftly to a crisis.[11] The Allies controlled the surface of every ocean and of all the strategically important narrow seas except the Dardanelles, the Baltic, and the southeastern rim of the North Sea.[12] Their commercial

[8] *ibid.*, Chaps. XII–XXI; Frothingham, *op. cit.*, Vol. II, Chaps. XII–XXV; Cruttwell, *op. cit.*, Chap. XVIII; Corbett, *op. cit.*, Vol. III, Chaps. XIII–XXI.

[9] German submarines were popularly called U-boats, a term derived from the German word "Unterseeboot."

[10] Frothingham, *op. cit.*, Vol. II, Chaps. XXVI–XXIX; Cruttwell, *op. cit.*, Chap. XXII; Henry Newbolt, *Naval Operations* (1928), Vol. IV, Chaps. I–VIII.

[11] Admiral Viscount Jellicoe (R.N.), *The Crisis of the Naval War* (1920), Chap. II; Admiral W. S. Sims, *The Victory at Sea* (1919), Chap. I; Newbolt, *op. cit.*, Vol. IV, Chap. IX; Liddell Hart, *The Real War,* Chap. V; Cruttwell, *op. cit.*, Chaps. XXI–XXII.

[12] Command of the Straits (connecting the Black Sea and the Aegean) would have restored military communications between Russia and the other Allies; command of the Baltic would have had a similar effect, and would also have

blockade promised in time to break the resistance of the Central Powers. But there were ominous indications that the Allies themselves might collapse under the strain. Their armies in France were still deadlocked after two and a half years of dreadful and useless sacrifice. The Russian Revolution (March 1917) foreshadowed an early collapse of the Allied Eastern Front. Military and civilian morale was everywhere low. And more alarming still, the German submarine offensive against merchant shipping was rapidly sapping the life of Great Britain, whose industrial and financial power and resources were alone sustaining the tottering Entente.[13]

Although Germany's initial assault on merchant shipping, back in the spring of 1915, had dramatically revealed the commerce-destroying potentialities of the submarine, the British Admiralty had shown little imagination in devising an effective system of defense.[14]

There were three more or less distinct approaches to the submarine problem. One was to seek means of making merchant vessels invulnerable to submarine attack. Another was to attempt to hunt down and destroy enemy U-boats at sea. And a third was to attack at the source by striving to prevent the under-water raiders from getting to sea at all.

The Admiralty's anti-submarine campaign had proceeded along two lines to the virtual exclusion of all others. Merchant vessels had been armed with small naval guns which were often effective if the attacking submarine approached its prey upon

---

cut Germany off from a vitally important trade with the neutral Scandinavian countries; and command of the southeastern rim of the North Sea would have greatly facilitated blockade or destruction of the principal German submarine bases.

[13] Newbolt, *op. cit.*, Vol. IV, pp. 370, 379; Jellicoe (*op. cit.*, p. 51), gives Allied and neutral shipping losses, Jan.–June 1917, as follows:

Jan.	324,016 tons	April	870,359 tons
Feb.	500,573 "	May	589,754 "
March	555,991 "	June	675,154 "

[14] Lieutenant Commander J. M. Kenworthy (R.N.) (Baron Strabolgi), *Sailors, Statesmen—and Others* (1933), Chap. IV; *War Memoirs of David Lloyd George* (1934), Vol. III, Chap. III.

the surface, but were useless against surprise torpedo attack by a submerged U-boat. The Admiralty had expended much greater effort in creating an anti-submarine patrol, consisting of destroyers, submarines, a miscellaneous array of auxiliary vessels, and even aircraft. The function of these forces was to hunt down and destroy enemy submarines at sea. This task, however, presented the greatest difficulties. There were rarely more than thirty U-boats abroad at once, and they were scattered over an immense area. In February 1917, for example, no less than 3,000 vessels were patrolling the Mediterranean and the waters surrounding the British Isles. Yet in that one month alone, Allied and neutral shipping losses rose above 500,000 tons. And the naval authorities of Great Britain, virtually admitting the failure of their anti-submarine campaign, were secretly predicting still greater losses in the months to come, and acknowledging their inability to cope with the crisis.[15]

This desperate situation was at least partially attributable to the Admiralty's consistent failure to take a large view of the submarine problem and to heed timely suggestions and advice from a highly intelligent group within the Navy, mostly younger officers who had had first-hand experience in combating submarines. While a respectable number of these officers strongly favored convoying merchant vessels in groups through the danger zones, the conservative men who dominated the Admiralty had raised various technical objections, and refused even serious consideration to this method of protecting shipping.[16] While competent officers urged well conceived plans for destroying the German submarine bases, blocking their exits, or mining their approaches, all these projects involved technical difficulties which the naval authorities considered insuperable,

[15] Newbolt, *op. cit.,* Vol. IV, pp. 347, 370.

[16] This statement is subject to slight qualification. Troop transports were regularly convoyed, as were certain vessels carrying especially valuable cargoes. Also, one function of the destroyers with the Grand Fleet was to guard the capital ships against submarine attack, a function analogous to that of convoying merchantmen.

or entailed risks which they were unwilling to assume.[17] One of their most frequently reiterated objections, both to a convoy system and to aggressive operations against the German submarine bases in the North Sea, was the inadequacy of Allied naval forces. Yet in the winter of 1916–1917, it was discovered that the Admiralty had absolutely no plans for utilizing naval reenforcements from America, although the entry of the United States into the war had been imminent during most of 1916, and was by now practically certain within the very near future.[18]

The American Navy's Approach to the War

The German submarine offensive forged the final link in the chain of events that transformed the United States from a neutral partisan into a belligerent partner of the Allies. American policy had necessarily envisaged this possible eventuality from the winter of 1915. War had been imminent during most of 1916. While the desperate plight of Great Britain in the winter of 1916–1917 was not widely appreciated in America, there was no dearth of information as to the general situation in the war area. Yet the Navy entered the great struggle in April 1917 materially unprepared and without plans for waging the kind of war then in progress.[19]

While it is easier in retrospect than it was in prospect to plot

[17] Kenworthy, *op. cit.*, Chap. IV; Lloyd George, *War Memoirs*, Vol. III, pp. 86*ff*.

[18] Kenworthy, *op. cit.*, p. 72.

[19] This section is based largely on testimony before a subcommittee of the Senate Naval Affairs Committee (66 Cong. 2 Sess.), published in two volumes as *Naval Investigation, 1920*. This investigation grew out of criticisms respecting the Navy Department's conduct of the war. The author of these criticisms was Admiral W. S. Sims who had commanded American naval forces in European waters during the war. The investigating committee held hearings from March to May 1920. The stenographic record thereof runs to nearly 3,500 closely printed, unindexed pages. A fairly adequate abridgement was printed in the *Army and Navy Journal* (Vol. LVII). And a brilliant, if rather partisan, analysis of the testimony is still more available in *Naval Lessons of the Great War* (1921), by Lieutenant T. B. Kittridge, a reserve officer on Admiral Sims' staff, who assisted Sims in preparing his evidence for the committee.

our fateful progress from neutrality to belligerency, many contemporary observers foresaw and predicted the eventual entry of the United States into the war. Such an eventuality was definitely perceivable after February 1915. The cloud upon the horizon grew distinctly larger following the *Lusitania* disaster. And no well informed observer could miss the ominous implications of Wilson's solemn threat, after the sinking of the *Sussex* in March 1916, "to sever diplomatic relations . . . altogether" unless Germany abandoned its ruthless war on merchant shipping.

Wilson's threats, the shortage of submarines, and other considerations forced the German government into successive compromises which compelled the U-boats to operate, at great disadvantage, with some regard for the safety of neutrals. But there were indications, especially after the Battle of Jutland, May 1916, that this shaky truce would not last. It was positively known that the German Admiralty was pushing forward a great submarine building program. And the Navy Department was receiving trustworthy reports during 1916 of Germany's "intention to carry on unrestricted attacks on merchant shipping, whether neutral or not, as soon as [enough of] their [new] submarines were ready."[20]

The Department had equally reliable information as to the general course of the war upon the sea. It was perfectly well known that the Allies had indisputable command of the ocean's surface. The Battle of Jutland had provided a convincing demonstration of the German Fleet's inability either to shatter the British Navy or to escape from the North Sea. Events had early revealed the commerce-destroying potentialities of the submarine. As already noted, the Navy Department had positive knowledge, after Jutland, that the German Admiralty was concentrating on the U-boat campaign. Although a rigid censorship partially concealed Allied and neutral shipping losses in

[20] Testimony of Captain Harris Laning who was serving in the Office of Chief of Naval Operations during the period in question. *Naval Investigation, 1920*, p. 384.

the winter of 1916–1917, it was no secret that the submarine campaign was taxing the defensive resources of the Allies. And the intensification of that campaign, following Germany's resumption of unrestricted submarine warfare in February 1917, served notice on neutrals as well as belligerents that the war upon the sea was moving swiftly to a crisis.[21]

These developments foreshadowed the rôle which the American Navy might play if the United States joined the Allies. With the German Fleet immobilized, there would be no fighting for American battleships to do on this side of the Atlantic. It was doubtless expedient to put the heavy ships into condition for oversea service to reenforce the British Fleet in case of need. But there was no reason whatever, connected with winning the war, for hastening the construction of additional capital ships to strengthen the American Fleet. There were urgent reasons, however, for concentrating on means for combating the submarines which were playing havoc with Allied and neutral shipping. Cooperation with the Allies in guarding troop ships and merchant vessels from enemy U-boats, and in driving these under-water raiders from the sea, would certainly be one of the Navy's functions, and might well be its chief contribution to winning the war. Such a prospect plainly called for concentration on anti-submarine weapons, and for a plan of operations that would enable the Navy, after a declaration of war, to enter promptly and effectively into the anti-submarine campaign.[22]

The Administration, however, took a different view. The 1916 naval program was justified as "normal" expansion, looking beyond the immediate conflict to the more distant future, and ostensibly envisaging war with no nation in particular. But specific preparation for early hostilities with Germany,

[21] Laning, *ibid.*, pp. 385, 388, 397; Admiral Sims' final summary of the evidence, p. 3215.

[22] Laning, *ibid.*, pp. 385*ff.*; Admiral A. P. Niblack, General Board member, pp. 1012, 1018; Admiral C. J. Badger, General Board member, p. 1142; Admiral W. S. Benson, Chief of Naval Operations, pp. 1824–5, 1841; and especially Admiral Sims, p. 3215.

such as systematically putting the existing ships on a war footing or laying down a great flotilla of destroyers and other antisubmarine craft, was flatly rejected. In defense of this policy of inaction, it was contended that such warlike measures would constitute "overt acts," likely to precipitate war, and certainly contrary to the spirit if not the letter of neutrality.[23]

There are indications that this novel interpretation of neutrality was at least partially attributable to domestic politics. As already noted, President Wilson, by the spring of 1916, was virtually committed to war if and when Germany should resume unrestricted attacks on merchant shipping. Democratic campaigners, however, in the summer and autumn of that year made much of Wilson's success in keeping the country out of war, and appealed for his reelection on the ground, among others, that he would continue to do so.[24] Politically minded statesmen naturally hesitated, while the pre-election campaign was in progress, to sanction warlike preparations that might be difficult to reconcile with their party's pacifistic pledges. And the Democratic victory at the polls, in November, widely interpreted as a mandate for peace, was cited as a further reason for avoiding acts which might seem to foreshadow an early renunciation of neutrality.[25]

Whether or not this policy of inaction originated, as was claimed, in the mind of Secretary of the Navy Josephus Daniels,[26] he apparently enforced it as strictly as he could from

[23] Niblack, *ibid.*, pp. 1010–11, 1025; Badger, pp. 1097, 1175, 1176, 1184–6; Captain W. V. Pratt, Plans Section, Office of Chief of Operations, pp. 1526, 1581, 1582.

[24] James Kerney, *The Political Education of Woodrow Wilson* (1926), pp. 381–2.

[25] Admiral H. B. Wilson, *Naval Investigation, 1920*, p. 894; Niblack, p. 1043; Badger, p. 1097; Pratt, p. 1465; Admiral J. S. McKean, Assistant for Material, Office of Chief of Operations, p. 1803. In his final summary, Admiral Sims noted that "practically everyone of the witnesses commented at length on the policy of neutrality, and declared that the Department thought that the country did not want to go into war; and that therefore the Department did not consider it wise to take any steps which might make the navy ready for war," p. 3297.

[26] This question was repeatedly raised by the investigating committee. For a positive summary of the affirmative case, see Kittridge, *op. cit.* The question

the outbreak of war in 1914 right down to our entry in 1917. He studiedly avoided even discussing the possibility that we might be drawn into the conflict.[27] He persistently ignored the recommendations of his professional advisers and obstructed their individual efforts to put the Navy in readiness for war.[28]

Under such conditions, relatively little could be done in the way of general preparations, and practically nothing in anticipation of the special exigencies of anti-submarine warfare. Many officers in higher administrative positions did what they could to put their respective branches of the service in condition for war.[29] The men assigned to the Office of Chief of Operations, created by Congress over Secretary Daniels's opposition,[30] labored despite the greatest handicaps to coordinate these individual activities.[31] But inertia, inaction, and opposition from above impeded them at every turn, and largely frustrated their efforts to accumulate war material, to put the ships in repair, and to relieve an acute personnel shortage which prevented manning many of the vessels in reserve, or assigning full war complements to those already in commission.[32]

---

of higher responsibility was also raised, but nothing definite was proved. *Naval Investigation, 1920,* pp. 2852–3.

[27] In his summary, Admiral Sims noted that, according to the Department's own witnesses, "the words 'war' or 'preparedness for war' were practically never used by the Secretary or his advisers . . ." and that "the Secretary conscientiously avoided any reference to a possibility of war in his plans and recommendations for the guidance of the Navy Department." *ibid.,* pp. 3213, 3216.

[28] For typical instances, see Captain L. G. Palmer, Chief of Bureau of Navigation, *ibid.,* p. 455; Captain J. K. Taussig, Assistant, Bureau of Navigation, p. 508; Admiral C. P. Plunkett, Assistant (in charge of gunnery), Office of Chief of Operations, pp. 517–19; Badger, pp. 1138–9; for record of all official recommendations from General Board, July 1914 on, and action of Secretary of the Navy thereon, pp. 1090*ff.* And for general situation, Sims' summary, pp. 3218, 3225, 3289.

[29] Such is the clear import of the testimony of practically every officer who appeared before the 1920 investigating committee.

[30] Admiral B. A. Fiske, *From Midshipman to Rear Admiral* (1919), pp. 567*ff.*, 599*ff.*

[31] Benson, *Naval Investigation, 1920,* pp. 1817*ff.*; Sims, *ibid.,* p. 3211.

[32] For representative cases, see Admiral W. F. Fullam's account of his efforts to mobilize the forces in the Pacific, *ibid.,* pp. 755*ff.*; the struggles of Captains Palmer and Taussig to relieve the personnel shortage, pp. 441*ff.*, 475*ff.*; Admiral

Especially serious was the Department's failure to envisage the problems that lay ahead, and to formulate plans with reference to actual conditions in the war area. While there was no pressing need for more battleships, the Department kept on with its regular building program, ignoring the imminent demand for large numbers of destroyers and other craft especially suited to the exigencies of anti-submarine warfare.[33] While certain officers individually gave thought to ways and means for combating submarines, the Department undertook no systematic official study of this problem which now overshadowed every other phase of the war upon the sea.[34] And when Congress declared war, April 6, 1917, the only official plan for war with Germany envisaged a campaign, not against submarines in European waters, but against a battle fleet in the Western Atlantic, with the probable focus of operations in the Caribbean.[35]

The American Navy in the War

The entry of the United States into the war forged a partnership for which neither our Navy Department nor the British Admiralty was prepared. The former's initial view of the war

---

Plunkett's labors with the gunnery problem, pp. 516*ff.*; Admiral A. W. Grant's struggle to improve inefficient submarines, pp. 531*ff*.

[33] In December, 1916, Secretary Daniels stated that "the department has . . . been carefully studying the occurrences of the European war, as affecting types of naval vessels. There have not developed, however, any facts which would cause the department to recommend any changes in the numbers or types of vessels as provided for in the [1916 building] program." Navy Dept., *Ann. Repts., 1916*, p. 11. Also testimony of Niblack, *Naval Investigation, 1920*, p. 1012; Badger, pp. 1099, 1142, 1176-7; Pratt, pp. 1209, 1464, 1525-6. According to Senator Key Pittman, minority member of the investigating committee, some of the opposition to suspending the capital-ship program was traceable to certain members of Congress who feared that this program once suspended would never be resumed, p. 565.

[34] Laning, *ibid.*, pp. 384, 385, 388, 397; Grant, p. 563. The first such study was undertaken by the Board of Devices and Plans in "May or June," and a report was submitted July 6, 1917, pp. 1209*ff*.

[35] Fletcher, *ibid.*, pp. 929, 939; Niblack, p. 1018; Badger, pp. 1098, 1142–3, 1193–4; McKean, pp. 1771*ff*.; Sims, p. 3214.

and of the American Navy's rôle therein, the latter's reactionary anti-submarine policy, and the unreadiness of both for a concerted attack on the submarine problem—these and other factors aggravated and prolonged the shipping crisis which carried the Allies almost to disaster.[36] Both organizations eventually rose to the emergency, and the American Navy, with which we are chiefly concerned, played a major part in devising and putting into execution an effective system of anti-submarine defense, which restored the threatened life lines of the British Empire and made possible the safe transportation of two million American soldiers to bolster the crumbling military front in France.[37]

A significant move, just prior to our formal entry into the war, was the Administration's decision to send a high-ranking American officer to confer with the British Admiralty and to report on conditions in the war area.[38] Admiral William S. Sims, the officer selected, was an ideal choice. He was well known and liked in England. He was unquestionably one of the ablest officers in the American Navy. And he became not merely an expert observer and spokesman for the Navy Department, but also a capable adviser and an invaluable accession to the group in England, who were struggling for a fresh approach to the submarine problem.[39]

Such an approach was desperately needed. As previously noted, the Admiralty's defensive measures were proving utterly inadequate to check the depredations of the U-boats. Arming merchantmen merely forced the enemy to attack without warn-

[36] There was much fruitless discussion before the investigating committee, as to whether the Navy's delay in getting under way prolonged the war. Sims, *ibid.*, pp. 36*f.*, 311; Wilson, p. 917; Fletcher, pp. 928, 871*ff.*; Strauss, pp. 1082*ff.*; Badger, pp. 1110, 1165; Pratt, pp. 1482–3, 1488–9, 1523–4; McKean, pp. 1754*ff.*, 1768; Benson, pp. 1942, 1957; Secretary Daniels, p. 2205.

[37] Frothingham, *Naval History of the War,* Vol. III; Sims, *Victory at Sea.*

[38] Result of a mutual if tardy desire on the part of British and American naval authorities to arrange for concerted action after the United States should have declared war. B. J. Hendrick, *Life and Letters of Walter Hines Page* (1922), Vol. II, p. 274; *For. Rels., 1917, Suppl. II,* Vol. I, p. 5.

[39] Kenworthy, *Sailors, Statesmen—and Others,* p. 106; Newbolt, *Naval Operations,* Vol. V, pp. 17, 32*ff.*, 56, 132.

ing. Patrolling the danger zones was like hunting needles in a hay stack. A more effective system of defense had to be devised or Great Britain would soon have to sue for peace. Such a system was found in a modern adaptation of the ancient practice of convoy.

It is clear in retrospect that convoy was the logical answer to the submarine. Torpedoing a moving vessel was at best a complicated business. The submarine commander had to gauge accurately the distance, course, and speed of his intended victim. Since a U-boat's torpedo equipment was immovable, the process of aiming involved maneuvering the whole ship into a position where the torpedo tube pointed toward the place at which it was calculated that torpedo and target would come together. If the latter was moving at high speed, the submarine captain would have scarcely enough time to make his calculations and to maneuver his ship into position. If the target was following an irregular or zigzag course, the process was still further complicated. Moreover, compared with a projectile fired from a gun, a torpedo travelled very slowly, about thirty knots, and the farther it travelled the more it was likely to vary from its true course. Hits were rarely scored beyond two thousand yards, and much shorter ranges were essential to good results. Furthermore, each torpedo cost several thousand dollars, and few submarines were equipped to carry as many as ten. None, therefore, could be wasted.

As a result of all these factors, a submarine commander was virtually forced to work at fairly short ranges. He had also to work with at least his periscope exposed, and he could not prevent his travelling torpedo from leaving a plainly visible wake upon the ocean's surface. These telltale signs did not seriously endanger a submarine as long as there was no swift enemy warship in the vicinity. But the presence of such a vessel radically altered the situation.

Even the largest and most powerful submarines were extremely vulnerable. They lacked the speed to run away from danger. Their thin steel plates afforded no protection against gunfire. They contained a great deal of intricate and delicate machinery. And they necessarily possessed little reserve buoyancy. A single well placed shell, even of small caliber, could sink a submarine floating upon the surface. And the invention of the depth charge provided a weapon of like potency against a submerged U-boat.

The depth charge consisted of a metal container filled with several hundred pounds of TNT and fitted with a mechanism which fired the explosive at any prearranged depth of water. A destroyer sighting either a submarine's periscope or the wake of its torpedo would rush to the spot where the enemy was believed to be, and drop a number of depth charges. If one of these exploded within a hundred feet of the submerged U-boat, the result was generally fatal. Even at greater distances the concussion was apt to cause serious damage, forcing the submarine to come to the surface where it would have to surrender or quickly succumb to gunfire. Even to attempt to torpedo a vessel in the presence of swift warships equipped with depth charges involved terrible risk for the submarine. But the latter's commander had either to accept the risk or to work at long range with a large chance of missing his target altogether.

The logical answer to the submarine offensive was, therefore, to escort merchant vessels in groups through the danger zones under protection of destroyers or other craft equipped to fight submarines. Whether or not the Allies could have operated a large-scale convoy system before the United States entered the war is a debatable question. Some of the highest naval authorities in Great Britain doubted its feasibility even with the aid of the United States. But the gravity of the crisis, together with the virtually admitted bankruptcy of the Admiralty's own anti-submarine campaign, forced the issue. The British Cabinet, largely at the instance of Prime Minister Lloyd George, and with strong support from Admiral Sims as well as from progressive British officers, in May 1917 ordered a trial the striking success of which marked the turning point of the submarine crisis.[40]

The next problem was to assemble enough anti-submarine craft—particularly destroyers—to operate a commercial convoy system on a large scale. Although Great Britain possessed nearly three hundred destroyers at this time, very few of them could be made available for convoy duty.[41] The United States, on the other hand, with less than seventy destroyers in commission,[42] could easily spare a considerable number for service overseas.[43] And within a few days after reaching England, Admiral Sims commenced bombarding the Navy Department with alarming reports of the desperate plight of the Allies and with appeals for all available destroyers and other suitable craft to strengthen the anti-submarine patrol and to assist in operating the projected convoy system.[44]

The Department, however, was both materially and psychologically unprepared for such large-scale oversea operations.[45] Secretary Daniels and his chief naval adviser simply could not believe that the situation was as desperate as Sims pictured it. They feared that German submarines would shortly appear in force off the American coast. They thought the German Fleet might come out again, and this time drive the British Fleet "off the sea." And they felt compelled to envisage the possibility of Allied defeat on both land and sea, leaving the United States alone to face a triumphant and hostile Germany.[46]

Holding such views, the Navy Department heads naturally hesitated to leave the United States coast unguarded and to

[40] Newbolt, *op. cit.*, Vol. V, Chap. I; Lloyd George, *War Memoirs*, Vol. III, Chap. III.

[41] The Grand Fleet alone required more than a hundred destroyers, and the remainder were variously employed on half a dozen different stations. Newbolt, *op. cit.*, Vol. V, pp. 387*ff*.

[42] *Naval Investigation, 1920*, p. 1236.

[43] Since there was no fighting in prospect for our battleship fleet, and no probability of large-scale submarine operations off the American coast, there would be comparatively little work for our destroyers on this side of the Atlantic.

[44] Sims, *ibid.*, pp. 1*ff*.; Pratt, pp. 1563*f*.

[45] Pratt, *ibid.*, pp. 1199*ff*., especially pp. 1226–9, 1237, 1252.

[46] Benson, *ibid.*, pp. 1843–7, 1850, 1880, 1898, 1905–6, 1941, 1965–6, 1971.

strip the Atlantic Fleet of its protective escort of destroyers. One division of six destroyers was promptly dispatched overseas, after which there was a pause. Still betraying inadequate grasp both of the extreme gravity of the crisis and of the methods of submarine warfare, the Department raised objections to the proposed convoy system, and suggested arming all merchant vessels instead.[47] And still possessed by unfounded fears of German aggression in this hemisphere, the Department labored to prepare the battleship fleet for active service, and to assemble forces to meet the expected submarine assault in American waters.[48]

It is clear in retrospect that this view of the war and of the Navy's rôle therein was based upon a number of profound misconceptions. The German Fleet presented no menace to the United States. That fleet was narrowly confined within the North Sea, and there was little prospect that it would again challenge Britain's surface command of the sea. There was only slightly greater danger of submarine attack in this hemisphere. A few of the larger German U-boats might cross the Atlantic and make a demonstration in American waters. But the ocean was too wide and Germany had too few submarines to do more than that. Moreover, the British Admiralty, through its highly efficient intelligence service, kept close track of U-boat sailings and destinations, and could give warning two or three weeks in advance of arrival, in case any of them started across the Atlantic. The real danger lay not in the scattered depredations which these raiders might commit in American waters, but rather in the possibility that such raids might divert American effort from the "critical area" of submarine operations, which, as Admiral Sims repeatedly stressed, was not in the Western but in the "Eastern Atlantic at the focus of all lines of communications" to the British Isles.[49]

[47] Sims, *ibid.*, pp. 87*ff.*; Pratt, p. 1558, Benson, pp. 1908*f.*, 1972*f.*; Daniels, pp. 2841*f.*

[48] Badger, *ibid.*, pp. 1144, 1161*f.*; Grant, pp. 550, 552, 556*f.*; Niblack, p. 1016; McKean, p. 1767; Benson, pp. 1844, 1907.

[49] Sims, *ibid.*, pp. 104*ff.*; Fletcher, pp. 928, 946, 974, 978.

Gradually, however, the situation clarified. Personal appeals to President Wilson expedited the dispatch of anti-submarine forces overseas,[50] overcame the Navy Department's opposition to the proposed convoy system,[51] and brought about a redefinition of the Department's war policy more in accord with actual conditions.[52] Thanks largely to the efforts of Captain (later Admiral) William V. Pratt, Assistant to the Chief of Operations, the handling of intelligence was reorganized and greatly improved.[53] The betterment of this service gave a clearer view of the situation overseas, as did also the visits to the war area in the autumn of 1917 by Admiral Henry T. Mayo, Commander of the Atlantic Fleet, and Admiral William S. Benson, Chief of Operations.[54] Meanwhile, after vacillation and delay, the government had suspended nearly all capital-ship construction, and was concentrating on destroyers and other anti-submarine craft.[55] And by the beginning of 1918, the Navy was at last becoming an efficient, smooth-running war machine.[56]

Simultaneously, while undergoing this transformation, the Navy Department was contributing in various ways and degrees to the struggle overseas. American cooperation had greatly facilitated the institution and operation of the convoy system.[57] The American and British Navies were cooperating in the unprecedented task of safely ferrying a great American army to Europe through submarine-infested waters.[58] Despite the Navy

[50] Hendrick, *Page,* Vol. II, p. 278; and Sims, *Naval Investigation, 1920,* pp. 40–3, 3236–43.

[51] Kittridge, *Naval Lessons,* pp. 434–6.

[52] *Naval Investigation, 1920,* pp. 56, 1220, 1221, 3237*ff.*

[53] For Admiral Sims' criticism of the Department's handling of his communications, and Captain Pratt's reply thereto, see *ibid.,* p. 1220; for the latter's reorganization of intelligence relating to operations, see *ibid.,* pp. 1263, 1533*ff.*

[54] For Admiral Mayo's report, Oct. 11, 1917, see *ibid.,* pp. 632*ff.*; indications as to the effects of Admiral Benson's trip are scattered through his testimony in *ibid.,* pp. 1817*ff.*

[55] Laning, *ibid.,* pp. 403, 417; Pratt, pp. 1206*ff.,* 1217, 1345; Sims, pp. 3240, 3256*f.*

[56] For the details of this difficult transition, see Pratt, *ibid.,* especially pp. 1205, 1229, 1252, 1263*ff.,* 1356.

[57] Pratt, *ibid.,* pp. 1256*f.,* 1450; Wilson, p. 904.

[58] Admiral Albert Gleaves, *History of the Transport Service* (1921). Altogether,

Department's extreme reluctance to disrupt its own fleet organization, a division of American battleships had been sent to reenforce the British Fleet in the North Sea, and was serving there with unostentatious distinction.[59] And steadily increasing numbers of American destroyers, submarines, gunboats, converted yachts, smaller patrol vessels, tugs, and aircraft were joining the anti-submarine patrol.[60]

An extremely important American contribution in connection with the anti-submarine patrol was the development of effective sound-detectors. These listening devices warned anti-submarine craft of the presence and approximate location of submerged U-boats, thereby overcoming the greatest single obstacle to hunting down submarines at sea. Wide use of sound detectors, together with the great increase of available patrol vessels, opened the way for development of a really efficient anti-submarine patrol in the final months of the war.[61]

Still another American contribution was the "antenna mine" and the Northern Mine Barrage. The German submarine bases were all on the southern coast of the North Sea. To reach the Atlantic shipping approaches to the British Isles, the U-boats had to pass either through the English Channel or around to the north of Scotland. Sealing these exits would solve the submarine problem. By 1917, the British Admiralty, using mines and a strong patrol, had made some slight progress toward closing Dover Strait, the narrow eastern end of the Channel, but they had achieved practically no success in their efforts to

---

the United States Navy transported 927,000 men, or 45% of all troops sent to France, "without the loss of a single soldier by the hand of the enemy." *ibid.*, pp. 29, 91.

[59] Sims, *Naval Investigation, 1920,* pp. 74*ff.*; Pratt, pp. 1223*f.*, 1537; Benson, pp. 1904*ff.*; Rodman, pp. 841*ff.*

[60] In November 1918, the United States had in European waters: eight battleships, five cruisers, five gunboats, sixty-eight destroyers, nine submarines, twenty-six converted yachts and other comparable patrol vessels, one hundred twenty-one so-called sub-chasers (small patrol vessels), thirty tugs and mine-sweepers, twelve auxiliary vessels, and seventy miscellaneous vessels, totalling altogether three hundred fifty-four vessels of all classes. *ibid.*, p. 1235.

[61] B. S. Beach, "Hunting Submarines with a Sound Detector," *Scientific American,* Vol. CXX (April 5, 1919), p. 335; Sims, *Victory at Sea,* Chap. VI.

blockade the wide northern exit of the North Sea. The British Fleet patrolled the passage extending from Scotland to Norway, but the German U-boats easily slipped through the patrol into the Atlantic.[62]

This failure had stimulated a search for other means of confining the U-boats within the North Sea. The most popular proposal was to plant a mine field across the northern exit. But its extreme width (250 miles) and depth (600 feet) presented insuperable obstacles. To explode a mine, it was necessary for a ship to collide with it. To block a channel against submarines, or even to create a serious hazard to their safe passage, would necessitate planting mines at frequent levels down to about 250 feet. To close the northern exit would require at least 400,000 mines of this type, a number far beyond the resources of the Allies in 1917.

The entry of the United States into the war and the Navy Department's perfection of a new type of mine brought this gigantic project within the realm of practicability. The new mine had a float and an anchor connected with a container of explosive by a copper wire or "antenna." Contact between the iron hull of a vessel and this antenna actuated an electric current which exploded the mine. The concussion of this explosion, like that of the depth charge, would destroy or damage a vessel within a considerable vertical as well as horizontal distance from the mine. It was estimated that 100,000 antenna mines, planted at three widely spaced depths, would present a barrier sufficiently formidable to close the northern passage. Even this was a project of unprecedented magnitude. But it was organized and undertaken by the Navy Department in the autumn of 1917, and, with some British assistance, was well on the way to completion when the Armistice terminated hostilities in November 1918.[63]

[62] Admiral Sir Reginald Bacon, *The Dover Patrol* (1919), Vol. II, Chap. XIV; Admiral Sir Roger Keyes, *Naval Memoirs* (1935), Vol. II, Chap. XI; W. S. Churchill, *The World Crisis, 1916–1918* (1927), Vol. II, Chap. XV.

[63] Testimony of Admiral Joseph Strauss who commanded the mine force, *Naval Investigation, 1920*, pp. 1050*ff.*; Pratt, *ibid.*, pp. 1373*ff.*; Sims, *Victory at*

Lessons and Consequences

The World War, like earlier conflicts, put naval theories, technology, and organization to the test. Much of the experience thus acquired was so technical as to be intelligible only to experts. But some of the naval lessons deducible from this as from previous wars lay fairly within the layman's grasp. And it was important then, as it still is today, that the lay public should have some appreciation of these lessons, which had profound implications for the United States, and which were constantly to enter into discussions of American naval policy during the ensuing years.

To begin with, events of the war period reemphasized the importance of correlating naval policy with foreign policy. It is difficult to discover much correlation between the Wilson administration's redefinition of American naval policy in terms of parity with, and hence implied potential enmity toward, the British Navy, and the anglophile attitude of this Administration. There was a similar lack of correlation between the President's neutrality policy and the Navy Department's approach to the war. While following a diplomatic course that envisaged our entry into the war on the side of the Allies as a possible and increasingly probable eventuality, the Administration persistently declined to authorize the specific preparations necessary to put the Navy in readiness for the kind of war then in progress.

Events preceding and following our entry into the war cast light upon the meaning of naval preparedness. To most Americans a navy was merely warships, and preparedness meant simply building more warships. Few people knew or cared whether there were enough officers and enlisted men to operate these ships; whether there was an adequate shore establishment

Sea, pp. 288*ff*.; Captain R. R. Belknap, "The Yankee Mining Squadron," *Proc. of U. S. Nav. Inst.*, Vol. XLV (Dec. 1919), pp. 1973*ff*.; *idem*, "The North Sea Mine Barrage," *Scientific American* (March 15 and 22, 1919), Vol. CXX, pp. 250, 288.

to service and repair the ships; or whether the Navy Department was organized with a view to the most efficient conduct of war or other operations that might result from the government's diplomacy and policies. The Navy Department's vacillating approach to the war as well as its delay in getting into the struggle, all set forth in the glare of the post-war congressional investigation, gave new force to the repeated warnings of forward-looking officers and laymen. A fighting navy, they had reiterated, could not be quickly improvised in an emergency. Modern warships required months or years to build. The best warships were useless without skilled officers and crews, whose training was a still longer process. Ships and personnel were helpless without a highly developed system of dockyards, factories, warehouses, and transportation and maintenance facilities, as well as an elaborate organization to plan and direct operations and to perform a thousand other functions involved in the administration of a vast fighting machine constantly ready for war.[64]

The Navy Department's approach to and conduct of the war also emphasized the need for naval reorganization and the difficulties of formulating and administering a sound naval policy under conditions prevailing in the United States. Foreign policy determination is a presidential or congressional function with which the professional naval bureaucracy has little legitimate concern. Design and construction of vessels, organization and management of the fleet, planning and direction of operations, and many other technical functions ordinarily lie outside the sphere of intelligent civilian control. Between these extremes there is a broad zone in which naval efficiency and a proper correlation of naval policy with foreign policy require close and harmonious cooperation between naval experts and statesmen, as well as intelligent criticism and support on the part of the public. The government's chronic

[64] See, for example, the testimony of Admiral B. A. Fiske, Dec. 17, 1914, 63 Cong. 3 Sess. House Naval Affairs Committee, *Hearings on Estimates for 1915*, pp. 999*ff*.

reluctance to define its foreign policy had traditionally embarrassed the Navy. The latter's encroachments upon the policy-determining function of President and Congress had periodically agitated public opinion. The national legislature's constant meddling with technical naval details, and the political spoilsmen's annual raids on the Navy, had impaired the efficiency and aroused the resentment of the fighting forces. Deep-seated popular distrust of the Military, as well as the exigencies of electioneering politics, had long stood in the way of concentrating technical administrative control in professional hands. These forces had perpetuated an unwieldy departmental organization, notoriously weak when it came to planning the work of the Navy as a whole, and to coordinating the functions of its many branches. The vacillation, delays, and mistakes of the Navy Department, while partially attributable to certain personalities in the Wilson administration, were also the logical results of the existing system of control and management. These results plainly called for fresh study of the methods of formulating and administering naval policy, with special attention on the respective rôles of the general public. Congress, the political executive, and the professional naval bureaucracy.[65]

Turning from organization to technology, probably the outstanding event of the war was the rapid development of the submarine. This weapon antedated the war, but even naval experts had failed in the main to foresee its immense potentialities for offense as well as defense.[66] The hazard of submarine torpedo attack rendered close blockade of enemy ports practically impossible, especially at night, and increased the

[65] Kittridge, *Naval Lessons*, pp. 454*ff*.

[66] A notable exception was Admiral Lord Fisher (R.N.) who, in May 1914, two months before the war, submitted a memorandum to the Prime Minister, in which he uttered a prophetic warning regarding the potentialities of the submarine, declaring, in part, that "with the advent of the long-range submarine . . . surface ships can no longer either maintain or prevent blockade . . . [and that] this submarine menace is a truly terrible one for British commerce. . . ." Lord Fisher, *Records* (1919), pp. 181, 182, 184.

difficulty of invading or even raiding the enemy's seaboard.[67] Submarines provided a fighting fleet with all but invisible scouts. Constant danger of surprise torpedo attack forced a fleet to strengthen its protective escort of destroyers, and to travel at higher speed through submarine-infested waters, thereby increasing the fleet's fuel consumption and correspondingly reducing its effective radius of operations. And finally, the submarine, early in the war, revealed tremendous potentialities as a commerce destroyer, even partial realization of which nearly paralyzed the life of Great Britain, in spite of the latter's indisputable supremacy upon the ocean's surface.[68]

Another virtually new weapon was the mine. This weapon also antedated the war, but like the submarine, its offensive as well as defensive potentialities had been sadly neglected. Mine fields added one more hazard to naval attacks on a hostile coast, and to close blockade of enemy ports.[69] Mine laying was also developed into a formidable offensive operation. By fitting out roving cruisers and especially submarines with mine-laying equipment, the weaker naval Power was able to plant mine fields at the enemy's portals and at the foci of ocean commerce. In the hands of the stronger naval Power, mine fields became a means of frightening neutral shipping into specified, easily patrolled lanes, and of blocking, at least temporarily, the exits of the enemy's naval bases. And finally, technological improvements culminating in the famous antenna mine, still further extended the sphere of offensive mine-laying operations for that Power which controlled the ocean's surface.[70]

Aircraft development introduced a third new factor into naval warfare. Airships and airplanes revealed great potentialities in the later stages of the anti-submarine campaign, both as

[67] See Lord Sydenham of Combe, "A Great Lesson of the Naval War," *Nineteenth Century,* Vol. LXXXIX (June 1921), pp. 1062, 1065.

[68] See J. M. Kenworthv and George Young, *Freedom of the Seas* (1928), Chap. II.

[69] See Sydenham of Combe, *op. cit.,* p. 1065; Churchill, *World Crisis, 1916–1918,* Vol. II, pp. 84*ff.*

[70] See Sims, *Victory at Sea,* p. 292.

scouts and as bombers. Aircraft were also employed to a limited extent as commerce destroyers, and as adjuncts to the fighting fleets. Development of the naval aircraft carrier greatly increased the plane's naval utility, especially its radius of operations. This development assured the future rôle of the plane as a component of the battle fleet. And it opened up new vistas of offensive action against an enemy's coast and commerce.[71]

These and other technological advances gave rise to heated discussion regarding the future of the capital ship. According to pre-war doctrine, the objective of strategy was to establish a command of the sea that would assure security to one's own coast and shipping, and destruction of the enemy's commerce "root and branch." The battleship was considered the index of a navy's power, and the backbone of its fighting fleet whose ability to destroy, or at least to immobilize, an enemy's fleet was the decisive factor in establishing command of the sea.

As a result of the war, there sprang up a new school of thought whose chief contention was that submarines and aircraft had sounded the death knell of the battleship. In future wars, it was argued, air and under-water attacks would either sink these massive floating forts or drive them from the sea. It was folly, therefore, to go on spending millions to build and maintain vessels which were fast becoming as obsolete as eighteenth century ships-of-the-line.[72]

This doctrine, which quickly acquired great vogue, especially in American congressional circles, was rejected by the British

[71] See Kenworthy and Young, *Freedom of the Seas,* pp. 108*ff*.; General Sir W. S. Brancker (R.A.), "Air Power and Sea Power," *Brassey's Naval Annual, 1921–1922,* pp. 103*ff*.; Squadron Leader C. H. K. Edmonds (R.A.F.), "Aerial Cooperation with the Fleet," reprinted in *Proc. of U. S. Nav. Inst.,* Vol. XLVII (July 1921), pp. 1114*ff*.

[72] The issue was competently debated in a series of letters published in *The Times* (London), during December 1920, with Admiral Sir Percy Scott leading the attack on the capital ship. The issue was just as vigorously debated in America. See, for example, Admiral W. F. Fullam, "Battleships and Air Power," *Sea Power,* Vol. VII (Dec. 1919), p. 274; L. O. Battle, "The Battleship and the Junk Heap," *Sci. Amer.,* Vol. CXXIV (April 16, 1921), p. 312. The post-war assault on the capital ship is well summed up in Kenworthy and Young, *Freedom of the Seas,* pp. 115*ff*.

Admiralty,[73] by the United States Navy Department,[74] and generally by practical students of naval warfare.[75] Submarines and aircraft, they maintained, had not prevented the British fleet from performing the function for which it had been designed. It had imprisoned Germany's fighting fleet within a narrow zone along the southern and eastern rim of the North Sea. One result of this achievement was to secure the British Isles against invasion. Another was to make the seas safe for the cruisers, destroyers, and other small warships which swept German merchant shipping from the ocean, and intercepted neutral shipping with cargoes destined for the Central Powers. A third result was to cover the operations of the anti-submarine forces. With German battleships and battle cruisers at large, Allied destroyers and other anti-submarine craft could not have kept the sea for twenty-four hours; the commercial convoy system would have collapsed; and the Northern Mine Barrage could never have been undertaken. Release of Germany's fighting fleet would have disrupted the Allies' long-range blockade. And it would have rendered utterly impossible the transporta-

[73] "Notes on Naval Policy," *Brassey's Naval Annual, 1920–1921,* pp. 303, 304, 313.

[74] "Report of the General Board," Navy Dept., *Ann. Repts., 1920,* pp. 211*ff.* In 1921, a joint Army and Navy board appointed to report on the experimental bombing of certain ex-German warships, concluded, among other things, that "the battleship is still the backbone of the fleet. . . . The airplane like the submarine, destroyer, and mine, has added to the dangers to which battleships are exposed but has not made the battleship obsolete." "Report on Bombing Tests," *Aviation,* Vol. XI (Sept. 5, 1921), pp. 276, 278. This conclusion was officially endorsed in the next annual report of the Secretary of the Navy. *Ann. Repts., 1921,* p. 3.

[75] "It is a very significant fact," noted Hector Bywater, distinguished British naval critic, "that the opponents of the big ship are, practically without exception, retired officers who have had no experience of modern warfare. On the other hand, nine out of every ten officers who served in the late war—from admirals down to sub-lieutenants—are convinced that great armored ships are as essential to the command of the seas as ever they were, and that their supremacy is still unchallenged, despite the admitted powers, actual and potential, of submarines and aircraft." "The Backbone of Naval Power," *Sci. Amer.,* Vol. CXXII (May 1, 1920), p. 490. And see Archibald Hurd, an equally competent British authority, "Is the Battleship Doomed?" *Fortnightly Review,* Vol. CXIII (Feb. 1920), pp. 222*ff.* For a strong defense of the capital ship by a competent American critic, see Captain D. W. Knox, "Bomber vs. Battleship," *Army and Navy Journal,* Vol. LIX (Feb. 25, 1922), p. 605.

tion of the American Army to France. Everything, in short, depended on the Grand Fleet's success in keeping the German High Sea Fleet, or detachments of it, off the open sea. And the former's ability to do this lay ultimately in the superior power of its battleship squadrons. In other words, to realize either the defensive or offensive aims of naval strategy, it was necessary to control the sub-surface as well as the surface of the sea. But to control the sub-surface, it was first necessary to control the surface. And events had shown that the battleship was still the decisive factor in exercising a surface command of the sea.[76]

The relation of such a surface command to war in the air was equally clear, at least in theory. The future power of aircraft, except within a fairly narrow coastal zone, would depend upon the ability of aircraft carriers to keep the sea. Vessels designed to carry a large number of planes would have to be large and, for technical reasons, could have little defensive power. Like cruisers and destroyers, they could never remain in waters controlled by an enemy's capital ships. And conversely, only a superior battleship fleet could keep an enemy's aircraft carriers from approaching one's own coast and vital shipping lanes. Thus it appeared that command of the air above, like that of the water beneath, depended upon controlling the ocean's surface. And there, despite the menace of submarine and aircraft, the battleship still reigned supreme.[77]

Defenders of the battleship freely acknowledged that technological developments had forced changes in warship design, in fleet organization, and in tactics. Further changes were in process or in prospect.[78] So far naval architects had managed to

[76] See editorial, "The Battleship Still the Ruler of the Waves," *World's Work*, Vol. XLI (April 1921), p. 534; Lieutenant Commander L. P. Warren, "The Battleship Still Supreme," *ibid.*, pp. 556*ff.*

[77] See John Leyland, "What of the Navy?" *Nineteenth Century*, Vol. LXXXVI (Oct. 1919), pp. 620*ff.*; and C. G. Moran, "Sea Power: the Senate and the Air," *Proc., U. S. Naval Inst.*, Vol. XLVII (1921), Spec. Suppl., pp. 1676*ff.*

[78] See, for example, Henry Newbolt, *Submarine and Anti-Submarine* (1919), Chaps. VI–VII; "The War's Influence on Naval Design," *Sci. Amer.*, Vol. CXX (Feb. 8, 1919), p. 112; Admiral D. W. Taylor, "War's Lessons in Naval Construction," *Army and Navy Journal*, Vol. LVII (May 1, 1920), p. 1079; *idem*,

keep pace with submarines and aircraft. And the majority of naval experts were confident that they could do so in the future.[79] But the storm continued to rage around the issue thus raised.[80] And this issue was to recur again and again in discussions of American naval policy during the ensuing years.

Finally, the war reemphasized the importance of geography as a factor limiting hostile operations against a strong naval Power. The British Navy's success in confining the German battle fleet within the North Sea was attributable not merely to the former's superior power, *but also to the size and configuration of the North Sea.* And it is extremely doubtful if even the British Navy could have duplicated this achievement against the smaller Navy of the United States.[81]

In the first place, instead of lying at anchor in its home ports or cruising within a short radius of those ports, the attacking fleet would have to steam thousands of miles overseas. A fleet numbering over one hundred and fifty combatant ships such as Admiral Jellicoe commanded at the Battle of Jutland[82] would require an immense train of auxiliaries to transport reserves of fuel, ammunition, food, fresh water, and other supplies, as well as floating foundries and machine shops to service and

---

"The Design of War Vessels as Affected by the World War," *Proc. of U. S. Nav. Inst.*, Vol. XLVI (1920), pp. 1663*ff.*; "Warship Design and Torpedo Attack," *Engineering* (May 20, 1921), reprinted in *Proc. of U. S. Naval Inst.*, Vol. XLVII (1921), pp. 1091*ff.*

[79] See, for example, Admiral Sir Cyprian Bridge (R.N.), "The Capital Ship: Is It Doomed?", *Nineteenth Century*, Vol. LXXXIX (Feb. 1921), pp. 307*ff.*; Sir George Thurston, "The Capital Ship of the Future," *Brassey's Naval Annual, 1920–1921*, pp. 70*ff.*; Commander E. G. Allen, "Weapons at Sea," *Sci. Amer.*, Vol. CXXV (July 9, 1921), p. 25.

[80] See, for example, the collection of comments on the experimental bombing of the ex-German battleship *Ostfriesland*, reprinted in *Proc. of U. S. Nav. Inst.*, Vol. XLVII (1921), pp. 1451*ff.*; pp. 1635*ff.*; pp. 1640*ff.*; and pp. 1824, 1826, 1828.

[81] "Battle fleets are only of use in certain geographical divisions where the bases are not far apart. They are no use for wars in which the combatant countries are separated by thousands of miles of ocean." Admiral Mark Kerr (R.N.), "What Will Command the Sea?", *Nineteenth Century*, Vol. XC (Sept. 1921), pp. 383, 390. See also Lord Sydenham of Combe, "A Great Lesson of the Naval War," *Nineteenth Century*, Vol. LXXXIX (June 1921), pp. 1062*ff.*

[82] See Frothingham, *Naval History of the War*, Vol. II, p. 318.

repair the ships at sea.[83] It may be doubted whether even the British Admiralty, with the world's greatest merchant marine at call, could have assembled enough fast auxiliary vessels to sustain a naval campaign in American waters for any length of time.

Such an armada as the British Grand Fleet in the war would cover an immense expanse of ocean. In spite of every precaution, it would present an increasingly vulnerable target for enemy submarines and other raiders, as it penetrated more and more deeply into hostile waters. The ever-present submarine menace would require steaming at sustained high speed, which would enormously increase the fleet's fuel consumption as well as wear and tear on propelling machinery. The enemy's fleet, operating much closer to its home bases, could pick the time and place for a general action. Or it could avoid such an action altogether, and resort to attrition tactics, wearing down the invading force by submarine and air raids, especially against its vulnerable train, and its long and precarious line of oversea communications.

These would not be the only dangers. As British war experience plainly showed, it is impossible to keep all the ships in active service all the time. A warship must periodically have its bottom cleaned and undergo more extensive repairs than can be done at sea. The longer the ship remains at sea, the lower its speed and general mechanical efficiency. Further, the problem of escorting damaged or disabled warships home across thousands of miles of submarine-infested ocean was one that defied solution. Then there would be the problem of relief for officers and crews. The nervous strain of prolonged service in hostile waters, especially on board destroyers, submarines, and other less habitable types of ships, would have a progressively depressing effect on health and morale, which would inevitably reduce fighting efficiency.

[83] See, for example, Captain A. W. Hinds, "Changes in the Naval Situation of the Pacific Due to the World War," *Army and Navy Journal*, Vol. LIX (Oct. 15, 1921), p. 149; Captain D. W. Knox, "Strategic Advantage to the United States of the French Pacific Islands," *ibid.* (Dec. 10, 1921), p. 341.

In short, while the British Navy brilliantly reaffirmed the classic doctrine of command of the sea, it did so at short range, with distance and geographical configuration decidedly in its favor. For the British Navy, or any other navy, to duplicate this achievement across several thousand miles of ocean would be without successful precedent in modern naval history.[84] And if, as previously suggested, such an enterprise would have been difficult prior to 1914, the rapid development of submarines and aircraft after that date would make it even more so in the future.

This outlook had profound implications for American naval policy. It seemed to indicate that our continental position, supported by a fighting fleet of sufficient strength, was henceforth strategically unassailable on either front. On the other hand, the technological developments which so enhanced the security of the continental United States, just as markedly diminished the security of our oversea possessions in the Western Pacific and just as markedly complicated the problem of supporting our real or speculative interests in Eastern Asia. This problem was rendered still more difficult by the war's disruptive effects on the political situation in the Far East. Prior to 1914, the United States had derived marked advantage not only from the comparative weakness of Japan but also from the multilateral balance of power which supported at least the semblance of a commercial open door and the pretence of China's political unity. The war had destroyed this multilateral equilibrium, and immensely strengthened the military power of Japan. These results, together with other developments, compelled American naval strategists to envisage a war fought under enormous technical difficulties, thousands of miles from home, in virtually the local waters of a militant and expanding Japan whose Navy seemed at that time to be rapidly approaching unchallengeable supremacy in the Western Pacific.

84 At least, since the introduction of steam.

CHAPTER TWENTY

☆ ☆

The Log Reviewed

THE World War closed an era in the naval epic of the United States. That epic, it will be remembered, opened with the American struggle for independence, which thus early revealed the important rôle which the Navy was to play in the national defense of the United States. The experiment, under the Articles of Confederation, of independence without sea power, dramatically emphasized the value of a navy as an instrument of policy in an era of international anarchy and lawlessness upon the ocean. The inception of the Federal government in 1789 foreshadowed the early rebirth of American naval power. That event took place in 1794, but under conditions which plunged the infant Navy into the current strife of domestic politics, and which also gave rise to strategic conceptions that impeded American naval development for generations to come.

Since the seaboard knew itself to be more exposed to armed aggression, that region showed an earlier and keener interest in the Navy than was discovered in the interior. This early sectional difference partially coincided with the economic and social cleavage which soon found political expression in the Federalist and Jeffersonian Parties. The commercial and maritime interests of the Middle and North Atlantic States, arrayed mainly under the Federalist standard, logically favored a strong sea-going navy not merely for local defense in war, but also to command respect in peace as well as in war for their property and other interests abroad. To this end, the Federalists sponsored a naval program which was rather ambitious for a country with the available resources of eighteenth century America. But the strategic doctrine which took form under Federalist leadership envisaged little more than a sort of guerilla warfare against an enemy's shipping, carried on by solitary roving cruisers and privateers. The Jeffersonians, especially the spokesmen of the agrarian interior, denounced this Federalist Navy as a costly and mischievous instrument of power, more likely to provoke than to prevent war. Desiring little more than security of their homeland against actual invasion from overseas, they evolved the doctrine of passive coast and harbor defense, which first found expression in Jefferson's gunboat policy. The issue thus joined as to the purposes for which the United States should maintain a navy, and as to the size and kind of navy needed, opened a debate which has raged incessantly to the present day.

The westward continental march of the United States, chiefly under the agrarian banners of Jeffersonian and Jacksonian Democracy, repeatedly encroached on the territorial or other interests of the British Empire. The resulting crises, one of which led to the War of 1812, time and again forced the Democratic leaders from their negative policy. Exigencies of domestic politics sometimes impelled the opposing party to abandon temporarily its regular strong-navy position. And in later years, especially after about 1880, the historic party cleavage on naval policy tended to, but did not quite, fade out altogether.

For nearly one hundred years this debate turned largely on ways and means to implement the commerce-raiding and passive-defense strategies. The lesson of the Revolutionary War and of subsequent conflicts—that neither of these strategies could save the country from blockade in case of war with a great sea Power—was ignored or neglected. Not until Captain Mahan's famous work of 1890 did any considerable number of civilians or even naval officers grasp the fundamental doctrine of command of the sea, and its corollary, concentration of power. And several more years elapsed before the earlier doctrines were finally and conclusively subordinated within this larger system of naval strategy.

In the meantime, westward expansion to the Pacific had greatly enlarged the problem of naval defense. The United States, it was urged, must either maintain an independent naval force in each ocean, or else build a trans-isthmian canal. But the matter was allowed to drift until 1898 when the Spanish War proved the need for such a canal, and the accompanying annexations enormously increased the Navy's responsibilities in the Pacific. These responsibilities were still further augmented by the government's Asiatic policy which began to assume an interventionist cast about 1900. Completion of the Panama Canal in 1914 vastly improved the strategic outlook in the Pacific. But the Canal itself created a new defense problem, since the whole system of American naval strategy in the twentieth century came to depend on that vital waterway.

The American political system, however, was none too well equipped to cope with this growing strategic problem. For reasons inherent in its structure and composition, Congress but rarely took a national view of naval defense. The President usually represented a somewhat broader viewpoint. But the constitutional separation of powers raised serious obstacles against executive initiative and leadership. Deference to Senators and Representatives on administrative appointments was one means of closing the gap between President and Congress. Executive acquiescence in local appropriations was another logrolling device to the same end. To popularize the Navy in the different sections of the country, and to secure the congressional votes necessary to pass naval appropriations, it early became established practice to distribute naval appointments, contracts, and other spoils as widely as possible. At best, when the Administration combined exceptional capacity for leadership with a definite naval program, and also enjoyed safe majorities and strong party support in Congress, naval development was correlated with international objectives in spite of patronage and the pork-barrel. At worst, national interests and policies were lost to sight in a sordid congressional scramble for spoils. At all times money was wasted on useless or unneeded "improvements." Political strategy rather than naval strategy too often dictated the location of navy yards and other works. Oversea bases were chronically neglected, largely, it would appear, because the insular possessions had no congressional votes with which to bargain. Under such a system the American people might have the most expensive navy, but it was certain that they would never have as good a navy as the steadily rising financial outlay might have led them to expect.

The irresponsibility and waste which figured so conspicuously in the process of naval policy determination afforded rich opportunties to private interests so situated as to derive pecuniary gain from large naval appropriations. The number and variety of such groups tended to increase with the growing size and complexity of the naval establishment. Aside from the purely patriotic concern of otherwise disinterested citizens, the groups working for larger naval appropriations came eventually to include shipbuilders, the leading metallurgical industries, manufacturers of naval machinery, and producers of innumerable other articles necessary to the equipment and maintenance of a modern navy. In some instances the government was an industry's principal customer. That industry's prosperity, if not its solvency, might well depend on progressive naval expansion. The strategic value of such industries came frequently to be cited as a reason against slackening the pace of naval construction. From this it was but a short step to justifying naval works as a stimulant to business and to the national economy as a whole.

From the beginning the Service naturally exercised a large and continuous influence on naval policy. Officers logically desired a strong and prosperous navy. In case of war they would have to bear the brunt of battle. And in time of peace the attractiveness and prestige of their chosen profession depended on the Navy's progressive expansion and improvement.

On the whole, therefore, the Service tended to ally itself with private groups working toward the same end. In general this liaison proved extremely effective. The private groups working through the Navy League and other organizations carried the issue to the country, and the Service supplied the technical information to justify and support further increases in naval expenditures.

In certain other respects, however, the Service at times retarded the Navy's rise to power. Certain officers in influential posts had resisted steam and other technological advances. With few exceptions, officers as well as civilians long ignored the strategic lessons of successive wars upon the sea. Senior officers in high administrative places too often resented constructive criticism from the lower ranks; and even more, criticism originating outside the Service altogether. The administrative organization of the Navy Department long gave ample scope to such bureaucratic tendencies. And despite numerous improvements, many of which originated within the Service, the administration of the Navy in the twentieth century still fell somewhat short.

Closely related thereto was the issue of Service participation in policy determination. As previously noted, certain questions—fleet organization, operating plans, ship and machine design, etc.—lay normally outside the range of the civilian amateur. Certain other questions—territories to be defended, foreign policies to be supported, etc.—lay just as clearly beyond the sphere of the professional expert. Between these two extremes lay a broad and ill-defined borderland, wherein close and harmonious cooperation between the Executive, Congress, and the Service was absolutely essential to an efficient and sufficient Navy. But despite undeniable progress toward such cooperation, the exigencies of party politics and the pork-barrel, the pressure of private groups, the rarity of informed political leadership, the professional ambitions of the Service, and other disturbing factors, all rendered it exceedingly difficult to secure the collaboration on which necessarily depended the development of a navy sufficient, but not excessive, for realization of the political objectives and policies of the government.

It is unnecessary to review in detail the revolutionary advances in naval architecture and technology which figured so conspicuously in the rise of American naval power. It will be sufficient to recall that the introduction of steam and the growing complexity of naval machinery and equipment had profound strategic implications. The radius of a navy's operations was never unlimited. Even wind-driven warships had to return to port for ammunition, supplies, and major overhauls and repairs. But their radius far exceeded that of the modern steam-driven warship. And as the Spanish War revealed, and the World War conclusively demonstrated, hostile transoceanic operations against a great naval Power would be, without well equipped and strongly fortified oversea bases, an enormously difficult undertaking, and one without successful precedent in modern naval annals. Mahan himself had clearly perceived the virtual impossibility of waging war across the ocean without secure oversea bases. And had he lived to the end of the World War, one may be sure he would have been the first to stress that conflict's fundamental lesson: that twentieth-century technical progress, especially the phenomenal development of submarines and aircraft, had progressively narrowed the geographical area within which any navy could establish an indisputable command of the sea.

All this had vital bearing on the strategic situation of the United States. At the close of the World War no European or Asiatic Power possessed the shore bases essential for major hostile operations within the Western Hemisphere. The United States Navy held indisputable sway over the Eastern Pacific and over that part of the Western Atlantic which lay north of the Equator. The continental United States, therefore, enjoyed a measure of security unapproached by any other great nation in modern times.

The developments which so strengthened the security of the continental United States just as decidedly weakened the strategic position of American territories and other interests in the Far East. A war with Japan, necessarily fought in Asiatic waters, would involve, for the United States, difficulties that were fearful to contemplate. These potential difficulties were vastly increased by the failure to build up adequate dockyards and other shore facilities either in Guam or in the Philippines. And there was competent opinion, at the close of the World War, that as a result of this failure the command of the Western Pacific had passed to Japan.

The strategic situation was further affected by the political outcome of the war. As frequently noted in preceding chapters, the United States had derived great strategic advantage before the war from the European balance of power in general, and in particular from the Anglo-German naval equipoise which virtually tied the world's two greatest fleets to European waters. According to one view, the destruction of German sea power removed the last serious threat of European aggression in this hemisphere. According to another, however, that event gave Great Britain a free hand once more, with the possibility of future trouble in the Atlantic. While the latter contingency was not widely regarded as a very serious menace, it sufficed to give fresh impetus to the current formula, "a navy second to none," adopted originally in 1916 when the possibility of German victory was generally accepted as justifying the great building program voted in that year. And it was a further notable fact that full naval equality with Great Britain became the Navy Department's minimum standard immediately following the armistice.

Ominous as was the prospect of an Anglo-American struggle for a theoretical supremacy upon the sea, more sinister still were the war's politico-strategic consequences in the Pacific. That conflict had destroyed or at least weakened the Far Eastern position of every European Power. At the same time, the war had immeasurably strengthened the position of Japan whose advance into China, Manchuria, and Eastern Siberia, antagonized the American people, challenged American claims and policies, and seemed at that time to foreshadow possible future aggressions against our insular possessions in the Western Pacific.

Confronted with this seeming menace, the United States might withdraw from the Far East while there was yet time. Such a course would involve granting complete independence to the Philippines, and renouncing armed support of American citizens, property, and intangible interests in Eastern Asia. Whatever the merits of such a course, it was doubtful whether the American people in 1918 were prepared to accept what would certainly have been widely felt to be a humiliating surrender to Japan.

Another possibility was to reestablish the pre-war balance of power in the Far East. But this would present great difficulties. Russia was torn and at least temporarily demoralized by social revolution. The European Powers were exhausted by the war. European reconstruction would necessarily absorb most of their energy for years to come. On the other hand, as already noted, the war had immensely strengthened Japan. And the political chaos in China raised doubts as to the possibility of longer maintaining even a pretense of political unity in that distracted country.

A third choice was singlehanded defense of American interests and policies in the Far East. As statesmen and naval experts then saw it, this would require a vast expansion of America's naval establishment in the Pacific. Yet the inevitable consequence of such a program would be to stimulate Japanese naval expansion, to heighten distrust and fear on both sides of the Pacific, and in turn to precipitate a desperate struggle for control of Asiatic waters. From this impasse, as from the comparable if less serious post-war naval crisis in the Atlantic, the vicious circle of armament competition offered little but the promise of future conflict.

Thus the war closed one and inaugurated another era in the naval epic of the United States. There might and would be further increases in the material strength of the Navy. But future development, even if but the continuance of trends already in process, seemed likely to differ in marked respects from what had gone before. The stage was now set for a new drama in which prolonged struggle for armed security upon the sea might threaten the great naval Powers with bankruptcy or war, if not both together; a drama in which the ominous drift toward such disaster would challenge both the imagination of political leaders and their capacity for constructive statesmanship; a drama in which men would begin to ask whether armies and navies were instruments of national policy, or whether, on the contrary, national policy was itself becoming an instrument of war and of the war machine.

☆ ☆

☆ ☆

Notes on Methods and Materials

THE historical exposition which has resulted from the investigation described in the Foreword rests mainly upon official and other primary sources, supplemented by all available secondary writings. Broadly speaking, these materials include executive documents, congressional proceedings, memoirs and correspondence of statesmen and naval officers, contemporary newspapers, magazines, and technical journals, as well as general histories, biographies, and special studies on particular subjects or periods. Of this vast mass of material, by far the greater part is available in published form, and it is no small surprise to discover that so much of all this has lain so long unused.

The exact nature and scope of these materials are fully set forth in the extensive documentation which accompanies the text. It has seemed unnecessary to append a formal bibliography that would merely duplicate this documentation to which ready access is provided by an analytical index at the end of the volume.

The initiation of naval policy early became largely an executive function. With the passage of time, the decisions of the political Executive came increasingly to be reached with the help and advice of the professional Service whose technical knowledge was indispensable to intelligent policy-formulation. To understand the tortuous course of American naval development, it was therefore necessary to ascertain the influence and ideas of both the political Executive and the professional Service at each stage in the rise of American naval power. And to achieve this result it was necessary to analyze year by year the messages of the Presidents, the annual and special reports of the Secretaries of the Navy, the reports and memoranda of Navy-Department officials and bureaus, the proceedings of special boards, the testimony of executive statesmen and naval officers before congressional committees, the reports of commanding officers, and, wherever feasible, the private correspondence and diaries of representative spokesmen of these different groups.

Special mention should also be made of congressional proceedings. The constitutional power "to provide and maintain a navy" is vested in Congress, and that body has always insisted on its right to amend or reject executive recommendations pertaining to the Navy. Thus to understand the course of American naval development, it was also necessary to study the proceedings of the national legislature. The committee hearings and reports as well as the debates and votes of the two houses are a mine of information hitherto largely unused in this connection, except for certain short periods. We have followed these proceedings year by year from 1789 to 1918, analyzing thousands of speeches, scores of parliamentary battles, and dozens of critical roll calls. The tabular summaries printed on pages 31, 48, and 65 illustrate the method used throughout in handling congressional votes. While these particular tables show only the sectional alignment, we have utilized the same technique to ascertain the partisan alignment as well.

We have supplemented research in the official records of congressional proceedings with extensive investigation into the economic and political background of Senators and Representatives. And we have sought further light on the legislative battles in Congress and on the drift of public opinion, in contemporary newspapers, magazines, and other sources.

Finally, to mention but one more of the significant methods employed, we have attempted at each stage to correlate naval policy with war experience and with the trend of American foreign relations. We have summarized from the best expert opinion available the strategic and technical lessons of each war, and investigated the impact of war experience on the post-war generation of officers, statesmen, and citizens in general. We have attempted to analyze as objectively as possible both the naval implications of the foreign policy in vogue at a particular time, and the actual effects thereof on naval legislation and development. And we have tried to state with equal objectivity what seemed to be the potential consequences of the occasional failure of statesmen to chart the course of future naval development with due regard for the country's foreign policy and for the drift of world politics.

Turning to other writing in the general field of American naval affairs, we offer not a comprehensive bibliography but simply a few notes and citations, for the possible interest of the general reader as well as of the prospective worker in the field. Perhaps the most numerous group of books consists of those dealing with the Navy in action. Within this group are many general naval histories. Among these we recommend Captain Dudley W. Knox's *History of the United States Navy* (1936), and Fletcher Pratt's *The Navy: The Story of a Service in Action* (1938). There are many accounts of American naval operations in particular wars. Among these one should mention G. W. Allen's *Naval History of the American Revolution* (1913, 2 vols.) and *Our Navy and the Barbary Corsairs* (1905). Dr. C. O. Paullin's *Navy of the American Revolution* (1906) must also be cited in this group although this work, with its discussions of policy, politics, and administration, is more than a descriptive history of operations. Admiral F. E. Chadwick's *Relations of the United States and Spain: The Spanish-American War* (1911, 2 vols.), is the standard work on the naval operations of that conflict. And the American Navy's rôle in the World War is well covered in two descriptive histories: Captain T. G. Frothingham's *Naval History of the World War* (1924–1927, 3 vols.), and Admiral W. S. Sims' *The Victory at*

Sea (1920). For the Navy as an instrument of, and adjunct to, diplomacy, one should make special mention of Dr. C. O. Paullin's pioneer study, *Diplomatic Negotiations of American Naval Officers, 1778–1883* (1912), and also of the recent work of Professor T. A. Bailey whose numerous scholarly articles and larger study of *Theodore Roosevelt and the Japanese-American Crises* (1934) illuminate the inter-relations of naval policy and diplomacy during the early years of the twentieth century.

In a special class are the three major works of Captain (later Admiral) Alfred Thayer Mahan. These are *The Influence of Sea Power upon History, 1660–1783* (1890); *The Influence of Sea Power upon the French Revolution and Empire, 1793–1812* (1893, 2 vols.); and *Sea Power in Its Relations to the War of 1812* (1905, 2 vols.). In these works, the narrative of operations is subordinated to Mahan's exposition of strategic principles in general, and in particular of his theory of command of the sea.

Another group of important studies deals with phases of the history of naval architecture and technology, and the relations thereof to naval policy and development. An excellent discussion of naval architecture in the era of sails is to be found in H. I. Chapelle's *History of American Sailing Ships* (1935). An exhaustive documented study covering one aspect of this subject is Professor R. G. Albion's *Forests and Sea Power, The Timber Problem of the Royal Navy, 1652–1862* (1926). For the transition from sails to steam, one should consult F. M. Bennett's *Steam Navy of the United States* (1896), an engineer's quasi-technical account of progress down to 1895. For the transition from "wooden walls" to armor, the definitive work is Dr. J. P. Baxter's *Introduction of the Ironclad Warship* (1933), which covers the critical period, 1830-1863. Admiral B. A. Fiske's autobiography, *From Midshipman to Rear Admiral* (1919), covers certain phases of technical progress, especially the introduction of precision methods in gunnery, etc., during the quarter century prior to the World War. In addition, there is a wealth of material on naval technology in the *Proceedings of the United States Naval Institute,* and in other technical and professional journals. There is still room, however, for further systematic studies, comparable to those by Albion and Baxter, to cover the later stages of the technological revolution.

Turning to the field of naval organization and administration, one finds little significant recent work. There is the series of articles published many years ago by Dr. C. O. Paullin, in Volumes XXXII-XL (1906–1914) of the *Proceedings of the United States Naval Institute.* These studies, however, come down only to 1911, and should be supplemented with further work utilizing recent advances in the technique of public administration research.

Although there are thus seen to be important books or other writing dealing with the Navy in action, with the principles of naval strategy and warfare, with the evolution of naval architecture and technology, and with naval administration, there has been no comprehensive work on the development and dynamics of American naval policy. And as stated in the Foreword, it is hoped that our own study will go some way toward filling this gap, and thereby contribute something at least to a reasoned public opinion on the great issue of national defense.

☆ ☆

Index

Adams, John, Pres., 38*f.*, 50; quoted, 101-2

Advisory Board (1881), 186, 195

African Squadron, 95

"Aid" system (1909-13), 296

Aleutian Islands, 242

Ammen, Daniel, Rear-Adm., 173, 179

Anglo-American relations, *see* Great Britain, U. S. relations with

Anglo-German naval rivalry, implications for U. S., 252, 299 and n., 300, 384; Churchill, W., "naval holiday" proposal, 308

"antenna mine," 366

appropriations, naval, U. S., (1799), 51; (1802-7), 57; (1816), 88; (1817-25), 97; (1827), 102; (1841-2), 124n.; (1902-5), 261; (1907-9), 269; (1909-13), 294; *see also* expenditures; fiscal situation

armaments, limitation of, Rush-Bagot Agreement (1817), 91; cong'l resolution favoring (1910), 287n.; Pres. Taft's views on, 287-8; Sec. of Navy Daniels' views on, 308; Hensley amendment, Act of 1916, 345; Problem of (1918), 385-6

armor, introduction of, Stevens Battery, 125; progress abroad, 145; Confederate ironclad policy, 156; Union ironclad policy, 158; strategic significance, 159; post-Civil War policy, 170; prejudice against, 194; New Navy, 189, 213

armored cruisers, strategic functions of, 260n.; *and see* naval architecture

armored ships, *see* battleships *and* naval architecture

Articles of Confederation, naval provisions of, 18; naval policy under, 15*ff.*, 24

Asiatic Fleet (1901-1907), 282*f.*

Asiatic Squadron, established (E. India Squadron, 1835), 95; (1898) 230, 231; (1899-1901) 246

Atlantic Fleet, antecedents of, 118, 217; established, 282; World Cruise (1907-9), 265, 285; disposition of (1909-13), 299; reviews of (1911, 1912), 291, 292; rôle of, in World War, 364*ff.*

Atlantic Ocean, politico-strategic situation in, (1845), 131; (1897), 222; (1899), 241; (1900-14), 251*ff.*; (1913), 305; (1915-16), 326; (1918), 384

Bailey, W. W., Rep., quoted, 343

balance of power, European, strategic implications of, 84, 176, 288, 299 and n., 307, 384; Far Eastern, strategic implications of, 245, 255, 257, 307, 384*ff.*

Bancroft, George, Sec. of Navy, 129, 133n.

Barbary Powers, *see* Mediterranean *and* Tripolitan War

bases, oversea, and domestic politics, 294; importance of, discussed, 119, 281; in Aleutian Islands, 242; China, proposed site on coast of, 247; Cuba (Guantanamo), 298; Guam, 243, 255, 301; Hawaii (Pearl Harbor), 241, 301; Philippines (Cavite and Olongapo), 244, 255, 301; Puerto Rico 241; Samoa (Pago Pago) 242; Virgin Islands (Danish West Indies), 329n.

battle cruiser, *see* naval architecture

battleships, early U. S., 189; "sea-going coastline," 211-13; strategic function of, 204, 207, 372*ff.*; future of, discussed, 372; *and see* naval architecture

Benson, W. S., Adm., 365

Benton, T. H., Sen., quoted, 106, 121, 143

Bernard, Simon, quoted, 100

Beveridge, A. J., Sen., 266

Bibb, William, Rep., quoted, 70

Blaine, J. G., Sec. of State, 185, 206

blockade, rôle of, in Revolutionary War, 11, 13, 14; in Tripolitan War, 57*f.*; in Napoleonic War, 72, 218*f.*; in War of 1812, 79*ff.*; in Mexican War, 135; in Civil War, 154, 163*f.*, 218*f.*; in Spanish-American War, 232, 237; in World War, 348*ff.*, 373*ff.*; *and see* submarine warfare

Board of Navy Commissioners, established, 92; influence on policy, 93, 118; report of, on naval policy (1836), 107*ff.*; report of on steam warships (1840), 115; abolition of, 118

Bocock, T. S., Rep., 146; quoted, 142

Borie, A. E., Sec. of Navy, 178

Boutelle, C. A., Rep., quoted, 211, 212

Buchanan, James, Pres., 146, 149

California, conquest, strategic implications of, 136

Campbell, P. P., Rep., quoted, 342

Canada, projected attack on (1812), 66, 74*ff.*; Rush-Bagot Agreement (1817), 89*ff.*

Cannon, J. G., Rep., 249, 260n., 267n.

Caribbean Sea, strategic importance of, 139, 241, 251*ff.*, 305; *and see* Atlantic Ocean

Cavite (Philippine Islands), 296; *and see* bases, oversea

Chandler, W. E., Sec. of Navy, 187, 192

Chesapeake, see ships (old)

Chesapeake Bay, strategic importance of, in Revolutionary War, 8; in War of 1812, 83; in the Civil War, 156

Cheves, Langdon, Rep., quoted, 66*ff.*

China, policy of U. S. as to, 244, 289; proposed site for naval base, 247; *and see* Far East *and* Japan, U. S. relations with

Civil War, Chap. X; naval resources of the Union, 151*ff.*; Union objectives and strategy, 154*f.*; Confederate objectives and strategy, 156; ironclads, rôle of, in, 157*ff.*; commerce raiding and the blockade, 162*ff.*; lessons of (summary), 151*ff.*, 160*f.*, 164

Cleveland, Grover, Pres., 189, 218, 221

coastal fortifications (U. S.), 59; report on, by Endicott Board (1886), 199; condition of (1915), 327

Collins, E. K., 133

commerce raiding, rôle of in Revolutionary War, 8, 10*ff.*; in Quasi-war with France, 41; in War of 1812, 78*ff.*, 83*ff.*; in Civil War, 162; *and see* submarine warfare

Congress, naval bills, debates and proceedings on, (1794) 29*ff.*; (1796) 36*ff.*; (1799) 44*ff.*; (1810) 63; (1811) 63*f.*; (1812) 66*ff.*, (1816) 89; (1827) 103*ff.*, (1839) 114; (1841) 117; (1842) 121*f.*; (1846) 132; (1854) 142*ff.*; (1858) 147; (1860) 147*f.*; (1861) 148; (1873) 171; (1881-5) 188n., 191n.; (1890) 211*ff.*; (1895-6) 221; (1899-1901) 248; (1902-5) 260; (1906) 262; (1907) 264*f.*; (1908) 266*f.*; (1909) 268; (1912) 292; (1913) 293; (1914) 312*ff.*; (1915) 319*f.*; (1916) 335*ff.*

Congress, special investigations, (1876) 180 and n., 185; (1879) 182; (1908) 277*ff.*; (1920) 354n.

Congress, votes on naval bills, (1794) 31 (table); (1798-9) 48 (table); (1812) 64*f.* (table); (1821) 97; (1827) 104; (1841) 117; (1842) 123; (1854) 143; (1858) 147; (1861) 148; (1873) 171n.; (1881-5) 188n., 191n.; (1890) 212; (1895) 221; (1908) 266; (1916) 338, 341, 344*f.*

Congress, *see also* naval policy, formulation of; party alignment; sectional alignment; patronage; "pork-barrel"

Constitution, Convention of 1787, 19; provisions of, on navy, 19; struggle for ratification of, discussions of navy, 20*ff.*

Continental Congress, revolutionary naval policy of, 9*ff*.; post-Revolutionary naval policy of, 15*f*., 18*f*.; sectionalism in, 9*f*., 19
Continental (Revolutionary) Navy, 10*ff*., 15
Convoy, rôle of in Revolutionary War, 10; in Quasi-war with France, 41; in War of 1812, 78; in World War, 361*ff*.
Crimean War, lessons of, 145, 149
Crowninshield, B. W., Sec. of Navy, quoted, 88
cruisers, strategic functions of, 204, 208, 218, 293, 338; *and see* naval architecture *and* strategic principles, discussions of
Cuba, Island of, *see* bases, oversea

Daniels, Josephus, Sec. of Navy, appointed, 308; views on naval policy (1913), 308*f*.; views on naval policy (1914), 318, 319, 335n.; neutrality and war preparation (1916), 357*f*.; attitude toward cooperation with Allies, 363*f*.
Danish West Indies, purchase of, 329n.
Dardanelles campaign (World War), lessons of, 328, 350
Delaware Bay, strategic importance of, in Revolutionary War, 8
Democratic Party, foreign policy of, 127, 132, 140; National conventions (1912) 292; (1916) 340; *and see* party alignment
depth charge, 362
destroyers, strategic functions of, 248n., 363
destroyers, *see* naval architecture
Dewey, George, Admiral, 230, 231, 340n.
Dickerson, Mahlon, Sec. of Navy, quoted, 112*f*.
distances (nautical miles), San Francisco-Key West (via Magellan Strait), 233; Hawaii-Guam, 243; Hawaii-Philippines, 243
Dobbin, J. C., Sec. of Navy, quoted, 141*f*., 145
domestic materials, use of, in naval construction, 35, 42, 120, 193*f*.
domestic politics, influences on naval policy, (1799-1801) 46*ff*.; (1842) 121*ff*.; (1870's) 175*ff*.; (1880's) 184, 190*f*.; (1890's) 206, 224, 249; (1901-13) 266, 290*ff*., 294, 299*f*.; (1916) 337, 357; *and see* party alignment
dreadnought, *see* naval architecture
Duane, James, quoted, 22

East India Squadron, 95; *see also* Asiatic Squadron *and* Asiatic Fleet
Ericsson, John, 125n.
Europe, *see* balance of power
Evans, R. D., Adm., quoted, 242n., 301
expenditures, trend of, 47, 54, 57, 87, 106n., 121, 344; *see also* appropriations *and* fiscal situation

Farragut, D. G., Adm., 145, 177, 179
Federalist, The, national interest in a navy, 21*f*.
Federalist Party, naval policy of, Chap. IV, 51, 71
Fillmore, Millard, Pres., 137
Fillmore, Millard, Rep., 122
fiscal situation, influence on naval development, (1797-1800) 46; (1801) 54; (1821) 97; (1835) 106; (1837) 113; (1849-1853) 137; (1858) 147; (1870's) 181; (1881) 183; (1893-1897) 219*f*.; (1907-1909) 269; (1909-1911) 290*f*.
Fiske, B. A., Rear-Adm., 315; quoted, 198
Fleet, development of, 118, 217, 282; composition of, 269, 293, 295; organization of, 295; training of, 295; maintenance of, 296; reviews of, 285, 291, 292
Fletcher, F. F., Rear Adm., 327, 335n.
"Flying Squadron" (1898), 234
France, Quasi-war with, 38-49; relations of U. S. with, crisis of 1835, 106; sea power of, in American Revolution, 12
frigate, *see* naval architecture

Gallatin, Albert, quoted, 45*ff*., 54*ff*.
Gardner, A. F., Rep., 318
Garfield, J. A., Pres., 183*ff*.
General Board, established, 247; building programs of, (1903-1914) 261*f*.,

310*ff*.; (1914) 319; (1915-1916) 335*ff*., 339; and Newport Conference, 279
general staff, proposals for a, (1901-1909) 275, 276*ff*., 280; (1909-1913) 296; (1915) 320; (1916) 345
Goldsborough, L. M., Rear-Adm., quoted, 169
graft and corruption, 180; *and see* patronage *and* "pork-barrel"
Gray, F. H., Rep., 342*f*.
Grayson, William, quoted, 23*f*.
Great Britain, military power in Western Hemisphere, 44; (1812) 85; (1846) 131; Great Lakes (1814), 90*f*.; W. Indies (1841), 117; Cent. America (1850's), 136; disposition of forces (1900-1914), 252
Great Britain, naval strategy of, 69; in War of 1812, 78, 83*ff*.; in Napoleonic War, 218
Great Britain, relations of U. S. with, Jay Treaty, 38; *Chesapeake* incident, 62; Rush-Bagot Agreement, 89n., 89*ff*.; crisis of 1840-1841, 116; Webster-Ashburton Treaty, 116; Oregon crisis, 128*ff*.; rivalry in Cent. America (1850's), 139, 143, 144; slave trade, 146; Venezuelan crisis (1895), 220; outlook in 1918, 384
Great Britain, sea power of, in American Revolution, 11*f*.; in War of 1812, Chap. VI
Great Lakes, strategic importance of, in War of 1812, 73-6; Rush-Bagot Agreement, 89n., 89*ff*.
Guam, Island of, strategic importance of, 243, 255, 301
Guantanamo (Cuba), strategic importance of, 298*f*.
Gulf of Mexico, strategic importance of, 139
gunboat policy, Jefferson's, 58*ff*.
gunboats, *see* naval architecture
gunnery (U. S.), in Spanish-American War, 239; improvement of (1901-1909), 273*ff*.
guns afloat *vs*. guns ashore, 239, 327

Hale, Eugene, Sen., 249, 260, 277*f*., quoted, 211
Hamilton, Alexander, quoted, 21*f*., 36*f*., 85n.
Hamilton, Paul, Sec. of Navy, quoted, 63
Hardy, Rufus, Rep., 342
Harrison, Benjamin, Pres., 206
Hawaiian Islands, strategic importance of, 215, 241*f*., 301
Hay, John, Sec. of State, 289*f*.
Hayne, R. Y., Sen., quoted, 103
Henry, Patrick, quoted, 23
Herbert, H. A., Sec. of Navy, 218, 220, 221
Hobson, R. P., Rep., 264n., 320; quoted, 264*f*., 312*f*., 335n.
Home Squadron, 95, 116*ff*.
House, E. M., Col., 306, 333
Hudson River, strategic importance of, in American Revolution, 8*f*.
Humphreys, David, quoted, 34
Hunt, W. H., Sec. of Navy, 186*f*.

inland lakes, *see* Great Lakes *and* Lake Champlain
interest, national, *see* national interest in the Navy
interests, influence on naval policy, 22, 35, 120, 122*f*., 139, 194, 204, 220, 257*ff*., 287, 298n., 300, 322*ff*., 324n., 342n., 381
ironclad, *see* armor *and* naval architecture
Isherwood, B. F., 178; quoted, 153n., 159, 199
isthmian canal, strategic need of, 247, 251; defense of, problem, 251; relation to strategic disposition of fleet, 284
Isthmus, strategic importance of, after 1803, 139; after 1848, 136, 214; after 1898, 251

Jackson, Andrew, Pres., views on naval policy, (1829), 105; (1837), 107
Jacksonian (Democratic) Party, naval policy of, 104*ff*.
Japan, U. S. relations with, 244*f*., 247, 262, 264, 265, 284, 289, 303, 306, 329, 377, 385
Jay, John, 18
Jay Treaty, 38
Jefferson, Thomas, views on naval policy, (1781), 14; (1785), 17; (1791),

26; (1794), 28, 32n.; (1801), 53, 55, 56; (1806), 61; (1807), 58*ff.*
Jeffersonian-Republican (Democratic) Party, naval policy of, 24, 47*ff.*, Chap. V, 71
Johnson, Cave, Rep., quoted, 121
Johnson, R. M., Rep., 68
Jones, John Paul, Captain, 11
Jones, William, Sec. of Navy, quoted, 87
Jutland, battle of, 350; effect on U. S. naval policy, 338*ff.*; lessons of, 340

Key, A. L., Comm., 278
King, T. B., Rep., 134
Kitchin, Claude, Rep., 260n., 324; quoted 343
Knight, A. M., Rear Adm., quoted, 326*f.*
Knox, P. C., Sec. of State, 289*f.*

LaFollette, R. M., Sen., 281n., quoted, 325n.
Lake Champlain, strategic importance of, in American Revolution, 9; in War of 1812, 74, 75
Laning, Harris, Capt., quoted, 355
legislation, *see* naval policy, formulation of, statutes, *and* Congress
legislative process, *see* naval policy, formulation of
Lenthall, John, quoted, 153n., 159, 199
Lloyd George, David, 362
localism in Congress, 106, 121*ff.*, 138, 276*f.*, 292n., 380*f.*; *and see* bases, oversea, Congress, domestic politics, interests, naval policy, formation of, patronage, *and* "pork-barrel" legislation
Lodge, H. C., Sen., 217, 226, 260n., 262, 266, 341n.; quoted, 212
Long, J. D., Sec. of Navy, 224, 249; quoted, 228, 229
Luce, Stephen B., Adm., 279

Macdonough, Thomas, Comm., 75, 86
McKee, Samuel, 68
McKinley, William, Pres., 224, 228, 249
Maclay, William, Sen., 28
Macon, Nathaniel, Rep. and Sen., 29; quoted, 103*f.*
Madison, James, views on naval policy, (1781), 13; (1787), 20, 21; (1789), 26; (1794), 32n.; (1809-1812) 62*f.*
Mahan, Alfred Thayer, Rear Adm., Chap. XIII; views of, on sea power and U. S. policy, 203*ff.*, 213*ff.*; writings of, 7, 73n., 145n., 183, 202, 202n., 218, 236n., 240n.; influence of, on U. S. policy, 205*ff.*, 217*ff.*; influence of, on Theodore Roosevelt, 226*f.*
Mallory, R., Sen. and Sec. of Confederate Navy, 146, 148; quoted, 156
manifest destiny, relation of, to naval policy, (1840's and 1850's), Chap. IX; (1890's), Chaps. XIII-XIV
Manila Bay, battle of, 231
Mason, J. Y., Sec. of Navy, quoted, 135
Maxim, Sir Hiram, quoted, 328n.
Maxim, Hudson, 328n.
Mayo, H. T., Rear Adm., 365
Mediterranean piracy, relation of, to establishment of the Navy, 17*f.*, 28*ff.*, 30, 36; effect of, on Jeffersonian naval policy, 55*ff.*, 58*ff.*; *and see* Jefferson; Tripolitan War *and* Mediterranean Squadron
Mediterranean Squadron, 94*f.*
Melville, G. W., Rear Adm., quoted, 240
merchant marine, relation of, to naval power, 133*ff.*, 153n., 203*f.*
Metcalf, Victor, Sec. of Navy, 280
Mexican War, lessons of, 135; strategic consequences of, 136
Meyer, George Von Lengerke, Sec. of Navy, 290*ff.*; "aid system," establishment of, 296; navy-yard policy, 297*f.*; oversea bases, improvement of, 298*ff.*; fleet, strategic disposition of, 299*f.*
Miles, N. A., Gen., quoted, 327n.
Mississippi River, strategic importance of, (1836), 108; (1861-1865), 155
Mondell, F. W., Rep., quoted, 342
Monitors, strategic function and value of, 160, 171*ff.*, 208, 239; *see also* naval architecture
Monroe, James, Pres., quoted, 98*ff.*
Monroe Doctrine, relation of, to naval policy, 184n., 185, 252
Moody Commission, 280
Morris, Gouverneur, 34
Morris, Robert, 13, 15

national interest in naval power, early discussion of, 14*ff*., 17*ff*., 20*ff*., 26*ff*., 29*ff*.; views of, Hamilton, 21*f*., 37, 85; Stoddert, 41*ff*.; Cheves, 66*ff*.; Upshur, 118*ff*.; Bocock, 143; Mahan, 203; Herbert, 220; Theo. Roosevelt, 227; summary, 380*ff*.

Naval Academy (U. S.), proposals to establish, discussion of, 102*ff*., 120; establishment of, 133n.

naval architecture, evolution of, Chap. I, 43, 110*ff*., 126, 145, 149*f*., 157*ff*., 164, 170, 188*f*., 213, 239, 263, 338
 types of ships, armored cruiser, 260n.; battle cruiser, 261, 339, dreadnought battleship, 263; destroyer, 248n., 338; frigate, 43; gunboat (Jefferson's), 58; monitor, 158, 171; protected cruiser, 188n.; scout cruiser, 261n., 338; screw frigate, 145; screw sloop, 144; ship-of-the-line, 43; sloop-of-war, 43; steam battery, 111; submarine, 356; super-dreadnought, 338
 fuel capacity, 167, 247
 sails *vs.* steam, 167, 194*f*.; *and see* steam power

naval functions, peacetime, 94*ff*., 96n., 166

Naval Operations, Office of Chief of, 320, 345

naval operations in Revolutionary War, Chap. II; Quasi-war with France, 40*f*.; Tripolitan War, 55*ff*.; War of 1812, Chap. VI; Mexican War, 135*f*.; Civil War, Chap. X; Spanish-American War, Chap. XIV; World War, Chap. XIX, *and see* oversea operations, problems and difficulties of

naval policy, formulation of, 6; (1849-1853), 138; (1917), 369; summary, 375*f*.; rôle of executive, (1837-1845), 111; (1853-1857), 145; (1880's), 186; (1901-1909), 259*ff*., 266; (1909-1913), 294; (1916), 336; rôle of Congress, (1841-1845), 121; composition of congressional committees, 29, 122, 281, 297, 340*f*.; importance of party control, (1841-1845), 124; (1870's), 177*ff*., 182; (1909-1913), 294; *and see* interests; press, *and* Service

naval policy, political and economic background of, (1776-1783), 7*ff*., (1783-1789), 18*f*.; (1789-1801), 25*ff*., 33*f*., 38, 47*ff*.; (1801-1812), 50*ff*., 55*f*., 64*ff*.; (1815-1837), 86*ff*., 96*f*., 104*f*., 106; (1837-1845), 113*f*., 116, 122, 124; (1845-1861), 127*ff*., 137, 139*ff*.; (1865-1881), 175*ff*., 181; (1881-1889), 183*ff*., 190*ff*.; (1889-1897), 205*ff*., 217*ff*.; (1897-1901), 224*ff*., 245*ff*.; (1901-1909), 250*ff*., 262*ff*.; (1909-1913), 286*ff*.; 290*ff*.; (1913-1914), 304*ff*.; (1914-1917), 317, 322*ff*., 329*ff*., 337*ff*.

Naval War College (U. S.), 202

Navy Commissioners, *see* Board of Navy Commissioners

Navy Department, Board of Navy Commissioners, *see* Board of Navy Commissioners

Navy Department, establishment of, 39; organization and administration of, 57, 76*f*., 92, 118, 189, 193, 247, 271, 275*f*., 277*f*., 279*f*., 296*f*., 320, 345

Navy Department, Office of Naval Operations, 320, 345

Navy League of U. S., 258*f*.

navy yards, location and number of, 35, 42, 51, 292*f*.; patronage and "pork-barrel," 122*f*., 138, 180, 192, 281, 297; policy as to, 55, 281, 297; condition of, 77, 102, 180

Newberry, Truman, Sec. of Navy, 280

New Navy, the, Chap. XII

Newport Conference, 278*f*.

North Atlantic Squadron, 217, 246, 282; *and see* Atlantic Fleet

Northern Mine Barrage, 366*f*.

Olongapo (Philippines), 301; *and see* bases, overseas

operations, naval, in war, *see* oversea operations, problems and difficulties of

ordnance, technical progress in, consequences of, 110, 125; Service opinion on (1861), 158; condition of U. S. (1865-1881), 170; ordnance *vs.* armor, 161

Oregon, significance of voyage of, 233

Oregon, strategic implications of annexation of, 136

oversea naval bases, *see* bases, oversea

oversea operations, problems and difficulties of, (1777), 12; (1801), 57; (1812), 67ff., 84f.; (1865), 166f.; (1890), 203f.; (1898), 238ff., 242ff., (1900), 253ff.; (1901), 280f.; (1909-1913), 287f., 301f.; (1916), 326; (1914-1918), 328, 375; summary, 383ff.

Pacific Fleet, 282, 291
Pacific Ocean, politico-strategic situation in, (1898-1914), 241ff., 253ff., 301f., 305f.; (1918), 377, 385
Pacific Squadron, 95, 135n.
Padgett, L. P., Rep., quoted, 294n., 341, 344
Page, R. N., Rep., quoted, 342
Pago Pago (Samoan Islands), 242f.; *and see* bases, oversea
Panama Canal, strategic importance of, 296, *and see* isthmian canal
party alignment on naval policy, (1794), 32; (1799), 47ff.; (1812), 68; (1827), 103f.; (1842), 123; (1854), 143; (1880's), 190f.; (1890), 212; (1891-1897), 217ff.; (1909-1913), 294; (1914-1915), 321; (1916), 337; summary, 379
patronage and favoritism, 35, 42, 121, 187, 191f.; *and see* Congress; domestic politics, graft and corruption; interests; naval policy, formulation of; navy yards, *and* "pork barrel" legislation
Paulding, J. K., Sec. of Navy, quoted, 114f.
peacetime functions, *see* naval functions, peacetime
Pearl Harbor (Hawaiian Islands) 301, *and see* bases, oversea
Pearson, Joseph, Rep., quoted, 81
Perry, M. C., Capt., 114, 144
Perry, O. H., Comm., 75, 86
personnel, increase of, (1841-1842), 116; naval academy, (1827), 102ff.; (1842), 120; (1845), 133; rank; (1801), 51f.; reduction of, (1801), 55; (1815 on), 98f.; shortage of, (1812), 76; (1853), 141; (1861), 152; (1901-1909), 271, 272f.; (1914), 319; (1917), 358
Philippine Islands, conquest of, 229f., 242; defense problem of, 243ff., 255, 300ff., 306; strategic value of, 244f.; *and see* bases, oversea
Pierce, Franklin, Pres., 141, 145
Pinckney, C. C., quoted, 20
Policy Board, (1890), 209ff.
politico-strategic situation, *see* Atlantic, Caribbean, *and* Pacific
Polk, J. K., Pres., 129f., 132f., 136n.
"pork-barrel" legislation, 121ff., 138, 191, 266, 281, 293f., 293n., 380f.; *and see* bases, overseas; Congress; domestic politics; interests; naval policy, formulation of; navy yards; *and* patronage
Porter, D. D., Adm., 177ff.; quoted, 170, 172, 174, 195
Pratt, W. V., Capt., 365
preparedness, movement for, (1915-1916), 317ff.; official propaganda for, 336; Wilson's conversion to, 332ff.
Preparedness Movement, the, (1915-1916), 322ff.; motivation of, 324; technique of, 324f.
presidential campaigns and elections, (1800), 49f.; (1824), 101f.; (1828), 105; (1844), 127ff.; (1848), 137; (1880), 182f.; (1884), 189; (1888), 206; (1896), 224; (1912), 292f., 304; (1916), 357
Presidents, *see names of*
press, the, (1881), 185n.; (1890), 211; (1898), 234; (1901-1909), 261n., 268; (1914), 318n., 321; (1915), 322f.
pressure groups, *see* interests
privateering, in American Revolution, 10; results of, 11
propaganda, organized groups, Administration, 323; American Bankers Association, 323; League to Enforce Peace, 323, National Association of Manufacturers, 323; National Security League, 322, Navy League, 322; Services, 323; U. S. Chamber of Commerce, 323
protected cruiser, *see* naval architecture
public opinion, and military operations, in War of 1812, 75; and naval operations, in Civil War, 162ff.; in Spanish American War, 223, 234ff.; and strategic disposition of ships in peace, 208f., 282f., 300; on naval policy, (1903), 257ff.; (1908), 267f.; (1911), 291f.; (1909-1913), 295; (1914-1915), 321; *and see* interests; pre-

paredness movement; *and* propaganda
Puerto Rico, (1898), 233

Quincy, Josiah, quoted, 69

radius, cruising, 166*f*., 247; *and see* oversea operations
Randolph, Edmund, quoted, 20
Reed, T. B., Rep., 206
Republican Party, platform, (1896), 224
Reuterdahl, Henry, 277*f*.
Revolutionary America, maritime interests of, 8
Revolutionary America, strategic situation of, 7
Revolutionary War, naval policy in, 7-9; navies of the States in, 10; British sea power in, 11; French sea power in, 12; naval lessons of, 13*ff*.; *see also* naval operations *and* sea power
Reynolds, John, Rep., quoted, 121
Robeson, G. M., Sec. of Navy, quoted, 178*ff*.; Rep., quoted, 196
Rodgers, John, Comm., quoted, 107*ff*.
Roosevelt, Theodore, personality and interests, 225*f*.; friendships, 217, 226; Asst. Sec. of Navy, 225*ff*.; views on naval policy (Naval War College lecture), 227; attempts to influence McKinley administration, 228; prepares the Navy for War, 229; measure of responsibility for conquest of Philippines, 230; elected Vice-President, 249; succeeds to presidency, 249
Roosevelt, Theodore, Pres., 250*ff*.; isthmian canal, views on, 251; fear of German aggression, 252*f*.; foreign policy, 257, 289; building programs, 259*ff*., 261*f*., 264, 271*ff*.; program of naval reforms, 271*ff*.; strategic views of, 282*f*.; World Cruise of the Fleet, 284*f*.
Rush-Bagot Agreement, (1817), 89n., 89*ff*.
Rutledge, John, quoted, 20

sails, reluctance to give up, (1880's), 194*f*.
sails *vs.* steam, (1865-1881), 167, 169; *see also* naval architecture
Samoan Islands, crisis of 1888-1889, 206; partition of, 242*f*.; *see also* bases, oversea
Sampson, W. T., Rear Admiral, 234, 237
Santiago, naval battle of, 233, 237
Scott, Sir Percy, R. N., gunnery, 273
scout cruiser, *see* naval architecture
screw frigate, *see* naval architecture
screw sloop, *see* naval architecture
sea power, rôle of, in American Revolution, Chap. II, 41; in Quasi-War with France, 38*ff*.; in Tripolitan War, 55*ff*.; in Napoleonic Wars, Chap. VI, 72, and discussion of, 218*f*.; in War of 1812, Chap. VI, (Atlantic Ocean), 76-85, (on inland lakes), 73-76; in Mexican War, 135; in Civil War, 151, and discussion of, 219; in Spanish American War, 231, 232*ff*.; in World War, 348*ff*.
sectional alignment on naval policy, 10, during the Revolution, 9*f*.; (1788) 20, 22*ff*.; (1791), 27; (1794), 29-32; (1799), 47*f*.; (1812), 64*f*., 68; (1821), 97; (1827), 103*f*.; (1842), 121*ff*.; (1846), 130; (1850's), 139; (1854), 143; (1858), 147; (1861), 148*f*.; (1890), 212 (1908), 267 and 267n.; (1909-1913), 294; (1912), 293; (1914), 313; (1914-1915), 321; (1916), 336; summary, 378*f*.
Service, the, rôle of in administration, 91; relations with Executive and Congress, 93; influence on policy, (1870's), 177*ff*.; summary, 381*f*.; *and see* naval policy, formulation of
Service opinions, on Jefferson's gunboat policy, (1807), 60; on war operations, (1812), 77; on control of naval policy and administration, (1815), 91; on policy and strategy (1836), 107*ff*.; on sails *vs.* steam, (1830's), 113*f*.; on policy and strategy, (1840), 115; on strategy, (1845), 131; on armor and ordnance, (1861), 158; on ordnance, armor, and steam, (1870's), 167-175; on naval reform (1870's), 185; on policy, (1880's), 195; on policy, (1890), 209*f*.; on operating policy,

(1899-1901), 246; on policy, (1913), 310*ff*.; on policy, (1915-1916), 326*ff*., 335; on lessons of World War, (1918), 369*f*.
ship-of-the-line, *see* naval architecture
shipbuilding policy, (1794), 30, 33, 35; (1796), 36; (1799), 48, 51; (1800), 52; (1801), 52, 55; (1805), 58; (1807), 62; (1813), 87; (1815), 88; (1816), 88; (1821), 97*f*.; (1826), 112; (1829), 105; (1834), 113; (1839), 114; (1841), 125; (1842), 120; (1845), 134; (1854), 143; (1857), 145; (1865), 168*f*.; (1872), 171*f*.; (1873), 171; (1882), 188; (1883), 188; (1885), 189; (1885-1889), 189; (1890), 213; (1891-1893), 217*f*.; (1898), 247; (1899), 248; (1900), 248; (1902-1905), 260*f*.; (1908-1909), 269; (1909-1913), 293; (1914), 315; (1915), 320; (1916), 344*ff*.; (1917-1918), 365
ships, British naval, *Dreadnought*, 263, 315
ships, Confederate naval, *Alabama*, 162, 162n., 195; *Virginia*, 157*ff*., *illus. 158*
ships, defects of design and/or construction, (1840's), 125; (1850's), 145, 149; (1870's), 168*ff*.; (1880's), 188, 192*f*.; (1900's), 270, 275, 277, 279
ships, strategic disposition of, policy as to, (1790's), 37*f*.; (1800's), 55, 62; (1810's), 77, 88, 89; cruising stations, (1815), 94*ff*.; (1820's-1830's), 96*ff*.; Home Squadron, (1841), 116; (1861), 152; (1870's-1880's), 166*ff*.; (1890's), 217; (1900's), 270*f*., 282*ff*.; (1909-1913), 299*f*.; in World War, 355*ff*.
ships, U. S. naval (built before 1881)
John Adams, 96n.
Argus, 58n.
Bonhomme Richard, 5
Boxer, 96n.
Brandywine, 96n., *illus. 43*
Brooklyn, *illus. 168*
Chesapeake, 40, 61
Constellation, 40, 96n.
Constitution, 40, 96n., *frontis.*, *illus. 43*
Demologos (1st *Fulton*), 111*f*.
Dolphin, 96n.
Enterprise, 96n.
Erie, 96n., *illus. 43*
Fairfield, 96n.
Fulton (1st) *see Demologos*
Fulton (2nd), 113, 114
Grampus, 96n.
Hornet, 58n.
Kearsarge, 163
Merrimac, *see also Virginia* (Confederate), 157*ff*.; *illus. 142*
Miantonomoh, 172n.
Mississippi, 114n., *illus. 142*
Missouri, 114n.
Monadnock, 172n.
Monitor, 158*ff*., 171, *illus. 158*
Nautilus, 58n.
North Carolina, *illus. 43*
Ontario, 96n., *illus. 43*
Peacock, 96n.
Potomac, 96n.
President, 40
Princeton, 125
St. Louis, 96n.
Shark, 96n.
Stevens Battery (unfinished), 126, 145
Syren, 58n.
Vandalia, 96n.
Vincennes, 96n.
Vixen, 58n.
Wampanoag, 169
Warren, 96n.
Wasp, 58n.
ships, U. S. naval (built after 1881) [battleships marked*]
*Alabama**, 221n.
*Arizona**, 293n.
*Arkansas**, 269n.
Atlanta, 188, 195
Baltimore, 231
Boston, 188, 231
Brooklyn, 218n., 237
*California**, 320n.
Charleston, 189
Chicago, 188, 195, *illus. 218*
Concord, 231
*Connecticut**, 260n.
*Delaware**, 263, *illus. 264*, 278
Dolphin, 188, 193
Fanning, *illus. 363*
*Florida**, 269n.
*Georgia**, 248n.
*Idaho** (1st), 260n., 315 and n.
*Idaho** (2nd), 315n.

*Illinois**, 221n., 270
*Indiana**, 213, 237
*Iowa**, 218n., 237
*Kansas**, 260n.
*Kearsarge**, 221n.
*Kentucky**, 221n.
L3, illus. 363
*Louisiana**, 260n.
McCulloch, 231
*Maine** (1st), 189, 229
*Maine** (2nd), 248n.
*Massachusetts**, 213, 237
*Michigan**, 260n., 261n., 263
*Minnesota**, 260n.
*Mississippi** (1st), 260n., 315 and n.
*Mississippi** (2nd), 315n.
*Missouri**, 248n., 274
*Nebraska**, 248n.
*New Hampshire**, 260n.
*New Jersey**, 248n.
*New Mexico**, 315n.
New York (renamed *Saratoga*, later *Rochester*), 190, 237
*New York**, 237
Newark, 189
*North Dakota**, 264, 278*f.*
*Ohio**, 248n.
Olympia, 190, 231
*Oregon**, 3, 213, 233, *illus. 234*, 237, 263
*Pennsylvania**, 292n.
Petrel, 189, 231
Raleigh, 231
*Rhode Island**, 248n.
Salem, illus. 260, 278
San Diego, illus. 260
*South Carolina**, 260n., 261n., 263
*Tennessee**, 320n.
*Texas** (1st) (renamed *San Marcos*), 189
*Texas** (2nd), 237
*Utah**, 269n., 279
*Vermont**, 260n.
*Virginia**, 248n.
*Wisconsin**, 221n.
*Wyoming**, 269n.
Yorktown, 189
Sims, W. S., Adm., 264n., 273*f.*, 277, 279*f.*, 349n., 362; quoted, 357n., 358n.
Sino-Japanese War (1894-1895), lessons of, 220
slave politics and naval policy (1853-1861), 139*f.*, 148
sloop-of-war, *see* naval architecture
Smith, Melancthon, quoted, 22
Smith, Robert, Sec. of Navy, 53n.
sound-detectors, submarine, 366
South Atlantic (Brazil) Squadron, 95
Southard, S. L., Sec. of Navy, quoted, 98
Spain, relations of U. S. with, *Black Warrior* crisis, 143; *Virginius* crisis, 175; Cuban crisis (1895-1898), 220; destruction of *Maine*, 229
Spanish-American War, Chap. XIV; U. S. forces, in Atlantic, 231, 232*f.*, 235, in Far East, 231; Spanish forces, in Atlantic, 232, in Pacific, 231; U. S. strategy and operations, in Pacific, 231, in Atlantic and Caribbean, 231*ff.*, 234*ff.*; Spanish strategy and operations, 233; lessons of the war, 224, 230*ff.*, 237*ff.*; political and strategic results, in Atlantic, 241, in Pacific, 241*ff.*
Squadron of Evolution, 217
standard of power, U. S., Board of Navy Commissioners on, (1836), 108; (1841), 120; (1853), 142; Service opinion on, (1913), 311; (1901-1915), 335, (1915 on), 335*ff.*, 384
stations, cruising, establishment of, 94*ff.*
statutes, U. S. (mentioned or discussed), (Act of 1789), 26; (1794), 28*ff.*; (1796), 36; (1799), 48, 51; (1800), 52; (1801), 52, 55; (Embargo Act of 1807), 62; (1809), 63; (1813), 87; (1815), 92; (1816), 88, 96, 102, 112*f.*; (1821), 102; (1839), 124; (1842), 126; (1845), 134; (1882), 188; (1883), 188, 188n.; (1890), 213; (1900), 248; (1910), 291; (1911), 291, 299; (1914), 304, 315; (1916), 329, 344*ff.*, 347
steam battery, *see* naval architecture
steam power, experiments with, 111*ff.*; early discussions of, 112; strategic implications of, 112, 117, 119; opposition to, (1830's), 115; *same*, (1870's), 167*ff.*; early progress abroad, 117, 130*f.*; sidewheel drive, naval limitations of, 124*f.*; screw propeller, naval implications of, 125; use of in Civil

War, 161, 167; radius of operations under, 166*f.*, 238, 383
Stockton, R. F., Capt., 125
Stoddert, Benjamin, Sec. of Navy, 39*ff.*, 50*ff.*; quoted, 41*ff.*
strategic doctrines, cruiser warfare and commerce raiding, 63, 70*f.*, 99*f.*, 131*f.*, 149*f.*, 156, 162*f.*, 168*ff.*, 194*f.*, 218, 374; passive coast and harbor defense, 59*f.*, 69, 71, 99*f.*, 160, 171*ff.*, 195*f.*, 374; command of the sea (concentration of power, blockade, etc.), 13*f.*, 84*f.*, 96, 101, 117*f.*, 141, 156, 159, 164, 168, 199*ff.*, 203*ff.*, 207*ff.*, 211, 217*ff.*, 282*ff.*, 295*f.*, 311, 370*ff.*
strategic principles, contemporary discussion of, (1781), 13*f.*; (1798), 41*f.*; (1809), 63; (1812), 69*ff.*, 83*ff.*; (1824), 99*ff.*; (1837), 107*ff.*; (1841), 117*f.*, 119*f.*; (1845), 131*f.*; (1853), 141; (1860), 149*f.*; (1861), 156, 159; (1870's), 168*ff.*; (1880's), 194*ff.*; (1890's), 203*ff.*, 207*ff.*, 211*f.*, 217*ff.*; (1900's), 282*ff.*; (1913), 311; (1914), 315*f.*; (1918), 370*ff.*
strategic situation and problem of U. S., in eighteenth century, 14, 21, 42, 44; early nineteenth century, 99, 119, 131; after 1848, 136; after 1898, 224, 241*ff.*, 250*ff.*, 305*ff.*, 316, 326*ff.*; after World War, 383*ff.*
Subig Bay (Philippines), 301; *and see* bases, oversea
submarine, *see* naval architecture
submarine warfare, 330*f.*, 350*f.*, 361*ff.*
subsidies, steamship, 133*ff.*
super-dreadnought, *see* naval architecture

Taft, W. H., Pres., foreign policy of, 286*ff.*; naval policy of, 288*ff.*, 291*ff.*, 293, 300*ff.*
technical progress, early stages of, 110*ff.*; resistance to, (1830's), 111, 113*f.*; (1870's), 168*ff.*; official attitude toward, (1880's), 194, 198*f.*; dreadnought battleship, 263; in World War, 370*ff.*; summary, 3*ff.*, 383
territorial expansion, continental, strategic implications of, 136; oversea, strategic implications of, 241*ff.*, 251*ff.*; summary, 380
Thompson, R. W., Sec. of Navy, quoted, 181
Tillman, B. R., Sen., 340
Totten, J. G., 100
Toucey, Isaac, Sec. of Navy, quoted, 146*f.*
Tracey, B. F., Sec. of Navy, 206, 211; quoted, 207*ff.*
Tripolitan "War," lessons of, 57*ff.*
Tyler, John, Pres., 110, 124

United States coastal fortifications, condition of, (1916), 322
United States, geographical isolation, naval implications of, 14, 21, 44, 85, 120, 238*ff.*, 253*ff.*, 326*ff.*, 375*ff.*, 383*ff.*
United States Navy, decline of, (1865-1881), Chap. XI
United States Navy, rank of, (1846), 130; (1853), 138; (1874), 171; (1881), 184; (1897), 222; (1908), 272; (1914), 313; (1918), 1
Upshur, A. P., Sec. of Navy, 124, quoted, 118

Van Buren, Martin, Pres., 110, 113, 115
vessels, *see* naval architecture; shipbuilding policy; ships; *and* ships, strategic disposition of
Virgin Islands, purchase of, 329n.
Vreeland, Charles, Rear-Adm., 311*f.*

War Department, administration of naval affairs, (1789-1798), 26*ff.*
"War Hawks" of 1812, 64, 74
wars, *see names of*
Washington, George, quoted, 13, 37
Wayland, Francis, quoted, 81*f.*
Weaver, E. M., Gen., quoted, 327n., 328n.
Welles, Gideon, Sec. of Navy, 163, 176, 177
West India Squadron, 95
Whig Party, 101, 104; naval policy of, (1841-1845), 118-23, 124*ff.*; (1849-1853), 137*f.*
"White Squadron," 188*f.*
Whitney, W. C., Sec. of Navy., 189
Whitthorne, W. C., Rep. and Sen., 194
Williams, W. E., Rep., quoted, 314

Wilson, H. B., Rear Adm., 357n.
Wilson, Woodrow, Pres., 304; foreign policy, (1913), 305*ff*.; naval program, (1913), 307*ff*.; (1914), 317*ff*.; neutrality policy, (1914-1917), 329*ff*.; conversion to preparedness, 332*ff*.; preparedness speeches, (1916), 336; building program, (1916), 335, 337, 341
world cruise (1907-1909), 265, 284*f*.
World War, Chaps. XVIII–IX; initial impact of, on U. S. naval policy, 317*ff*.; rôle of sea power in, 348*ff*.; naval resources of the antagonists, (1914), 348; Allied strategy and operations, 349; German strategy and operations, 350; naval crisis, (1917), 351*ff*.; anti-submarine defense problem, 352*ff*.; British Admiralty's anti-submarine operations, 352*ff*.; shipping losses, (1917), 352*f*.
World War, lessons of, naval policy and foreign policy, 368; meaning of preparedness, 368*f*.; policy formulation, 369*f*.; naval administration, 370; potentialities of submarine, 370*f*.; potentialities of mines, 371; potentialities of aircraft, 371*f*.; rôle and future of capital ship, 372*ff*.; radius of operations, 375*ff*.
World War, politico-naval consequences of, 377
World War, U. S. Navy, approach to, 354*ff*.; naval implications of Wilson's neutrality policy, 354; knowledge of naval crisis, 355; policy of inaction, 356; service efforts to prepare for war, 358; lack of planning, 359
World War, U. S. Navy, rôle in, Sims' Mission, 360; convoy system, 361*ff*.; Navy Dept.'s war policy, 363*f*.; submarine raids in American waters, 364; increasing aid and cooperation, 365*ff*.; forces in European waters, (Nov. 1918), 366n.
Wright, Robert, Rep., quoted, 70